Encyclopedia of Cuba

Encyclopedia of Cuba

People, History, Culture

Volume II

Edited by
Luis Martínez-Fernández,
D. H. Figueredo, Louis A. Pérez, Jr.,
and Luis González

An Oryx Book

Greenwood Press
Westport, Connecticut • London

Library of Congress Cataloging-in-Publication Data

Encyclopedia of Cuba : people, history, culture / edited by Luis Martínez-Fernández . . . [et al.].
 p. cm.
 Includes bibliographical references and index.
 ISBN 1–57356–334–X (set: alk. paper)—ISBN 1–57356–572–5 (v. 1: alk. paper)—
 ISBN 1–57356–573–3 (v. 2: alk. paper)
 1. Cuba—Encyclopedias. I. Martínez-Fernández, Luis, 1960–
F1754.E53 2003
972.91′003—dc21   2002070030

British Library Cataloguing in Publication Data is available.

Library of Congress Catalog Card Number: 2002070030
ISBN: 1–57356–334–X (set)
ISBN: 1–57356–572–5 (v. 1)
ISBN: 1–57356–573–5 (v. 2)

First published in 2003

Greenwood Press, 88 Post Road West, Westport, CT 06881
An imprint of Greenwood Publishing Group, Inc.
www.greenwood.com

Printed in the United States of America

The paper used in this book complies with the
Permanent Paper Standard issued by the National
Information Standards Organization (Z39.48–1984).

10 9 8 7 6 5 4 3 2 1

Copyright Acknowledgments

The editors and the publisher gratefully acknowledge permission for use of the following
material:

Every reasonable effort has been made to trace the owners of copyright materials in this book,
but in some instances this has proven impossible. The author and publisher will be glad to
receive information leading to more complete acknowledgments in subsequent printings of this
book and in the meantime extend their apologies for any ommissions.

Contents

List of Entries

Introduction

The study of Cuba and its people attracts attention—and elicits passions—disproportionate to the country's numbers. With its 42,845 square miles (roughly equivalent to the area of Pennsylvania or Guatemala) and its 11.2 million inhabitants (about the population of Ohio or Metropolitan London), Cuba has captured worldwide attention among scholars and the general public—increasingly so since the triumph of the Cuban Revolution in 1959. The Cuban Revolution, in fact, is credited with igniting the ensuing boom in Latin American studies in U.S. universities, think tanks, and government agencies. The unexpected establishment of a pro-Soviet regime in an island state so near to, and with so many affinities with, the United States sparked interest among those who wanted to know "What happened in Cuba?"—either to keep it from happening again or to demonstrate that its alternative path was viable and replicable. Paradoxically, the same circumstances that increased U.S. scholarly interest in Latin America turned the study of Cuba into a challenging and difficult task as the United States imposed a trade embargo on the wayward island and as revolutionary leaders pursued a path of isolation from the West. Increased attention to Cuba, much of it responding to Cold War era political agendas, coupled with difficult access to information and obstacles to sustained research, as well as the absence of dialogue and exchange between island-based and foreign-based Cubanists, hampered the development of Cuban studies over the first few decades of the Cuban Revolution.

Over the last decade many of the old barriers to Cuban studies have begun to crumble, allowing the production of many valuable studies. Yet, some of the grotesque distortions that dominated the first few decades of the revolutionary era linger stubbornly and continue to influence the way many individuals—informed or otherwise—speak, write, and teach about Cuba's past and present. Although the catalogue of distortions is a long one, some of the most prevailing and harmful are highly politicized approaches producing polarized interpretations; a teleological view of Cuba's history that reduces the past to a mere prologue to the Revolution; a before-and-after narrative that fails to recognize continuities before and after 1959; a static view of the Revolution as if 1960s realities are the same as those of the dawn of the twenty-first century; a romanticized and exoticizing portrayal of the island and its people; and the notion that the more than one in ten Cubans who live abroad have somehow turned into something other than Cuban.

The Scope of this Encyclopedia

The editors and authors of this *Encyclopedia* have sought to prevent these distortions by striving to produce a collective work that is balanced and thus avoids a politicized depiction of the Cuban past and present reality. While not shying away from controversial topics—so much about Cuba is controversial—a concerted effort was made to include a variety of entries in which individual contributors could provide information and interpretation on the achievements and shortcomings of various epochs in Cuba's history: colonial, republican, and revolutionary. Biographical entries were selected on the merits and historical relevance of each biographee regardless of where each stood, or stands, vis-à-vis the Revolution or whether they lived, or live, on the island or abroad. Although many more individuals may warrant inclusion in a reference work of this kind, space limitations forced us to select a limited number of people to profile. Although the selection was subjective and certainly not perfect, no one was left out or forced in because of political considerations. Furthermore, much care went into the selection of the *Encyclopedia*'s eighty-one contributors, to ensure not only that each author possessed the necessary knowledge and skills but also that as a whole the contributions presented a balanced and objective picture.

Although the Cuban Revolution and Cuba's recent past has been the overwhelmingly primary object of attention from scholars as well as the general public, the editors of this *Encyclopedia* stress that Cuba has had a long and rich history that merits attention for its own importance and not only as a background to the tumultuous revolutionary period that began in 1959. This work points to the extraordinarily rich and vibrant contributions of generations of Cubans to the arts, literature, the sciences, sports, and many other fields. It also tells of the Cuban peoples' struggles, achievements, and failures, all of which deserve attention (even had the Revolution not taken place) and which will continue to deserve notice long after the Revolution comes to an end.

A related distortion is the before-and-after syndrome that continues to dominate the narrative of Cuban history. Rather than portraying the Cuban Revolution as a profound abyss separating heaven from hell, or conversely hell from heaven, we set out to trace the historical continuities that transcend the different periods of Cuban history. Undoubtedly, Cuba's Revolution was built upon a preexisting culture, and it inherited a tempestuous and complex past. For example, Cuba's contemporary emphasis on medical research and its laudable goal to make health care accessible to the entire population cannot be fully understood without recognizing that even if most physicians left the island shortly after the Revolution—more than half emigrated between 1959 and 1964—Cuba's health revolution grew out of a preexisting ethos of socially conscious medicine and a long tradition of medicine as science dating back to the nineteenth century. Similarly, the recent wave of official corruption and malfeasance is not simply a response to the crisis of the so-called Special Period but rather is heir to an ingrained political culture—again dating back to the colonial era—that has historically viewed political power as the primary source of individual profit and privilege. This *Encyclopedia* also seeks to provide a nuanced and historical view of the revolutionary period which recognizes that much has changed in the forty-odd years since Fidel Castro assumed power. It also seeks to emphasize that one should not generalize for the entire period but should rather be sensitive to change over time when looking at a host of matters ranging from nutrition to foreign relations and from government repression to internal support for the regime. Because the entries on the revolutionary period and contemporary era draw upon the latest available sources and publications, they provide up-to-date information and trace the most recent transformations in Cuban society.

The before-and-after perspective often leads to two related distortions: one that credits all areas of progress in Cuba to the Revolution and another that blames it for all of the island's misfortunes. Comparing pre-1959 Cuba with the island's present reality is both ahistorical and distorting—it assumes that all changes over a four-decade period were the result of actions by the revolutionary regime. It also ignores, for example, that the position of women has changed over the past forty years in Puerto Rico, Venezuela, and other societies that did not go through a revolution. The other side to this distortion, which I call the James Dean distortion, perpetuates a frozen and idealized picture of a late 1950s Cuba that was violently truncated suddenly and unexpectedly. Marlon Brando, we all know, grew old, fat, and bald; but the only James Dean we will ever know is the handsome twenty-four-year-old Hollywood icon who died tragically in 1955. Applied to Cuba, this distortion assumes that the island nation would not have suffered severe economic and social traumas had Castro not taken over in 1959. To conclude that all would have gone well in a Cuba without Revolution is a counterfactual exercise that ignores the past four convulsed and troubled decades of Latin American history.

Comparing Cuba to other neighboring societies, meanwhile, can be equally problematic. Much of what is said and written about the island nation, particularly by those who wish to highlight the achievements of the Revolution, implicitly or explicitly compares Cuba with nations like Guatemala or even Haiti. Such comparisons not only fail to recognize Cuba's particular historical trajectory but also ignore the fact that, dating back to the late eighteenth century, Cubans used European and North American frames of reference for their cultural, political, social, and technological aspirations. Thus, eighteenth-century planters purchased the latest European technology, nineteenth-century annexationists aspired to freedoms similar to those enjoyed in the United States, and present-day scientists and athletes pursue accomplishments comparable to those of their European and U.S. counterparts. When someone highlights Cuba's recent achievements in reducing illiteracy and child mortality, for example, by comparing them to those of, say, El Salvador, that person is engaging in overlapping distortions: first, implying that both societies stood at the same educational and health level fifty years ago—which was not the case; second, assuming that both societies aspire to the same standards—which is not the case either.

Yet another distortion that the editors have sought to avoid is the one that extrapolates the political differences separating Cuba's diaspora from the Cuban regime to the point that Cubans are bifurcated into two distinct peoples, each with its own culture, set of values, and aspirations for the island's future. Cuba has had a long history of massive and recurrent exile and emigration. José Antonio Saco, Félix Varela, José Martí, Tomás Estrada Palma (Cuba's first president), and thousands of other Cubans spent the bulk of their lifetimes abroad. In 1898, as the Cuban War of Independence raged on, one in ten Cubans—roughly the same proportion as today—lived in exile in the United States. These experiences forged a Cuban culture that could remain Cuban and continue to thrive even during prolonged periods of exile. Similarly, the estimated two million Cubans who are scattered throughout the world today continue to contribute to—and arguably preserve—many aspects of Cuban culture. In that vein, anthropologist Fernando Ortiz, one of Cuba's most influential scholars, asserted in 1940 that Cuba was "both a land and a people; and that 'lo cubano' are those things belonging to this country and to its people." Likewise, Guillermo Cabrera Infante later wrote "To be Cuban is to go with Cuba everywhere." Echoing these beliefs, the editors of this work did not separate the contributions of Cubans abroad from those of Cubans on the island. We recognized that what unites Cuban writers, musicians, and even *peloteros* on both sides of the Straits of Florida is more than what sets them apart. That is why, for example, the entry on Cuban American novelist Cristina García—who writes in English—appears in the same chapter as that of writer Cabrera Infante, who sought exile in 1966 and now lives in London, and poet Nicolás Guillén, who died in Havana in 1989, to the end apparently loyal to the Revolution. In short, this *Encyclopedia* subscribes to the notion that there is one Cuban literature, and it includes not only what has been written on the island but also what the Countess of Merlín wrote in mid-nineteenth-century Paris and what Martí later wrote in New York as well as what Oscar Hijuelos writes today in New York and what Zoé Valdés writes in Paris. Given the massive nature and historical importance of the Cuban diaspora, however, we have chosen to include a separate section on the Cuban diaspora that chronicles the activities of Cubans abroad, particularly in the realms of business and politics.

Arrangement of the Encyclopedia

A few words on the *Encyclopedia*'s organization: Rather than structure these volumes along a strict A-to-Z format, the editors decided to arrange the work's more than 700 entries into twelve topical chapters so that readers could easily find clusters of entries touching upon similar topics. Entries within each chapter appear alphabetically. The chapters include a brief opening explanation on Cuba's national symbols, followed by a chapter on geography, the environment, and urbanization. These are followed by three historical chapters, each focusing on a particular period (colonial, republican, and revolutionary) and a sixth chapter covering aspects of the island's contemporary economy and society. Chapters 7, 8, and 9 provide information on literature, the performing arts, and the plastic arts, respectively. Chapter 10 addresses popular culture and religion, and Chapter 11 covers sports. A final chapter is dedicated to the Cuban diaspora. Because of this thematic structure, a reader seeking information on, say, baseball Hall of Famer Atanasio (Tony) Pérez, will find next to his entry those of other Cuban sports legends ranging from Cuba's first Olympic star, fencer Ramón Fonst, to contemporary sluggers Orestes Quindelán and Omar Linares. Pérez's entry also leads to a series of cross-referenced entries such as **Camagüey Province** (where he was born) and related entries such as **Baseball** and **Cubans in the U.S. Major Leagues**. This format also allows someone interested in learning about a given topic, for example, Cuban painting, to encounter information on the leading painters and related subjects within a specific section of the *Encyclopedia*. By reading all the entries in that particular section, the reader will get a good sense of the trajectory and richness of Cuban painting. Most entries include cross references that point to other entries and also include a list of suggested further readings where students and researchers can find expanded information on any particular person or subject matter. All cross references within the entry appear in **bold type**. For those who wish to find information alphabetically in the *Encyclopedia*, there are both a detailed index at the end of the second volume and a list of all the entry headwords in alphabetical order at the front of the volumes. A number of appendixes are also included to provide extra information on some particular topics. The appendixes include historical documents, a chronology of Cuban history and lists of all colonial governors and presidents.

Acknowledgments

This project has been a collective labor of love that has brought together nearly a hundred scholars, photographers, and artists from all over the globe who share a passion for Cuba and its people. Luis González deserves credit for the idea of producing this comprehensive Cuban encyclopedia, the first since the mid-1970s and the first ever in English. He drafted the original proposal for the book and also took the first steps in putting together the team of four editors, which besides him included Louis A. Pérez, Jr., of the University of North Carolina, D. H. Figueredo, of Bloomfield College, and myself, Luis Martínez-Fernández, of Rutgers University. At the early stages of this project, the editors sought the advice of some of the world's foremost experts on Cuban subjects and invited them to join the *Encyclopedia*'s advisory board, which includes Antonio Benítez Rojo, Wilfredo Cancio Isla, Cristóbal Díaz Ayala, Jason Feer, Ada M. Isasi-Díaz, Peter T. Johnson, Juan A. Martínez, Félix Masud-Piloto, Consuelo Naranjo Orovio, Silvia Pedraza, Paula J. Pettavino, Armando H. Portela, and Alan West-Durán. They were instrumental in shaping the work's structure and in tackling the difficult task of establishing the master list of entries. They also wrote a number of the work's entries and recommended many of the other contributors. Consuelo Naranjo Orovio in particular was key to the selection of the Spanish contributors. The team of eighty-one scholars who wrote the work's more than 700 entries includes writers, researchers, and scholars from various parts of the world; we received contributions from Spain, the United Kingdom, Australia, Canada, Cuba, Puerto Rico, and from several states of the United States. The authors ranged from advanced graduate students to middle career scholars to professors emeriti, and they came from various fields: geography, history, literary criticism, journalism, and filmmaking, to name but a few. Unusual for a collaborative project of this magnitude, we had virtually no *embarcadores*—on the contrary, the authors were reliably punctual—and despite the bewildering back-and-forth of hundreds of diskettes and attachments over a three-year period, no cyber-viruses were ever received. Although the editors remain responsible for the selection of the team of contributing scholars and the structural balance of the work, all authors retained the prerogative to write their entries as they saw fit. The editors of the *Encyclopedia* wish to acknowledge their gratitude to the advisers and authors who generously poured their energy and knowledge into this project.

We are also grateful to a number of institutions and individuals who collaborated with and supported the project in a variety of ways. Rutgers University's Research Council provided a grant that helped fund some of the research. The Center for Latin American Studies of the University of Florida awarded a Library Travel Grant to the University of Florida's Smathers Libraries, where Richard Phillips and his staff were enormously helpful. Pat Roos, former Area Dean for Social and Behavioral Sciences at Rutgers University, allotted funds that paid for graduate student assistance. Aracely García Carranza of the Biblioteca Nacional José Martí in Havana, Esperanza Varona of the Cuban Heritage Collection at the Otto G. Richter Library of the University of Miami, and Peter T. Johnson and AnnaLee Pauls of Princeton University's Firestone Library also provided invaluable assistance, as did Lourdes Vázquez and Fernanda Perrone of Rutgers University's Alexander Library. Myra Torres Alamo and the staff of the Digitalization Project of the *El Mundo* Photograph Collection at the University of Puerto Rico, Río Piedras, granted access to their collection. Also generous with his collection was Cristóbal Díaz Ayala of Fundación Musicalia in San Juan, a unique collection of recordings and other materials documenting the trajectory of Cuban and Latin American music. This collection was donated to the Florida International University Library in 2001, which also made these materials available for our use. Frank Argote-Freyre served as assistant editor, writing entries and laboring in various research and administrative tasks.

Numerous cartographers, photographers, and editors allowed us to reproduce their work so that the *Encyclopedia*'s visual component would match the quality of its text. Geographer Armando H. Portela produced many of the maps specially for the *Encyclopedia*. Michael Siegel of Rutgers University Cartography produced the map of nineteenth-century Havana. Jason Feer, former editor of *CubaNews*, graciously allowed us to reproduce several graphs, tables, and maps. My father, Celestino Martínez Lindín, traveled to Havana—his first visit in four decades—to take many of this book's photographs of contemporary Cuba. And my oldest son Luis Alberto Martínez, despite never having worn one, drew the sketch of the traditional Cuban *guayabera* shirt. Dania del Sol of Art & Photo Retouching gave of her technical expertise in photo retouching to improve the quality of many of the illustrations. Alejandro Anreus, Ada Ferrer, and Julio César González Pagés graciously loaned us photographs from their collections. Many other photographers whose work graces the pages of the *Encyclopedia* are properly credited in the captions.

Anne Thompson and the other editors and staff members of the Greenwood Publishing Group took special interest in and devoted particular care to these volumes. We thank them for their support, guidance, and assistance during the various stages leading to their publication.

Numerous other individuals—too many to mention here—contributed to the final result in large and small ways: providing hard-to-find facts, giving leads about illustrations, suggesting potential contributors, or simply encouraging us about the relevance of this work.

We trust that this work will fill an important gap among works of reference on Cuba and that it will serve as the first step in many future studies that shall continue to increase our knowledge and understanding about that alluring and complex island and its brave, tenacious, and creative people. We especially hope that these volumes will find their way to the bookshelves and hearts of Cuban and Cuban American homes so that new generations may get a taste of the *ajiaco* (Cuban stew) with which Fernando Ortiz compared the complex Cuban culture and find ways to connect with the island which Columbus described as "the most beautiful land human eyes have ever seen."

This work, whose publication coincides with the centennial of Cuba's ill-starred independence in 1902, is humbly dedicated to all Cubans, wherever they may live.

Luis Martínez-Fernández
Senior Editor

8

Performing Arts

Afro-Cuban Jazz

Afro-Cuban jazz, the wedding of Cuban rhythm, ensemble style, and structural elements with jazz-based melody and harmony, gelled just after World War II and grew into a dominant genre within jazz (see **Afro-Cubans**).

Scott Joplin's ragtime and Jelly Roll Morton's piano jazz were early attempts to assimilate Latin American (principally Cuban) rhythmic elements in U.S. music; Puerto Rican trombonist Juan Tizol's work with Duke Ellington in the 1930s, including such compositions as "Perdido," furthered the enterprise. But only in the 1940s did musicians move beyond simply adding conga drums or simple rhythmic motifs onto a swing-jazz base, instead weaving a tight fabric of Afro-Cuban percussion and rhythmic structures with jazz instrumentation, melody, and harmony. Crucial rhythmic functions were played by Afro-Cuban ostinatos (reiterated rhythmic figures) on percussion and piano; the two-measure *clave* pattern of alternating 3-2 or 2-3 stresses; and the syncopated bass style, *bajo anticipado*. The movement's founding moments were the formation of "Machito's Afro-Cubans" in the mid-1940s and Dizzy Gillespie's 1946 record-ing of **Luciano "Chano" Pozo**'s "Manteca" with Pozo on congas.

Afro-Cuban jazz was an international, collective creation by such musicians as Cubans **Frank Grillo ("Machito")**, Mario Bauzá, "Patato" Valdés, Pozo, **"Cachao" (Israel López), Arsenio Rodríguez**, Chico O'Farrill, and "Mongo" Santamaría; Puerto Ricans Tito Puente, Tito Rodríguez, and Noro Morales; and North Americans "Cab" Calloway, Gillespie, Stan Kenton, and Cal Tjader. Machito's orchestra was particularly seminal; its musical director, his brother-in-law trumpeter Mario Bauzá, had played in jazz orchestras such as Calloway's and tapped black jazz arrangers. The genre is often referred to as "Cubop," testimony to its contemporaneity with bebop.

Afro-Cuban jazz can be defined via its boundaries with certain kindred musical forms. It differs from traditional Cuban folk and popular forms such as **guajira** and **son** in being almost strictly instrumental, jazz-based, and heavily improvisational; from jazz by its percussion instrumentation and structural elements; and from the Cuban-derived dance music known as **salsa** (with which it is often confused) in not being primarily a danceable genre and the virtual absence of lyrics.

After its foundation in the 1940s, Afro-Cuban jazz developed in concert with **mambo** and **cha-cha-chá** in the 1950s, went into relative eclipse in the 1960s (though Cachao with his **descargas**, Santamaría, and vibraphonist Tjader all continued its development), coexisted with salsa in the 1970s, and reemerged beginning in the 1980s particularly under the influence of Puente, New York Puerto Rican musician Jerry González, and others.

Further Readings

Loza, Steven. *Tito Puente and the Making of Latin Music*. Urbana: University of Illinois Press, 1999.
Roberts, John Storm. *The Latin Tinge*. 2nd ed. New York: Oxford University Press, 1999.

Pablo Julián Davis

Almendros Cuyás, Néstor (1930–1992)

One of the world's greatest cinematographers, Néstor Almendros was born in Barcelona and immigrated to Cuba with his parents when he was eighteen years old. After graduating from the **University of Havana**, Almendros studied film, photography, and editing at the City College of New York; later on, he continued his film studies at Rome's Centro Sperimentale de Cinematografia, where **Tomás Gutiérrez Alea** was also a student. When the Cuban **Revolution** triumphed in 1959, he returned to Cuba where he shot a few documentaries. Encountering censorship in 1961 of his films *Gente en la playa* and *Tumba francesa*, Almendros relocated to Paris where he worked with Eric Rohmer, Francois Truffaut, and other New Wave filmmakers. His Hollywood phase began in 1978 when he won the Oscar for best cinematography for the film *Days of Heaven*. He used his cinematographic and photographic talents in the making of two anti-**Castro** documentaries, *Conducta impropia*, in 1983, and *Nadie escuchaba*, in

1988. Besides an Oscar, he also received the Cesa award for the *Last Metro* and was made Chevalier of the French Honor Legion. He died in New York City in 1992. *See also* U.S. Entertainment Industry, Cubans in the

Further Reading

Chanan, Michael. *The Cuban Image: Cinema and Cultural Politics in Cuba*. London: British Film Institute, 1985.

Jesús Vega

Alonso, Alicia (1921–)

Alicia Alonso was born Alicia Ernestina de la Caridad del Cobre Martínez Hoya in Havana. Considered one of the great classical ballerinas in the history of dance, she is also a choreographer and founder of the Ballet Alicia Alonso (1948) and of the **Ballet Nacional de Cuba**. Alonso has been enormously influential due to her educational and artistic contributions and is probably the best-known Latin American figure associated with theatrical dance.

Strongly motivated at a young age, she was trained at Pro Arte Musical in Havana, where she met Cuban dancer Fernando Alonso, whom she married at sixteen. Defying negative social stereotypes associated with ballet at the time, the Alonsos moved to New York to initiate a professional career. They arrived in New York at a time when U.S. artists, recently out of the Great Depression, were probing into North American indigenous themes in order to give new meaning to the foundations and traditions of the past. Ballet Theatre, the first "American" ballet company founded in the United States in 1939 under the direction of Lucia Chase and Richard Pleasant, was Alonso's professional beginnings. There she met an innovating avant-garde of choreographers, dancers, designers, and musicians. She also came into contact with the leading Russian masters, including Michael Fokine, and studied with Enrico

Alicia Alonso is considered one of the world's greatest ballerinas of all time (1977). AP/Wide World Photos.

Zanfretta and Alexandra Fedorova and at the School of American Ballet with George Balanchine, Anatole Oboukhoff, Anatole Vilzak, and others.

Her spectacular rise to stardom as a young dancer with Ballet Theatre in spite of great odds (including blinding eye sight problems since her early twenties) was one of the most important accomplishments for Latin American dance traditions. Alonso's interpretation of *Giselle* established her as a "prima ballerina" in the history of romantic ballet. She was partnered by some of the most important prominent classical dancers of the time: Anton Dolin, Igor Youskevitch, André Eglevsky. She also excelled in neoclassical and contemporary ballets. Balanchine choreographed *Theme and Variations* for her, and she interpreted works by Eugene Loring, Leonide Massine, and Antony Tudor.

In spite of her triumphs in the United States, Alonso always returned to Cuba, where she cofounded the Ballet Alicia Alonso in 1948 (later named Ballet de Cuba). Many dancers joined her, including Youskevitch. Ana García, cofounder of Puerto Rico's Ballets de San Juan, was also among them. Alonso's influence in the development of dance in other Spanish-speaking countries is one of her greatest contributions. Since 1948 she has been acclaimed by critics and audiences worldwide. Later, in the early stages of the **Revolution**, she chose to return to her homeland to direct the Ballet Nacional de Cuba (1960). This ambitious project, which brought together a group of distinguished artists, was subsidized by the revolutionary government. Alonso has been recognized as an inspiring national figure by Cuba's cultural critics and writers **Alejo Carpentier, Fina García Marruz, José Lezama Lima, Jorge Mañach, Juan Marinello**, and **Cintio Vitier**, who have paid tribute to her art. In a broader spectrum, Alonso has been included by scholars among the exceptional women artists of Latin America and has been the recipient of numerous awards, honors, and medals including the *Dance Magazine* Award (1958) and the Prix Pavlova (1966).

Further Readings

Hechevarría, María del Carmen. *Alicia Alonso: más allá de la técnica*. Valencia: Universidad Politécnica de Valencia, 1998.

Parera Villalón, Célida. *Historia de la Sociedad Pro-Arte Musical de La Habana*. Montclair, NJ: Senda Nueva Ediciones, 1990.

Simón, Pedro y Rey Alfonso. *Alicia Alonso: órbita de una leyenda*. Madrid: Autores del Siglo XX, 1996.

Terry, Walter. *Alicia and Her Ballet Nacional de Cuba*. Garden City, NY: Anchor, 1981.

Alma Concepción

Álvarez, Adalberto (1948–   )

Adalberto Álvarez established himself as the leading modernizer of the **son**, as well as its most popular composer, beginning in the 1980s.

Born in **Camagüey**, Álvarez grew up in a musically nourishing home; he first performed with Avance Juvenil, the band led by his father. He studied at the Escuela Nacional de Arte, directing its **charanga**-style Orquesta Típica, and later became a professor in the Escuela Provincial de Música de Camagüey. He was deeply influenced by the master of the *tres*, **Arsenio Rodríguez**, and other Cuban artists of the early to middle twentieth century. Álvarez first achieved renown with his band Son 14, whose express aim was to modernize the traditional son. Álvarez's orchestrations tended to seek stylistic balance between such traditional Cuban elements as the tres and contemporary instruments including synthesizers. His compositions gained enormous influence; as early as 1985, they were the most widely recorded worldwide of any son composer's, a notable achievement given his young age and having at that time toured little outside Cuba. Álvarez's work has been recorded by an array of groups and artists including La Sonora Ponceña (Puerto Rico), Juan Luis Guerra (Dominican Republic), **Willy Chirino** (Cuba–Florida), and Oscar D'León (Venezuela). In 1984, now based in Santiago de Las Vegas, **Havana Province**, he established a new band, Adalberto Álvarez y Su Son, which began to tour widely; performances in the United States began in 1988. Álvarez's status as a *babalao* (priest) in the Afro-Cuban rites of **Santería** also informed his music.

Further Reading

Martínez, Mayra A. *Cubanos en la música*. Havana: Editorial Letras Cubanas, 1993.

Pablo Julián Davis

Álvarez, Paulina (1912–1965)

Paulina Álvarez is known as "the empress of the *danzonete*." Her voice and ability for improvisation brought the danzonete, created by composer **Aniceto Díaz**, to its

most complete expression. Born in **Cienfuegos** on June 29, 1912, Álvarez started to sing at the age of nine, performing in social and school events. In 1926, she arrived in Havana with her family, and in 1929 she was the first female performer to sing the danzonete. With the development of the radio in Cuba during the 1930s, she became a professional singer. She founded her orchestra in 1939, performing Cuban music at Havana's Teatro Auditorium; it was the first time popular music was played at a theater known for only showcasing classical works. Álvarez died in Havana in 1965.

Further Reading

Orovio, Helio. *Diccionario de la música cubana: biográfico y técnico*. Havana: Editorial Letras Cubanas, 1981.

Jesús Vega

Álvarez Guedes, Guillermo (1928–)

Arguably the best-known Cuban stand-up comic, Guillermo Álvarez Guedes has recorded dozens of comedy albums and written several volumes of joke books. Born in the town of Unión de Reyes, in **Matanzas Province**, he made his artistic debut at the age of five. He left home at the age of thirteen, working with small orchestras and traveling circuses. During the late 1940s he lived in New York, returning to Cuba in 1949. In the 1950s, he appeared in many Cuban television shows and created a character known as *el borrachito* (the little drunkard).

Álvarez Guedes left Cuba, seeking exile in the United States in 1959. In 1973 he began recording his stand-up comedy albums. He has recorded twenty-nine albums and has three films to his credit. Álvarez Guedes is known for using so-called bad-words in his act. His style is so natural, however, that few find them offensive.

One of his best-known albums, *El día que cayó Fidel Castro*, is actually a serious piece dramatizing what it might be like in the United States and in Cuba the day **Fidel Castro** is overthrown.

Further Reading
Álvarez Guedes, Guillermo. *De la vida, de la muerte, y otras mierdas más*. Caracas: Publicaciones Seleven, 1984.

Luis González

Anacaona, Orquesta

The Orquesta Anacaona was a Cuban dance band composed entirely of women of mixed Asian and Afro-Cuban descent. It was representative of one of many female ensembles popular in Havana of the 1930s including the Orquesta Ensueño and the Orquesta Orbe. Initially, the Castro sisters, who first formed La Anacaona in 1932, played *sones* in a traditional *sexteto* style (see **Son**). Concepción played guitar, Ada the *tres*, Olga the maracas, Flora the *clave*, Millo the *bongó*, and Ondina the trumpet, while Caridad sang lead vocals. Anacaona made its musical debut playing in open-air cafés on the Prado near the **capitol building** such as the El Dorado, the Saratoga, and the café of the Hotel Pasaje. Though well received, they eventually decided to change their format and repertory. Beginning in 1934 they played *danzones, danzonetes*, and related ballroom music as a **charanga**, and in the later 1930s they changed again to form a jazz band (see **Danzón**). It is this final format, retained through the 1950s, that brought them greatest success. The repertory of the Orquesta Anacaona included a surprising diversity of genres including North American fox trots and swing tunes, Spanish *paso dobles*, tangos, waltzes, and son-influenced dance music. Because of its versatility, the group was able to perform in virtually any venue in Havana, from popular beer gardens to exclusive gatherings in the Casino Español. Beginning in 1933, they also toured abroad regularly in Puerto Rico, Mexico, and other Latin American countries and also the United States in 1938 with Cuban musician Alberto Socarrás as director. The orchestra has remained active in Cuba with new generations of performers.

Further Reading
Orovio, Helio. *Diccionario de la música cubana: biográfico y técnico*. 2nd ed. Havana: Editorial Letras Cubanas, 1992, 322–323.

Robin Moore

Anckermann, Jorge (1877–1941)

Pianist and theater orchestra director Jorge Anckermann is one of the most well-known musicians associated with Cuba's *teatro vernáculo*, or comic theater, during the early twentieth century. Amazingly prolific, Anckermann wrote over 700 musical reviews for **theaters** including the Martí, Actualidades, Payret, Tacón, Lara, and mostly the Alhambra. Born in Havana to German parents, Anckermann studied music with his father Carlos and by his late teens had already established himself as a composer and conductor of distinction. He began his professional career on tour as director of the **Narciso López** comedy troupe that spent several years in Mexico beginning in 1892. Anckermann's original works consist of a diversity of genres including **zarzuela** arias, *canciones*, **criollas, boleros, puntos cubanos, guajiras** (he is considered the creator of this genre), and comic sketches. He is perhaps best remembered for his tenure in the Alhambra theater before its closure in 1935 and the many *sainetes*, or one-act musical plays, he wrote that parodied contemporary political events. Unfortunately a surprising number of his scores have been lost; the Centro Odilio Urfé in Havana houses the largest collection of those that are still available. *See also* Teatro Bufo

Further Reading

Orovio, Helio. *Diccionario de la música cubana: biográfico y técnico*. 2nd. ed. Havana: Editorial Letras Cubanas, 1992, 32–33.

Robin Moore

Aragón, Orquesta

The Orquesta Aragón was founded in 1939 by *contrabajista* Orestes Aragón under the name of Rítmica Aragón. As usual at that time, it was an amateur group composed of musicians who worked at other jobs to help earn a living. A year later, thirteen-year-old Rafael Lay substituted as one of the orchestra's violinists. In 1948, upon Aragón's retirement, Lay became the orchestra's director and conductor. During this time, Orquesta Aragón's reputation grew, and in 1953, it began to record for RCA Victor. The musicians recorded *danzones* as well as a new dance called the **cha-cha-chá**. With the help of the arrangements of the creator of cha-cha-chá, Enrique Jorrín, the orchestra played on radio stations and gave live performances, and its recordings were played on jukeboxes across the island. In 1955, the orchestra moved to Havana, and it added to the group the flutist, composer, and arranger Richard Egües, as well as the singers Pepe Olmo and Rafael Bacallao. With its musical discipline, professionalism, arrangements, soloists, and selected repertory, the orchestra became emblematic of the cha-cha-chá. In 1982, the director died, and his son Rafaelito took over the orchestra. He expanded the repertory, adding other musical genres, including such original works as the *Chaonda*, created by the orchestra's cellist, Tomasito Valdés. The orchestra has traveled widely. Sixty years old, and with many of the original members either dead or retired, Orquesta Aragón remains the embodiment of cha-cha-chá and the most influential musical group of its period.

Further Reading

Díaz Ayala, Cristóbal. *Música cubana del areyto a la nueva trova*. Miami: Ediciones Universal, 1993.

Cristóbal Díaz Ayala and Marisa Méndez

Arcaño y sus Maravillas, Orquesta

Antonio Arcaño (1911–1991), also called el Monarca, was a flutist who performed with several orchestras that primarily played *danzones* until creating his own group Arcaño y Sus Maravillas in 1937 (see **Danzón**). He was an accomplished musician, as were the members of his group: the violinists Miguel Tachit, Félix Reina, and Enrique Jorrín; cellist Orestes López; and his brother, bass player **"Cachao" (Israel López)**. All these musicians also doubled as composers, proving true the appellation *Maravillas*. The group innovated the danzón, making the dance more dynamic, fast moving, and more appealing to the dancer. They also incorporated the use of drums. It is believed that the **mambo** originated in some of the danzones written by Orestes and Cachao López and that the **cha-cha-chá** evolved out of the pieces composed by Jorrín.

Arcaño y Sus Maravillas was highly successful during the 1940s and 1950s, forming part of a musical triumvirate called "Los Tres Grandes," which included the orchestras Melodías del 40 and the Conjunto de **Arsenio Rodríguez**. The orchestra was featured regularly at the famous dance parties at Jardines de la Tropical.

Due to health reasons, Arcaño ceased to perform in 1945 but remained as the orchestra's director. He retired in 1958.

Further Reading

Díaz Ayala, Cristóbal. *Música cubana del areyto a la nueva trova*. Miami: Ediciones Universal, 1993.

Cristóbal Díaz Ayala and Marisa Méndez

Desi Arnaz, musician, bandleader, actor, and producer. Photograph by Ernest Bachrach. Images of Desi Arnaz courtesy of Desilu, too, LLC.

Arnaz, Desi (1912–1986)

Desi Arnaz was a television pioneer, bandleader, singer, and actor best remembered for his appearances as Ricky Ricardo in the popular series *I Love Lucy*. Arnaz pioneered the use of the three-camera film technique for television shows as well as the concept of filming a situation comedy before a "live" audience. He is also credited with leading the way in the creation of syndicated reruns.

Desiderio Arnaz was born in **Santiago de Cuba**, where his father was the mayor. In 1933, Arnaz and his family moved to Miami as a result of the **Revolution of 1933** against dictator **Gerardo Machado**, whom his father supported. In Florida, Arnaz attended private school and worked at different jobs. His musical training, pleasant voice, and good looks landed him a spot as a guitarist at a nightclub. Eventually, he met bandleader **Xavier Cugat**,

joining his orchestra. He helped popularize the **conga** dance in the United States.

In the late 1930s, he performed in the Broadway hit *Too Many Girls*. In 1940, he appeared in the movie version of the play. During the filming, he and the leading lady, Lucille Ball, fell in love and later married. Arnaz had minor roles in several movies but spent most of his time touring the country with his own orchestra. Back in California, his wife was busy pursuing a successful career in Hollywood and on the radio. The constant separations strained their marriage, and the couple decided to work together on a radio show for CBS. Initially, network executives believed that the U.S. public would not accept a program where the housewife was married to a Cuban. To prove them wrong, Arnaz and Lucille Ball staged a husband-and-wife show, which they took on a national tour. Audiences loved the couple.

I Love Lucy premiered in 1951 and ran for six years. Arnaz and his wife formed their own productions company, Desilu. As head of the studio and producer, Arnaz produced or coproduced several popular television shows, including *The Untouchables, Make Room for Daddy*, and *Star Trek*. He and Lucille Ball starred in two movies, *The Long Long Trailer* (1954) and *Forever Darling* (1956). In 1960, Arnaz and Ball were divorced.

Arnaz was the first Hispanic superstar in U.S. television. Since his death in 1986, his reputation has grown. Arnaz was portrayed in the novel *The Mambo Kings Play Songs of Love*, by **Oscar Hijuelos**, as well as in the film adaptation. His radio performances with his orchestra were recently released as CDs. *See also* U.S. Entertainment Industry, Cubans in the

Further Reading
Arnaz, Desi. *A Book*. New York: Morrow, 1976.

D.H. Figueredo

Avilés, Orquesta Hermanos

Founded in 1882 by the Avilés brothers, the Orquesta Hermanos Avilés is possibly the oldest orchestra in Latin America. It originally consisted of eleven musicians who exclusively performed *danzones* (see **Danzón**). Most of the musicians joined the Cuban army during the **War of Independence**, playing in the military band. Under the direction of trombonist Manuel Dositeo Aguilera, the band premiered on November 14, 1895, the anthem "El Himno Invasor," considered Cuba's second **national anthem**. "El Himno Invasor" was composed by General Enrique Loynaz del Castillo and orchestrated by Aguilera.

After the war, the orchestra was reorganized as a jazz band. It remained a local group with few recordings. In 1982, however, the orchestra recorded a long play in celebration of its centennial.

Further Reading

Díaz Ayala, Cristóbal. *Música cubana del areyto a la nueva trova*. Miami: Edicions Universal, 1993.

Cristóbal Díaz Ayala and Marisa Méndez

Azpiazu, Orquesta

The orchestra of Justo Ángel "Don" Azpiazu (1893–1943) received international recognition for helping to initiate the "rumba craze" of the 1930s in the United States and Europe (see **Rumba Complex**). Born into an elite Cuban family, Azpiazu began performing with the Havana **Orquesta Casino**, a group of his own creation, in 1921. In the wake of global depression after 1929, Azpiazu chose to leave Cuba for potentially more lucrative markets abroad. His ensemble opened on April 26, 1930, at the Palace Theater in New York. It came with exhibition rumba dancers, apparently the first who had ever performed in the United States. The shows they presented were well received and resulted in a record contract with RCA Victor. Azpiazu's ensemble consisted of what is now standard Afro-Cuban percussion in addition to those more typically associated with jazz bands. Their renditions of "Ay Mamá Inés" and "El manicero" (The Peanut Vendor) became hits in the United States in 1930 and 1931. They went to New York in 1932 and thereafter to France with great success, but Don left the band in 1934 in the hands of his brother Antobal, who back in New York reorganized it under his own name. Don came back to Cuba, but in 1937 he worked for a while with Rudy Vallee and Glen Gray's Casa Loma Orchestra. Azpiazu is credited as one of the first Cuban jazz bandleaders to accept dark-skinned **Afro-Cubans** as performers in his ensemble. He died of a heart attack in Havana a few days before his fiftieth birthday. *See also* Afro-Cuban Jazz

Further Reading

Orovio, Helio. *Diccionario de la música cubana: biográfico y técnico*. 2nd ed. Havana: Editorial Letras Cubanas, 1992, 43.

Robin Moore

Ballet Nacional de Cuba (Formerly Ballet de Cuba)

Originally founded in 1948 by **Alicia Alonso**, the Ballet Alicia Alonso was later renamed Ballet Nacional de Cuba and was subsidized by the revolutionary government that came into power in 1959. The National Ballet encompassed an ambitious project conceived not only for the establishment of a dance company but for making the art of ballet accessible to all Cubans. Goals included the long-term education of dancers under a rigorous discipline to ensure an artistic and technical level of international stature. The Escuela de Cubanacán, housed in an arts complex on the outskirts of Havana, recruited talented candidates and offered them scholarships. The project expanded nationwide, and Alicia Alonso devoted herself to transmitting her art and her knowledge to a new generation of dancers that included Aurora Bosch, Josefina Méndez, Mirta Plá, Loipa Araujo, Orlando Salgado, Lázaro Carreño, Andrés Williams, and Jorge Esquivel, who rose to be Alonso's partner. Some members have been recipients of gold, silver, and bronze medals in international competitions, including Aurora Bosch, Loipa Araujo, Amparo Brito, Josefina Méndez, Marta García, Mirta Plá, and María Elena Llorente. Many more have made outstanding contributions to Cuban and international dance.

The National Ballet renovated the classical tradition and expanded classic and contemporary currents by integrating a diverse cultural heritage. By establishing from the beginning their own aesthetic and pedagogical ideas, Cuban teachers and choreographers developed a series of traits, including a distinct style, a different way of dancing, called the *escuela cubana de ballet* (Cuban ballet school), which has earned a place in the history of dance. As part of their educational outreach, the company and its teachers have collaborated with dance projects in Colombia, Mexico, Puerto Rico, and Spain. The National Ballet did not adopt prevalent physical stereotypes but incorporated the physical and kinetic heritage of the multiracial and multicultural Caribbean region, respecting individuality at the same time. The company promoted collective effort over stardom and gave male dancers increased visibility. Its repertoire has always included the classics, such as *Giselle* and *Swan Lake*, as well as contemporary works by renowned choreographers. The National Ballet also stimulated new artists. Alberto Méndez, its main choreographer for many years, created a varied repertoire with works such as

Plasmasis, El río y el bosque, and *Tarde en la siesta*, in which he reinvented myths, rituals, and traditions within a classical vocabulary. Several major pieces were created by Alberto Alonso, including *Carmen*, originally composed for the Bolshoi Ballet. Political ties with the Soviet Union fostered choreographic and educational exchanges as well as dancing partnerships. Other Cuban choreographers, including Alicia Alonso herself, as well as several generations of dancers, designers, and musicians, have contributed to a vast repertoire that has earned the National Ballet many distinctions and honors worldwide. *See also* Soviet Union, Cuba's Relations with the

Further Readings

Cabrera, Miguel. *Órbita del Ballet Nacional de Cuba/1948–1978*. Havana: Orbe, 1978.

Terry, Walter. *Alicia and Her Ballet Nacional de Cuba*. Garden City, NY: Anchor, 1981.

Alma Concepción

Bola de Nieve (Ignacio Villa) (1902–1971)

Ignacio Villa (commonly referred to as "Bola de Nieve" or "Snowball") stands out as the only dark-skinned Cuban to achieve recognition as a performer and composer of commercial salon music in the 1930s. Born in Guanabacoa, outside of Havana in 1902, Villa pursued classical music studies from an early age, at first privately with Gerardo Guanche and later in the Conservatorio de José Mateu. He studied flute and mandolin in addition to the piano. Villa's professional keyboard career began in silent movie theaters as a means of supporting himself (see **Theaters**); he continued to study the piano intensely and by the 1930s had established a reputation as a classical accompanist. In 1933, **Rita Montaner** contracted Villa for a tour of Mexico. It was during this time that he began

Famed entertainers Bola de Nieve and Rita Montaner. Photograph courtesy of the Biblioteca Nacional José Martí, Havana.

to sing himself on occasion, interpreting the **Eliseo Grenet** compositions for which he would become most famous. In later years he spent a great deal of time abroad and befriended African American performers Lena Horne, Paul Robeson, and Teddy Wilson. His performance included a wide repertory, including his own songs, **boleros**, and Afro-Cuban songs; some of his musical performances resembled those of Tin Pan Alley contemporaries Jerome Kern and Cole Porter. As an Afro-Cuban classical musician who became famous for interpreting songs of the white middle classes that depicted black street culture, Ignacio Villa personifies the complexities and ironies of early-twentieth-century popular song in Cuba. He died in 1971 while on tour in Mexico. *See also* Afro-Cubans

Further Reading
Ojeda, Miguelito, ed. *Bola de Nieve*. Havana: Editorial Letras Cubanas, 1998.

Robin Moore

Bolero

The *bolero*, a genre for dancing and listening Caribbean and Mexican musical repertoires, shares its name with an ancient Spanish dance for solo couples and castanets, introduced in Cuban **theaters** by the end of the eighteenth century. A century later, Cuban troubadours gave that name to songs of love, nature, and patriotic devotion. Its melodic phrasing and contours revealed—within a binary form and a dual meter—a strong influence of Italian *cantilenas* and the Spanish *tonadilla* to the accompaniment of a guitar. This accompaniment incorporated a balance of simple harmonies and rhythmic patterns like the Cuban *cinquillo*, a feature that markedly evoked a Latin American and Caribbean identity in its African stream. Originally, composers like the legendary Pepe Sánchez made boleros as a medium for listening along with the **habanera**, the *canción*, and the **criolla**, created for solo singers and later by duets. The **Trío Matamoros** introduced the *bolero-son* as a dance genre in the urban dance halls of Cuba during the late 1920s. In courtship rituals and other musical events, the bolero evolved into forms like the *danzonete* and the *danzón cantado* and eventually displaced the **danzón** and the waltz to become the slow counterpart of genres like the *guaracha* and the **son**. Much like the prominence of Argentinean tango in Buenos Aires, Paris, and North American cities, the popularity of bolero as a form of dance spread rapidly through Mexico and the Caribbean, whose marginal enclaves of brothels and *cantinas* helped inspire a new thematic development with songs of love, nostalgia, solidarity, treason, friendship, solitude, infidelity, and jealousy.

With the development of the radio, and the impulse of the recording and movie industries in the 1930s and 1940s, the bolero catapulted to international exposure, led by a formidable group of composers, mostly from Cuba, Mexico, and Puerto Rico. Their songs became an indispensable element in Cuban-style *cuartetos, quintetos, sextetos* and *septetos*, **charangas**, and innumerable Latin American orchestras that adopted the format of North American big bands. The prominence of bolero in recordings occurred at the cost of some rhythmic simplification that responded to the demands of the international market. In the dance halls, however, the adoption of boleros drastically changed the old repertoire of dances in ways that revolutionized the codes of gender and sexual interaction. With the help of bandleaders, composers, and music performers, the emerging modern middle-class audience avidly adopted the close-embrace approach of couples dancing in slow motion, so common in brothels and bars. The fashion of embraced and slow dancing, "on one tile" (*en una loza*), came to be emblematic of the bolero. This gendered impetus brought momentum to new musical developments like the appearance of the modern **tríos** (e.g., Los Panchos) and the emergence of the *filin* (feeling).

Further Readings

Aparicio, Frances. *Listening to Salsa: Gender, Latin Popular Music, and Puerto Rican Cultures.* Middletown, CT: Wesleyan University Press, 1998.

Loyola Fernández, Jaime. *En ritmo de bolero: el bolero en la música bailable cubana.* San Juan: Ediciones Huracán/Ateneo Puertorriqueño, 1996.

Rico Salazar, Jaime. *Cien años de boleros: su historia, sus compositores, sus mejores intérpretes y 600 boleros inolvidables.* 4th ed. Bogotá: Centro de Estudios Musicales, 1994.

Edgardo Díaz Díaz

Bolet Tremoleda, Jorge (1914–1990)

Jorge Bolet was one of the last representatives of the Romantic tradition in classical piano. His name is nearly synonymous with the work of composer Franz Liszt.

Bolet was born in Havana in 1914. He began playing the piano at age nine, and by twelve he had become a scholarship student at the Curtis Institute of Music in Philadelphia. He studied under David Saperton, Fritz Reiner, Leopold Godowsky, and Moriz Rosenthal. Bolet's European debut came in Amsterdam in 1935. His U.S. debut was in Philadelphia in 1937. He continued his studies under Rudolf Serkin. He won the Naumberg Prize (1937) and the Joseph Hofmann Award (1938). Beginning in 1939, he taught for a period of about three years as Serkin's assistant at the Curtis Institute. He served in World War II, and in 1946 he conducted the Japanese premiere of *The Mikado*. After the war, he resumed his career, spending much of his time working with Abram Chasins.

Throughout the 1950s, 1960s, and 1970s, when the works of Bach and Beethoven were in favor, Bolet remained faithful to the Romantic stylings. Bolet was renowned for both his artistry and virtuosity. In 1988, Bolet received the Liszt Medal of Honor from the American Liszt Society.

Further Readings

Noyle, Linda J. *Pianists on Playing: Interviews with Twelve Concert Pianists.* Metuchen, NJ: Scarecrow Press, 1987.

Orovio, Helio. *Diccionario de la música cubana: biográfico y técnico.* Havana: Editorial Letras Cubanas, 1981

Luis González

Borja, Esther (1913–   )

Esther Borja is one of Cuba's most famous singers. Born in Santiago de las Vegas, **Havana Province**, she attended normal school in Havana where she studied pedagogy and music. In 1935, she sang in concerts organized by **Ernesto Lecuona** and performed in Lecuona's **zarzuela** Lola Cruz. In 1936, she traveled to Argentina, where she remained until 1939. She toured the United States during the 1940s, performing in musical works created by Sigmund Romberg. In 1953, Borja recorded an album emblematic of Cuban music: *Rapsodia cubana*. She has performed on the radio and on the stage and has appeared in films and nightclubs. Her recordings of vocal duets, triplets, and quartets, using her own voice, have not been equaled in Cuba or abroad. Borja retired in 1984.

Further Reading

Orovio, Helio. *Diccionario de la música cubana: biográfico y técnico.* Havana: Editorial Letras Cubanas, 1981.

Cristóbal Díaz Ayala and Marisa Méndez

Brindis de Salas, Claudio (1852–1911)

Claudio José Domingo Brindis de Salas, one of the world's most prominent violinists of his time, was born and raised in Havana. He received his first violin lessons from his father, Claudio, and later with José Redondo. As he played at the age of eleven with **Ignacio Cervantes** at the Liceo de La Habana, he surprised the audience with his unique performance at the

Claudio Brindis de Salas was a world renowned violinist. Photograph courtesy of the Biblioteca Nacional José Martí, Havana.

violin. Eminent European artists like José Bousquet and José Van der Gutch led him to the latest stylistic developments of the French school, already in vogue among Cuban violinists. In 1869, he entered the Paris Conservatory, where he studied with Ernest Sivori—a pupil of Nicolo Paganini—and later obtained the first prize. As the French school gained momentum due in part to his technical and stylistic contributions, Brindis de Salas was proclaimed in Italy as the "Black Paganini." His tours in Italy, France, and Germany earned him numerous honorary titles like the Baron de Salas and member of the French Legion of Honor. Back in the Americas, he toured in Haiti, Venezuela, Cuba, Mexico, Puerto Rico, the Dominican Republic, and Argentina. In the 1890s he established his residence in Germany and became a naturalized citizen, married a lady of the local aristocracy, and was appointed violinist of the chamber orchestra of the Court of Emperor William II. But his marriage ended abruptly in 1898, and his tour schedule gradually waned until his life ended desolately in Buenos Aires, afflicted by tuberculosis, in 1911.

Further Reading

Toledo, Armando. *Presencia y vigencia de Brindis de Salas.* Havana: Editorial Letras Cubanas, 1981.

Edgardo Díaz Díaz

Brouwer, Leo (1939–   )

Leo Brouwer is a leading figure in contemporary Cuban music. Born in Havana on March 1, 1939, he is the grandson of **Ernestina Lecuona** and the grandnephew of composer **Ernesto Lecuona**. Brouwer studied guitar and composition as a youth and attended Juilliard Music School and Hartford University, where he majored in composition. He was director of the Departamento Experimental del Instituto de Arte e Industria Cinematográfica (ICAIC) and taught music at the Conservatorio Nacional **Amadeo Roldán** (see **Cinema**).

Brouwer is regarded as one of the most prolific composers for the classical guitar featuring a style that displays serialism, postserialism, aleatory influences, and new trends. He has also composed for ballet and has written operas and works of ensemble. He has recorded many albums with Deutsche Grammaphon, Erato, and the Musical Heritage Society.

As a performer, he has appeared in scores of concerts worldwide, and as a conductor, he has performed with the Berlin Philharmonic. In 1987, he was made honorary member of the United Nations Educational, Scientific, and Cultural Organization (UNESCO), a distinction that has been awarded only to a handful of musicians, including Isaac Stern, Joan Sutherland, and Yehudi Menuhin.

Further Readings

Carpentier, Alejo. *La música en Cuba*. Mexico City: Fondo de Cultura Económica, 1993.

Orovio, Helio. *Diccionario de la música cubana: biográfico y técnico*. Havana: Editorial Letras Cubanas, 1981.

Jesús Vega

"Cachao" (Israel López) (1918–   )

Cachao, the most famous and influential bass player in twentieth-century Cuban music, helped found the **mambo** genre and led the improvisational **descarga** movement of the 1960s; like Alberto Socarrás, Mario Bauzá, and other popular musicians of his generation, he had played for Havana's **Philharmonic Orchestra**.

Born in Havana, Cachao, with **Arcaño y Sus Maravillas** (the first **charanga** orchestra to add conga drums) in the late 1930s, he and his brother Orestes helped create the mambo by transforming a section of the stately **danzón** into a more

heavily syncopated, percussive, and driving rhythm. The mambo genre finally crystallized with **Dámaso Pérez Prado**, who gave it worldwide popularity. But Cachao's greatest contribution to Afro-Cuban music was his refashioning of the bass in a more percussive and syncopated direction, accentuating its *anticipado* role (strongly marking the downbeat) in its rhythmic pattern, or *tumbao*. In 1962, Cachao left Cuba for the United States, eventually settling in Miami. In the 1960s, he spearheaded the descarga movement toward more fiery and free jazz improvisation over the Afro-Cuban rhythmic base (See **Afro-Cuban Jazz**). Cachao tasted glory again late in his career with a sold-out 1994 concert at New York's Radio City Music Hall and a 1994 Grammy for his *Master Sessions, Vol. 1*. The 1990s also brought widespread recognition through **Andy García**'s documentary production *Cachao—como su ritmo no hay dos*. In 1995, the National Endowment for the Arts accorded him its highest honor, the National Heritage Fellowship Award. He resides in Miami, where he continues to perform and work on musical projects.

Further Readings

Galán, Natalio. *Cuba y sus sones*. Valencia, Spain: Pre-Textos, 1997.

Loza, Steven. *Tito Puente and the Making of Latin Music*. Urbana: University of Illinois Press, 1999.

Roberts, John Storm. *The Latin Tinge*. 2nd ed. New York: Oxford University Press, 1999.

Pablo Julián Davis

Carrillo, Isolina (1907–1996)

A composer, Afro-Cuban pianist Isolina Carrillo played music accompaniment to silent films at the age of ten. She was a member of Cuba's first all-women band the Septeto Trovadoras del Cayo. In 1940 Carrillo also founded el Conjunto Vocal

Siboney, consisting of four singers with Carrillo at the piano. This was the first all-women vocal quartet assembled in Cuba. In 1937 she began to work for the radio station RHC, playing the piano but also training and tutoring such popular singers as **Olga Guillot**. Encouraged by the station's president, Armando Trinidad, she began to write commercial jingles; later on, Trinidad convinced her to compose her first romantic ballad, "Miedo de ti," which yielded her the 1948 award for the best composer of the year. That same year, she composed her most famous song, "Dos gardenias." In 1949, the Puerto Rican singer Daniel Santos recorded the song, making it an international hit.

She provided medicines to combatants during the **Struggle against Batista** and played an active political role after the triumph of the **Revolution**. She organized a choir for a labor union and put together concerts for various **committees for the defense of the Revolution (CDRs).**

Further Reading

Díaz Ayala, Cristóbal. *Música cubana del areyto a la nueva trova*. Miami: Ediciones Universal, 1993.
Valdés, Enrique. Interview with Isolina Carrillo. *Bohemia*. Dec. 16, 1977, p. 20.

Cristóbal Díaz Ayala and Marisa Méndez

"Cascarita" (Orlando Guerra) (1920–1975)

Orlando Guerra "Cascarita" was born in **Camagüey** on September 14, 1920. He became a soloist for the Hermanos Palau orchestra during the 1940s, developing a distinct phrasing and pacing on **son** and **guaracha** genres. He carried over what **Miguelito Valdés** had been doing but with his own particular style. In 1944, he joined the orchestra of trombonist Julio Cueva. From there, he moved on to the **Orquesta**

Casino de la Playa. With each move, his fame grew. His early recordings featured Casino de la Playa above his name, but subsequent releases listed him as the main attraction. He introduced **Dámaso Pérez Prado** to the orchestra and the Cuban public as pianist and arranger.

Cascarita's star diminished as the singer **Benny Moré**'s popularity grew. Cascarita moved to Mexico, where he died in obscurity.

Further Reading

Orovio, Helio. *Diccionario de la música cubana: biográfico y técnico*. Havana: Editorial Letras Cubanas, 1981.

Cristóbal Díaz Ayala and Marisa Méndez

Casino de la Playa, Orquesta

Founded in 1937 as an offshoot from the Hermanos Castros' orchestra, the Casino de la Playa became an overnight sensation, thanks to its pianist Anselmo Sacasa, who developed a "montuneo sonero" sound that was widely emulated, and a vocalist, **Miguelito Valdés**, who had a distinct voice and style along with a charismatic personality. He began the dynasty of the Cuban *soneros* (see **Son**). In 1939, the orchestra toured Puerto Rico, Curaçao, Venezuela, Colombia, and Panama, becoming the most influential musical group in the Caribbean. But a year later, the pianist and the vocalist left Casino de la Playa, and while the orchestra continued to perform, its popularity began to wane. In 1945, another singer and another pianist rescued Casino de la Playa. The singer was **Orlando Guerra "Cascarita"** and his ludic singing and his choice of **guarachas** over sones attracted new fans. The pianist was **Dámaso Pérez Prado** who during his time with the orchestra developed the sound and feel of the **mambo**. Three years later, both performers left Casino de la Playa.

This time, however, the orchestra was not able to regain a foothold in the music world, and within a short period, was disbanded.

Further Reading

Díaz Ayala, Cristóbal. *Música cubana del areyto a la nueva trova*. Miami: Ediciones Universal, 1993.

Cristóbal Díaz Ayala and Marisa Méndez

Cervantes Kawanagh, Ignacio (1847–1905)

Ignacio Cervantes Kawanagh was Cuba's most important composer of the nineteenth century. Unlike **Manuel Saumell Robredo**, Cervantes Kawanagh did not have economic barriers that curtailed his music vocation. In 1859, he studied under Nicolás Ruiz Espadero. In 1865, he traveled to France, where he enrolled in Paris' Conservatory, and studied under such prestigious professors as Antoine François Marmontel and Charles Valentin Arkan and received awards and recognition for his ability for interpretation and harmony. In 1870, he returned to Havana where he performed as a pianist. Five years later, Spanish authorities forced him to leave Cuba accusing him of raising funds for the Cuban insurrection (see **Political Exile [Nineteenth Century]**). He resided in the United States and Mexico, going back to Cuba at the end of the **Ten Years' War**. Again, he left the island in 1895 and returned in 1900 when he was appointed conductor of the Teatro Tacón's orchestra (see **Theaters**). In 1905, he died as a result of a brain illness.

Cervantes Kawanagh is better known for his work as a composer rather than a concert pianist. His major accomplishments are the *danzas*, which express melodic originality and richness. Says **Alejo Carpentier** of Cervantes's music, "Noth-

ing in it is false—it has a feminine and restless touch that emerges out of the 'criollo.' The style is clean and lucid, creating a small world of sounds."

Further Reading

Carpentier, Alejo. *La música en Cuba*. Mexico City: Fondo de Cultura Económica, 1993.

Jesús Vega

Cha-Cha-Chá

Generally considered the invention of violinist and composer Enrique Jorrín, the *cha-cha-chá* is a genre of Cuban dance music that first became widely popular in the early 1950s. In a musical sense, it derives primarily from the **danzón**, a form of ballroom dance music that tended in the early twentieth century to feature prominent melodies on the violin and flute accompanied by piano, bass, *timbales*, and *güiro*. The cha-cha-chá uses the same instrumental format but also incorporates significant influences from the **son**, *son guajiro*, and **mambo**, most notably through the inclusion of *montuno*-like call-and-response sections and characteristic percussion rhythms in later sections. The cha-cha-chá is performed in a moderate tempo and is associated with a unique dance step; while not a simple dance, it is less elaborate than the mambo. Its melodies tend to be more lyrical and less syncopated than those of the *son*. According to Jorrín, the cha-cha-chá's moderate tempo and relative lack of syncopation in both melody and accompaniment are due to his desire to create a style of music that was easier to dance to than the danzón and mambo.

Further Reading

Díaz Ayala, Cristóbal. *Música cubana del areyto a la nueva trova*. Miami: Ediciones Universal, 1993.

Robin Moore

Charanga

The *charanga* is a type of orchestra popular in Cuba in the nineteenth century that included in its repertoire a variety of Haitian, French, and Cuban quadrilles (*contradanzas*). These diverse influences paved the way in the 1870s for a new form of dance music, known as the **danzón**. Charangas were influenced by a wide array of traditions, including military band music and Afro-Cuban music. The typical orchestra consisted of a clarinet, a coronet, a trombone, a bombardone, a bass, kettledrums, and a *güiro* (a gourd used as an instrument). Just prior to the twentieth century, charangas began to shun the use of metal instruments and instead incorporated the piano. They also began to experiment with the melodic use of the flute and violin, while retaining the bass, kettledrums, and güiro. The experimentation led to the development of the so-called *charanga francesa* (French charanga). In the 1920s, they incorporated popular dance music, such as sones (see **Son**) and **guarachas**, with the idea of competing with bands specializing in sons. This popular instrumental style reached its zenith in the 1950s and 1960s. One of the high points was the early 1950s with the popularity of the **cha-cha-chá**. The style remained popular with the development of new musical forms such as the **mambo**, the *pachanga*, the charanga, and the *bugalú*.

Willy Chirino makes handprints in cement at the Walk of Stars, Miami Beach (2001). AP/Wide World Photos. Photograph by Wilfredo Lee.

Further Readings

Acosta, Leonardo. "Los formatos instrumentales en la música popular cubana." In *Del tambor al sintetizador*. Havana: Editorial Letras Cubanas, 1983.

Argeliers, León. *Del canto y el tiempo*. 2nd ed. Havana: Editorial Letras Cubanas, 1984.

Edgardo Díaz Díaz

Chirino, Willy (1956–)

Cuban-born, U.S.-raised musician and producer Willy Chirino helped create the "Miami Sound" beginning in the 1980s and became strongly identified, both personally and artistically, with the anti-Castro cause.

Born in Consolación del Sur (**Pinar del Río Province**), Chirino left Cuba as a child under "**Operation Pedro Pan**," an early 1960s campaign by which some 14,000 children were sent by their parents to the United States. In school, Chirino formed rock bands; he launched his Latin music career in the 1970s in New York City, working with Tito Puente and others. His first album was released in 1974. His compositions were widely interpreted by other artists; "Soy," a kind of anthem of rootlessness, was recorded by some sixty singers worldwide. Chirino's music alternated rock, pop, samba, and other influences with **son** and other Cuban styles; as political convictions came increasingly to inform his work, the music became more Cuban. On the 1989 album *Oxígeno*, the song "Ya viene llegando" (It's Almost Here) alluded to an impending end to the **Fidel Castro** regime; *Habana, D.C.* (1992) was even clearer in its prophesizing (the initials meant "Después de Castro" [After Castro]), and Chirino used the title song as a fund-raiser for **Hermanos al Rescate**. He also declared enmity to Cuban artists like **Silvio Rodríguez** and **Pablo Milanés** who publicly supported Fidel Castro. In 1995, the City of Miami named a stretch of N.W. 17th Avenue "Willy Chirino Way." By the 1990s, remarkably, Chirino's music began to be widely heard in Cuba itself.

Further Readings

Conde, Yvonne. *Operation Pedro Pan: The Untold Exodus of 14,048 Cuban Children.* New York: Routledge, 1999.

Pérez Firmat, Gustavo. *Life on the Hyphen: The Cuban-American Way.* Austin: University of Texas Press, 1994.

Pablo Julián Davis

Cinema

In January 1897, Frenchman Gabriel Veyre brought films from Mexico City to Havana. For the first showing, which took place at the Paseo del Prado #126, the following shorts were featured: "The Card Game," "The Train," "The Water Hose and the Young Boy," and "The Funny Hat." A few days later, on February 7, Veyre made the first Cuban film. It was titled *Simulacro de incendio*, and it portrayed firemen fighting a fire. Soon, several movie houses were established by the actor José A. Casasús, who was also a producer and impresario.

Film scholars see the historical recreation film as the first popular film genre in Latin America. In 1914, Enrique Díaz Quesada made the movies *El capitán mambí* and *Libertadores o guerrilleros* (see **Mambises**); the enterprise received

help from General **Mario García Menocal**. Later on, Díaz Quesada adapted for the screen several classics from Spanish literature, a popular practice at the time. This silent phase of Cuban cinema lasted until 1937 when talkies were finally produced. From this period, and until 1959, two notable films emerged, *La Vírgen de la Caridad* and the *Romance del palmar*, filmed by Ramón Peón, a legendary figure in Cuban cinema.

In 1959, the Revolutionary government passed its first cultural law, resulting in the founding of the Instituto Cubano del Arte e Industria Cinematográficos (ICAIC), which controlled, and still controls, the Cuban movie industry. The years immediately following the creation of the ICAIC are known as the Golden Age of Cuban Cinema. It was a time when prominent international filmmakers visited the island: the Italian neorealist Cesare Zavattini, the French Chris Marker, Agnes Varda and Armand Gatti, the Dutch documentary maker Joris Ivens, and the Soviets Roman Karmen and Mijail Kalatazov. Their visits fostered productive debates, exchanges, and learning experiences for Cuban cinematographers.

In 1962, director **Tomás Gutiérrez Alea** produced *Las doce sillas*, a satire about bourgeois ambitions within a revolutionary setting. In 1966, *La muerte de un burócrata*, also by Gutiérrez Alea, targeted socialist bureaucracy; *Las aventuras de Juan Quinquín*, directed by Julio García Espinosa in 1967, celebrated the rich peasant heritage and picaresque attitudes; *La Primera carga del machete*, directed by Manuel Octavio Gómez in 1969, was a historical epic. But the two most important features of this period were Gutiérrez Alea's *Memorias del subdesarrollo* (1968), a study of the role intellectuals played within the revolutionary struggle, and **Humberto Solás**'s *Lucía* (1968), a story of three different women in different stages of Cuban history; these two films

Scene from *La última cena* (1976). Still photograph courtesy of Instituto Cubano del Arte e Industria Cinematográficos, Havana.

remain as relevant and engaging today as when they were first produced.

The decade of the 1970s was characterized as a particularly repressive period throughout Cuba. The government censored many works, most notoriously the books *Fuera del juego* by Heberto Padilla (see **Padilla [Affair], Heberto**) and *Los siete contra Tebas* by **Antón Arrufat**. Yet, within the ICAIC, artists still enjoyed relative freedom. In 1972, Humberto Solás filmed *Un día de noviembre*, a complex story about suffering from frustration and resentment. Sara Gómez and Gutiérrez Alea made in 1974 *De cierta manera*, about men and women who had not become integrated into the **Revolution**. In 1974, Gutiérrez Alea directed *La última cena*, a film about **slavery** and the hypocrisy of power and perhaps the island's best-made film. In 1978, Gutiérrez Alea shot the satire *Los sobrevivientes*. A year later, Pastor Vega filmed *Retrato de Teresa*, on the contradictions between revolutionary and *machista* attitudes (see **Machismo**).

Other major films from the decade included *Los días del agua*, by Manuel Octavio Gómez, 1971, and *El hombre de Maisinicú*, filmed by Manuel Pérez in 1973 and about the campaign against the so-called bandits, anti-**Castro** forces that took refuge in the Cuban countryside (see **Segundo Frente del Escambray**).

The 1980s brought the exodus of tens of thousands of Cubans and was marked by many controversies and contradictions within the government (see **Mariel Boatlift**). These controversies spilled into the film industry. In 1981, the making and the release of the epic *Cecilia*, loosely based on the classic novel *Cecilia Valdés* by **Cirilo Villaverde**, produced heated debate between the public, the filmmakers, and the government, as authorities questioned the production of what they called the most expensive film ever made in Cuba. As a result of the controversy Alfredo Guevara, president and founder of ICAIC, resigned from his post. Julio García Espinosa replaced Guevara, allowing the government to exert more control and influence over ICAIC. This was the beginning of a period of mediocre productivity and adherence to the government's bureaucratic culture and tendencies. A positive development during this era was the production of feature films made by directors who had been trained as documentary and news producers. There was also the participation of a new generation of actors. About seventy films were shot during the 1980s. The more relevant were *Se permuta*, directed by Juan Carlos Tabío in 1983; *Lejanía*, by **Jesús Díaz** in 1985; *Amada* (1983) and *Un hombre de éxito* (1985) by Humberto Solás; Fernando Pérez's *Clandestinos*, in 1987; Orlando Rojas's *Papeles secundarios*, in 1989. The most successful film made was *La bella de la Alhambra*, shot by Enrique Pineda Barnet in 1989; the movie was an international hit. The documentary continued to excel as art form, as witnessed by Enrique Colina's *Vecinos* and *Estética*, as did the animated film with the works of Juan Padrón. By the end of the 1980s, ICAIC established the so-called Grupos de Creación, directed by Gutiérrez Alea, Humberto Solás, and Manuel Pérez, who attracted filmmakers who worked within dictated stylistic lines.

The so-called **Special Period**, when Cuba's socialist project hit rock bottom, marked the island's film production during the 1990s. The decade opened with the production of *Alicia en el pueblo de maravillas* (1999) by Daniel Díaz Torres. The film incorporated a variety of convoluted situations and veiled elements to evade official censorship at a time when the ICAIC was still headed by Julio García Espinosa. The controversial film had a limited screening: only three days in two cinemas. The theaters in which it played were virtually taken over by forces of the state security apparatus, who repressed any manifestation of sympathy for the film. Paradoxically, Díaz Torres, who was a militant communist and member of the

ICAIC's most "red" creation team, was accused of being a counterrevolutionary. At the time, ICAIC became the object of organized harassment and threats of being closed down. These threats were counteracted by the unified stance of Cuba's filmmakers led by Tomás Gutiérrez Alea and Humberto Solás. García Espinosa, meanwhile, yielded to government pressures but later resigned from his post, thus allowing the return of Alfredo Guevara, who remained at ICAIC's helm until 2000. That year he resigned and went on to preside at the Festival of Latin American New Cinema. An obscure cultural bureaucrat replaced him as head of ICAIC.

Other 1990s films that subtly denounced the regime were *Madagascar* (1994, Fernado Pérez), *Reina y Rey* (1994, García Espinosa), and the much debated *Fresa y chocolate* (1993, Gutiérrez Alea and Tabío), the latter the recipient of an Oscar nomination for best foreign film. Other films included *Hello, Hemingway* (1990, Fernando Pérez), *María Antonia* (1990, Sergio Giral), *Mascaró* (1992, Constante Diego), *El siglo de las luces* (1992, Solás), and *Adorables mentiras* (1991, Gerardo Chijona), a satire of socialism's shortcomings and the so-called double morality, evident among Cubans. Later in the decade other films made an impact, among them *El elefante y la bicicleta* (1994, Tabío) and *Guantanamera* (1995, Gutiérrez Alea and Tabío). The latter was Gutiérrez Alea's swan song against tyrannical rule over Cuba. Among the decade's young filmmakers Arturo Sotto distinguished himself with films such as *Pon tu pensamiento en mi* (1995) and *Amor vertical* (1997).

The advent of the twenty-first century finds Cuban cinema at a low point with reduced production and toned-down criticism sifted through the censorship by Cuba's cultural bureaucracy. Among the latest works of note one finds *Hacerse el sueco* (2000, Daniel Díaz Torres) and *Lista de espera* (2000, Tabío). The future of Cuba's film production hangs in the balance and will require the creative input of the island's young filmmakers, particularly the graduates of the School of Film and Television and Cuban filmmakers living abroad. *See also* Film Posters

Further Readings

Chanan, Michael. *The Cuban Image: Cinema and Cultural Politics in Cuba*. London: British Film Institute, 1985.

García Borrero, Juan Antonio. *Guía crítica del cine cubano de ficción*. Havana: Editorial Arte y Literatura, 2001.

Mazón Robau, Antonio. *Cine notas*. Havana: Editorial Arte y Literatura, 1999.

Jesús Vega

Compadres, Los

A Cuban musical group from Oriente, Los Compadres was formed in 1942 by Lorenzo Hierrezuelo (1907–1991) and his relative Francisco Repilado ("Compay Segundo"), replaced in 1955 by Reinaldo, Lorenzo's brother. The duo played traditional music of the region where they were born and raised, primarily based on the **son, guaracha**, and **bolero**. The entire Hierrezuelo family was very musical, and they learned to play and sing at home in family gatherings. Lorenzo began his musical career in the 1930s performing **vieja trova** with the Trío Lírico Cubano and later accompanying **María Teresa Vera**, while also playing with Los Compadres, until illness brought Vera's career to an end in 1962. Most recordings of Los Compadres feature small acoustic ensembles of guitar, *tres, bongó*, and maracas in addition to vocals. They are noteworthy for their lively rhythms as well as lyrics that openly support revolutionary activities in many cases. Along with Carlos Puebla y Sus Tradicionales, the duo Los Compadres represents one of the first ensembles to adopt overt political messages in the early

1960s and to use music as a means of fostering support for **literacy campaigns, agrarian reform acts**, and other socialist programs.

Further Reading

Orovio, Helio. "Hierrezuelo, Lorenzo." In *Diccionario de la música cubana: biográfico y técnico*. 2nd. ed. Havana: Editorial Letras Cubanas, 1992, 246.

Robin Moore

Conga

The *conga* is a danceable musical genre associated with **carnival**; the name also applies to a kind of musical group and to the drum central to Afro-Cuban percussion. Beginning in the 1930s, conga became a dance craze in the United States and beyond.

The conga, a term widely believed to be derived from the African region of Congo, is both a lyrical and danceable genre, rooted in the music of carnival troupes or *comparsas*. In the carnival context, a conga group is mostly percussive. Beginning in the late 1930s, and intensely in the 1940s, it became wildly popular in the United States, due in no small measure to Hollywood's "Latin" musicals. RKO's offerings were particularly influential, notably *Too Many Girls* (1940), in which **Desi Arnaz** appeared as a conga-playing Argentine student. Spanish-Catalan bandleader **Xavier Cugat**, who gave Arnaz his musical start, helped to popularize the dance, but the biggest impact belonged to Arnaz himself. With its simple march step, the interlinking of dancers snaking about in single file, and a one-two-three-hump rhythm with the fourth beat strongly marked, the conga was not only attractive but also readily accessible to U.S. and other foreign audiences. One of the earliest and most successful of twentieth-century Cuban musical exports, the conga lacked the polyrhythmic sophistication or subtlety of the **son**, **mambo**, or **salsa** but served to nurture the future receptivity of an international public to the wider gamut of Cuban musical styles.

Further Readings

Leymarie, Isabelle. *La música latinoamericana, ritmos y danzas de un continente*. Barcelona: Ediciones B, 1997.

Roberts, John Storm. *The Latin Tinge*. 2nd ed. New York: Oxford University Press, 1999.

Pablo Julián Davis

Criolla

The *criolla* is a type of song that idealizes Cuban rural life from an urban perspective. Its beginnings date to 1909 with compositions by band director Luis Casas Romero. The criolla is characterized by the use of alternating major and minor modes and the simultaneous use of melodies in 6/8 with an accompaniment in 3/4. This metric ambiguity—known as *sesquialtera*—distinguished the criolla from most of the vast repertoire of Afro-Cuban genres characterized by the use of polyrhythms and binary meters and highlights the marked similarities between the criolla and other Latin American musical expressions like the Colombian *bambucos* and the several versions of *valses criollos*. With the reference of its texts to the romantic and idyllic world of the Cuban rural landscape, during the early days of the Republic, the criolla and its generic antecedent, the *clave*, gained a reputation as a cover-up of the harsh realities of racial and economic discrimination. Eventually, with the influence of genres like the **son**, the criolla acquired a special meaning as a syncopated waltz, *a la cubana*.

Further Readings

Alén Rodríguez, Olavo. *De lo afrocubano a la salsa: géneros musicales de Cuba*. San Juan: Editorial Cubanacán, 1992.

León, Argeliers. *Del canto y el tiempo*. Havana: Editorial Letras Cubanas, 1984.

Edgardo Díaz Díaz

Salsa star Celia Cruz performs at the Ringling Bros. and Barnum & Bailey Circus at the Miami Arena (2000). AP/Wide World Photos. Photograph by Ed Cox.

Cruz, Celia (1924–   )

Commonly known as "la Guarachera of Oriente" and the "Queen of Salsa," Celia Cruz was born on October 21, 1924, into a family of fourteen children. She began her musical career upon winning a talent show known as "La Hora del Te" (The Tea Hour) in Havana. Her education focused on literature, a field that she would later teach for some years. Her artistic career began early when she sang in school and entered radio contests and performed at the **Tropicana Nightclub**.

In 1950, Cruz began to sing with the musical group **Sonora Matancera**. During the next fifteen years, the band toured extensively in Latin America and became one of the most popular musical groups of the time. It was with her fellow band mates that she fled revolutionary Cuba in 1960 and took up residence in New York City. She has since been vocal against the **Fidel Castro** government, which did not allow her entry to attend her father's funeral on the island.

During her more than four decades in exile, she has recorded over fifty albums, many with some of **salsa** music's most internationally acclaimed artists. She has also participated in various films and Mexican soap operas. She has recorded with salsa legends Tito Puente, with whom she recorded eight records, and Johnny Pacheco. During the 1970s Cruz sang with Pacheco's Fania All Stars, an ensemble that brought together salsa's greatest. Since then, she has been at the forefront of salsa music and today continues to be one of the most sought-after performers in the world.

Her trademark yell of "Azúcar!" along with her unique voice, fashion, and hairstyles have made Celia Cruz a legend and earned her many accolades, including a Grammy Award.

Further Reading

Valverde, Umberto. *Celia Cruz: Reina Rumba*. Bogotá: Editorial La Oveja Negra, 1981.

Nilo Jorge Barredo

Cugat, Xavier (1900–1990)

Xavier Cugat stands out as one of the most commercially successful bandleaders associated with Cuban music of the 1930s and 1940s. Born in Catalonia, Spain, Cugat moved with his family at an early age to Havana. Uninterested in popular music as an adolescent, he dedicated himself instead to the study of classical violin repertory, but critical success eluded him. In 1932 the managers of the Waldorf Astoria Hotel in New York contracted him as their house dance band leader. His live coast-to-coast radio broadcasts from the hotel began later that decade, called *Dinner at the Waldorf Show*, generating tremendous demand for stylized Latin music in the United States, as did frequent film appearances. The Waldorf served as a forum for introducing new singers and dancers to the North American public; **Frank "Machito" Grillo, Miguelito Valdés**, Tito Rodríguez, and others first established themselves as national Latin celebrities in the ensemble. While criticized as "inauthentic," Cugat did not claim to play in a traditional style and in fact freely admitted that his renditions of Afro-Cuban music had little to do with street culture in Havana or elsewhere. The repertory of his orchestra included arrangements of Spanish, Mexican, Argentine, Venezuelan, and Brazilian folk songs, in addition to those from the English- and French-speaking Caribbean. The band also played North American jazz standards, quasi–Middle Eastern "exotic" numbers, and even the "Chiquita Banana" song. He continued to perform into the 1980s along with wife and fellow entertainer Charo.

Further Reading

Cugat, Xavier. *Rumba Is My Life*. New York: Didier, 1948.

Robin Moore

Danzón

The *danzón* figures as one of the most important Cuban musical forms of the late nineteenth and early twentieth centuries and is one of Cuba's oldest national musical genres. Although primarily derived from European traditions, it remained controversial in early years as a result of its strong associations with **Afro-Cubans** and Haitians. The genre seems to have first been performed by working-class musicians in **Matanzas**, but was appropriated by members of middle-class black social clubs and transformed into a respectable ballroom dance. The first recognized danzón is Miguel Faílde's "Alturas de Simpson" (1879). Stylistically, *danzones* are descended from the *bailes de cuadros*, such as the *danza* and *contradanza*, popular among the white and black middle classes beginning at the turn of the nineteenth century. The overall sound of the danzón is virtually identical to these earlier genres. The majority are performed in duple-meter by orchestras of European instruments such as the violin, acoustic bass, clarinet, and occasionally horns, as well as the *timbal*, which plays a constant isorhythmic pattern. The most common timbal rhythm consists of a *cinquillo* figure followed by four quarter notes. Choreographically, danzones are performed by couples holding each other in a loose embrace.

Further Reading

Castillo Faílde, Osvaldo. *Miguel Faílde, creador musical del danzón*. Havana: Editora del Consejo Nacional de Cultura, 1964.

Robin Moore

De la Vega, Aurelio (1925–   )

Composer Aurelio de la Vega was born in Havana on November 28, 1925. He studied composition with Fritz Kramer and later took advanced courses with Ernest Toch in the United States. Besides being one of the most influential and articulate musical experimenters of his generation, he has had a successful career as a professor and administrator. His compositions include thirty-two chamber pieces and five choral compositions, among others. De la Vega's works reflect his inclination toward contemporary techniques such as free atonalism, dodecaphonism, serialism, and electronic music. He left Cuba shortly after the triumph of the **Revolution** resettling in Los Angeles. During the late 1970s he introduced in his music various elements of Cuba's popular traditions that had been absent from his earlier compositions. Salient examples of such works are *Septicilium* (1974), for clarinet and seven instruments; *Adiós* (1977), for orchestra; *Asonantes* (1985), for soprano, electronic sounds, and seven instruments; and *Canciones transparentes* (1995), for soprano, clarinet, cello, and piano. His symphonies have been interpreted by leading orchestras in the United States, Europe, and Latin America. He has received two Friedheim Awards from the Kennedy Center. He remains an active speaker and is professor emeritus at California State University, Northridge.

Further Reading

Béhague, Gerald. "Aurelio de la Vega." *Latin American Music Review* 22, no. 1 (Spring–Summer 2001): 1–3.

Edgardo Díaz Díaz

Descarga

Descarga, a term used by Cuban musicians to refer to the act of collective improvisation, came to designate a strongly jazz-influenced genre created in the 1950s.

In naming the improvisational section of a musical number, or an entire musical session made up of such improvisations, the term descarga is akin to U.S. musicians' term "jam session." Beginning in the 1950s but in a more fully developed way in the 1960s, bassist Israel López—better known as "**Cachao**"—led the way in forging a new musical style. Rhythmically and structurally, descarga was rooted in **rumba, danzón, son, mambo**, and other Cuban forms; melodically, it unleashed an improvisational power and freedom drawn largely from the bebop and hard-bop currents of jazz. In a sense, the descarga can be considered an approach and a sensibility, as much as a genre in the strict sense. Ethnomusicologist John Storm Roberts considers the descarga an intermediate form between **salsa** and Latin jazz in that it "tend[s] to preserve the Cuban structure yet contain[s] far more jazz soloing than does salsa." Into the twenty-first century, descarga continued to influence both salsa and Latin jazz. *See also* Afro-Cuban Jazz

Further Readings
Loza, Steven. *Tito Puente and the Making of Latin Music*. Urbana: University of Illinois Press, 1999.
Roberts, John Storm. *The Latin Tinge*. 2nd ed. New York: Oxford University Press, 1999.

Pablo Julián Davis

Díaz, Aniceto (1887–1964)

Aniceto Díaz was a composer, flautist, saxophonist, and the indisputable creator of the Cuban *danzonete*. Born in **Matanzas** in 1887, he developed and combined elements of the **son** and the **danzón** (other Cuban musical creations), and especially the danzón's introduction and uses of violin arrangements, to create the danzonete. He also amplified the role of the singing voice in the danzonete. A crucial influence in Díaz's life was his association with Miguel Faílde, the father of the danzón, and his orchestra.

In 1929, Díaz, who was performing at the Casino Español, premiered his piece "Rompiendo la rutina," introducing to the public his first danzonete; later on the singer **Paulina Álvarez** sang the composition and from that moment on became known as the "Empress of the Danzonete." If with time the danzonete did not achieve the artistic heights of the danzón, it did play an important part in the popularization of Cuban music, and it opened avenues of musical expressions for other genres.

Further Readings
Carpentier, Alejo. *La música en Cuba*. Mexico City: Fondo de Cultura Económica, 1993.
Galán, Natalio. *Cuba y sus sones*. Valencia, Spain: Pre-Textos, 1997.
Orovio, Helio. *Diccionario de la música cubana: biográfico y técnico*. Havana: Editorial Letras Cubanas, 1981.
Urfé, Odilio. *Síntesis del danzón*. Havana: Biblioteca Nacional José Martí, n.d.

Jesús Vega

Díaz, Cameron (1972–   )

Cameron Díaz is one of the more popular and sought-after young actresses in the United States in the late 1990s and the new century. Born in San Diego, California, to a father of Cuban descent and a mother of German, English, and Native American descent, Díaz grew up in Long Beach. One night at a Hollywood party she met a photographer who linked her with the Elite Modeling Agency and Díaz dropped out of high school to pursue modeling full-time at the age of sixteen. For the next five years, she traveled the world, working in Japan, Australia, Mexico, Morocco, and Paris. She did commercial work for such products as Coca Cola, Nivea, and L.A. Gear. She returned to California to pursue acting. Along the way, she earned her high school diploma.

Díaz was barely twenty-one when she landed the leading female role opposite superstar comedian Jim Carrey in *The Mask* (1994). Then she chose to act in a series of small independent films including *The Last Supper* (1995), *She's the One* (1996), *Feeling Minnesota* (1996), and *Keys to Tulsa* (1997). That was followed by what many considered her scene-stealing performance opposite Julia Roberts in *My Best Friend's Wedding* (1997), endearing her to audiences and critics. She immediately returned to more quirky films like *A Life Less Ordinary* (1997) and *Fear and Loathing in Las Vegas* (1998). But it was the offbeat box office hit *There's Something about Mary* (1998) that earned her the widest recognition. The following year critics hailed her performance in *Being John Malkovich* (1999), and although many said it was Oscar worthy, a nomination never materialized. That same year she performed opposite Al Pacino in *On Any Sunday*. Díaz began the new century in the Hollywood extravaganza *Charlie's Angels* (2000) and followed with a starring role in *Vanilla Sky* (2001). Many believe she is destined to become one of Hollywood's leading ladies.

Further Readings

Kieran, Scott. *Cameron Diaz*. Philadelphia: Chelsea House, 2001.

Penning, Lars. *Cameron Diaz*. Berlin: Bertz, 2001.

Ray Blanco

D'Rivera, Francisco "Paquito" (Francisco Jesús Rivera Figueras) (1948–   )

Saxophonist and bandleader who first rose to fame with legendary Cuban fusion band **Grupo Irakere**, Paquito D'Rivera sought exile in the United States in the early 1980s and became one of the most influential Latin American jazz musicians.

Born in Havana, he was raised in a musical family; his father Tito was a bandleader and local representative for the instrument manufacturer Selmer. The child prodigy studied at the Havana Conservatory from age twelve. A charter member of Irakere, founded in 1973, he left Cuba not long after a Grammy went to the 1979 album *Irakere*. He settled in New York City and began a period of intense and creative work in a range of settings. In 1988, Dizzy Gillespie made him a charter member of his fifteen-piece United Nations Orchestra, whose reins the saxophonist took up after Gillespie's death in 1993. Carnegie Hall honored him with a Lifetime Achievement Award in 1991. In his first two decades in the United States, D'Rivera issued twenty-two releases, including *Portraits of Cuba*, which won a 1996 Grammy (Best Latin Jazz Performance). D'Rivera's best-known work is on alto saxophone and

Paquito D'Rivera playing Charlie Parker's horn in 1995. Photograph © 1995 by Michael Wilderman/ Jazz Visions.

clarinet where he creates a brilliant, luminous sound. His music combines a crisp, virtuoso attack, clearly forged in the study of the classical literature (he performed with symphony orchestras in Cuba, the United States, and Europe), long phrasing, and a predilection for the high, even altissimo melodic range, combined with Afro-Cuban rhythmic complexity, all leavened by a ready musical wit and idiosyncratic sense of humor.

Further Reading

D'Rivera, Paquito. *Mi vida saxual*. Barcelona: Seix Barral, 2000.

Pablo Julián Davis

Duarte, Ernesto (1922–1988)

Composer and pianist Ernesto Duarte began his music studies in his native **Matanzas** before moving on to the Conservatorio Municipal de La Habana at fifteen years of age. He played the piano on radio stations and in 1943 joined first the orchestra Hermanos Lebatard and then the Orquesta Continental. Later on, he formed his own musical group. During the 1950s, he developed in three important areas: as distinguished composer of **boleros**, such as "No lo digas," "Anda, dilo ya," "Ven aquí a la realidad," and "Como fue," regarded as a classic composition of Cuban music; as a composer of dance music, such as "Miguel," "El baile del pingüino," and "Nicolasa"; and as arranger, working for the **Benny Moré** orchestra.

Duarte was also instrumental in discovering and nurturing new talents. Through his help and musical arrangements, many singers, including **Rolando Laserie**, Fernando Álvarez, Celeste Mendoza, Tata Ramos, Rolo Martínez, and others, achieved fame.

In 1961, Duarte relocated to Spain, taking along his orchestra, Sabor, and singer Tata Ramos. In Spain they performed in clubs and cabarets until he disbanded the group to accept the position of musical director for RCA Victor. In 1974, he launched a recording company, Duher; he remixed his hits from the late 1950s and released them in Madrid.

Further Reading

Díaz Ayala, Cristóbal. *Cuando salí de La Habana.* San Juan: Fundación Musicalia, 1998.

Cristóbal Díaz Ayala and Marisa Méndez

Estefan, Gloria (1957–)

One of the most successful crossover performers in Latin music history, Gloria Estefan was born Gloria Fajardo in Havana. Her mother (also named Gloria) was a schoolteacher. Her father, Jose Manuel, was a security officer for **Fulgencio Batista**.

Gloria and her parents fled for Miami in 1959 soon after **Fidel Castro** had overthrown Batista. The family settled in an impoverished area. Her father took part in the failed **Bay of Pigs Invasion** in 1961. He was captured and imprisoned. He was released by the Cuban government two years later. Shortly thereafter, he joined the U.S. Army and was sent to Vietnam in 1967. When her father returned from the war, he had succumbed to the effects of Agent Orange, leaving him mentally and physically impaired. While still a young girl, Estefan helped her mother care for her father as well as look after her younger sister, Rebecca. Having been studying the guitar for some years, she found strength in her music.

In 1975 Estefan entered the University of Miami. That same year she met her future husband, Emilio Estefan. They met at a wedding where Emilio's band, the Miami Latin Boys, was playing. Emilio asked Gloria to sing and then to join the band. She did, and the band was renamed Miami Sound Machine. Three years later Gloria graduated with honors and married Emilio. The year 1980 was a bittersweet year for Estefan. Her father passed way, her first child, Nayib, was born, and Miami Sound Machine landed its first recording contract.

The group recorded four Spanish-language albums between 1981 and 1983 for Discos CBS International, the Hispanic division of CBS records. In 1984, the single "Dr. Beat" went to number ten on the charts, prompting CBS to switch the band to its international rock music division, Epic Records. "Conga" (1985) became their first international smash hit—it was the first single to ever make *Billboard's* pop, dance, black, and Latin charts concurrently. Several more hits followed. By the end of the 1980s, Estefan had reached new levels of crossover success as no Latin artist before her. In 1989, Estefan released her first solo album, *Cut Both Ways*.

Just as Estefan seemed to have reached a pinnacle in her success, she suffered temporary paralysis, having broken her back in two places when a semitrailer crashed

Estefan's song "Reach" from her *Destiny* album became the official song of the 1996 **Olympics**. She performed the song at the closing ceremonies before an estimated audience of 3 billion TV viewers.

In 2000, Estefan received an Oscar nomination for *Music of the Heart*. In 2001 she released her *Greatest Hits, vol. 2* and won the Grammy Award for Best Traditional Tropical Latin Album for *Alma Caribeña*. In total, Estefan has sold more than 45 million records.

Further Readings

Gourse, Leslie. *Gloria Estefan: Pop Sensation*. New York: Franklin Watts, 1999.

Nielsen, Shelly. *Gloria Estefan: International Pop Star*. Edina, MN: Abdo and Daughters, 1993.

Luis González

Gloria Estefan and husband Emilo Estefan (1997). AP/Wide World Photos. Photograph by Alan Díaz.

into her tour bus in March 1990. She underwent surgery and physical rehabilitation for about a year.

In 1992 Estefan won the Humanitarian of the Year award from B'nai B'rith and a Lifetime Achievement Award from Premio Lo Nuestro. That same year, she released her *Greatest Hits* album.

In 1993, Estefan recorded *Mi Tierra* for which she earned her first Grammy award (Best Latin Tropical Album). That same album sold 4 million copies worldwide and was Spain's bestselling album of all time. In that same year she received the Congressional Medal of Honor, was honored by the Alexis de Tocqueville Society for her outstanding philanthropy, and received an honorary doctorate in music from the University of Miami as well as a star on the Hollywood Walk of Fame (see **U.S. Entertainment Industry, Cubans in the**).

In 1995, she earned another Grammy award, this time for *Abriendo Puertas* (Opening Doors), also in Best Latin Tropical Album category.

Fernández "Trespatines," Leopoldo (1910–1985)

One of Cuba's most popular and beloved comedians, Leopoldo Fernández began his career in the **Teatro Bufo**, a type of entertainment akin to vaudeville, but in 1940 he left the theater to pair off with another comic, Anibal de Mar, and work on the radio. Their show was called *La tremenda corte* (The Great Court), and it was broadcast over the station RHC. With an ingenious script by Castor Vispo, *La tremenda corte* depicted the misadventures of an Afro-Cuban named Trespatines—portrayed by Fernández—who always ended up in municipal court before de Mar, acting as judge. Their hilarious antics received support from other excellent performers, such as the actress Mimi Cal, portraying a *mulata*, and Adolfo Otero, playing a Spaniard. The show was an immense hit, and the radio station sold its rights to networks in Puerto Rico and the United States; thus fifty years after first airing, the show is still popular throughout Latin America.

After the death of Castor Vispo, and due to certain copyright restrictions, the

"Trespatines," one of Cuba's most famous comedians. Courtesy of Fundación Musicalia, San Juan, Puerto Rico, and the Library of Florida International University, Miami.

Poster for *Retrato de Teresa* (1979) by Servando Cabrera. Luis Martínez-Fernández Collection.

two comedians created two new characters, Pototo y Filomeno, who were two working-class rogues. Besides performing on radio, Fernández and de Mar resurrected for the stage and television old Teatro Bufo skits that always ended with a song. The act proved so popular during the 1950s that it always made the Hit Parade listings. Going into exile in 1960, the pair revived *La tremenda corte*, but this time on Mexican television. Eventually, the two comics parted company. Fernández worked on the stage until his death in Miami in 1985.

Further Reading

Díaz Ayala, Cristóbal. *Música cubana del areyto a la nueva trova*. Miami: Ediciones Universal, 1993.

Cristóbal Díaz Ayala and Marisa Méndez

Film Posters

The art of making posters for Cuban cinema dates to 1943 when Eladio Rivadulla designed posters to promote films, using for the first time the serigraphy technique, or silkscreen. With the creation of Cuba's film institute (Cuban Institute of Art and Motion Picture Industry, ICAIC) in 1959, poster art headed in new directions. The poster designed by Eduardo Muñoz for the film *Historias de la Revolución* (1960) pointed a new way for artists who now attempted to create an aesthetics that not only captured what the film was about but that were also instruments of suggestion, provocation, and reflection. Initially, the posters department at ICAIC was a modest space with three artists—Rivadulla, Muñoz, and Rafael Morante—but then others—including René Azcuy, Antonio Fernández Reboiro, Alfredo Rostgaard, Holbein López, Ricardo Reymena, Humberto Peña, and Luis Vega—joined the effort.

The 1970s were a period of flowering as these and other artists used their experiences and experimented with pop art, psychodelic art, and retro. It was a time when Cuban film was transcending national context, creating a "Cuban school." But in 1989, there was a violent fall as several poster artists fled Cuba and art materials became scarce; the fall also coincided with the decline of production quality in Cuban films. Today, the Cuban cinema poster is a bittersweet memory of what once was. *See also* Cinema

Further Readings

Rivadulla Pérez, Eladio. *La serigrafía artística en Cuba*. Havana: UNEAC, 1996.

Sontag, Susan. "Posters: Advertisements, Art, Political Machinery, Commodity." In *The Art of Revolution*. By Dugall Stermer. New York: McGraw-Hill, 1970.

Vega, Jesús. *El cartel cubano del cine*. Havana: Letras Cubanas, 1996.

Jesús Vega

Hollywood leading man Andy García. © Timothy White/Paradigm.

García, Andy (1956–)

Born Andrés Arturo García-Menéndez, Andy García is one of Hollywood's leading actors, yet maintains a fervent interest in his Cuban roots.

García was born in Havana on April 12, 1956. In 1961, shortly after the triumph of the **Revolution**, his family was exiled to Miami Beach when Andy was just five years old. His family struggled financially for some years until García's father (formerly a lawyer) established a successful cosmetics business. García attended Florida International University. After college, he left for Los Angeles to pursue a career as a stand-up comic. He worked several jobs, including as a waiter, to earn a living.

In 1981 he landed his first television role, a small part on *Hill Street Blues*. Two years later he worked in his first film, *Blue Skies*, a baseball comedy. In 1985 he caught the attention of critics and moviegoers alike with his role as a drug kingpin in *8 Million Ways to Die*. He was then seen in *The Untouchables* (1987) and *Stand and Deliver* (1988). García earned both Oscar and Golden Globe nominations for best supporting actor for his role as Michael Corleone's nephew in *The Godfather, Part III* (1990). Most recently, he has been featured in *Oceans 11* (2001) and *Basic* (2002).

In addition to films, García's other passion is Cuban music. He combined the two when he made his directorial debut with *Cachao—Como su ritmo no hay dos* (Like His Rhythm there Is No Other), a documentary concert film on Cuban bass player and composer **"Cachao" (Israel López)**. García produced the film under CineSon, his own production company. García also produced and performed on *Cachao Master Sessions*, Volume I, which won a Grammy award in 1994. Volume II of the same work received a Grammy award nomination in 1995. He again combined film and Cuban music in an original film based on the life of Cuban trumpeter **Arturo Sandoval** for HBO in 2000. García played Sandoval.

García's many honors include the Harvard University Foundation Award for outstanding contributions to the American Performing Arts and Intercultural Relations, a Star on the Hollywood Walk of Fame, and a Hispanic Heritage Award for the Arts. *See also* U.S. Entertainment Industry, Cubans in the

Further Reading

Reyes, Luis and Peter Rubie. *Hispanics in Hollywood: An Encyclopedia of Film and Television.* New York: Garland, 1994.

Luís González

García Caturla, Alejandro (1906–1940)

García Caturla was an influential composer with a vast legacy of musical works, including *La Rumba* (1933), one of his best-known works. Born in Remedios, García Caturla collaborated on some of his earliest works with Fernando Estrems and María Montalván. In 1922, he went to Havana to study law but also studied musical composition with Pedro San Juan. His love for music led him to Paris in 1928 to study with Nadia Boulanger, a renowned teacher who counted among her students some of the most accomplished composers of the era. He returned to Havana to practice law, but he quickly emerged as a promising young composer. García Caturla was influenced by Hector Villalobos, Carlos Chávez, and Aaron Copland, and he would collaborate with all of them throughout the course of his career. Sensitive to Afro-Cuban rhythms, he assimilated the **son** and **rumba** into his music. Along with **Amadeo Roldán**, he succeeded in securing international acclaim for Cuban concert music. *La Rumba* remains one of the most important repertory works produced in Latin America. Assassinated at age thirty-four by a criminal over whose case he was ruling, García Caturla left behind hundreds of diverse musical works, including seventeen symphony pieces, some thirty instrumental and vocal works, an opera, three band compositions, a ballet, a theatrical work, two cinemagraphic music scores, and innumerable other works for the violin, piano, saxophone, and organ.

Further Readings

De la Vega, Aurelio. "Historia de la música cubana de concierto." In *Notas para el festival Sonido de las Américas: Cuba,* ed. Eric Caraballo. New York: American Composers Orchestra, 1999. 13–17.
Orovio, Helio. *Diccionario de la música cubana: biográfico y técnico.* Havana: Editorial Letras Cubanas, 1981.

Edgardo Díaz Díaz

González, Celina (1928–   )

Celina González was born in Jovellanos **Matanzas Province** on March 16, 1928. At the age of eight her family relocated to **Santiago de Cuba**. She later married Reutilio Domínguez with whom she formed the musical duo Celina y Reutilio. Together they performed for Cadena Oriental radio, RHC Cadena Azul, and various cabarets and other venues. Their composition "Que viva Changó" brought them much acclaim, and their performances earned them seven duo of the year awards. The duo broke up in 1963, but Celina continued as a solo performer and often in the company of her son Reutilito. The elder Reutilio died in 1971.

Until the production of "Que viva Changó" in the late 1940s, Celina y Reutilio had been essentially a Cuban country music duo. With her mastery over the difficult genre of *punto guajiro* (see **Punto Cubano**) and improvisation along with her husband's gifted guitar playing, the duo invoked the Afro-Cuban deity Changó and thus helped bridge the divide between the country genres and Afro-Cuban musical forms (see **Afro-Cubans** and **Santería**). She credits **Ñico Saquito** with helping her master the *clave* and the secrets of the **son**.

With the collaboration of Reutilio, Celina composed a succession of hits in both the Afro-Cuban and Cuban country traditions. Among the former, she wrote "A la Caridad del Cobre," "Antonia Gervasio," "A la reina del mar," and "El hijo de Eleguá." Among the latter she composed "Yo soy el punto cubano," "uQiero bailar con Celina," "Que bueno baila Celina," "Ese es mi orgullo," and "Canto a Borinquen." During the early years of the **Revolution**, Celina was permitted to perform and develop only the country side of her works; only in the 1980s, when Afro-Cuban folklore became a tourist attraction (see **Tourism**), was she allowed to continue with the more Afro-Cuban part of her work. She remains active as a performer but has failed to earn the international recognition that Compay Segundo has gained. *See also* Compadres, Los

Further Readings

Díaz Ayala, Cristóbal. *Cuando salí de La Habana: 1898–1997: cien años de música cubana por el mundo.* San Juan: Fundación Musicalia, 1998.

Díaz Ayala, Cristóbal. *Música cubana del areyto a la nueva trova.* Miami: Ediciones Universal, 1993.

Rodríguez, Lil. *Bailando en casa del trompo.* Caracas: Euroamericana de Ediciones, 1997.

Cristóbal Díaz Ayala and Marisa Méndez

Gramatges, Harold (1918–   )

Harold Gramatges was born in **Santiago de Cuba**, where he studied music as a child. Later in Havana, he studied under **Amadeo Roldán** and José Ardevol. In 1942 he went to the United States and studied at the Berkshire Music Center under Aaron Copland and Serge Koussevitsky. Upon his return to the island, Gramatges dedicated himself to musical composition and became a member of a group of Cuban composers known as "Renovación Musical" (1943–1948). He founded and directed the Orquesta Juvenil del Conservatorio Municipal de La Habana (Youth Orchestra of the Municipal Conservatory of Havana).

Gramatges initially adopted *neoclassical* forms as a means to merge popular Cuban styles with contemporary techniques, such as microtonality and indetermination. The special adaptation of these techniques led him to create an innovative musical notation. But Gramatges's most recent works have moved away from complex rhythmic textures and gone back to elements of popular tradition. Overall his body of work includes symphonic pieces, chamber music, choral works, instrumental pieces, and compositions for the **theater**, ballet, and movies. Gramatges's catalog of works, which numbered 124 compositions as of 1996, illustrates the evolution of Cuban concert music from the 1940s to the present day. In 1996, he was awarded the Premio Iberoamericano de la Música Tomás Luis de Victoria, one of the most important honors in the field of Latin American concert music. After the **Revolution**, Gramatges was appointed to a series of government posts, including ambassador to France (1960–1964). He serves as president of the National Music Association and as a member of the Technical Advisory Council of the Ministry of Culture.

Further Readings

Amer, José, ed. *Catálogo de compositores: Harold Gramatges.* Madrid: SGAE/Fundación Autores, 1996.

Caraballo, Eric, ed. *Sonido de las Américas: Cuba.* New York: American Composers Orchestra, 1999.

Edgardo Díaz Díaz

Granados, Daisy (1942–   )

Granados is one of Cuba's most revered actresses. After studying drama at the Escuela Nacional de Arte de Cubanacán, her first role was in the movie *La decisión*, directed by José Massip, in 1964. It is, however, her appearance in 1968 in the renowned *Memorias del subdesarollo*, directed by **Tomás Gutiérrez Alea**, that

Daisy Granados in scene from *Retrato de Teresa* (1979). Still photograph courtesy of Instituto Cubano del Arte e Industria Cinematográficos, Havana.

demonstrated her acting abilities. Eleven years later, her role in Pastor Vega's *Retrato de Teresa* established her as a major international star. Since then she has matured as an actress in the films *Cecilia* (**Humberto Solás**, 1981), *Habanera* (Pastor Vega, 1984), *Plaff* (Juan Carlos Tabío, 1988), and *Vidas paralelas* (Pastor Vega, 1992). Recently, she worked in Spain in *Cosas que dejé en La Habana* (Manuel Gutiérrez Aragón, 1997), *Cuarteto en La Habana* (Fernando Colomo, 1998) *Las profecías de Amanda* (Pastor Vega, 1999), and *Nada* (Juan Carlos Cremata Malberiti, 2001). She has received numerous awards and prizes, including the Catalina de Plata award for best actress and the award Premio Coral de Honor for lifetime accomplishments in Latin America cinema. *See also* Cinema

Further Reading

Chanan, Michael. *The Cuban Image: Cinema and Cultural Politics in Cuba.* London: British Film Institute, 1985.

Jesús Vega

Grenet, Eliseo (1893–1950)

Cuban composer and bandleader Eliseo Grenet was born in Havana on June 12, 1893; he studied music from an early age with Raimundo and Pablo Valenzuela and began his professional career as a young teenager writing popular *danzones*. At age sixteen he was asked to direct the orchestra of the Politeama Habanero theater where he wrote humorous Afro-Cuban–inspired works for the stage (see **Teatro Bufo**; **Theater**). In 1926, Grenet became director of the blackface troupe of Arquímedes Pous, which performed in the Teatro Cubano. Following Pous's death that same year, he served as director of the house orchestra of the Casino Nacional and organized an Afro-Cuban entertainment troupe called Cubanacán. Grenet had no desire to leave Cuba but was forced to flee in 1932 when his song "Lamento cubano" (Cuban Lament) was judged to be subversive by the government of **Gerardo Machado**. The composer first went to Madrid, where he continued to perform and write **zarzuela**-like theater productions with much critical and financial success. Encouraged by his success in Spain, Grenet decided in 1934 to move to Paris. Within the year, as a result of clever promotional techniques, he managed to become the talk of the city by consciously reinventing *comparsa* music for the French ballroom and salon. In this way he single-handedly helped to generate interest in the salon **conga** internationally. In 1936 he moved to New York, founding the Yumurí cabaret and popularizing the conga around the city. Back in Cuba in 1947, he added to his long list of hit compositions, including "Ay, Mamá Inés," "Facundo," and "Las perlas de to boca." He also revived the old folk genre, *sucu-sucu*, with Felipe Blanco.

Further Reading

Orovio, Helio. *Diccionario de la música cubana: biográfico y técnico*. 2nd ed. Havana: Editorial Letras Cubanas, 1992, 225–226.

Robin Moore

Grillo, Frank ("Machito") (1908–1984)

An orchestra leader born in Havana in 1908, Machito established himself in the United States and became the seminal figure in the creation of a new and dynamic amalgam known as **Afro-Cuban jazz**.

Machito began his musical career in Cuba, then emigrated to the United States in his teens in 1937. Among his first jobs was with the orchestra of Catalan bandleader **Xavier Cugat**, who had earlier established himself in Cuba and was, at the time, the dominant Latin bandleader in the United States. Together with his brother-in-law, the experienced jazz trumpeter and arranger Mario Bauzá (an alumnus of Cab Calloway's orchestra), he established "Machito and his Afro-Cubans" in 1940 and grew in popularity throughout the decade. The orchestra's popularity climaxed

Jazz musician Machito (Frank Grillo). Photo courtesy of Izzy Sanabria (SalsaMagazine.com) Archives.

in the early 1950s; it regularly played New York City's Palladium dance hall, "ground zero" of the **mambo** sensation. It would be difficult to overstate the importance of Machito's orchestra; the roster of its alumni and collaborators included Tito Puente, Charlie Parker, Dizzy Gillespie, Buddy Rich, Harry "Sweets" Edison, and Cannonball Adderley, and an entire jazz genre derived its name from the "Afro-Cubans." Long past its peak of popularity, Machito's orchestra continued to work and tour. In 1976, Bauzá left to form his own orchestra. The year 1982 brought recognition in the form of the Grammy award for Best Latin Recording, for *Machito & His Salsa Big Band–82*. Waiting to take the bandstand at a London club in 1984, the tireless pioneer was felled by a fatal stroke.

Further Readings

Leymarie, Isabelle. *La música latinoamericana, ritmos y danzas de un continente*. Barcelona: Ediciones B, 1997.

Loza, Steven. *Tito Puente and the Making of Latin Music*. Urbana: University of Illinois Press, 1999.

Roberts, John Storm. *The Latin Tinge*. 2nd ed. New York: Oxford University Press, 1999.

Pablo Julián Davis

Guajira

One of the more traditional Cuban musical forms, the *guajira* is a rural-inspired music genre associated most closely with Spanish influence.

Taking for its usual themes country matters, and retaining in its tempo the pace of bucolic life, the guajira bears the marks of its rural origin even when incorporated into urban forms such as the **son**. Its lyrics take the form of the *décima*, a poetic scheme possessed of a long improvisational tradition in the folklore of the Spanish-speaking world. The genre's name derives from the Cuban term for country folk, *guajiro*, which is conventionally understood to refer to the mainly Spanish-descended dwellers of the island's interior (see **Guajiros**). Yet the guajira, if markedly less African than such styles as the son, and generally lacking *clave*, is far from being simply a Spanish music transplanted to Cuban soil; it has its hybrid qualities. Its instrumentation is that of Cuban musical traditions of the countryside, dominated by strings, particularly guitar and *tres*; however, Afro-Cuban percussion may be used in varying degrees. The incorporation of substantial Afro-Cuban rhythmic elements, particularly clave, under the influence of the son, gave rise by the middle of the twentieth century to the subgenre *son-guajira*. It is not to be confused with the *punto guajiro*, a vocal genre of decidedly Iberian origin (see **Punto Cubano**).

Further Readings

Orovio, Helio. *Diccionario de la música cubana: biográfico y técnico*. Havana: Editorial Letras Cubanas, 1981.

Roberts, John Storm. *The Latin Tinge*. 2nd ed. New York: Oxford University Press, 1999.

Pablo Julián Davis

"Guantanamera, La"

"La guantanamera" (or "La guajira guantanamera") is a song written in the 1930s by composer and *música* **guajira** singer Joseíto Fernández (1908–1979). The title of the song might be translated as "Country Woman from Guantánamo." Essentially, "La guantanamera" consists of a repeated refrain or chorus that alternates with *coplas*, two-line phrases of text, which are typically improvised by a soloist. Melodies of the coplas vary to some degree but tend to consist of stock phrases; the emphasis in this artistic form is on the spontaneous creation of lyrics. The practice of improvising poetry to instrumental accompaniment in música guajira, or Cuban "country music", is derived from southern Spanish culture and ultimately from the Arab world.

Fernández first developed the composition as a closing piece for a dance band with which he performed; he would teach others a chorus that named each new city they played in and then invent rhymed coplas about the beauty of women from that area. Later in the 1940s the song became famous on live radio broadcasts in Havana, used by Fernández as a means of commenting on current political events. The version promoted by Pete Seeger that has become famous internationally since the 1960s uses precomposed coplas by poet and Cuban independence martyr **José Martí** from his work *Versos sencillos* (Simple Verses).

Further Reading

Sánchez Oliva, Iraida. *La guantanamera*. Havana: Editorial José Martí, 1999.

Robin Moore

Guaracha

Guaracha is the name given to a musical dance genre that traditionally employs humor and satire in its lyrics. The satire is typically directed at popular personalities or on aspects of urban life (see **Choteo**). The origins of guaracha may be found in the Afro-Cuban tradition of employing satire in the playful interplay between chorus and soloist. The guaracha came to be associated with a variety of dances including the *chuchumbé*, the *sacamandú*, and the *maracumbé* as early as the eighteenth century. The unity of the guaracha can be traced to the rhythmic patterns of the **habanera** or the *cinquillo*. The meter is based on a beat of two by four, although originally a beat of six by eight was common. During the second half of the nineteenth century the guaracha was employed during the intermission of Cuban minstrel productions known as the *bufos habaneros* and acclaimed throughout Latin America. Additionally, composers in Cuba and Puerto Rico received commissions from cigar and liquor producers to arrange guarachas as commercial jingles to be played by Spanish military bands. In the context of the **tobacco industry** the workers created guarachas as a powerful vehicle for social political expression. In these cases, the use of a chorus and soloist is abandoned, and the guaracha concentrates on the expression of one central idea or commentary. The guaracha later evolved and was used in different musical formats by **tríos** and Cuban orchestras. In these later formats a specialized singer, known as the *guarachero*, alternates with the *bolerista* (see **Bolero**) in orchestras. In recent times the guaracha has been absorbed into **salsa** music.

Further Readings

Díaz Díaz, Edgardo. "Música para anunciar en la sociedad sanjuanera del Siglo XIX." *Revista Musical Puertorriqueña* 1(1987): 6–13.

León, Argeliers. "La Guaracha." In *Del canto y el tiempo*. 2nd ed. Havana: Editorial Letras Cubanas, 1984. 166–184.

Edgardo Díaz Díaz

Guaracheros de Oriente, Los

Around 1945 Antonio Fernández, better known as **Ñico Saquito**, founded the musical group Los Guaracheros de Oriente, in great measure as a venue to perform his own hits. Among the first to join the group were Florencio Santana "Pícolo" and Gerardo Macías "El Chino." The group's first voice was not fixed but varied over time; since Ñico did not have a soloist's voice, he organized the ensemble with Macías as first guitar and third voice, Pícolo as second guitar and second voice, and himself in the maracas and singing chorus. Whenever recording, the trio was expanded to include a bongo player and a first voice, Máximo Sánchez "Bimbi," who had successfully led his Trío Oriental until 1943 (see **Tríos**). Los Guaracheros recorded a succession of hits: "Silverio," "Facundo y la luna," "El Jaleo," "Adiós Compay Gato," "El muñequito." Later the group's principal voice was Orlando Vallejo, one of Cuba's foremost *boleristas* (see **Bolero**), who surprised his fans with renditions of the **guarachas** "Qué bobo es Juan" and "El berrinche de María," the *quasi-guaguancó* "Mamá Belén," the **son montuno** "Estoy hecho tierra," and the sweet boleros "Qué humanidad" by Ñico and "Siempre te adoraré" by Humberto Suárez. Another of the group's bolero singers was Jack Sagué, who did not receive the acclaim he deserved. He was followed by Alfredito Valdés, one of Cuba's most distinguished soloists and member of various bands including jazz orchestras.

In 1950 Ñico Saquito offered Félix Escobar, "El Gallego," the opportunity to play the bongo drums for Los Guaracheros during a tour of Tampa, Florida. El Gallego surprised the group and their audiences with a secret weapon: his delightful first voice. Thus far, bongo players did not sing in quartets because of the difficulties associated with keeping a rhythm and singing at the same time. El Gallego, however, avoided these difficulties by singing and playing small timbales or *pailas* with sticks instead of the bongo drums, a development that gave Los Guaracheros a unique sound and the ability to perform dance music numbers. The Tampa tour was a success and was followed by a visit to New York. Among Los Guaracheros' greatest hits were "Mujer perjura" "Las perlas de tu boca," "Frutas del Caney," "Tres cositas nada más," and "Yereyé."

In 1960, while in Venezuela, El Gallego, El Chino, and Pícolo decided not to return to Cuba, but Ñico did. The three exiled Guaracheros retained the group's name and continued to tour in the United States, Puerto Rico, and other countries. In 1966 El Chino died and Pícolo retired. El Gallego then reorganized the group with Puerto Rican musicians and continued to record and tour.

Further Reading

Díaz Ayala, Cristóbal. *Cuando salí de La Habana: 1898–1997: cien años de música cubana por el mundo*. San Juan: Fundación Musicalia, 1998.

Cristóbal Díaz Ayala and Marisa Méndez

Guillot, Olga (1929–   )

Affectionately known as "Olga de América" and "La Reina del Bolero" (Queen of the **Bolero**), Olga Guillot has performed throughout Latin America and the United States for several decades. Guillot was born on October 9, 1929, in the old Oriente Province. As a young girl, she moved with her family to Havana and performed with her sister Ana Luisa under the name Duo Hermanitas Guillot. Under the guidance of Cuban musician Facundo Rivero,

Guillot became a soloist, debuting in 1945 at Havana's Zombi Club. Well-known singer **Miguelito Valdés** took her to New York to record under the Decca label. The following year she gained fame with her recording of the Spanish version of "Stormy Weather" ("Lluvia gris").

In 1948, René Cabel arranged for her to travel to Mexico, where she made her motion picture debut and continued to make records. It was in 1954 that she recorded what is her best-known song, "Miénteme" (Lie to Me). In 1958 she toured throughout Europe.

Guillot left Cuba in 1961 with her daughter Olga María. They settled in Caracas, Venezuela, for a brief period. Shortly thereafter, she set up residence in Mexico. In 2000, after a fifteen-year hiatus from recording, Guillot signed an exclusive record contract with Warner Music. Guillot has performed worldwide, including New York's Carnegie Hall. She has appeared in sixteen films and has recorded fifty-eight albums, twenty of which are gold and ten platinum. In **Little Havana** a street has been named after her.

Further Reading

"Olga Guillot." *People en Español*, June–July 1999 V2 p60.

Luis González

Güines, Tata (1930–   )

Born Arístides Soto, Tata Güines is one of Cuba's most legendary percussionists. Güines, who plays the conga drums, began his career at the age of twelve playing bongos with the group Ases del Ritmo (Aces of Rhythm). At age eighteen, he left for Havana, attempting to join a group but worked at odd jobs for four years.

Güines got his big break in 1952 when he joined Fajardo y Sus Estrellas (Fajardo and his Stars). The group made several international appearances, most notably a tour in Venezuela in 1956. The following year, Güines joined the Chico O'Farrill group. Güines then left for New York City, where he appeared at the Waldorf Astoria and other nightclubs.

In 1959 he returned to Cuba, performing as a solo act at the Habana Libre hotel. He later joined Frank Emilio's jazz band. Güines has recorded with numerous artists, including **Paquito D'Rivera, Arturo Sandoval**, and more recently, Jane Bunnet and Julio Padrón. Güines currently leads a band that bears his name.

Further Reading
"Tata Güines: maestro de la percusión." Andaluciajazz. com.

Luis González

Gutiérrez, Julio (1912–1985)

Regarded as the most versatile and multi-talented Cuban composer who worked in almost every genre, Julio Gutiérrez also discovered and mentored many singers and performers. A conductor, composer, and pianist, Gutiérrez learned to play the piano as a young child. By the time he was fourteen years old, he had already formed a musical group. In 1940, he moved from his native Manzanillo to Havana, where he joined the famous orchestra **Casino de la Playa**. During this time, he wrote some of his best songs, the **boleros** "Cuando vuelves a quererme" and "Macurijes"; he also composed several **congas**.

By 1948, Gutiérrez had his own orchestra. While touring Mexico and other Latin American countries, including Brazil and Argentina, where he spent three years, he continued to compose boleros, such as "Desconfianza," "Llanto de luna," and "Inolvidable." When he returned to Cuba in 1950, the **mambo** was the musical craze, and so he composed the boleros-mambos "Un poquito de tu amor," "Qué es lo que pasa," "Así así," and "Pero qué te parece." He conducted several orchestras, performing for radio, television, and cabarets.

Always creative, adaptable, and prolific, he wrote **cha-cha-chá** numbers when this dance became popular at the end of the 1950s; he modified the bolero when fans preferred romantic ballads; and he directed and recorded jam sessions when this type of performance gained popularity in the early 1960s.

Further Reading
Díaz Ayala, Cristóbal. *Revista la Canción Popular*, 6 (1991): 81.

Cristóbal Díaz Ayala and Marisa Méndez

Gutiérrez Alea, Tomás (1928–1996)

Tomás Gutiérrez Alea was a film director, scriptwriter, editor, writer, and film theorist whose movie *Memorias del subdesarrollo* (1968) is considered one of the best films ever made in international **cinema.** Born in Havana, Gutiérrez Alea graduated with a law degree from the **University of Havana** to please his father but loved movies, making his first film in 1947, a humorous short titled *El faquir y la Caperucita Roja*. In 1950, he founded the Sociedad Cultural "Nuestro Tiempo," an association that attracted leftist intellectuals. In 1951, he traveled to Rome to study directing in the Centro Sperimentale di Cinematografia. In 1955, he collaborated with Julio García Espinosa in the direction of the documentary *El Mégano*, a denunciation of the working conditions of the charcoal workers from the Ciénaga de Zapata in southern Cuba. He filmed documentaries and humorous shorts for Cine Revista, and upon the triumph of the **Revolution**, he organized, with other directors, the film department of the Dirección de Cultura del Ejército Rebelde; there he took charge of the filming of the documentary *Esta tierra nuestra*. He was also one of the founders of Cuba's film institute (Instituto Cubano del Arte e Industria Cinematográficos [ICAIC]). In 1960, he shot *Historias de la Revolución*, the ICAIC's first

Director Tomás Gutiérrez Alea and wife actress Mirtha Ibarra. Courtesy of Instituto Cubano del Arte e Industria Cinematográficos, Havana.

feature movie. His most distinguished films and documentaries include *Las doce sillas* (1962); *La muerte de un burócrata* (1966); *Memorias del subdesarrollo* (1968); *El arte del tabaco* (1974), *El camino de la mirra y el incienso* (1975); *La última cena* (1976); *Fresa y chocolate* (with Juan Carlos Tabío, 1993). His last film was *Guantanamera* (with Juan Carlos Tabío, 1994).

Gutiérrez Alea was nominated for the 1995 Best Foreign Picture Oscar for his *Fresa y chocolate*. He was the recipient of the 1973 National Critics Award for *Memorias del subdesarrollo* and the first prize winner of the Biarritz Award in 1979. He received numerous honors and awards in Cuba.

Gutiérrez Alea said of his work: "For me, film making is not just taking a picture of reality. To film is to manipulate; it affords you the opportunity to manipulate different aspects of reality and create new meanings. Through that game, one can learn about the world."

Further Reading

Chanan, Michael. *The Cuban Image: Cinema and Cultural Politics in Cuba.* London: British Film Institute, 1985.

Jesús Vega

Habanera

The *habanera* is a danceable musical genre born in nineteenth-century Cuba and characterized by a gently syncopated rhythmic pattern of uncertain origin, which achieved worldwide influence.

The habanera is typically set in 2/4 time, with a dotted eighth note, a sixteenth note, and two eighth notes. Another popular variant of the pattern ties the sixteenth note over to give a lilting, swaying effect. The name, meaning "of Havana," is a contraction of "*contradanza* (or *danza*) habanera*." The subject of its ultimate origins has given rise, for more than a century, to the wildest diversity of conjecture; North African Arab, sub-Saharan African, Basque, and Cuban sources have all been put forward. Its fundamental rhythmic pattern has enjoyed probably the widest diffusion of any Latin American musical idea. Its influence marked the tango; U.S. country music and "rhythm and blues"; Latin American rural styles; and the work of European composers including Isaac Albéniz, Maurice Ravel, Georges Bizet, and Claude Debussy. One of the best-loved pieces set to this rhythm was the famous habanera from Bizet's opera *Carmen*. It also appeared, early in the twentieth century, in ragtime; Scott Joplin used the pattern most famously in his graceful, melancholy piece "Solace: A Mexican Serenade." The habanera became a strictly vocal genre (**Eduardo Sánchez de Fuentes**'s "Tú" was a famous example) and vanished as a living genre by the middle twentieth century, surviving only in the rhythmic traces it left on other musical forms worldwide.

Further Readings

Galán, Natalio. *Cuba y sus sones*. Valencia, Spain: Pre-Textos, 1997.
Roberts, John Storm. *The Latin Tinge*. 2nd ed. New York: Oxford University Press, 1999.

Pablo Julián Davis

Ibarra, Mirtha (1948–   )

One of the most important actresses in Cuban film, Mirtha Ibarra attended the Escuela Nacional de Art de Cubanacán, followed by intensive training at Grupo **Teatro Estudio**, Teatro Político Bertolt Brecht, and Teatro de Arte Caribeño. She met filmmaker **Tomás Gutiérrez Alea** in the 1960s and established a long-term relationship until his death in 1996. Her credits are numerous: *La última cena* (1976), *Se permuta* (1983), *Otra mujer* (1986), *Hasta cierto punto* (1983), *Cartas del parque* (1988), *Adorables mentiras* (1991), *Fresa y chocolate* (1993), and *Guantanamera* (1995). Abroad, she worked in Venezuela in *Golpes a mi puerta* (1993); in Colombia in the film *Ilona llegó con la lluvia* (1996); in Spain, *Cuarteto de La Habana* (1998); and in Canada, *Ruleta* (1999). Her script *Éramos tan vírgenes*, about homosexuals in Cuba, awaits production (see **Gays and Lesbians**).

Ibarra has received the Premio Coral Best Actress award in 1983 and the Premio Coral Best Supporting Actress award in 1993.

Further Readings
Ebert, Roger. *Movie Yearbook 1999*. Kansas City, MO: Andrew McMeel Publishing, 1999.
Vizcaíno Serrat, Mario. "La actriz y el maestro." *La Gaceta* (Havana), no. 5 (September–October 1998).

Jesús Vega

Ichaso, León (1945–   )

Renowned director, producer, and scriptwriter, León Ichaso's film *El súper* (1979), which tells of the life of Cuban exile in Manhattan, gave him entry to Hollywood. Born in Havana, Ichaso arrived in the United States when he was fourteen years old and lived in New York and Miami. In Cuba, his family had held prominent positions in radio, television, and the press.

His father, Dr. Justo Rodríguez-Santos, was a prominent literary figure whom Ichaso honored in his film *Bitter Sugar* (1996) by quoting one of his poems. His publicity work in New York City helped him realize a cinematographic vision and concept, and his first film, *El súper*, received kudos from critics and the general public. The film was shown at the Venice Film Festival and won awards at Biarritz and Manheim festivals. His movie *Crossover Dreams* (1985) boosted the Hollywood careers of actress Elizabeth Peña and singer Rubén Blades. His most recent feature film, *Bitter Sugar*, is a realistic criticism of the Cuban **Revolution**.

Ichaso has also worked in television, including the popular series *Miami Vice*, in 1984, and the productions *Free of Eden* and *Execution of Justice*, both in 1999, *Ali: An American Hero* (2000) and *Hendrix* (2000). *See also* U.S. Entertainment Industry, Cubans in the

Further Reading
Reyes, Luis and Peter Rubie. *Hispanics in Hollywood: An Encyclopedia of Film and Television*. New York: Garland, 1994.

Jesús Vega

Irakere, Grupo

Grupo Irakere was formed in 1973 under the direction of pianist (**Jesús**) **Chucho Valdés** and quickly emerged as one of the most accomplished jazz ensembles of the period. Among its original members were saxophonist **Paquito D'Rivera**, trumpeter **Arturo Sandoval**, and flutist Carlos Averhoff. One of the first goals of the group was to bridge the divide between listeners and dancers. This challenge emerged from Irakere's dual role as a jazz group and a dance orchestra. As a dance orchestra, the group incorporated traditional dance rhythms into their repertoire, including **rumba, son**, and **danzón** and a modern instrumental format for **charangas**. In

Cuba, the group was renowned as a dance orchestra, garnering an award as the best dance group, but internationally they were recognized for their jazz playing. The unique nature of the group made it a musical laboratory of innovation and experimentation. The group consisted of twelve members skilled in thirty-five different instruments. Without abandoning the traditional Cuban charanga, Irakere incorporated a wide range of different rhythms, phrases, and fragments from European concert music and ritual *santero* music (see **Santería**) to jazz, funk, **salsa**, and rumba. The stylistic versatility of the group earned it a multimillion-dollar contract from Columbia Records. Irakere was awarded a Grammy in 1980. The group played in concert with the likes of Dizzy Gillespie and Stan Getz. Some of the original members, including D'Rivera, Sandoval, and Averhoff, have left the group and established solo careers. *See also* Afro-Cuban Jazz

Further Reading

Orovio, Helio. *Diccionario de la música cubana: biográfico y técnico.* Havana: Editorial Letras Cubanas, 1981.

Edgardo Díaz Díaz

La Lupe (Yoli Guadalupe Victoria Raymond) (1936–1992)

The Cuban entertainer Yoli Guadalupe Victoria Raymond, better known as La Lupe, was born in **Santiago de Cuba** on December 23, 1936.

Known as La Lupe, or endearingly by fans as La Yi Yi Yi, Lupe Victoria recorded approximately twenty-nine albums (two while living in Cuba) and made numerous U.S. television talk show appearances including the *Merv Griffin Show* and the *Tonight Show*. In addition, she collected several top awards and gold albums—all of which resulted in her crowning as "La

Reina de la Música Latina" (Queen of Latin Music). A Havana schoolteacher by profession, La Lupe entered Cuba's music scene as a singer with the famed Trío los Tropicales (see **Tríos**) Her stage performance style, distinct and furious, included La Lupe often shouting "Ahí, na má!" to the four winds, throwing her shoes into the audience, laughing and crying while pulling her hair, ripping her clothes, or even slapping herself or fellow musicians. La Lupe performed with such energy that some of her concerts reportedly ended with her being carried off stage with an oxygen mask. Critics called her a genius and a musical animal, attributing her stage personality to both drugs and **Santería** (the Afro-Cuban religion in which La Lupe was deeply involved and on which she spent her savings to undergo varying initiation rituals). In describing her unique musical presence, La Lupe offered this statement: "When I sing, I feel trapped in an almost insane fascination, which, at the same time, sets me free."

La Lupe's tumultuous stage presence, which initially propelled the singer into Cuban stardom, became condemned by the increasingly rigid Cuban revolutionary government. In 1962, La Lupe finally left Cuba, moving first to Mexico before relocating to New York City in 1963. Collaboration with compatriot Mongo Santamaría on the 1963 album *Mongo Introduces La Lupe* impelled Tico Records to sign La Lupe to its list of performing artists and paired her with another rising star—Tito Puente. Their joint album *Tito Puente Swings, the Exciting Lupe Sings* (1965) catapulted La Lupe into U.S. stardom, with New York's Latin press naming her "Singer of the Year" in 1965 and 1966.

During the mid-1970s, Fania Records acquired Tico Records, and in endorsing another star, **Celia Cruz**, La Lupe's career soon faltered. Despite further releases between 1977 and 1980, including another collaboration with Puente, La Lupe failed

La Lupe in one of her characteristically dramatic performances. Photo courtesy of Izzy Sanabria (SalsaMagazine.com) Archives.

to recapture her former success. Having retired from performing in the early 1980s, La Lupe was reportedly paralyzed following an accident, healed by an Evangelical preacher, converted to Evangelical Christianity in 1986, and thereafter sang Spanish Gospel until her death. Contemporary **salsa** singer La India pays tribute to La Lupe in her 1999 album *Sola*, interpreting two of La Lupe's best-known songs, "¿Qué te pedí?" and "Si vuelves tú." In 2001 the Puerto Rican Travelling Theater Company produced a musical drama chronicling the life of La Lupe. *See also* U.S. Entertainment Industry, Cubans in the

Further Reading
Salazan, Max. "Remembering La Lupe" *Latin Beat Magazine*, 10 (May 2000), 24.

Nanette de Jong

Laserie, Rolando (1923–1998)

Rolando Laserie was a popular entertainer who started his music career as drummer and singer. Born in Las Villas, Laserie played drums with several orchestras until the early 1950s when he was invited to sing on the radio show *Olga y Tony*. But his real opportunity came in 1956 when he recorded the melodic and soft **bolero** "Mentiras tuyas," which he adapted to his own style. Over 30,000 copies of the sin-

gle were sold in a matter of days. Subsequently, he recorded over thirty long plays.

Laserie earned the nickname of "El Guapo de la Canción," meaning the daring singer, for the liberties he took. He accented the lyrics and modified the song's timing to fit his delivery style. While visiting Argentina, he was applauded for his interpretation of such classic tangos as "Las cuarenta" and "Esta noche me emborracho."

Further Reading
Díaz Ayala, Cristóbal. *Revista la Canción Popular*, no. 14 (1999):172.

Cristóbal Díaz Ayala and Marisa Méndez

Lecuona, Ernestina (1882–1951)

The older sister of composer **Ernesto Lecuona**, Ernestina was her brother's first piano teacher. A concert pianist, she performed solo as well as with her brother. She was a composer herself, writing scores of songs that were gently erotic and daring for their time (1920s and 1930s). At the time, it was usual for composers to write songs in response to those of other composers. And thus, to the torrid song written by composer Félix B. Caignet ("Te odio" [I Hate You]) she countered with the glacial "Me odias" (You Hate Me). It turned out to be a perfect combination of songs. Other popular songs by Lecuona included "Ya que te vas," "Cierra los ojos," and "Ahora que eres mía."

Further Reading
Díaz Ayala, Cristóbal. *Música cubana del areyto a la nueva trova*. Miami: Ediciones Universal, 1993.

Cristóbal Díaz Ayala and Marisa Méndez

Lecuona, Ernesto (1895–1963)

Born in Guanabacoa, Ernesto Lecuona was a pianist and orchestra leader whose most lasting fame came as a composer

Stamp commemorating the 100th anniversary of Lecuona's birth. Luis Martínez-Fernández Collection.

with a special gift for melodic creation rooted in Cuban and Spanish soils and whose remarkable career straddled the boundary between classical and popular musical forms.

Lecuona developed his gift early in a musical family and imbibed deeply the influences of nineteenth-century Cuban composers such as **Manuel Saumell** and **Ignacio Cervantes**. Graduated from the National Conservatory of Music of Havana at seventeen under Hubert de Blanck, Lecuona then appeared widely at the keyboard in Spain, the United States, and France. Among his teachers was Cuban Spanish composer Joaquín Nin, and he won high praise from such luminaries as Maurice Ravel and Joaquín Turina. His technical mastery of the keyboard was considerable. He achieved renown with his

touring dance orchestra, Lecuona's Cuban Boys. However, Lecuona did not limit himself to creating melodic and dance music; in 1926, he premiered his first major piano concert composition, *The Andalucía Suite*. Though he drew much of his inspiration from the Spanish sources of Cuban musical culture, he composed "Six Afro-Cuban Dances," and among his more than 100 lieder are eight song settings of poems by **José Martí**. He is best remembered for such popular songs as "Malagueña," "Andalucía" (also known as "The Breeze and I"), "María la O," and "Siboney." He composed a good deal of music for the movies and was nominated for an Academy Award in 1942 for the song "Always in My Heart" from the film of the same name, though the Oscar went to Irvin Berlin's "White Christmas." In 1943, Lecuona was made cultural attaché of the Cuban embassy in Washington. He cultivated a staggering range of forms, including **son, bolero, habanera**, tango, *pasodoble*, waltz, and more—some 850 compositions in all. In spanning the popular and classical realms, his creative achievement has warranted comparisons with the work of his contemporary George Gershwin. Lecuona left Cuba in 1960 amid public denunciations of **Fidel Castro**'s **Revolution** and died three years later in the Canary Islands, having become the best known of all Cuban composers worldwide.

Further Readings

Gómez Cairo, Jesús, et al. *El arte musical de Ernesto Lecuona*. Havana: Sociedad General de Autores y Editores, 1995.

Martínez, Orlando. *Ernesto Lecuona*. Havana: Unión de Escritores y Artistas de Cuba, 1989.

Roberts, John Storm. *The Latin Tinge*. 2nd ed. New York: Oxford University Press, 1999.

Pablo Julián Davis

Lecuona, Margarita (1910–1981)

Composer and singer Margarita Lecuona spent her childhood traveling with her father, who was a diplomat. After graduating from college, she chose a career in music. She played the guitar and studied classical ballet. During the 1930s, she started to write songs. From this period came the piece "Tabú," inspired by an elderly Afro-Cuban who had been a slave and who had befriended Lecuona when she was little. The singer Guyun made the song popular, and in 1934, Oscar de la Rosa and Antonio Machín recorded it in New York City. A year later, the Lecuona Cuban Boys recorded it in Europe. The song became a "standard" hit.

A similar fate occurred with "Babalú," which was also inspired by Afro-Cuban liturgical music and some exotic flavor. In 1939, singer **Miguelito Valdés**, performing with the orchestra **Casino de la Playa**, recorded it, featuring it as his opening song. Consequently, Valdés came to be known in the United States as Mr. Babalú.

Lecuona wrote over 300 songs, though none achieved the fame of "Tabú" and "Babalú." She resided in Buenos Aires for many years, performing solo or in a trio that traveled throughout Latin America. In 1960, she moved to the United States.

Further Reading
Díaz Ayala, Cristóbal. *Dicconario de la música española e hispanoamericana*. Madrid: Editorial Autor, 2000.

Cristóbal Díaz Ayala and Marisa Méndez

León, Tania (1943–   )

Tania León has an impressive trajectory as a composer and orchestra director. Born in Havana on May 14, 1943, she was trained in piano, violin, and music theory. Between 1964 and 1967 she played the piano and served as musical director for Cuban television, while composing popular music. In 1967 she emigrated to the United States; in New York City she accepted Arthur Mitchell's invitation to found and direct the music department of the Dance

Theater of Harlem. In 1980 she organized and directed the Community Concert Series of the Brooklyn Philharmonic Orchestra. Prominent individuals in the music world such as Gian-Carlo Menotti, Kurt Masur, and Lukas Foss have sought her to engage in important artistic roles.

As of 2001 León's compositions included seven works for orchestra, an opera, two works for musical theater, three ballets, and two chorales. She has also composed theater pieces for voice and ensembles, and one for voice and piano, eight for chamber orchestra, and fifteen for small ensembles. Among the many distinguished entities that have commissioned her work are the Munich Biennial, the Hamburg Hammoniale Festival, the Philharmonic Orchestra of Cincinnati, and the Berlin Music Biennial. Some twenty of her compositions have been recorded by interpreters such as **Paquito D'Rivera**, Ana María Rosado, the Continuum ensemble, and the Trío Jubal.

Further Reading
Labes, Jason. *Profile of Tania León*. New York: Peermusic Classical, 2001.

Edgardo Díaz Díaz

Mambo

The *mambo*, a musical hybrid, Cuban in origin but consolidated as a genre in Mexico and the United States, conquered dance floors in North America, particularly in and around New York City, beginning in the 1950s.

The word *mambo* derives from Afro-Cuban religious rites where it means "conversation with the gods" (see **Santería**). Its origin has been long disputed, with some tracing it to the **danzón** and others to a section of the **son**. Orestes López, with the collaboration of his bassist brother Israel (**"Cachao"**), composed a danzón called "Mambo" in 1938 while with **charanga** orchestra **Arcaño y Sus Maravillas**. The figure most closely associated with mambo's development, however, is **Dámaso Pérez Prado**, "El Rey del Mambo." The mambo as it became popularized by Pérez Prado was marked by vibrant rhythm, usually a fast tempo, and a pulsating flow of sixteenth notes in the accompaniment, baritone saxophone figures, blaring and wailing trumpets often rising to an almost unbearable peak of gaudy, reckless dissonance, and grunts by the bandleader signaling a new section of a number. As shaped by Pérez Prado, mambo was an almost hypnotic dance music with only rudimentary lyrics, usually a recurring word or short phrase. The origin of the grunt, curiously, lay in poor acoustics; Pérez Prado was actually shouting out the word "¡Dilo!" (Say it!), but when the recording became popular, the grunt became a kind of trademark, helping make the mambo instantly identifiable to a nonspecialized public. In the mid-1950s it was partially supplanted in popularity by the **cha-cha-chá**.

Further Readings

Galán, Natalio. *Cuba y sus sones*. Valencia, Spain: Pre-Textos, 1997.

Pérez Firmat, Gustavo. *Life on the Hyphen: The Cuban-American Way*. Austin: University of Texas Press, 1994.

Roberts, John Storm. *The Latin Tinge*. 2nd ed. New York: Oxford University Press, 1999.

Pablo Julián Davis

Matamoros, Trío

One of Cuba's longest-lived groups, Trío Matamoros (see **Tríos**) performed from 1925 until it disbanded in 1969. The group was formed by Miguel Matamoros, a guitarist and composer from **Santiago de Cuba**. The two other original members were percussionist Siro Rodríguez and guitarist Rafael Cueto. The group made popular the *bolero-son* style, mixing rich harmonies and melodies and rhythms into the traditional romanticism of **bolero**. Over the years the trio sometimes evolved

into a septet or an orchestra. In the 1940s founder Matamoros began having difficulty with his voice and therefore recruited other singers, the most famous of which was **Benny Moré**. Among Matamoros' greatest hits are: "Juramento," "Triste muy triste," "Mamá son de la loma," and "El que siembra su maíz."

Further Reading

Orovio, Helio. *Diccionario de la música cubana: biográfico y técnico*. Havana: Editorial Letras Cubanas, 1981.

Luis González

Milanés, Pablo (1943–   )

Pablo Milanés, a performer associated with the emergence of **nueva trova**, or Cuban protest music, was born in 1943 in **Bayamo** in the eastern part of the country. As is the case with most musicians from this region, his first musical experiences involved playing traditional acoustic music for dancing (**son**) as well as romantic pieces (**boleros, vieja trova**); in general, his work has been strongly grounded in Cuban folklore, and he has consistently promoted the work of such entertainers. As a teenager, Milanés was already singing on Cuban television as a result of invitations from guitarist José Antonio Méndez and singer Marta Valdés. In the 1950s he performed in dance bands in Havana as well as in the Cuarteto del Rey (Quartet of the King), a group dedicated to interpreting North American spirituals. Milanés's early solo repertoire is noteworthy for its engaging melodies, the influence of jazz harmonization, his adaptation of folkloric rhythms into unique fingerpicking patterns on the guitar, and the straightforward but engaging lyrics discussing intimate relationships, love of country, as well as more political matters. More than any other figure, Milanés is credited with bridging the generational divides that separate nueva trova from popular song of the 1950s. He

Singer-song writer Pablo Milanés attending a tribute to his music at the University of Puerto Rico, Río Piedras (1997). AP/Wide World Photos. Photograph by John McConnico.

wrote the first piece recognized as nueva trova by music historians, "Mis 22 años" (My Twenty-two Years), in 1965. *See also* Rodríguez, Silvio

Further Reading

Díaz Pérez, Clara. *Sobre la guitarra, la voz. Una historia de la nueva trova cubana*. Havana: Editorial Letras Cubanas, 1994.

Robin Moore

Modern Dance

Dancer and choreographer Ramiro Guerra (Havana, 1922) is the founding figure in the evolution of modern dance in Cuba, which he studied in New York with Martha Graham, Doris Humphrey, and Katherine Dunham. Guerra returned to head the Department of Modern Dance at the Teatro Nacional de Cuba, where he created the Conjunto Nacional de Danza Moderna (1959), now called Danza Contemporánea de Cuba. This organization dedicated its efforts to developing a modern dance vocabulary with Cuban musical/dance traditions. In this effort, American choreographer Lorna Burdsall was instrumental, especially for her staging of dances by Doris Humphrey. Guerra holds a law degree from the **University of Havana** and

has received many honors including Doctor Honoris Causa in Dance (1989) and the Premio Nacional de Danza de Cuba (1999).

With *Suite Yoruba* (1960), a seasoned piece inspired by the Afro-Cuban legacy, Guerra rose as a national figure (see **Afro-Cubans**). Beginning with the establishment of the National School of Art, a number of schools developed throughout the island to train students in Cuban modern dance technique. Guerra is an outstanding figure not only as teacher and choreographer but also as a scholar and critic of dance history and aesthetics. He is editor of a quarterly journal *Toda la danza, la Danza Toda* and author of several books on Cuban dance. *Coordenadas danzarias* (1999) is one among several publications that provide an analysis of diverse themes on twentieth-century dance.

Guerra promoted new artists, such as Eduardo Rivera, principal dancer and choreographer of Conjunto Nacional for many years and later director of Teatro de la Danza del Caribe in **Santiago de Cuba**. Rivera's piece *Sulkary* (1980) exemplified the search for a Caribbean aesthetic, an aesthetic that connects with similar expressions in Jamaica, where Rivera shared his quests with Rex Nettleford and his National Dance Theater Company. New generations of Cuban choreographers continued to spring out of Danza Contemporánea in the 1980s, each expressing an extensive range of themes through diverse body languages. Among them, Marianela Boan, founder of DanzaAbierta (OpenDance), is well known for her experimental approach to dance/theater and her pioneering, risk-taking choreographies. In 1996, the first national festival of Cuban modern dance was held in Havana, showcasing a vibrant group of contemporary dancers and choreographers who have added new dimensions to modern dance in Cuba. *See also* Ballet Nacional de Cuba (Formerly Ballet de Cuba); Theater

Further Readings

Guerra, Ramiro. *Teatralización del folklore y otros ensayos*. Havana: Editorial Letras Cubanas, 1989.

Historia de un Ballet. Havana: Instituto Cubano del Arte e Industria Cinematográficos, 1962. Video.

Pajares Satiesteban, Fidel. *Ramiro Guerra y la danza en Cuba*. Quito: Casa de la Cultura Ecuatoriana, 1993.

Alma Concepción

Montaner, Rita (1900–1958)

Rita Montaner was Cuba's first entertainment superstar, receiving popular and critical acclaim in Cuban radio and television, in Mexican movies, and on the international stage. She performed with popular Latin American actors, the likes of Pedro Infante, and the U.S. crooner and show business legend Al Jolson. Montaner was the first to introduce to the world numerous popular songs associated with Cuba such as "Ay, Mamá Inés," "El Manicero," and "Siboney."

Born in Guanabacoa on May 14, 1900, Montaner demonstrated a talent for music at an early age. She studied piano and voice as a child and considered a career either as a concert pianist or in the opera. In her late teens, however, she opted to sing popular ballads and recorded a few singles that proved popular throughout the island. The recordings brought her some attention in Europe, and in the early 1920s she toured in Spain and France. In Paris, she became the talk of the town and one of the most popular foreign performers to grace the city.

In the early 1930s, Montaner signed a contract with Al Jolson and toured the United States with the North American singer. She introduced "El Manicero" to foreign audiences in New York City. While she sang the song, about a peanuts vendor in Havana, Al Jolson mingled with the audience, handing out bags of peanuts. She returned to Cuba a consecrated star and performed as a singer, an actress, and comedienne on the radio and the stage. One of her most popular appearances was on the radio show *La tremenda corte*, where she portrayed a *mulata* who was often the target of the scheming Trespatines (**Leopoldo Fernández**).

During the 1940s, Montaner became involved in labor issues, advocating better salaries and opportunities for Cuban performers, and promoted the creation of a Cuban cinematic industry (see **Cinema**). Toward the end of the decade, she starred in the film *Angelitos negros*, a Mexican production. This was one of the first films in Latin America to examine the subject of racism. The decades of the 1950s saw Montaner poking fun on the stage at the international star Josephine Baker, who had just visited the island, and starring in the adaptation of Noel Coward's play *Spring Fever*. While performing in this production, Montaner lost her voice. It was discovered later on that she was suffering from cancer.

Montaner died in Havana in 1958. She is still admired in Cuba, where many books have been written about her work. In the United States, a Cuban American drama club bears her name.

Further Reading

Fajardo, Ramón. *Rita Montaner, testimonio de una época*. Havana: Casa de las Américas, 1997.

D.H. Figueredo

Moré, Benny (1919–1963)

Known as "El Bárbaro del Ritmo" (The Tremendous One of Rhythm), Benny Moré gained fame and popularity as a singing sensation in the 1940s and 1950s. Born Bartolomé Moré on August 24, 1919, in Santa Isabel de las Lajas, **Cienfuegos**, Moré spent much of his childhood playing the guitar and singing at parties in his home town.

Moré began his professional career in the late 1930s. In the early 1940s, he sang

Singing sensation Benny Moré.

with Conjunto Matamoros (see **Trío Matamoros**), soon becoming the band's featured singer. The Matamoros toured Mexico, and in 1945 Moré decided to settle there to sing and appear in films. It was in Mexico that he performed with **Dámaso Pérez Prado**. In the 1950s he returned to Cuba, forming his own band. Moré also performed with Mariano Mercerón and **Bebo Valdés**. He soon became one of Cuba's most popular entertainers and signed a recording contract with RCA.

At the height of his career Moré had achieved worldwide recognition. But fame proved to be tragic for Moré, however, who suffered from a heavy drinking problem. He died in Cuba on February 19, 1963.

Further Reading

Martínez Rodríguez, Raúl. *Benny Moré*. Havana: Editorial Letras Cubanas, 1999.

Luis González

NG La Banda

NG La Banda is an innovative and popular orchestra founded in 1988. The initials "NG" stand for Nueva Generación (New Generation) emphasizing the orchestra's ambitious goal of creating the Cuban music of the future. Its founder is José Luis Cortés, born in 1951 and known as El Tosco, a classical flutist who interprets popular music. The orchestra is known for its fusion of the **son**, a classic Cuban slow dance, the **guaracha**, the **mambo**, jazz, and rap. The songs the orchestra favors deal with contemporary political issues on the island while attempting to reproduce the vernacular of the common people. Likewise, the gesture and the dance of the musicians reflect contemporary Cuban dancing style and beat.

The orchestra became a national sensation in the early 1990s, and the subsequent release of more than thirty CDs brought NG international recognition. Some of the titles are *En la calle* (1993), *La bruja* (1995), and *Veneno* (1998). Critics agree that the CD *No se puede tapar el sol* (1988) is the orchestra's best and most representative of its unique style. The band performs regularly at Havana's Marina Hemingway.

Wilfredo Cancio Isla

Nueva Trova (New Song)

Nueva trova (new song) is the term given to acoustic music performed by young Cubans beginning in the mid-1960s. Since the early 1970s it has been the genre most closely associated with the Cuban **Revolution**. Nueva trova retains a devoted audience today, but the peak of its popularity extends from the mid-1970s through the mid-1980s. The early movement has been described as a "culture of contestation"; by growing long hair, wearing torn "hippie" clothing, performing on sidewalks or other nonstandard venues, and through other forms of nonconformity in addition to songwriting, artists challenged social and artistic norms on multiple fronts.

Some music scholars suggest that the most direct predecessor of nueva trova is **vieja trova**. This is the term for the music of individual singer-songwriters from the turn of the century such as Sindo Garay and Alberto Villalón. Both styles are intended to be listened to rather than danced—a fairly atypical characteristic of Caribbean popular music—and are performed by small groups in informal settings. Other influences come from traditional Cuban folklore, genres such as the **son** and *música* **guajira**. However, folk rock from the United States and Britain has been most central to the development of this repertoire, a fact that contributed to the movement's controversial reception in its formative years. Because of the extent of international rock and pop influences in many pieces, some of the best-known songs do not sound overtly "Cuban" but instead strike the listener as cosmopolitan and eclectic.

Lyrics are a central feature of nueva trova music, but the lyrical themes with which it is associated are difficult to generalize. Some artists have been strongly influenced by nationally and internationally recognized poets (**Nicolás Guillén**, César Vallejo, Pablo Neruda). Most typical, however, is the use of fairly simple and direct original verse. Love is a prominent subject, but writers tend to avoid **machismo** and the objectification of women as well as stereotypically romantic imagery. Some pieces are overtly political, contemplating the valor of revolutionary insurgents or paying homage to slain labor activists of past decades. Others are entirely tender and personal, while in yet others one finds a powerful linking of public and private spheres.

The nueva trova movement began as—and some might say remains—a rebellious one that supported some government policies and openly criticized others. During its early development it was known merely as "canción protesta" or "protest song" and provided an alternative perspective on the revolutionary experience for those willing to listen. As a result of their nonconformity, young musicians suffered harassment, blacklisting, and even jailings through about 1971. After that time, however, the government's attitude toward them began to change. Within a few years they had received dramatically increased exposure through government-controlled media, eventually becoming international symbols of a new Cuban culture (see **Communications**). The leading composers-performers of nueva trova are **Pablo Milanés, Silvio Rodríguez**, Noel Nicola, Sara González, and Vicente Feliú, among others.

Further Readings

Díaz Ayala, Cristóbal. *Música cubana del areyto a la nueva trova*. Miami: Ediciones Universal, 1993.

Díaz Pérez, Clara. *Sobre la guitarra, la voz. Una historia de la nueva trova cubana*. Havana: Editorial Letras Cubanas, 1994.

Robin Moore

Orbón (de Soto), Julián (1925–1991)

Composer Julián Orbón was born in Avilés, Spain, on August 7, 1925. While in his teen years, Orbón moved to Cuba with his family, completing his earliest musical studies in Havana under the guidance of **University of Havana**'s composer-in-residence José Ardévol—another Spanish expatriate. A central member of the Cuban musical movement, Orbón, with mentor Ardévol and other young composers (including **Harold Gramatges**, Hilario González, Argeliers León, Serafín Pro, Edgardo Martín, and Gisela Hernández), established Grupo de Renovación Musical (Group for Musical Renewal), a musicians' collective aimed to create a school of composition engendering Cuban-specific elements. Initially supportive of the group's ideologies, a 1946 invitation to study with U.S. composer Aaron Copland at Tanglewood led Orbón to experiment with atonality and leave Grupo de Renovación Musical in 1949 to pursue a more personal and independent musical style. From 1946 to 1960, he was director of the Orbón Conservatory in Havana, a school founded by his father; and from 1960 to 1963 Orbón taught music theory and composition at the National Conservatory in Mexico City. In 1964, he relocated to New York City, where he taught at Columbia University.

Orbón's compositional style encompasses broad musical influences, ranging from Gregorian chants and sixteenth-century Spanish dances to Afro-Cuban rhythms and Copland-inspired sonorities. His best-known composition "*Tres versiones sinfónicas*" won the Juan José Landaeta Prize at the first Latin American Music Festival, held in Caracas in 1954. *Tres versiones sinfónicas* propelled Orbón into the international music scene. Other notable compositions include his *Danzas sinfónicas* (1955), *Himnus ad Galli Cantum* (1956), *Concerto grosso* (1958), and "*Tres cantigas del rey*" (1960). He died in Miami Beach on May 20, 1991.

Further Reading

Orovio, Helio. *Diccionario de la música cubana: biográfico y técnico*. Havana: Editorial Letras Cubanas, 1981.

Nanette de Jong

Pérez Prado, Dámaso (1916–1989)

Pianist, composer, and bandleader Dámaso Pérez Prado was the musician most responsible for the **mambo**'s elaboration and worldwide popularization in the 1950s; his name became eponymous with the genre.

Dámaso Pérez Prado, popularizer of the *mambo*, in 1958. AP/Wide World Photos.

Born in **Matanzas**, Pérez Prado began his musical studies there before moving to Havana, where he performed and arranged for such groups as the Orquesta **Casino de la Playa**. In the late 1940s, Pérez Prado resettled in Mexico, whose active film industry and proximity to the Caribbean made it a Latin American musical mecca, formed his own orchestra in 1950, and spent most of the rest of his career there. Pérez Prado's love affair with the mambo—whose origins lay in the late 1930s innovations of Orestes López and Israel "**Cachao**" López with Antonio Arcaño's **danzón** orchestra—began in 1949; that year's "Qué rico el mambo" introduced this musical form to the world; a wave of popular successes included "Mambo No. 5" and "Caballo negro." (Ironically, the "Mambo King's" biggest hit was a 1955 **cha-cha-chá**, "Cherry Pink and Apple Blossom White.") **Benny Moré** sang on some of these seminal, early 1950s recordings. Mambo's eclipse and rock 'n'

Vladimir Cruz and Jorge Perugorría in scene from *Fresa y chocolate* (1993). Still photograph courtesy of Instituto Cubano del Arte e Industria Cinematográficos, Havana.

roll's ascendancy led to some ill-fated attempts at "updating" his sound in the late 1950s. Even his brilliant re-creation of the mambo in the early 1950s had been criticized by some as too "commercial," or less authentically Cuban than the work of such orchestras as Machito's Afro-Cubans (see **Frank Grillo**). Indeed, Pérez Prado's mambo lacked classic Afro-Cuban poly-rhythmic complexity; but it was original, irresistibly danceable, and absolutely compelling. When the mambo started to fade he created other genres such as *dengue, chunga,* and *suby*, none of which approximated the success of the mambo. His serious explorations included *Mosaico cubano* (1956) and *Suite de las Américas* (1958–1959). His achievement was one of the most important in twentieth-century Cuban music. He had a younger brother, Pantaleón, whom he sued over the latter's use of the Pérez Prado name, and the "Mambo King" title, in France. Dámaso Pérez Prado died in Mexico City of a stroke in 1989.

Further Readings

Gutiérrez Barreto, Francisco. *¡Qué le pasa a Lupita! . . . No sé.* Managua: Hispamer, 1998.

Pérez Firmat, Gustavo. *Life on the Hyphen: The Cuban-American Way.* Austin: University of Texas Press, 1994.

Roberts, John Storm. *The Latin Tinge.* 2nd ed. New York: Oxford University Press, 1999.

Pablo Julián Davis

Perugorría, Jorge (1965–)

His appearance in the film *Fresa y chocolate* (*Strawberry and Chocolate*, 1993) made Jorge Perugorría an international star and one of Cuba's most sought-out actors in the Spanish-speaking **cinema**. He began acting in secondary school, performing in classic drama and contemporary **theater**, but what turned him into a professional actor was his appearance in the play *Perra vida* in 1987. From there, he went on to television and appeared in his first film in 1991, in the short-feature *Bocetos* (Tomás Piard). Two years later, he played the sophisticated and refined gay man in *Strawberry and Chocolate* (see **Gays and Lesbians**). Since then, he has acted in dozens of Cuban and foreign films, including *Guantanamera* (1994), the last feature film made by the great director **Tomás Gutiérrez Alea**. Some of his recent credits are *Doña Bárbara* (Betty Kaplan, 1998), *Volavérunt* (Fernando Bigas Luna, 1998), *Tierra del fuego* (Miguel Littin, 1999), the Cuban production *Lista de espera* (Juan Carlos Tabío, 1999); and *Miel para Oshún* (2001). His major awards are the Premio Coral Best Actor prize in 1993; Los Angeles Critics Award for leading man, 1995; and the Festival de Cine de Viña del Mar's Best Actor award for the film *Amor vertical* (1997).

Jesús Vega

Philharmonic Orchestra of Havana (Orquesta Filarmónica de La Habana)

The Philharmonic Orchestra of Havana was founded on June 8, 1924, with the Spanish conductor Pedro San Juan as its founder-director. Past conductors in residence of the Orchestra have been Pedro San Juan (1924–1932), **Amadeo Roldán** (1932–1938), Massimo Freccia (1939–1943), Erick Kleiber (1943–1947), Juan J. Castro (1947–1948), Artur Rodzinski (1949–1950), Frieder Weissmann (1950–1953), Alberto Bolet (1956–1957), and Igor Markevich (1958).

Among its invited conductors were Joaquín Turina (1929), Leopold Stokowski (1932), Igor Stravinsky (1946), Bruno Walter (1948), Herbert Von Karajan (1949), and Heitor Villalobos (1953). Among the famous soloists invited to perform with the Philharmonic were Jasha Heifetz (1942, 1947, 1949) and Arthur Rubinstein (1942, 1945, 1950–1951).

Works of living composers were premiered in Cuba and performed on a regular basis. Some of these composers were Jean Sibelius in 1928; Manuel de Falla, George Gershwin, Arthur Honegger, and Arnold Schoenberg in 1933; Amadeo Roldán in 1934; Shostakovich in 1938; Igor Stravinsky in 1951; and **Alejandro García Caturla** in 1953.

During the first twelve years of its existence, the Philharmonic Orchestra of Havana had its residence at the Teatro Nacional (National Theatre), now the Gran Teatro de La Habana. After that it moved to the Teatro Auditorium (Auditorium Theater), now Teatro Amadeo Roldán (see **Theaters**).

On November 11, 1960, the orchestra offered its first performance under its new name Orquesta Sinfónica Nacional (National Symphonic Orchestra). Since then, Enrique González Mántici, Manuel Duchesne Cuzán, and **Leo Brouwer** have been its musical directors.

Further Reading

Sánchez Cabrera, Maruja. *Orquesta Filarmónica de La Habana, memoria 1924–1959*. Havana: Editorial Orbe, 1979.

Yavet Boyadjiev Collado

Piñeiro, Ignacio (1888–1969)

Cuban performer and composer Ignacio Piñeiro was an innovator of the **son**; he incorporated into the genre longer verses including *décimas*. He also combined the son with the **bolero, guajira**, and **rumba**, thus expanding the repertoire of the traditional sextet. An Afro-Cuban working-class artist with no formal training in music, he spent most of his life toiling as a manual laborer—as a stevedore, brick layer, cigar maker—in addition to performing music. Best known today as a composer of Cuban son, Piñeiro was also very involved with secular drumming groups and Afro-Cuban religious music (see **Afro-Cubans**). Long before his involvement with the commercial dance bands, he was recognized in his **Matanzas** barrio of Pueblo Nuevo as a virtuoso drummer and singer, joining the *clave y guaguancó* ensemble Timbre de Oro as early as 1906, playing in carnival bands, and forming the rumba group Los Roncos. He let his involvement with **Santería** and **Abakuá** societies influence the lyrics of later compositions such as "No jueges con los santos" (Don't Play with the Saints), "Canto Lucumí" (Yoruba Chant), and "Iyamba bero." In 1926 singer **María Teresa Vera** contracted Piñeiro to play in the son band Sexteto Occidente. After his return to Cuba in 1927 he formed a similar ensemble under his own direction, the Sexteto Nacional. Together with the Sexteto Habanero under the direction of Guillermo Castillo, Piñeiro's ensemble came to be one of the most popular and influential in the country. His most influential compositions include "Échale salsita" (Put a Little Sauce on It), "Suavecito" (Nice and Easy), and "Esas no son cubanas" (Those Aren't Cuban Women).

Further Reading

Orovio, Helio. *Diccionario de la música cubana: biográfico y técnico* 2nd. ed. Havana: Editorial Letras Cubanas, 1992, 355–356.

Robin Moore

Pozo, Luciano "Chano" (1915–1948)

Luciano "Chano" Pozo was a renowned percussionist, dancer and composer who played a key role in the creation of Latin Jazz. Pozo was born in Havana on January 7, 1915. Among his early hits were the *guarachas-rumbas* "Blen-blen-blen," "Pin-pon-pan," and "Manteca." He moved to New York in 1946 and the following year he performed at Carnegie Hall with Dizzy Gillespie. During his career he also performed with Charlie Parker, **Miguelito Valdés**, Chico O'Farrill, and other famed musicians. With Gillespie he composed the hit song "Manteca." Pozo was killed in a Harlem bar a month short of his thirty-fourth birthday. *See also* Afro-Cuban Jazz

Further Reading

Varela, Jesse. "Chano Pozo: The Original Conga King" *Latin Beat Magazine*, 11 (November, 2001): 30.

Luis González

Pumarejo y Sunc, Gaspar (1913–1969)

Gaspar Pumarejo was a well-known entertainment impresario and communications mogul. Born in Santander, in northern Spain, on November 8, 1913, he settled in Cuba in the 1930s, where he found employment as a radio announcer. Having established himself as a leading voice in Cuban radio, he became head of the programming department at the CMQ radio network, where he created the concept of "Radio Reloj," an innovative format in which live news and commercials were broadcast every minute with the background sound of a ticking clock. In 1941 he created the popular program *La tremenda corte*, starring **Leopoldo Fernández "Trespatines."** In October 1950, Pumarejo founded Cuba's first TV station (Radio Unión, Channel 4), the second station of its type in the world; a few years later he brought color television to the island. Before and after his exile to Puerto Rico in 1959, Pumarejo used his influence to launch the careers of several actors, singers, and bands. In Puerto Rico Pumarejo left a profound imprint, as he helped propel the careers of many artists whom he introduced in Peru to a broader Latin American audience. While in Peru, he established broad commercial networks that continue to play a major role in the world of entertainment. He returned to Puerto Rico, where he hosted the variety show *Viernes de Gala*; he died in 1969. *See also* Puerto Rico, Cubans in

Further Reading
Santiago, Javier. *Nueva ola portorricensis.* San Juan: Publicaciones del Patio, 1994.

Edgardo Díaz Díaz

Punto Cubano

The *punto cubano*, also known as the *punto guajiro*, is the musical genre distinctive to the Cuban peasants and the oldest of Cuba's musical genres. The punto cubano uses as lyrics a classical strophic form of Spanish origin called *décima espinela*. Guitars, *bandurria*, or *laúd* provide the musical accompaniment. *Claves, güiro, tres*, and other instruments can also be used. The décima is expressed through a melodic line known as the *tonada*. There are two types of punto: the *punto fijo* (fixed) and the *punto libre* (free). In the punto fijo, text and tonada must follow the metric pattern of the musical accompaniment, usually in 6/8 and 3/4. In this type of punto the décimas are generally sung from memory in *tempo giusto*. In the punto libre, the text is completely improvised and is expressed through a tonada *a piacere*. The instrumental accompaniment follows the improvisation and can be interrupted at any time by the *repentista* (also called *poeta*), the person who improvises and sings his own décimas. *See also* Guajiros

Further Reading
Linares, María Teresa. *El punto cubano.* Santiago de Cuba: Editorial Oriente, 1999.

Yavet Boyadjiev Collado

Rico, Alicia (1898–1967)

One of Cuba's best-known actresses, Alicia Rico was born on October 7, 1898, in **Pinar del Río Province**. Her family soon moved to Havana. At age eleven she debuted at the Martí Theater (see **Theater** and **Theaters**).

In 1921 Rico went to Mexico and in 1929 visited New York City, performing at the Apollo Theater, among other venues. In 1931 she returned to Cuba to perform popular theatrical pieces such as *Cecilia Valdés* and *María La O*. Rico performed not only on stage but also on radio and television and in films. In 1966, at the end of a performance at the Martí Theater, before a full house, Rico collapsed and was pronounced dead a short time later at a nearby hospital.

Further Reading
Rosell, Rosendo. "Mundo de estrellas." *Diaro Las Américas*, July 13, 1986, 4B.

Luis González

Roblán, Armando (1931–   )

Born as Franciso Armando Rodríguez on February 4, 1931, in Bejucal, **Havana Province**, Armando Roblán is one of Cuba's best-known comedic actors. He is renowned for his satirical impersonation of **Fidel Castro**. In 1950 he was discovered on an amateur TV show. Throughout his career he has written, acted, and produced a variety of television shows in Cuba, Puerto Rico, Venezuela, Panama, and the United States. In addition to his imitation of Castro, Roblán has also performed as the **Caballero de París**, the legendary character of Havana.

Roblán is currently part of the cast of *Sábado gigante,* one of the most popular shows in Latin America and among U.S. Hispanics. He is also part of the ensemble cast of Univisión's *Los Metiches,* a popular satire that pokes fun at world leaders and celebrities.

Known as "Castro's double" for his impeccable impression, Roblán performs his one-man stage show in **Little Havana**. Roblán's recent parodies have included "En el 2000 se tiene que ir" (In 2000 he must leave), "En el 2001 no queda uno" (In 2001 not one is left), and "Un tal Iván" (A so-called Ivan), which features a sketch involving the Taliban.

Comedian Armando Roblán mocking Fidel Castro. Photograph courtesy of Alina Productions.

Roblán is also a painter and sculptor. He was trained at the **San Alejandro Academy of Fine Arts** in Havana. His artwork and caricatures have been featured at the annual Cuba Nostalgia exhibits in Miami.

Further Reading

Clary, Mike. "A City that is Still Consumed by Castro." *Los Angeles Times*, January 1, 1997.

Luis González

Rodríguez, Albita (1962–   )

Singer, guitarist, and composer Albita Rodríguez was born in Havana, where she was considered the "queen of the punto guajiro" (see **Punto Cubano**). She revitalized the genre with new interpretations, the use of jazz and modern sounds, which she performed with melodious phrasing and improvisations.

Rodríguez became a professional musician at the age of seventeen when she gained popularity through the television show *Palmas y cañas*. In 1986, she founded her own group, performing only Cuban country music, including a modernized version of **guajira**, mixing elements of rock and jazz. In 1988 she recorded the CD *Habrá música guajira*, which made her an international star. It sold more copies on the international market than any other Cuban record up to that time.

With the sanction of the Cuban government, Albita and her band moved to Colombia in 1991, where they signed a recording contract. There they performed for two and a half years. In 1993, while recording in Mexico, Albita and her band defected by crossing the Río Grande into El Paso, Texas (see **Dissent and Defections [1959–   ]**). In the United States she immediately became a top Latina performer. Her highly personal style made her a regular feature in magazines. In 1993, her composition "Dicen que . . . " earned her a Grammy award. In 1995, she wrote the music score for the Hollywood film *The Specialist*. Her albums include *Son, Cuba de dos épocas*, and *Si se de la siembra*.

She continues to perform throughout the world and lives in Miami.

Further Reading

Díaz Ayala, Cristóbal. *Música cubana del areyto a la nueva trova*. Miami: Ediciones Universal, 1993.

Wilfredo Cancio Isla

Rodríguez, Arsenio (1911–1970)

Cuban composer and bandleader Arsenio Rodríguez was born in Güira de Macurije, **Matanzas Province**, on August 30, 1911. One of the most prolific figures in the history of Cuban music, Rodríguez was a distinguished composer (writing nearly 200 songs), *tresero* (*tres* is a Cuban six-string guitar), percussionist, and bandleader. Regarded as the father of the *conjunto* (a type of ensemble), Rodríguez transformed

Latin music, with his compositions becoming standards in Cuban and New York **salsa** repertoires.

The third-generation descendant of Congolese slaves, Rodríguez was blinded by a horse's kick at age eight. During adult years, Rodríguez's blindness earned him the title El Ciego Maravilloso (The Marvelous Blind Man). Composing already during his teens, he formed El Sexteto Boston in the early 1930s, joining trumpeter José Interain's Septeto Bellamar and **Orquesta Casino de la Playa** in 1937. The first recordings of Rodríguez's compositions were made in 1937 with **Miguelito Valdés**, accompanied by the Orquesta Casino de la Playa, singing "Bruca Manigua," "Ven acá Tomás," and "Fumandó." In 1940 Rodríguez again established his own ensemble, expanding the sextet format to include conga drums a (which had previously been considered taboo because of their African origin), a second (and later a third) trumpet, more percussion, and piano, revolutionizing the **son** while giving birth to the conjunto. Rodríguez also changed the structure of the son form, introducing the *son montuno*, which featured improvised vocals (and later instrumental) over a repeated chorus. Rodríguez, along with bandleaders Antonio Arcaño and **Dámaso Pérez Prado**, was credited with developing the **mambo** rhythm and with laying the roots of **salsa** (see **Arcaño y Sus Maravillas**). His impressive list of band members included vocalists Miguelito Cun, Marcelino Guerra, and Ren Scull; trumpeters Chocolate Armenteros and Félix Chappotín (brother of **Chano Pozo**); and pianist Lilí Martínez.

An unsuccessful attempt to restore his sight brought Rodríguez to New York in 1947, where he recorded with Chano Pozo, Miguelito Valdés, and members of Machito's orchestra (see **Grillo, Frank ["Machito"]**). His return to Cuba was brief. Turning over the band to Chappotín, Rodríguez permanently relocated to New York City in 1953, where his musical innovations continued. Rodríguez again expanded the conjunto by adding flute and timbales; he initiated *swing son*, which utilized horn arrangements favored by U.S. swing bands of that period; and he fused jazz, son, and Afro-Cuban religious elements into a music style he termed *quindembo* (a Congolese word meaning "mixture of things").

Rodríguez's popularity in New York, though strong, never matched what it had been in Cuba, and he died in the city in near obscurity on December 31, 1970. *See also* Afro-Cubans

Further Reading

Díaz Ayala, Cristóbal. *Música cubana del areyto a la nueva trova.* Miami: Ediciones Universal, 1993.

Nanette de Jong

Rodríguez, Silvio (1946–   )

Singer-songwriter Silvio Rodríguez was a central figure in the **Nueva Trova (New Song)** movement of the 1960s and 1970s and continues to be one of Cuba's most widely recognized performers.

Born at San Antonio de los Baños, Rodríguez showed musical inclinations early, winning a radio prize at age four and beginning conservatory studies at eight, but graphic art engaged him throughout his adolescence. His public musical debut came only in 1967, in the format for which he would become best known: that of *cantautor* (singer-songwriter), accompanying himself with simplicity on the guitar. The same year, a protest-song festival took place in Havana, and 1972 saw the foundation of Nueva Trova, a school whose usual characterization as leftist protest song is incomplete: in Rodríguez's work, social conscience and a political temperament supportive of Cuba's **Revolution** and

Silvio Rodríguez is the leading singer-song writer of Cuba's Nueva Trova. Photograph of a 1997 concert in Buenos Aires, Argentina. AP/Wide World Photos. Photograph by Daniel Muzio.

of resistance to the Chilean and other contemporary military dictatorships were wedded to serious lyrical exploration and to an eclectic, modern musical identity drawing on folk and popular forms of Cuba, Latin America, and Spain and on such rock influences as John Lennon, Paul McCartney, and Bob Dylan. Rodríguez's clear, delicate, Spanish-influenced tenor voice became one of the most recognizable in all of Spanish-language song in the last quarter of the twentieth century; his compositions, such as "Rabo de nube" and "Unicornio," were recorded widely. Past the era of Nueva Trova, Rodríguez continued to search and innovate musically. A signal achievement was the critically acclaimed trilogy *Silvio, Rodríguez*, and *Domínguez* (1992–1996), exploring his family heritage. Rodríguez served as a deputy in the **National Assembly of People's Power** beginning in 1993. *See also* Milanés, Pablo

Further Readings

Díaz, Clara. *Silvio Rodríguez*. Havana: Editorial Letras Cubanas, 1993.
Zapata, Sandra. *Silvio para letra y orquesta*. Caracas: Alfadil Ediciones, 1996.

Pablo Julián Davis

Roig, Gonzalo (1890–1970)

Gonzalo Roig was one of Cuba's greatest musical talents of all times. Raised by his grandmother, Roig started working at an early age while still managing to study music. When he was seventeen years old, he played the piano at a movie house and wrote his first song. In 1911, he composed "Quiéreme mucho," his most famous work. He was conductor of the orchestra at the legendary Alhambra Theater and in 1922 was elected director of the Sociedad de Conciertos de La Habana, successfully creating the **Philharmonic Orchestra of Havana** (see **Theaters**). In 1927, he was appointed director of the Escuela de Música de La Habana and of the Municipal Band. In 1931 he organized a repertory company in the Martí theater where many **zarzuelas** were staged, including his own *Cecilia Valdés*, Cuba's most important operetta. In 1943, he conducted a concert of Cuban music at Carnegie Hall. Over the years, he wrote dozens of zarzuelas and songs while also directing radio programs, television shows, and stage productions.

Further Readings

Cañizares, Dulcila. *Gonzalo Roig*. Havana: Editorial Letras Cubanas, 1976.
Roig, Gonzalo. "La música." In *Historia de la nación cubana*. By Ramiro Guerra. Havana: Editorial Historia de la Nación Cubana, S.A. 1952. 7:433–484.

Cristóbal Díaz Ayala and Marisa Méndez

Roldán, Amadeo (1900–1939)

Along with **Alejandro García Caturla**, Amadeo Roldán was the creator of Cuba's modern symphonic art. His *Obertura sobre temas cubanos* (1925) earned him recognition as Cuba's first symphonist. Born in Paris, it was his mother, a pianist, who introduced him to music. At the age of five, he attended the Conservatorio de Madrid, and at the age of sixteen, he received the Sarasate violinist award. He played with the Orquesta Filarmónica de Madrid, and then in 1919, he went to Havana where he worked as a music professor. Two years later, he was a violinist for the Sociedad de Música chamber orchestra. In 1922, he moved on to the Orquesta Sinfónica de La Habana, which was under the direction of **Gonzalo Roig**. At the **Philharmonic Orchestra of Havana** he assumed the post of concert violinist in 1924; there conductor Pedro San Juan taught him technical formation and premiered his *Obertura*. It was regarded as the most important musical event of the period. In 1932, Roldán was appointed director of the Philharmonic Orchestra, a position he kept until his premature death due to illness before reaching the age of forty.

Roldán wrote symphonic works for diverse instruments; he also composed an Afro-Cuban ballet. In his works, Roldán recognized the African and Spanish influences in Cuban culture.

Professional rumba stage dancers, Havana circa early 1930s. Louis A. Pérez, Jr. Collection.

Further Readings

Carpentier, Alejo. *La música en Cuba*. Mexico City: Fondo de Cultura Económica, 1993.

Orovio, Helio *Diccionario de la música cubana: biográfico y técnico*. Havana: Editorial Letras Cubanas, 1981.

Jesús Vega

Rumba Complex

The *rumba* has its origins in Cuban **slavery** and colonial society, yet its impact reaches twenty-first-century global commercialized music markets. The word rumba itself is used not only for the traditional music-dance performance in the Cuban context; it is also used for other tropical musical forms and also as a term to describe social gatherings or celebrations in Cuba and other Caribbean societies. As a music-dance complex with strong African influence, the rumba emerged in mid-nineteenth century Cuba in the western provinces of **La Habana** and **Matanzas**. Ethnic groups from West Central Africa contributed to its development, and two particular dances have been identified as influential in the rumba: the *yuka* and the *makuta*. It developed as an urban phenomenon, although it was also practiced in rural areas near the **sugar plantations**. Its main performers in colonial times were lower-class free blacks in the city of Havana; in addition, slaves sometimes performed it in their spare time (often under surveillance). As most cultural expressions from the working classes, rumba was a secular manifestation of explicit and implicit social commentary in its dancing and songs. That characteristic, along with its association with people of African heritage and other Afro-Cuban cultural practices, prompted its prohibition by colonial and neocolonial authorities at different stages.

Rumba's traditional performance in Cuba combines song, music, and dance. A lead singer and chorus perform in a call-and-response style. The singer usually begins with a *diana*, a starting line announcing the beginning of the rumba, to which the chorus responds with different verses. Wooden sticks, or *claves*, mark the rhythm at the beginning and throughout the performance. Drumming is central to the rumba whether it is on wooden boxes, on improvised instruments, or on conga drums such as the *tumbador* (low pitch) and the *quinto* (high pitch). The best-known rumba styles are the *yambú*, the *guagancó*, and the *columbia*. The dance performance of the yambú and the guagancó includes the participation of male and female dancers who display their grace and sensuality. In the guaguancó the music is faster and dance can be more expressive than in the yambú. The couple interacts in a game of sexual acceptance and rejection and constant flirtation that reaches a climax with the *vacunao*, a movement of the male pelvis that mimics the sexual act. The female uses her dance skills to accept or reject the vacunao. Dance performance in the columbia involves the interaction between the male dancer and the drums. The dancer enters in a dialogue with the quinto where every movement is designed to show off his skills and abilities, often in competition with other male dancers. Improvisation, interaction, and dialogue are central to the rumba, whether it is in the dance itself or between singers and dancers or drummers and singers. The traditional social setting of the rumba has been in yards and *solares* (urban tenements), as well as on street corners or at specific social events and gatherings. Through the more recent commercialization and institutionalization of rumba, more formal, organized, and regular presentations of this music-dance are taking place in Cuba as well as internationally.

Further Readings

Acosta, Leonardo. "The Rumba, the Guaguancó, and the Tío Tom." In *Essays on Cuban Music: North American and Cuban Perspectives*, ed. Peter Manuel. Lanham, MD: University Press of America, 1991. 51–73.

Crook, Larry. "The Form and Formation of the Rumba in Cuba." In *Salsiology: Afro-Cuban Music and the Evolution of Salsa in New York City*, ed. Vernon W. Boggs. Westport, CT: Greenwood Press, 1992. 31–42.

Daniel, Yvonne. *Rumba: Dance and Social Change in Contemporary Cuba*. Bloomington: Indiana University Press, 1995.

Moore, Robin D. *Nationalizing Blackness*: Afrocubanismo *and Artistic Revolution in Havana, 1920–1940*. Pittsburgh: University of Pittsburgh Press, 1997.

Jorge L. Giovannetti

Salas, Esteban (1725–1803)

Esteban Salas is among the most important composers in the history of colonial Latin America. He was born in Havana on December 25, 1725. When he was fifteen years old, he enrolled at the Seminario San Carlos in Havana, majoring in philosophy and law, preparing to become a priest. He sang at la Parroquia Mayor while studying music. He lived in Havana until 1764 when he relocated to **Santiago de Cuba** where he reorganized the music collection in the Cathedral. From this period emerged his musical output, consisting of masses, hymns, motets, Christmas carols, and other musical pieces; this body of work was discovered in the twentieth century by novelist and musicologist **Alejo Carpentier**.

All of Salas's works belonged to the baroque movement and were linked with the Neapolitan school, the result of Salas's friendship with choir singer and mariner Cayetano Pagueras who brought to Salas musical works published in Italy.

Further Readings

Carpentier, Alejo. *La música en Cuba*. Mexico City: Fondo de Cultura Económica, 1993.

Orovio, Helio. *Diccionario de la música cubana: biográfico y técnico*. Havana: Editorial Letras Cubanas, 1981.

Jesús Vega

Salsa

Salsa is a marketing term that developed in 1960s New York City to denote a genre of dance music fusing musical elements of the Cuban **son** with influences from Puerto Rico and elsewhere. It is associated with a number of distinct musical characteristics. The incorporation of *bomba* and *plena* rhythms in many pieces, the use of *güiro* patterns derived from Puerto Rican *seis*, and the foregrounding of instruments such as the Puerto Rican *cuatro* represent only a few examples. These significant factors notwithstanding, the essence of the musical style is derived from Cuban *conjuntos de son* of the 1940s and 1950s. Features derived from these bands include the prominence of Cuban percussion instruments (bongo and conga drums, *timbales*), characteristic rhythms (the basic *tumbao* pattern on the conga; *cáscara* rhythms derived ultimately from Cuban **rumba**; the *clave* rhythm itself), anticipated bass figures, characteristic piano *montunos*, and others.

Salsa in New York became popular during a moment of unprecedented grassroots activism on a national scale. In the context of anti–Viet Nam protests, Black Power, the Young Lords movement, and a general politicization of minorities, salsa emerged as a symbol of a new pan-Latino identity in the United States. Bombarded with mainstream U.S. commercial culture and living in an environment frequently inhospitable to their traditional music, Latinos embraced salsa as an assertion of self, a form of resistance. This is the context that led to the emergence of biting social commentary in the compositions of Tite Curet, Willie Colón, Rubén Blades, Eddie Palmieri, and others in the 1970s and 1980s. Please see color insert in Volume I for photograph.

Further Readings

Aparicio, Frances. *Listening to Salsa: Gender, Latin Popular Music, and Puerto Rican Cultures*. Middletown, CT: Wesleyan University, Press, 1998.

Boggs, Vernon W., ed. *Salsiology: Afro-Cuban Music and the Evolution of Salsa in New York City*. Westport, CT: Greenwood Press, 1997.

Díaz Ayala, Cristóbal. *The Roots of Salsa: A History of Cuban Music*. Westport, CT: Greenwood Press, 1996.

Robin Moore

Sánchez de Fuentes, Eduardo (1874–1944)

Composer, musicologist, and lawyer Eduardo Sánchez de Fuentes represents one of the best-known classical music personalities of early-twentieth-century Cuba. He was born in Havana on April 3, 1874. He began his musical training at age eleven in the Conservatorio Hubert de Blanck and in subsequent years studied with **Ignacio Cervantes** and **Carlos Anckermann**. Sánchez de Fuentes was a founding member of the Academia Nacional de Artes y Letras and the Sociedad de Estudios Folklóricos Cubanos. In 1922 he organized the first Festivals of Cuban Song in **Cienfuegos** and Havana. The compositions of Sánchez de Fuentes, which have never been well cataloged, include the **habanera** "Tú" (1892), the operas *Yumurí* (1898) and *Dorea* (1918), and a number of *canciones cubanas* including "Corazón," "Vivir sin tus caricias," and "Mírame así."

Sánchez de Fuentes was a gifted composer but fundamentally biased as a music critic. For many years he refused to consider any Afro-Cuban musical genre as a valid form of national expression. In published essays through the 1930s, the author insisted that indigenous Siboney and Arawak Indians had contributed to the development of Cuban music rather than African slaves and their descendants (see **Afro-Cubans**; **Indigenous Inhabitants**).

Further Readings

Lapique Becali, Zoila. *Figura musical de Eduardo Sánchez de Fuentes*. Havana: Biblioteca Nacional José Martí, 1974.

Sánchez de Fuentes, Eduardo. *Folklorismo: artículos, notas y críticas musicales*. Havana: Molina y Cía., 1928.

Robin Moore

Sandoval, Arturo (1949–)

A protégé of legendary jazz musician Dizzy Gillespie and a founding member of the Grammy Award–winning **Grupo Irakere**, Arturo Sandoval was born in Artemisa, **Havana Province** on November 6, 1949. He began studying the trumpet at age twelve. Early in his career, prior to forming Irakere, he performed with the Cuban Orchestra of Modern Music.

In 1981 Sandoval left Irakere to form his own band, which was well received by audiences and critics alike throughout Europe and Latin America. He was voted Cuba's Best Instrumentalist from 1982 to 1984.

Sandoval, his wife, and their teenage son were granted political asylum in the United States in 1990. Since leaving Cuba, Sandoval has increased his classical performances. He has performed with the National Symphony, the Los Angeles Philharmonic, and the Pittsburgh Symphony. In 1992, while performing with the Dizzy Gillespie United Nations Orchestra, the group earned a Grammy Award for their album *Live at Royal Festival Hall*.

In addition to performing, Sandoval is also a professor at Florida International University. He has lectured internationally and has performed at the Conservatoire de Paris and the Tchaikovsky Conservatory. There are three scholarships named for Arturo Sandoval: The Arturo Sandoval's

Dizzy Gillespie Trumpet Scholar Award at the University of Idaho, the Sandoval Trumpet Scholarship at the Central Oklahoma University, and the Sandoval Trumpet Scholarship at Florida International University.

In 2000, Home Box Office produced an original film based on Sandoval's life (*For the Love of Country*), with **Andy García** playing Sandoval.

Further Reading

Mandel, Howard. "Comes Out Swinging" *Downbeat Magazine*, October, 1996.

Luis González

Saquito, Ñico (Antonio Fernández) (1902–1982)

Antonio Fernández, better known as Ñico Saquito, is regarded as Cuba's best **guaracha** composer ever. Through his compositions, he also chronicled Cuban daily life and his compatriots' idiosyncrasies. Born on January 17, 1902, he moved between his hometown of **Santiago de Cuba** and Havana, founding several musical groups over the years. Following the great success of his hit "Cuidadito Compay Gallo," he formed the Conjunto Compay Gallo with musicians Maximiliano Sánchez and Florencio Santana "Pícolo." In 1945 he founded his most famous ensemble, the **Los Guaracheros de Oriente**, along with Pícolo and master guitarist Gerardo Macías. Los Guaracheros later included other gifted performers and achieved international acclaim. Among Ñico's other great compositions are "El jaleo," "Adiós Compay Gato," and "Que humanidad." When Los Guaracheros disbanded in Venezuela in 1960, Ñico returned to Cuba. He died in 1982.

Further Readings

Martínez Rodríguez, Raúl. "Un cronista de su tiempo: Ñico Saquito." *Revista Salsa Cubana*, no. 6 (1998):30.

Rodríguez, Lil. *Bailando en casa del trompo*. Caracas: Euroamericana de Ediciones, 1997.

Cristóbal Díaz Ayala and Marisa Méndez

Saralegui, Cristina (1948–   )

Cristina Saralegui became a household name as the host and producer of the number-one talk show on Spanish-language television, *El show de Cristina* (The Cristina Show 1989–2001). She is seen daily by more than 100 million viewers worldwide. She is a household name and a leading role model for Hispanic women in the United States and around the world.

Saralegui was born in Havana on January 29, 1948. She left for Miami as an exile in 1960, when she was eleven years old. When she was of college age, Saralegui attended the University of Miami, majoring in mass communications and creative writing. She was preparing to follow in the footsteps of her grandfather, Francisco Saralegui, who was a prominent magazine publisher. While in college, Saralegui took an internship with *Vanidades*, the leading women's magazine in Latin America.

In 1979 Saralegui was named editor in chief of *Cosmopolitan en Español* (the Spanish-language edition of *Cosmopolitan*). In 1989 came the debut of her television talk show, *El show de Cristina*, on Univisión. Three years later, CBS aired *The Cristina Show* in English for a thirteen-week run. In 1998 Warner Books published her autobiography, *My Life as a Blonde*, in English and Spanish-language editions simultaneously.

In addition to her ongoing work on television on *El show de Cristina* and numerous other appearances, Saralegui hosts a daily radio show, *Cristina Opina* (Cristina Says), and is copublisher of *Cristina La Revista* (Cristina the Magazine).

Saralegui's work as a television personality and her charitable endeavors have brought her many honors and distinctions.

Talk show host and publisher Cristina Saralegui receiving Gracie Allen Tribute Award in 2001. AP/Wide World Photos. Photograph by Matt Moyer.

Among them are a Star on the Hollywood Walk of Fame, a Nosotros Golden Eagle Award for outstanding achievement, and several awards from the American Federation for **AIDS** Research for whom she has raised a considerable amount of money and awareness. *See also* U.S. Entertainment Industry, Cubans in the

Further Reading
Saralegui, Cristina. *My Life as a Blonde*. New York: Warner Books, 1998.

Luis González

Saumell Robredo, Manuel (1817–1870)

Pianist and composer Manuel Saumell Robredo is one of the pillars of Cuba's musical identity. He was born in Havana on August 14, 1817. A piano student of Juan Federico Edelman, Saumell Robredo participated in numerous musical activities, from playing the organ to teaching music and organizing music symposiums. If his many activities did not allow time to compose, he certainly achieved recognition as the father of the *contradanza*, not because he was the creator of the genre but because he perfected it. His melodic creations and rhythms were extraordinary. Saumell Robredo's genius, however, went beyond the contradanza. His compositions included the genres the **habanera**, the **danzón**, the *clave*, the **criolla**, and the **guajira**, along with certain modification to the contemporary song. Because of him, according to novelist and musicologist **Alejo Carpentier**, disperse musical elements that made up a Cuban sound came together to create a national musical identity. Among his best known compositions are "La amistad," "La celestina," "Los ojos de Pepa," "La Nené," and "La Luisiana."

Further Readings

Carpentier, Alejo. *La música en Cuba*. Mexico City: Fondo de Cultura Económica, 1983.

Orovio, Helio. *Diccionario de la música cubana*: *biográfico y técnico*. Havana: Editorial Letras Cubanas, 1981.

Jesús Vega

Secada, Jon (1962–   )

Winner of two Grammy awards, Jon Secada (born Juan Secada) is a leading singer and songwriter in Latin music. Secada was born on October 4, 1962, in Havana, where he lived until 1971, when he left with his family for the United States. The Secada family opened a coffee shop in Miami Beach. Growing up, Secada admired the songs by Stevie Wonder, Billy Joel, and Elton John, among others. Secada went to school in Florida and earned both a bachelor's and a master's degree in jazz vocal performance from the University of Miami.

Secada remained in Miami, taking a teaching position at Miami Community College while pursuing a career as a performer. **Gloria Estefan**'s husband Emilio heard one of Secada's demo tapes and proceeded to hire him to write for Gloria and to sing backup for her. Secada cowrote a number of Estefan's greatest hits, including "Coming Out of the Dark."

Secada has recorded his own albums, selling more than 20 million copies. His first album, titled *Jon Secada*, was certified triple platinum in the United States. His single from that album, "Otro día más sin verte" (titled "Just Another Day" in English), went gold. The album was number one on Billboard's charts and earned Secada a Grammy for Best Latin Pop Album in 1992. In 1994 Secada released his second album, *Heart Soul and a Voice* (which went platinum), and performed with Frank Sinatra on the *Duets II* album. His 1995 album *Amor* (Love) earned him his second Grammy (Best Latin Performance). Secada has written hit songs for Ricky Martin and Jennifer López. In 2000, Secada released *Better Part of Me*, which contained elements of pop, rock, and Latin music.

Further Reading

Morales, María. "Un nuevo amanecer." *People en Español*, November 2002, 63.

Luis González

Simons, Moisés (1888–1945)

Moisés Simons was a musical composer who gained worldwide fame for his compositions, most notably "El manicero." Born Moisés Simón in Havana in 1888, he began to take music lessons from his father at age five. By ten he was the organist at a Havana church, and five years later, he directed his own company of children musicians. He later joined a Spanish **zarzuela** company with which he composed his first operetta: *Deuda de amor*.

By the 1920s, Simons had already established himself as a renowned director-composer. Among the works he created during the decade were *Revista de 1914* and *El pescador de corales*. His musical reviews contained a variety of Cuban genres from Afro-Cuban pieces like "Lamento negroide" and "Vacúnala" to highly lyrical compositions like "Serenata cubana." Two of his most popular songs of the period were "Qué es el danzón" and "Palmira," an ode to the Cuban *mulata*. Several of these songs were recorded by famed entertainer **Rita Montaner** in 1927 and 1928.

In 1928 Simons composed his spectacular hit, the *pregón*-**son** "El manicero." There is, however, disagreement about the authorship of its lyrics, with some crediting Gonzalo G. de Mello with them. The noted anthropologist **Fernando Ortiz** traced them to an anonymous nineteenth-century street vendor's call. "El manicero" became an overnight world sensation. Montaner recorded it in 1928, and it was later recorded by **Orquesta Azpiazu**. This orchestra's live performances in New York helped establish the song as a megahit in the United Sates, where it became part of the score for the film *Cuban Love Song*. Montaner helped popularize the song throughout Latin America and Europe. The Italian tenor Tito Schipa made it part of his repertoire. Another of Simons's great hits was "Marta," a lyrical composition that has been routinely interpreted by some of the world's best tenors and baritones.

Simons spent much of the 1930s in Europe, particularly France and Spain. There he composed musical reviews like *Toi c'est moi* and *El canto del trópico;* among the individual pieces of the period were "Cubanakán," "Yamba-O," "Colibrí," and "Danza del fuego." In Spain he composed film scores and other works. He died in Spain on June 28, 1945.

Further Reading
Díaz Ayala, Cristóbal. "Moisés Simons." *Revista la Canción Popular*, no. 4 (1989): 55.

Cristobál Díaz Ayala and Marisa Méndez

Solás, Humberto (1941–   )

The film *Lucía* (1968) earned Humberto Solás international recognition as a director, and together with **Tomás Gutiérrez**

Alea he is recognized as Cuba's best filmmaker.

Born in Havana in 1941, Solás made his first film when he was eighteen years old. He joined the Cuban Film Institute (Instituto Cubano del Arte e Industria Cinematográficas, ICAIC) in 1960, and after studying cinematography at Centro Sperimentale de Cinematografia de Roma, in 1966 he directed the short film *Manuela*, which attracted critical attention, not only for his craft but also because it was filmed in Cuba to explore feminist themes. His movie *Cecilia* (1980), sparked a controversy as the most expensive film ever made in Cuba. His production of *El siglo de las Luces* (1991) was conceived as a miniseries for French television and then adapted for the screen. His most recent endeavor is *Miel para Oshún* (2001).

Solás has received numerous awards, including the 1998 best film award from Festival Internacional de Cine de Cartagena—for the film *Cantata de Chile* (1975)—and best script from Premio Coral for the film *Horcón. See also* Cinema; Film Posters

Further Reading
Chanan, Michael. *The Cuban Image: Cinema and Cultural Politics in Cuba*. London: British Film Institute, 1985.

Jesús Vega

Son

The *son* arose early in the twentieth century and became the island's central, and most fully Afro-Cuban, musical genre (see **Afro-Cubans**).

Originating in Oriente, the son reached Havana before World War I and became a popular urban genre by the teens. The sextets Habanero, Occidente, Boloña, and Nacional and the **Trío Matamoros** consolidated son in the 1920s, the genre's classical era. One of the most famous early compositions in the genre was **Moisés Simons**'s *son-pregón* "El manicero." Legendary *tres* player **Arsenio Rodríguez** revolutionized the genre in the 1940s and beyond by Africanizing the rhythmic base and infusing arrangements with fiery dynamism, particularly in the horns. The genre's centrality to Cuban music might well be compared to that of blues in U.S. musical culture; an almost infinite array of variants has proliferated, including *son-guaguancó, son montuno*, **guajira** *son*, and *son-afro*; the **rumba** is often understood to be another variety. Indeed, son forms the core of **salsa**, the originally New York City–based, Cuban-derived idiom. Though performed in a variety of orchestral configurations, son oftentimes uses congas and other Afro-Cuban percussion and displays consistent structural elements, including pronounced polyrhythm; the fundamental rhythmic pulse of clave (3-2, i.e., three marked beats in one measure, two in the next; or reverse, 2-3, *clave* pattern); and *bajo anticipado*, the syncopated bass pattern stressing the downbeat as opposed to the first count of each measure. The son's influence is illustrated by the use, in salsa and other Cuban-influenced forms, of the term *sonero* to mean "lead singer."

Further Readings

Galán, Natalio. *Cuba y sus sones*. Valencia: Pre-Textos, 1997.

Orovio, Helio. *Diccionario de la música cubana: biográfico y técnico*. Havana: Editorial Letras Cubanas, 1981.

Roberts, John Storm. *The Latin Tinge*. 2nd ed. New York: Oxford University Press, 1999.

Pablo Julián Davis

Sonora Matancera, La

La Sonora Matancera, one of the oldest continually existing orchestras of twentieth-century Cuba—indeed of all of Latin America—was best known for its work with Bienvenido Granada and Daniel Santos and, later on, **Celia Cruz**.

The orchestra was founded in 1924 in **Matanzas** by *timbalero* Valentín Cané (its first director) and Pablo Vázquez. They were later joined by Rogelio Martínez, who at the end of the 1930s became musical director due to Cané's failing health; he served for more than fifty years as guitarist, director, and business manager. La Sonora (as it was widely known) spent its first quarter-century of existence mainly working as a house band, accompanying singers, and so on. In 1950, a young woman of about twenty years of age first performed with the orchestra, singer Celia Cruz. The orchestra entered a golden era in the 1950s, appearing on radio and television, headlining at Havana's famed **Tropicana nightclub**, and touring extensively to Mexico and elsewhere. In 1960, La Sonora Matancera left Cuba for Mexico, but its sojourn there was brief, less than two years in length. In 1962, the orchestra settled in the United States.

Through some combination of Martínez's superb ear for talent and the orchestra's pronounced stylistic versatility, La Sonora's durability was remarkable, and its knack for launching brilliant singing careers was unparalleled in Latin American music. Among the singers who achieved fame with La Sonora Matancera behind them were Leo Marini and Carlos Argentino of Argentina, Nelson Pinedo of Colombia, Puerto Rican Daniel Santos, Bienvenido Granada, Celio González, Puerto Rican Bobby Capó (composer of the popular **bolero** "Piel canela"), and Dominican singer Alberto Beltrán (whose "Negro del batey" and other hits helped give the merengue genre of his homeland its first broad diffusion in the Americas). The most enduring, and celebrated, combination was that of La Sonora Matancera with Celia Cruz. Also among its most famed members was Carlos Díaz Alonso, "Caíto," who contributed a distinctive vocal style to the accompanying voices, or *coro*.

Because of its recordings, touring, and the many nationalities of its lead singers, La Sonora Matancera achieved enormous influence throughout Latin America. One index of that influence has been the proliferation of orchestra names beginning with "Sonora" including the distinguished Puerto Rican **salsa** orchestra La Sonora Ponceña.

Further Readings
Galán, Natalio. *Cuba y sus sones*. Valencia, Spain: Pre-Textos, 1997.
Pérez Perazzo, Alberto. *Ritmo afrohispano antillano 1865–1965*. Caracas: Editorial Sucre, 1988.
Roberts, John Storm. *The Latin Tinge*. 2nd ed. New York: Oxford University Press, 1999.

Pablo Julián Davis

Teatro Bufo (1868–1930)

Beginning in 1868 a series of theater bouffe companies were established throughout the island to promote Cuban works. The **theaters** were known for the **guaracha** (dance), the *sainete* (one-act comedies), dramas, costume period pieces (*costumbristas*), and their bold and experimental style. All of the important social and national issues of the period were incorporated into the productions. Politicians, prostitutes, and immigrants were frequently depicted on stage. From these comical/satirical productions emerged a powerful social and political critique. Because of the challenges that Teatro Bufo productions posed to the Spanish colonial regime, their performances sometimes led to confrontations, as was the case in the Teatro Villanueva affair, when a theater performance culminated in a riot (see **Ten Years' War**). In a classic format, actors representing popular stereotypes, typically people of lower socioeconomic standing, were depicted in scenes with a host of problems, which would be resolved in comic fashion. Among the comic archetypes utilized were the *negrito* (the black man), the *mulata* (the

mulatto woman), the *gallego*, (used as a symbol for all Spanish immigrants from the Iberian Peninsula), the *isleño* (used as a symbol for immigrants from the Canary Islands), and the *chino* (used as a symbol of Chinese immigrants). The negrito and mulata were typically portrayed as streetwise and mischievous, while the others were frequently portrayed as naive or dense. The satirization of the gallego centered on depicting him as stubborn, ignorant, crude, stingy, sloppy, and having a weakness for dark-skinned women. The theatrical productions frequently concluded with an appreciation and understanding of the gallego and on occasion with his triumph in the face of adversity. The most typical theater of the genre was El Teatro Alhambra (Havana, 1890–1935). These works declined in popularity at the end of the 1920s. *See also* Theater

Further Readings
Arrom, José Juan. *Historia de la literatura dramática cubana*. New Haven, CT: Yale University Press, 1944.
La Bella del Alhambra. Cuban film. Enrique Pineda Barnet, 1989.
Leal, Rine. *La selva oscura. De los bufos a la neocolonia (Historia de teatro cubano de 1868 a 1902)*. Havana: Editorial Arte y Literatura, 1982.
Leal, Rine. *Teatro bufo, siglo XIX. Antología*. Vol. 2. Havana: Editorial Arte y Literatura, 1975.
Robreño, Eduardo. *Como lo pienso lo digo*. Havana: Ediciones Unión, 1985.
Robreño, Eduardo. (Selección, prólogo y notas. Estudio complementario de Álvaro López). *Teatro Alhambra. Antología*. Havana: Editorial Letras Cubanas, 1979.

Consuelo Naranjo Orovio

Teatro Estudio

In 1958, director and actor Vicente Revuelta, along with seven other **theater** professionals, founded Teatro Estudio, a collective that has become one of Cuba's most enduring and influential theater groups. The majority of revolutionary

Cuba's foremost theater practitioners, such as Sergio Corrieri, Berta Martínez, Roberto Blanco, and Flora Lauten, can be traced to Teatro Estudio. The group's richly varied repertory marks significant moments in the development of a national theater movement in Cuba. By experimenting with the techniques of Bertolt Brecht and Constantine Stanislavsky, and by staging avant-garde European and North American works as well as the classics and the most recent Cuban plays, Teatro Estudio has shown a strong commitment to both the **Revolution** and the renovation of the Cuban stage. Some of the group's noteworthy productions include its 1958 inaugural production of Eugene O'Neill's *A Long Day's Journey into Night* and its 1959 performance of *The Good Woman of Setzuan*, the first production of a play by Brecht in Cuba. In 1963, Teatro Estudio's production of Lope de Vega's *Fuenteovejuna* drew tens of thousands of spectators, including **Fidel Castro**. Teatro Estudio was Cuba's central theatrical institution during the first decade of the Revolution, a period characterized by intense creative activity. The group's permanent home, the Hubert de Blanck Theater in Havana, remains an important site for quality theater viewing. *See also* Theaters

Further Reading

Leal, Rine. *Breve historia del teatro cubano*. Havana: Editorial Letras Cubanas, 1980.

Camilla Stevens

Theater

From its origins to the present, Cuba has had a rich history of theatrical activity shaped by the historical and sociopolitical conditions of the island. Although conquerors and missionaries brought the Spanish dramatic tradition to Cuba, performance in the Caribbean predated the arrival of the Europeans in the form of *areítos*, rituals representing the cultural heritage of the **indigenous inhabitants** that incorporated dance, music, and costumes. Colonizers judged the areítos heretical, and in 1512, such performances were banned, setting the stage for the imposition of Spanish cultural patterns. Accordingly, the history of Cuban theater represents the development of an autochthonous tradition (see **Conquest**).

The theater constituted a primary source of entertainment for all social classes in the cities during the colonial period, although it was not until the end of the eighteenth century that the first fine playhouse appeared in Havana. The first known drama by a Cuban, *El príncipe jardinero y fingido Cloridano*, by Santiago Pita, was performed in Havana in 1791. The play was a great success in part because it was written in the spirit of the Spanish Golden Age *comedias* that had formed the tastes of Cuban theatergoers. During this period, the players were mainly peninsular, and the theaters performed a repertory similar to that of the contemporary Spanish stage: adaptations of Golden Age plays or works by Spanish or foreign authors. The actor-author Francisco Covarrubias (1775–1850) was the first Cuban playwright to dramatize local themes and settings. His pieces, many from the 1820s to 1840s, introduced Cuban types such as the *negrito* (the white actor in blackface). Although none of his plays survive, Covarrubias is considered the father of Cuban theater because he transformed the Spanish *género chico* into a theatrical form with national characteristics.

The artistic and social rebellion of Romanticism dominated Cuban theater during the first half of the nineteenth century. In 1836, the performance of *Don Pedro de Castilla*, by Francisco Foxá y Lecanda, a Dominican exile in Havana, created a scandal because conservatives believed it represented an attack on Spain. In the same year, **José Jacinto Milanés** premiered *El Conde Alarcos*, a technically superior romantic play also based on a Spanish medieval legend and also critical of despotism. One outstanding writer of the moment was Cuban-born poet, novelist, and dramatist **Gertrudis Gómez de Avellaneda** (1814–1873), whose fame in the theater rests primarily on her comedy *Hija de las flores* (1852) and her biblical tragedy *Baltasar* (1858). **José María Heredia** and **José Martí**, other important nineteenth-century figures in Cuban letters, made their mark in the theater as well. Although few of his plays were staged, critics consider **Joaquín Lorenzo Luaces** (1826–1867) the best and the most authentically Cuban playwright of the period. His plays such as *El becerro de oro* and *El fantasmón de Aravaca* are incisive comedies that examine Cuban societal ills and attack colonial oppression. Luaces marks the end of Romantic drama in Cuba and, like Covarrubias, anticipates a popular national theater.

During the latter half of the nineteenth century, an essentially Cuban genre, the **teatro bufo**, developed in response to the political unrest in the colony and an increasing desire for independence from Spain. The term bufo comes from the Italian verb "to puff out one's cheeks in mockery." This musical dance theater specialized in humorous satire and parody and in representations of stock folk characters such as *el negrito, la mulata*, and *el gallego. Bufomanía* swept the island, but the anti-Spanish sentiments of the texts garnered censorship, and the **Ten Years' War** (1868–1878) suspended productions of the plays. A second cycle of bufos returned between 1879 and 1900, but by the advent of the Republic in 1902, the political aim of the pieces had been lost. The twentieth-century version of the bufo, however, flourished, and authors such as Federico Villoch and Carlos and Gustavo Robreño wrote hundreds of the sketches. Teatro bufo became increasingly superficial, and

in the famous Teatro Alhambra, the genre degenerated into risqué spectacle.

Amidst the commercial theater of the early years of the Republic, groups such as the Sociedad de Fomento de Teatro (1910) and the Teatro Cubano (1912) attempted to create a serious national theater movement. The works of José Antonio Ramos (1885–1946) stand out for their psychological and social realism. Ramos's *Tembladera* (1917), which deals with a family divided over the sale of their sugar mill, represents one of the important works of the early Republican period. In 1936, Luis Baralt founded the group Teatro la Cueva, sparking a decade of theatrical education in which more than fifteen new private theater institutions trained directors, actors, and technicians. Teatro de las Máscaras initiated a "little theater" movement between 1954 and 1958 with the four-month run of one of its productions. Following the las Máscaras success, a variety of small theaters offering consecutive performances opened in Havana, which created a larger spectatorship and allowed the artists to fine-tune their performances. In the late 1940s by combining modern techniques with national themes, **Virgilio Piñera**'s *Electra Garrigó* (1947), and works by Carlos Felipe, Paco Alonso, and Rolando Ferrer, signaled the future of Cuban drama.

Many artists were well prepared to participate in the institutionalization of Cuban theater that came with the 1959 **Revolution**. The Revolution's Marxist ideology dramatically altered the sociopolitical and cultural structures of the island. Government subsidies and the decommercialization of the arts immediately produced a new generation of theater schools, groups, and dramatists. The early years of the Revolution saw Cuban productions of classic and avant-garde plays by international dramatists, as well as works by a new generation of Cuban authors such as José Brene, Manuel Reguera Samuell, and

Abelardo Estorino. Estorino (b. 1925), revolutionary Cuba's most important contemporary playwright, has staged over a dozen plays over the course of four decades. His play *El robo del cochino* (1961) is a classic realist drama about a family torn apart by the Revolution.

By 1967, a climate of ideological orthodoxy permeated the theater, and plays that did not represent a recognizable social reality came under suspicion as elitist and potentially counterrevolutionary (see **Padilla [Affair], Heberto**). José Triana's *La noche de los asesinos* (1965) won the **Casas de las Américas** prize, but its ambiguous message led critics to question his ideological stance. Other playwrights working with nonrealist forms such as Virgilio Piñera and **Antón Arrufat** were also accused of privileging individual artistic commitment over political responsibility to the Revolution.

The new position on the role of art in a socialist society moved Cuban theater in new directions. In 1968, Sergio Corrieri initiated the Cuban Teatro Nuevo movement by founding Grupo Teatro Escambray. Teatro Nuevo refers to a popular, antibourgeois theater that emerged from an interactive relationship between theater practitioners and their public. These groups abandoned the proscenium stage in search of new spaces and audiences for their collectively created pieces. Corrieri's troupe worked in the remote **Escambray Mountains**, as did Flora Lauten's Teatro La Yaya. Other groups worked in **Santiago de Cuba** (Teatrova and Cabildo Teatral de Santiago) or in working-class neighborhoods in Havana (Teatro de Participación Popular). Teatro Nuevo plays share such characteristics as uncomplicated forms, clear conflicts, colloquial language, and themes that deal with immediate issues relevant to the island's socialist transformation: **land reform acts**, the changing role of women, and the clash between new and old morals and behaviors. Among the many participants in this movement, representative figures include Albio Paz, Gilda Hernández, and Roberto Orihuela. Along with Abrahán Rodríguez, Héctor Quintero, **Eugenio Hernández Espinosa**, and Freddy Artiles, playwrights who staged their plays in more traditional settings, Teatro Nuevo constitutes the most innovative Cuban theater of the ideologically charged climate of the 1970s.

In the 1980s, a new theater generation began to combat the overuse of realism, schematic formulas, and didactic messages that had invaded Cuban dramaturgy. For example, rather than focusing on immediate social conflicts, plays such as *La verdadera culpa de Juan Clemente Zenea* (1986) by **Abilio Estévez** present complex character sketches, individual conflicts, and the connections between Cuba's past and present. In the 1990s, playwrights have continued to renovate theatrical form and content by using a postmodern approach to history, myth, language, and dramatic structure. The unresolved conflicts and ambiguities of contemporary works contrast with the dialectical resolutions in earlier revolutionary plays. In addition, new theater collectives such as Flora Lauten's Teatro Buendía and Víctor Varela's Teatro del Obstáculo have attracted young people wishing to explore realities not expressed by the official voice of the Revolution. The survival of theatrical activity in spite of a lack of materials, electrical blackouts, and the problem of transportation that has plagued the island since the onset of the **Special Period** (1990) testifies to the strength of Cuba's national theater tradition. *See also* Cinema; Theaters; Teatro Estudio

Further Readings

Leal, Rine. *Breve historia del teatro cubano*. Havana: Editorial Letras Cubanas, 1980.

Martin, Randy. *Socialist Ensembles: Theater and State in Cuba and Nicaragua*. Minneapolis: University of Minnesota Press, 1994.

Camilla Stevens

Elegant interior of Havana's Tacón Theater, one of the finest and largest of its time. Nineteenth-century sketch by Samuel Hazard.

Theaters

Before the construction of theaters in colonial Cuba, plays were performed in churches, plazas, and private homes. To the dismay of the Church, however, prosperous Havana residents began to desire an actual theater. The Marqués de la Torre helped the cause by arguing that the income from the theater could support the Church's charities; thus, Cuba's first theater, El Coliseo, was built in 1775. Although El Coliseo was beautifully restored as Teatro El Principal in 1803, Governor Miguel Tacón determined that Havana needed an even more luxurious playhouse. With money earned from taxing **slavery**, Teatro Tacón, a magnificent, five-tiered horseshoe auditorium, was completed in 1838 and was one of the world's largest and most well appointed. Other theaters built during this period include the Circo del Marte (1800), which later became the politically charged Teatro Villanueva

(1853), the Diorama (1820), Teatro José Payret (1877), and the Irijoa (1884). Other important theaters were built outside of Havana, among them El Sauto (1863) in **Matanzas**.

A cultural decline during the Republic followed the nineteenth-century boom in theater construction. From 1900 to 1934, the Teatro Alhambra offered light, bawdy musical theater. During the 1930s and 1940s, the few groups producing serious plays staged their productions in El Auditorium and El Principal de la Comedia, both built in the 1920s. In the late 1940s El Teatro Blanquita (today Carlos Marx) was inaugurated; it had 6,000 seats, 500 more than New York's Radio City Music Hall. In the 1950s, a series of small theaters ranging from 80 to 400 seats appeared, sparking a "little theater" movement. Many movie houses also served as theaters including El América, Campoamor, Radio Cine, and Radio Centro (El Yara, today).

The 1959 **Revolution** provided Cuban

theater with state support. El Teatro Nacional de Cuba was inaugurated in 1960. This striking, modern complex contains the Sala Avellaneda (2,500 seats) and the Sala Covarrubias (800 seats). Other noteworthy theaters include El Gran Teatro de La Habana (formerly the Teatro Tacón), Teatro Mella, and Teatro Buendía. *See also* Cinema; Teatro Bufo

Further Readings

Arrom, José Juan. *Literatura dramática cubana.* New York: AMS Press, 1973.

Leal, Rine. *Breve historia del teatro cubano.* Havana: Editorial Letras Cubanas, 1980.

Camilla Stevens

Tríos

Tríos originated as a type of musical ensemble in Cuba and the Caribbean during the 1920s, as three-member groups consisting of two voices and one or two guitars. These early tríos were composed of a soloist voice carrying the main melody and another voice, no less important, singing the melodic part known as the *contracanto.* The two voices were accompanied by a third member who played the guitar. Some tríos, like the **Trío Matamoros** in Cuba and the Trío Borinquen in Puerto Rico, followed a slightly different arrangement, with a second guitar played by the second voice. While the Puerto Rican repertoire for tríos consisted of **criollas**, songs, and **guarachas**, its Cuban counterpart alternated guarachas and **boleros** and also incorporated the more lively genre of *boleroson* (see **Son**). The two-voice trío with guitars gradually accepted percussion instruments and introduced the bolero as rival to the **danzón** and *danza.*

Another version of the trío, also known as *trío romántico*, emerged in Mexico in the 1930s, integrating three parallel voices in traditional harmony. This variation has served as a model for *contemporary* tríos that later became generalized throughout Latin America. Los Panchos was the most widely acclaimed of these romantic tríos. Like the earlier Cuban version, the more modern romantic tríos also incorporate percussion instruments when recording more lively pieces such as guarachas, *son-montunos*, and *merengues.*

Further Readings

Fernández, José Loyola. *En ritmo de bolero: el bolero en la música bailable cubana.* San Juan: Ediciones Huracán, 1996.

Ortiz Ramos, Pablo Marcial. *A tres voces y guitarras: los tríos en Puerto Rico.* Santo Domingo: Editora Corripio, 1992.

Edgardo Díaz Díaz

Tropicana Nightclub

The famous Tropicana nightclub opened to the public in 1939 in a suburb of Havana on the site of what was a small farm. The cabaret became the flagship of a number of first-rate nightclubs including the Sans Soucí, Capri, and Montmarte, among others. The Tropicana was originally known as "Beau-Sister," but the name was changed after composer and musician Alfredo Brito dedicated and played the song "Tropicana" at the cabaret. After several years, the floor shows at the Tropicana became a thing of legend throughout Latin America and the United States. Among the most dazzling features of the cabaret are the dancing water fountains accentuated by multicolored spotlights. The effect is multiplied by the eight female marble sculptures that dance around the stage nude, like tropical water spirits, in front of startled visitors. There are various salons inside the Tropicana, including the Arcos de Cristal, a **theater** with glass on the walls and ceiling. The cabaret can accommodate up to 500 patrons. Approximately 200,000 people visit the Tropicana annually. It takes about 160 workers, including the orchestra, the stage personnel, and performers, to put on the world-famous floor show. The performances are typified

Postcard depicting the Tropicana Nightclub, Havana (1950s). Luis Martínez-Fernández Collection.

by splashy, choreographed dance numbers performed by thirty-two dancers. *See also* Organized Crime; Tourism

Further Reading

Lam, Rafael. *Tropicana: A Paradise under the Stars*. Havana: Editorial José Martí, 1999.

Araceli García Carranza

U.S. Entertainment Industry, Cubans in the

Cubans have played a significant role in the motion picture and television industries of the United States since at least the 1930s. The best-known example is **Desi Arnaz**, or Ricky Ricardo as he is best known to most North Americans. Born Desiderio Alberto Arnaz y de Acha III, Arnaz was forced to leave Cuba after the **Revolution of 1933** landed his father, the mayor of **Santiago de Cuba**, in jail and stripped the Arnaz family of wealth and property. After his father's release, the family fled to Miami. While enjoying suc-

cess as a bandleader and musician, Arnaz landed a role in the Broadway play *Too Many Girls* in 1939. The following year he met and married Lucille Ball when both were making the movie version of the play.

By the time Arnaz arrived in Hollywood, another Cuban was already making movies there. The New York–born César Julio Romero, Jr., better known as Cesar Romero, was the grandson of **José Martí**, the nineteenth-century Cuban writer and revolutionary leader. Romero made his film debut in *The Thin Man* in 1934. In the 1940s, he was a staple in 20th Century Fox musicals, usually cast as a Latin lover, but he never achieved star status at the time. That would take several decades.

Desi Arnaz made television history in 1951 and provided a constant presence for Cuban culture on U.S. television for the greater part of the twentieth century. In 1950, Lucille Ball and Arnaz bankrolled the pilot of their hit television series *I Love Lucy*, which never ranked lower than third in the ratings during its six-year run. Behind the scenes, Arnaz single-handedly revolutionized the business of television by taping programs with live audiences, creating the three-camera technique, and establishing television syndication. In 1960, Desi and Lucille Ball ended their twenty-year marriage and split their interests in their studio Desilu.

In the 1960s, the children of Desi Arnaz emerged in their own right. Lucie Desiree Arnaz became a regular on her mother's hit TV series *Here's Lucy* as her TV daughter Kim Carter. Lucie went on to star in *Billy Jack Goes to Washington* (1977) and *The Jazz Singer* (1980). Her younger brother, Desiderio Alberto Arnaz IV, made national headlines the day he was born, which was the same night Little Ricky was born on *I Love Lucy*. After several appearances on *The Lucy Show* (1962–1968), he, too, became a regular on *Here's Lucy*.

At about the same time, Cesar Romero finally landed his most memorable role as "The Joker" on the television series *Batman* (1966–1968). Throughout his career, he starred in over sixty films and remained active in film and TV until his death on January 1, 1994. Another Cuban character actress of note of the period was Antonia Rey, whose credits include *Popi* (1969), *Klute* (1972), *Moscow on the Hudson* (1986), and *Gloria* (1999).

The 1970s saw the emergence of many young Cubans in the U.S. entertainment industries. In 1972, Luis Ávalos, the Havana-born actor, gained national attention in the public television children's series *The Electric Company* (1972–1977) opposite Rita Moreno and Morgan Freeman. Since then he has been a regular guest star on numerous television programs and motion pictures. At the same time another Cuban actor became a trailblazer on television. While he has been identified as African American, George Stanford Brown was born in Cuba to a Cuban mother and Jamaican father. In 1972, he became the

first Cuban to star in a prime-time network television series, *The Rookies*. Brown also starred in *Roots* (1977), *Roots: The Next Generation*, and *North and South* (1985). As a director, he received the Emmy Award for *Cagney & Lacey* (1982–1988).

Meanwhile, in Miami a group of talented young Cubans created the landmark television series *Qué Pasa, USA?* in 1978. Written by Cuban Luis Santiero, the sitcom captured the life of three generations of a Cuban family and their adaptation to life in the United States. A ten-time Emmy winner, Santiero has written such award-winning plays as *Our Lady of the Tortilla* (1987) and *The Lady from Havana* (1992) as well as for the legendary children's series *Sesame Street* for more than twenty years (see **Cuban Playwrights in the United States**).

In New York, Cuban playwright Iván Acosta wrote *El súper* (1977), a play about a Cuban exile working as a building superintendent in New York who longs to return to his homeland—or at least Miami, where it doesn't snow. In 1978, it was staged and received glowing reviews. The following year Acosta wrote the film script that fellow Cubans **León Ichaso** and Orlando Jiménez-Leal codirected as a film. Ichaso has directed other Cuban-themed independent feature films including *Crossover Dreams* (1985) and *Bitter Sugar* (1996). Jimínez-Leal continued to work in commercial production.

In Europe at the time, **Néstor Almendros** was building a reputation as one of the world's most talented cinematographers. Though born in Spain, Almendros identified himself as Cuban his entire adult life. At age eighteen he moved to Cuba to join his exiled anti-Franco father. In the late 1950s, he went to study in Italy but returned to Cuba after the 1959 **Revolution**, where he made several documentaries. But after two of his short films were banned by the **Fidel Castro** government, he moved to Paris where he immediately produced *Six in Paris* (*Paris vu par*, 1965) a documentary about six Cuban dancers adjusting to life in exile. By the end of the 1970s, he had already earned his place in world cinema by photographing such French classics as François Truffaut's *L'enfant sauvage* (*The Wild Child*, 1969), Eric Rohmer's *La genou de Claire* (*Claire's Knee*, 1971), and Barbet Schroeder's *Idi Amin Dada* (1974). Hollywood took notice of the man with the extraordinary eye. In 1978, he shot his first U.S. film, *Days of Heaven*, for which he was nominated and won the Oscar for best cinematography. Almendros thus became the only Cuban ever to win an Academy Award in the twentieth century. Thereafter he earned nominations for *Kramer vs. Kramer* (1979), *The Blue Lagoon* (1980), and *Sophie's Choice* (1982).

In 1984, Oscar-winning cinematographer Néstor Almendros produced a controversial documentary titled *Conducta impropia* (*Improper Conduct*), featuring a series of powerful interviews with Cuban intellectuals and homosexuals who had been persecuted under the Castro government (see **Gays and Lesbians**). In 1989 Almendros directed *Nadie escuchaba* (*Nobody Listened*) in which some thirty victims of oppression in Fidel Castro's Cuba give dramatic testimony. Nominated for an Academy Award for Best Documentary, the film was codirected by fellow Cuban Jorge Ulla, a commercial advertising producer.

In the 1980s, Miami resident Steven Echevarría, better known as Steven Bauer, was still in college when he won his first television role in the landmark series, *Qué Pasa, USA?* (1978–1980), then billed as Rocky Echevarría. He was quickly lured to Hollywood where he landed guest spots. By 1982, Bauer landed the showy role of Al Pacino's right-hand man in *Scarface* (1983), which portrayed Mariel Cubans as America's newest criminals (see **Mariel Boatlift**). His other credits include *Thief*

of Hearts (1984), *Wiseguy* (CBS-TV, 1989), and the movie *Traffic* (2000).

Another noted Cuban American actor, Julie Carmen, born to Cuban parents, made her film debut in John Cassavetes's *Gloria* in 1980. The following year, she landed the lead in the made-for-TV movie *Can You Hear the Laughter? The Story of Freddie Prinze* (1981). Her other screen credits include *The Milagro Beanfield War* (1988), *Fright Night: Part Two* (1989), and *In the Mouth of Madness* (1995).

In 1984, a young Cuban actress named María Conchita Alonso was winning over audiences and critics alike. Born in Cuba, but raised in Caracas, Venezuela, she was crowned Miss Venezuela at eighteen and went on to become a model, actress in *telenovelas* (soap operas), and singer. In 1982, she moved to the United States. Two years later, Alonso made her Hollywood feature film debut opposite Robin Williams in *Moscow on the Hudson*. She then starred in *Running Man* (1987), *Predator 2* (1990), and *House of the Spirits* (1993).

It was Lucie Arnaz who became the first Cuban American actress to headline her own television series, *The Lucie Arnaz Show*, in 1985. After that short-lived experience, Arnaz found success on Broadway for her performances in *They're Playing Our Song, Master Class*, and *My One and Only*. In 1993, she won an Emmy for producing *Lucy & Desi: A Home Movie*, a loving but honest tribute to her parents.

By the mid-1980s, music producer Emilio Estefan had had several Top Ten hits with Miami Sound Machine and his wife **Gloria Estefan**. Now he was lured by Hollywood to compose songs for such movies as *Top Gun* (1986). *The Specialist* (1999), and *Evita* (1996).

In 1986, New Jersey–born Elizabeth Peña gained national recognition for her performance as the maid-turned-revolutionary in *Down and Out in Beverly Hills* (1986). Peña was raised in Cuba and moved to

Manhattan at the age of eight. After success on the New York off-Broadway stage, Peña tackled her first film role in the ground-breaking Cuban American production *El súper* (1979). Since then, she has starred in *Crossover Dreams* (1985), *La Bamba* (1987), *Jacob's Ladder* (1990), and *Lone Star* (1996).

Toward the end of the 1980s, a young Cuban-born actor named Andrés Arturo García-Menéndez, better known as **Andy García**, took Hollywood by storm. After dropping out of college and performing in regional theater, García moved to Los Angeles in the late 1970s. By 1989, he had already appeared in *8 Million Ways to Die* (1986), *The Untouchables* (1987), *La Bamba* (1988), and *Black Rain* (1989). In 1990 his performance as the cold-blooded nephew of Michael Corleone in *The Godfather: Part III* won him an Academy Award nomination. He has also produced award-winning films and CDs of Cuban music.

In 1992, Hollywood made *The Mambo Kings*, based on **Oscar Hijuelos**'s Pulitzer Prize–winning novel *The Mambo Kings Play Songs of Love*. Hollywood producers cast a then relatively unknown Spaniard named Antonio Banderas and Italian American Armand Asante in the lead roles. Many in the Cuban and Latino artistic community expressed their resentment. The most notable Cubans in the cast were **salsa** singer **Celia Cruz** and Desi Arnaz, Jr., who won much praise for his moving portrayal of his father.

In New Jersey, meanwhile, Daisy Fuentes was studying communications and journalism at a community college when she was selected as the weather person for a local Spanish-language television station. In 1988, she was hired to host *MTV Internacional*. The first Latina VJ (video jockey), Fuentes also became the first crossover VJ to work on both MTV US and MTV Latino. She has hosted a variety of television programs including *America's Funniest Home Videos* (1992–1999) *Dick Clark's New Year's Rockin' Eve '98*, and the Miss Universe pageant.

In 1993, **Tomás Guitiérrez Alea**, whose films had challenged Cubans on the island and Cuban Americans in the states since the 1960s, made his most critical and important film. *Fresa y chocolate* (*Strawberry and Chocolate*). The film focused on the relationship between a young, heterosexual, homophobic communist and an older, intellectual gay man who becomes a political dissident. In 1995, it became the first Cuban-made film nominated for an Academy Award for Best Foreign Language film.

In 1994, **Cameron Díaz** seemed to come out of nowhere when she made her screen debut opposite comedian Jim Carrey in *The Mask*. With *My Best Friend's Wedding* (1997), Díaz, whose father is of Cuban descent, endeared herself to audiences and critics with her performance. But it was the quirky box office success *There's Something about Mary* (1998) that earned her the widest recognition. She was critically well received in *Being John Malkovich* (1999). She has recently starred in *Vanilla Sky* (2001).

Two other young Cuban actors gained much praise in the late 1990s. René Lavàn, who had left Cuba as a teenager during the **Mariel boatlift**, was introduced to American television audiences in a recurring role on *One Life to Live* in 1993 and starred in the bitterly anti-Castro film *Azúcar amarga* (*Bitter Sugar*) in 1996. The other was Cuban American Mel Gorham (Mel Schnier) who had appeared in small roles in *Do the Right Thing* (1989) and *Carlito's Way* (1993). In 1995, Gorham finally found her breakthrough role as a Latina spitfire in *Smoke*. That same year, Gorham played a demented refugee in *The Perez Family*, in which once again non-Cuban and non-Latino actors portrayed the Cuban lead roles. This time, Italian American actress Marisa Tomei played a Mariel Cuban.

German filmmaker Wim Wenders's documentary *Buena Vista Social Club* (1999), about a group of aging legendary Cuban musicians, featuring Ibrahim Ferrer and Omara Portuondo, was the brainchild of American musician Ry Cooder, who went to Havana to record with them. Nominated for an Academy Award for Best Documentary, the film earned an unprecedented $7 million in the United States, and its soundtrack was an international sensation (see **Compadres, Los**).

Behind the scenes in Hollywood, two Cuban Americans have had very important roles in the industry. Emanuel Núñez, an agent with the powerful Creative Artists Agency in Beverly Hills, was among a handful of big-time Hollywood agents who could determine the success of many actors. The other was Cuban American Pancho Mansfield who became senior vice president of Programming at Showtime Television Networks after being a documentary filmmaker. Mansfield oversaw the network's high-profile series the Latino-themed *Resurrection Boulevard* and the groundbreaking *Queer as Folk*.

In 2000, the plight of Elián González (see **González Case [Elián]**) dominated the nation's media, and Hollywood was no exception. Gloria Estefan, who made her movie debut in *Music of the Heart* (2000), was thrust into the Elián controversy. At the same time, she appeared with Andy García in the television movie *For Love or Country: The Arturo Sandoval Story*. García joined with Estefan and most of Miami's Cuban community demonstrating to keep the boy in the United States.

That same year, artist-turned-filmmaker Julian Schnabel filmed *Before Nightfall* (*Antes que anochezca*), based on the 1993 autobiography of Cuban writer **Reinaldo Arenas**. Mariel refugee Arenas was portrayed by Spaniard Javier Bardem who was nominated for an Academy Award for Best Actor. The film became one of the surprise hits of the year.

The new millennium has seen the emergence of a new group of Cuban Americans becoming more visible on television. Most notable among them was Gina Torres who was born in New York City to Cuban parents. This classically trained actress played the lead in *Cleopatra 2525*, which was followed by a recurring role in *Any Day Now* (2001). Another talented Cuban actor was the handsome David Fumero who left Cuba during the Mariel exodus in 1980. After a stint as a model in Paris, Fumero appeared in a Mariah Carey music video, which led to a recurring role on the soap opera *One Life to Live*. Finally, Cuban-born Judge Marilyn Milián became the first woman to preside over the longest-running court show, *The People's Court*, in 2001. The Cuban-born attorney had been a real-life judge in Florida prior to her television debut.

After a century of consistent immigration by Cubans into the United States, the influence of Cuban culture and its artists on U.S. movies and television appears destined to grow with succeeding decades.

Further Reading

Reyes, Luis and Peter Rubie. *Hispanics in Hollywood: An Encyclopedia of Film and Television*. New York: Garland. 1994.

Ray Blanco

U.S. Music Industry, Cubans in the

Since the 1930s, Cuban music had been heard on U.S. radio and in nightclubs. There were countless Cuban musicians in the United States throughout the early part of the twentieth century. One of the earliest Cuban musicians in the United States was Desiderio Alberto Arnaz y de Acha III, better known as **Desi Arnaz**, who was forced to leave Cuba after the **Revolution of 1933**. After some menial jobs, he landed a job with the **Xavier Cugat** Orchestra. A year later, he started his own orchestra. In the 1950s, he became a pioneer in U.S. television with *I Love Lucy*.

One of the most well known singers in Cuba and New York in the late 1930s, **Frank "Machito" Grillo** started his own band, The Afro Cubans, who regularly recorded with such leading jazz musicians as Charlie Parker and Stan Kenton. Machito had a number of successful records of his own. In 1942, he asked his brother-in-law Mario Bauzá to join his band as its musical director and arranger. The relationship lasted more than thirty-five years. Bauzá is one of the outstanding, if unsung, section men of the swing era, often cited as the man who invented Latin jazz. Throughout his long career, he performed with such legendary American musicians as Chick Webb, Cab Calloway, Dizzy Gillespie, Charlie Parker, Cannonball Adderley, Doc Cheatham, and Buddy Rich (see **Afro-Cuban Jazz**).

Arturo "Chico" O'Farrill moved to the United States and became an arranger after playing trumpet in several Cuban-based bands throughout the 1940s. His work was played and recorded by Benny Goodman, Count Basie, Dizzy Gillespie, and Stan Kenton during the 1950s. An outstanding exponent of Latin American music, O'Farrill's arrangements consistently demonstrated his comprehensive grasp of the music's potential and were often far more imaginative than those of others who worked in this field.

By 1950 U.S. audiences were going crazy for the **mambo. Dámaso Pérez Prado**, whom many hail as the King of the Mambo, left Cuba to work in Mexico in 1948. He scored moderate hits with "Que rico el Mambo" and "Mambo No. 5" in the United States in 1950. Pérez Prado's first performance in the United States was at the Teatro Puerto Rico in the Bronx in New York City in 1951 with fellow Cuban **Benny Moré**. In 1955, he scored his first number-one hit in the United States with "Cherry Pink and Apple Blossom White,"

which stayed on the pop charts for twenty-six weeks including ten weeks at number one.

The Cuban **Revolution** of 1959 saw the exodus of many Cuban musicians from the island. Among them was **Celia Cruz** who had been singing with **La Sonora Matancera** at Havana's world-famous **Tropicana nightclub** for over fifteen years. Cruz and her band fled Cuba in 1960 pretending that they were going on tour but settling in Mexico. They entered the United States the following year. Cruz's early years in the United States were less than memorable. She did not sell many records during the 1960s. It was in the late 1970s when she found an audience in the United States, performing with Tito Puente, Johnny Pacheco, and Ray Barreto.

If Celia Cruz is Cuba's **salsa** queen, **Olga Guillot** is Cuba's undisputed queen of **bolero**; she melted Cuba, Mexico, and the rest of Latin America with rip-your-heart-out melodrama throughout the 1950s. In 1961, she left Cuba with her eight-month-old daughter in her arms and settled in Mexico. In 1964, she made history by becoming the first Hispanic artist to perform at Carnegie Hall and on Broadway.

Born and raised in Cuba, Ramón "Mongo" Santamaría arrived in New York at the end of the 1940s and worked with orchestra leaders **Gilberto Valdés**, Pérez Prado, Tito Puente, and Cal Tjader in the 1950s. Santamaría first came to prominence as a solo artist in 1963, when he rocked the charts with "Watermelon Man," written by his keyboard player Herbie Hancock. With negligible promotion, the single became a Top Ten hit. That same year, he introduced U.S. audiences to the exotic, eccentric singer **La Lupe**. Born Victoria Lupe Yoli, she left Cuba at the beginning of 1962; after a brief stay in Mexico, La Lupe went to New York where she joined Santamaría. Eventually, she worked with the Tito Puente Orchestra as their singer for over six years. Her unique voice and outrageous performing style garnered fans beyond Latin Americans. La Lupe, who had retired from the music industry in 1980, died in poverty from a heart attack at the age of fifty-two. At the time of her death, she was a Pentecostal preacher.

The son of Desi Arnaz, Desiderio Alberto Arnaz IV, hit the music charts when he was still a teenager in the 1960s. As part of the teen rock band Dino, Desi and Billy, Desi Jr. had several Top 40 hit singles.

In the late 1970s in south Florida, Gloria Fajardo, later **Gloria Estefan**, and Emilio Estefan were two young Cuban refugees who were mixing the music of their homeland with a distinctive U.S. sound and creating a unique Miami sound. Fajardo left Cuba with her parents immediately after **Fidel Castro** took power. In the late 1970s, Emilio started the Miami Latin Boys, a local band in Miami. He and Fajardo met, and she joined the band, which was renamed the Miami Sound Machine. In 1980, they had their first smash hit with "Bad Boy." But it was their next album and its huge hit "Conga" that firmly established them.

In New York, Ángela Bofill hit the charts with her first album, *Angie*, in 1978. Bofill inherited some of her musical talent from her Cuban father, who sang with Cuban bandleader "Machito" in the 1940s. Between 1978 and 1984, she had consistent success on the R&B charts as well as five albums making the Top 100 on the pop charts. Her hit singles included "Something about You," "Holding Out for Love," and "I'm on Your Side," which reached number twelve on the pop charts.

In 1981, jazz great **Paquito D'Rivera**, who had established himself in Cuba by the age of nineteen, sought asylum at the U.S. embassy while on tour in Spain. Upon his arrival in the United States, D'Rivera quickly earned respect among U.S. jazz musicians and has recorded many jazz albums.

The year 1989 saw the murder of Cuban-born executive José Menéndez by his sons Lyle and Erik. After successful stints at Coopers & Lybrand and Hertz Rent-a-Car, Menéndez had taken over RCA Records in 1981 and was responsible for signing the Eurythmics and Jefferson Starship to the label. By 1985, at the age of forty-one, he had become executive vice president and chief operating officer for their worldwide operations. At the time of his murder, he was the president of LIVE Entertainment. Two films and several books have been produced about his death.

The year 1990 saw more Cuban artists seeking asylum in the United States. Among them was **Arturo Sandoval** who, along with saxophonist Paquito D'Rivera and pianist **Chucho Valdés**, had co-founded **Grupo Irakere**, Cuba's most important jazz ensemble, in 1973. In 1990, while on tour with Dizzy Gillespie's United Nations Orchestra in Rome, Sandoval requested political asylum. Sandoval settled in Miami, became a professor at Florida International University and soon recorded his first U.S. album, *Flight of Freedom*.

In the late 1980s, Cuban-born **Jon Secada** met Gloria and Emilio Estefan and joined their Miami Sound Machine band. His debut album in 1992, *Just Another Day*, sold more than 6 million copies worldwide and scored a number-five pop hit. Secada, the Grammy Award–winning singer, has also written hit songs for Gloria Estefan, Ricky Martin, and Jennifer López and performed on the soundtracks of many major motion pictures.

In April 1993, Cuban country singer **Albita Rodríguez**, already famous internationally, was in Mexico when she went to the U.S. border and casually walked over the bridge into El Paso, Texas. Upon her arrival, many celebrities including Madonna, Rosie O'Donnell, and Sylvester Stallone were mesmerized by her vocal ability. Since then, Albita has recorded several albums and won a loyal following of both U.S. and Cuban American fans. One of those fans was Emilio Estefan, who quickly signed her to his record label. By the mid-1990s, the Estefans' business empire included a publishing house, artist management, recording studios, production facilities, and restaurant management. Their success had also inspired many young Cubans in south Florida. One of them was music producer Rudy Pérez. Born in Cuba, Pérez came to Miami with his parents and grew up in a housing project in Liberty City, one of Miami's predominantly black neighborhoods. He has produced such artists as José Feliciano, Plácido Domingo, Luis Miguel, Christina Aguilera, and Jaci Velásquez.

Further Readings

Fernández, Raúl A. "The Course of U.S. Cuban Music: Margin and Mainstream." *Cuban Studies* 24 (1994): 105–122.

Gerard, Charley. *Mongo Santamaría, Chocolate Armenteros, and Other Stateside Cuban Musicians*. Westport, CT: Praeger Publishers, 2001.

Ray Blanco

Valdés, Bebo (1918–)

Bebo Valdés was born in 1918 in the town of Quivicán, in **Havana Province**, where he studied piano at an early age. In 1936, he moved to the capital city, finishing his music studies. By 1940, he was a well-known pianist and arranger. From 1945 to 1947, he orchestrated music for conductor Julio Cuevas and his orchestra. His musical arrangements had the sound and rhythm of what later on would become the **mambo**; in fact, one of his own pieces, "Rareza del siglo" (1946), though dubbed a "montune beguine" was a mambo.

In 1952, Valdés recorded the first **descarga** (Cuban jam session) with his own sextet. He also developed a new musical genre known as the *batanga*. His musical group and arrangements were responsible

for launching the recording career of artists such as **Rolando Laserie**, Fernando Álvarez, and Celeste Mendoza. He became musical director of the legendary nightclub **Tropicana**, and after ten years, he took a similar position at the Hotel Seville Biltmore. Leaving Cuba in 1960 for Mexico, he then relocated to Spain. He partnered with Chilean singer Monna Bell, directing two of her long-play recordings and touring Europe with her. In 1962, he joined the Lecuona Cuban Boys orchestra and while on tour stayed in Stockholm, marrying for the second time. For thirty-three years he remained there, earning a living as a pianist at luxury hotels. In 1994, he emerged out of his long hibernation to record a CD with **Paquito D'Rivera**. Since then, he has completed several recordings, one with his son **Chucho Valdés**, and appeared in the recent film *Calle 54* (2000). *See also* Lecuona, Ernesto

Further Reading

D'Rivera, Paquito. "Un premio viviente llamado Bebo Valdés." *Latin Beat Magazine* (March 1997): 26.

Cristóbal Díaz Ayala and Marisa Méndez

Valdés, (Jesús) Chucho (1941–)

Chucho Valdés is a group director and pianist with a special ability to integrate styles as diverse as jazz, Afro-Cuban music, and European concert music. Born in Quivicán, **Havana Province**, in 1941, he soon began his musical training under the tutelage of his father, **Bebo Valdés**. At the age of four he made his first piano incursions, later mastering the instrument with Zenaida Romeu and Rosario Franco as his teachers. While still an adolescent, he formed his first jazz trio, and by the age of eighteen, he had already recorded with the RCA label. As its composer and pianist, he organized the Música Moderna orchestra in 1967. In his grandest composition,

Misa Criolla (1969), Valdés integrated elements from the traditions of jazz, European romantic music, and the dense tunes of the Afro-Cuban *tumbao*. He also demonstrated his mastery of improvisation. In 1973 Valdés founded the legendary **Grupo Irakere**, which brought together some of Cuba's finest jazz musicians. Through Irakere, Valdés perfected his mastery of the keyboard. Eventually he established himself as a soloist and, according to some, as the world's foremost jazz pianist. In 1979 his Grupo Irakere won a Grammy, and he won another one as a soloist in 2001 for his twelfth album, *Live at the Village. See also* Afro-Cuban Jazz

Edgardo Díaz Díaz

Valdés, Gilberto (1905–1972)

Noted for his contributions to classical as well as popular music, Gilberto Valdés is also the inventor of the *valdímbula*, an Afro-Cuban musical instrument. Valdés was born in the town of Jovellanos, **Matanzas Province**, in 1905. He began his formal musical education at age twelve when he entered the Conservatorio Peyrellade de **Cárdenas**. He later studied under Pedro San Juan in Havana, at the Conservatorio Raventos, and at schools in the United States.

In 1936, Valdés presented an innovative series of concerts that blended classical compositions with popular Afro-Cuban rhythms. Soprano singer **Rita Montaner** performed alongside many of the finest percussionists of the time.

From 1946 to 1957 Valdés served as director and composer of the Catherine Dunham ballet company, touring through much of Europe.

Further Reading
Salazar, Max. "La Descarga Cubana: The Beginning and its Best." *Latin Beat Magazine*, February 1997.

Luis González

Valdés, Miguelito (1912–1978)

Miguelito Valdés was the vocalist who first introduced the song "Babalú," which later became **Desi Arnaz's** trademark song. Valdés performed in nightclubs, on radio and television, and in film, working both in Cuba and the United States.

Valdés began to sing on the radio in his late teen years. His voice was soft and romantic, and his preference for love tunes made him a popular entertainer; he also performed danceable Afro-Cuban tunes. In 1936, Valdés joined the Orquesta los Hermanos Castro; in 1939, he and other band members left to form another orchestra, **Orquesta Casino de la Playa**, probably the most influential dance band in Cuba.

In 1940, Valdés moved to New York City to work in **Xavier Cugat**'s band. His looks and affable personality made him quite an attraction. He worked with other musicians, such as **Frank Grillo "Machito,"** and finally established his own group. His appearances in Hollywood films such as *Panamericano* (1942) and *Suspense* (1946) were restricted to musical numbers that usually served as background to the main story line.

Valdés also hosted Latin television shows produced by Spanish stations in the United States, and his renderings were always popular with the Spanish-speaking communities there.

Further Reading
Reyes, Luis, and Peter Rubie. *Hispanics in Hollywood: An Encyclopedia of Film and Television*. New York: Garland, 1994.

D.H. Figueredo

Van Van, Los

Formed in 1969, Los Van Van (literally, "the go go") is credited with creating the *songo* rhythm—a fusion of **son** with ritual Yoruba rhythms and American pop (see **Santería**). The group was founded by Juan

Formell, a bassist, composer, and arranger. Prior to forming the group, Formell played with Elio Reve's orchestra, a classic **charanga** band. Under Formell's direction, Reve's band became Changui-68. Shortly thereafter, he formed Los Van Van.

Los Van Van is said to be the first Cuban charanga to incorporate trombones, synthesizers, drum machines, and vocal trios. Members of the group include music veterans such as César "Pupi" Pedroso, a pianist who has been with the band since its inception, as well as younger talents like Samuel Formell, son of the group's founder. Los Van Van has performed at major music festivals throughout Europe, Japan, Mexico, Central and South America, and more recently, the United States.

Further Reading

Varela, Jesse. "Los Van Van." *Latin Beat Magazine* 11 (October 2001): 30.

Luis González

Vera, María Teresa (1895–1965)

Singer, guitarist, and composer María Teresa Vera is regarded as the most representative performer of Cuba's **vieja trova**; her interpretations of songs, such as her own composition "Veinte años," are classics of the genre.

Vera was born in Guanajay on February 6, 1895. Her first guitar teacher was José Díaz, a cigar worker. As a youth she and Rafael Zequeira formed a duo and recorded many records in New York City. After Zequeira's death in 1924, Vera continued singing on her own, pairing on and off with other singers. She organized and directed Sexteto Oriente in 1926 with Miguelito García, **Ignacio Piñeiro** and other musicians and recorded several *sones* (see **Son**). In 1935, she founded another duo. This time her companion was Lorenzo Hierrezuelo, and they worked together for twenty-seven years, performing on radio and other venues. From their partnership came the hits "Veinte años," "Yo quiero que tú sepas," "Por que me siento triste," and "No me sabes querer." Vera retired in 1962 and died in 1965, fondly remembered by her family and legions of fans.

Further Reading

Orovio, Helio. *Diccionario de la música cubana: biográfico y técnico*. Havana: Editorial Letras Cubanas, 1981.

Jesús Vega

Vieja Trova (Old Song)

The *vieja trova*, also known as the traditional trova, dates to the latter part of the nineteenth century, when urban, working-class troubadours gathered to play guitar and sing **criollas** and **guarachas** of their composition. These singers–songwriters engaged in serenades and street performances, as they were denied access to the musical spaces of high society. They played at friends' homes, barbershops, and cafés, on street corners, and at other public spaces, where they developed patriotic themes in a context of comradeship. Just like their Puerto Rican counterparts, Cuba's troubadours developed a distinctive style of two-voiced polyphony (each voice following a different text) in what is known as *contracanto*. Among the most salient practitioners of the vieja trova are Pepe Sánchez, Sindo Garay, Manuel Corona, Juan de la Cruz Echemendía, Alberto Villalón, and Eusebio Delfín. The vieja trova was most widely developed in the larger cities: Havana, **Santiago de Cuba, Sancti Spíritus**. Because of its collective and social character, the vieja trova has often been associated with more recent genres like the feeling (*filin*) and **nueva trova**.

Further Readings

Cañizares, Dulcila. *La trova tradicional*. Havana: Editorial Letras Cubanas, 1995.

León, Argeliers. "La canción y el bolero." In *Del canto y el tiempo*. Havana: Editorial Letras Cubanas, 1984. 185–232.

Edgardo Díaz Díaz

White, José (1836–1918)

A versatile musician, José White mastered sixteen different instruments, including the violin, the cello, the guitar, the piano, the base, the flute, and the trombone. He was also gifted in the areas of composition, timbre, and harmony. White's composition *La bella cubana* placed him in the company of the most important composers of the nineteenth century.

White was born in **Matanzas** on January 1, 1836. When he was fifteen years old, he composed the mass *Misa para dos voces y orquesta*. Four years later, he made his first appearance as concert violinist, accompanied by Gottschalk. In 1855, he enrolled at the Paris Conservatory with the objective of improving his performance as a violinist and perfecting his knowledge of harmony and composition. The following year, he received the Primer Violín Prize from the conservatory.

White taught at the conservatory, made himself a name as violinist, and journeyed back and forth to Cuba. In 1875, while on the island, he found himself accused of conspiring against the Spanish authorities. He then traveled to Venezuela, Brazil, and several other countries before returning to Paris in 1888. He never left France again, composing numerous pieces for the violin, his favored instrument, including a concert for violin and orchestra. He died in Paris on March 12, 1918.

Further Readings

Carpentier, Alejo. *La música en Cuba*. Mexico City: Fondo de Cultura Económica, 1993.

Orovio, Helio. *Diccionario de la música cubana: biográfico y técnico*. Havana: Editorial Letras Cubanas, 1981.

Jesús Vega

Zarzuela

The arrival of the *zarzuela* to Cuba, a form of musical drama originating in Spain, can be traced to 1853 with the establishment of a theater company by José Robreño and José Freixas. Some of the first zarzuelas performed in Cuba debuted at the Gran Teatro de La Habana, known at the time as the Teatro Tacón. Among the works that premiered there were *El duende, La castañera, El tío caniyita, El grumete y la estrella de Madrid*, and *Todos los locos o ninguno*, the first zarzuela written in Cuba. Cuban artists adapted and redefined the zarzuela, and one of the breakthrough works in this regard was *Niña Rita o La Habana de 1830*, which was written by Aurelio G. Riancho and Antonio Castells with music by **Ernesto Lecuona** and **Eliseo Grenet**. This Cuban zarzuela premiered in 1927 at the Teatro Regina. Prior to that, artists such as **Jorge Ankermann** experimented with the zarzuela format. Lecuona, **Gonzalo Roig**, and Rodrigo Prats redefined the zarzuela in Cuban terms and created an important body of work. Among the classic works composed by Lecuona were *El cafetal, María la O, La tierra de Venus, Rosa la china, Lola Cruz, Sor Inés, El maizal, Julián el gallo, El torrente*, and *La Plaza de la Catedral*. The works by Roig include *Perlas, La hija del sol, La guayabera, El clarín*, and his most renowned work, *Cecilia Valdés*, based on the nineteenth-century Cuban novel. Prats composed *Soldedad, María Belén Chacón, La Habana que vuelve*, and *Amalia Batista*. In an effort to preserve this lyrical tradition, an organization was established in 1962 to promote and plan performances of the best-known national and international works. Since 1970, the organization bears the name of Gonzalo Roig. Meanwhile, Cubans abroad have established the Sociedad Pro Arte Getelli (Miami) and Pro Arte Lírico (San Juan) to produce zarzuelas.

Further Readings

Comedia lírica de Cuba Gonzalo Roig: tradición y universalidad. Havana, Ministerio de Cultura, Impr. de la Dirección de Información, 1989.

Molina, Antonio J. *150 años de zarzuela en Puerto Rico y Cuba*. San Juan: A.J. Molina, 1998.

Araceli García Carranza

9

The Plastic Arts

Abela Alonso, Eduardo (1889–1965)

Eduardo Abela was one of the pioneers of the modernist movement in Cuban art and one of its foremost caricaturists. He graduated from Havana's **San Alejandro Academy of Fine Arts** in 1921 and continued his artistic formation in Madrid, from 1921 to 1924, and Paris, from 1927 to 1929. His Parisian stay culminated with an exhibition at the Galerie Zak, which paintings and drawings, such as *Triunfo de la rumba* (ca. 1928), represent one of the earliest expressions of Afro-Cuban popular culture in Cuban modern art (see **Afro-Cubans**). Abela turned to political and social cartooning from 1929 to 1933, inventing the character El Bobo, which appeared in the pages of *El Diario de la Marina* nationwide. In the late 1930s he returned to painting, concentrating on a naturalistic yet idealized representation of the Cuban peasant and the countryside, as seen in his best-known work of that time, *Los Guajiros* (1938). In the 1940s and early 1950s, he served as Cuba's cultural attaché to Mexico, Guatemala, and the UNESCO (United Nations Educational, Scientific, and Cultural Organization) in France, returning full time to painting in 1955. In

Los Guajiros (*Peasants*) by Eduardo Abela (1938) oil on canvas. Courtesy of the Museo Nacional de Bellas Artes, Havana.

the late and most productive phase of his artistic career, the last decade of his life, he developed a mild expressionistic language to create a poetic and magical world, where children and animals usually reign. Abela began to exhibit regularly in Havana in 1919 and won purchase awards in the National Exhibition of Painting and Sculpture of 1938 and 1956. His paintings are found in private and public collections in Cuba and the United States, including the **National Museum of Fine Arts** in Havana. *See also* Newspapers (Republican Era)

Further Readings

Oraá, Pedro de. *Abela: dibujos de Eduardo Abela.* Havana: UNEAC, 1987.

Seoane Gallo, José. *Eduardo Abela, cerca del cerco.* Havana: Editorial Letras Cubanas, 1986.

Juan A. Martínez

Acosta León, Ángel (1930–1964)

Ángel Acosta León's paintings represent an adaptation and synthesis of the Surrealist aesthetic to a Cuban ethos. Born into a working-class family, Acosta León's father was a barber who encouraged his son's artistic talents. In order to support his art studies, Acosta León worked first as an auto body shop specialist and later as a bus driver. He studied painting and sculpture at the **San Alejandro Academy of Fine Arts** and graduated at the top of his class (1956), earning a traveling scholarship to visit Europe. Acosta León received awards in exhibitions at the Círculo de Bellas Artes (1958 and 1959) and the Salón Nacional (1959). In 1960, as part of an award for a poster contest, the Cuban National Institute of **Tourism** granted him a travel scholarship to Paris. In Paris he became the protégé of the Chilean Surrealist painter Roberto Matta. Acosta León's early work is in a style reminiscent of both Paul Klee and Joan Miró. His mature style (1959–1964) is brooding, transforming toys, coffeepots, and carriages into sinister objects. His preferred media were oil, on either cardboard or canvas, and ink and watercolor. Acosta León had solo exhibitions in the Galería de Bellas Artes in Havana (1960); in **Casa de las Américas**

(1961); and in major galleries in both Paris and Amsterdam (1963). In 1964, due to his active homosexual life and outspoken criticism of the Cuban government, he was recalled to the island (see **Gays and Lesbians**). En route home by ship, Acosta León committed suicide by drowning off the Havana Bay.

Further Reading

Hurtado, Oscar, and Edmundo Desnoes. *Pintores cubanos.* Havana: Ediciones R, 1962.

Alejandro Anreus

Alfonzo, Carlos José (1950–1991)

Carlos José Alfonzo was a neoexpressionist painter known in Cuba for developing a fable-based expressionist mode of painting. Born in 1950 in Havana, he studied painting in 1974 at the **San Alejandro Academy of Fine Arts** and the **University of Havana**. Early-twentieth-century avant-garde Cuban artist **Wifredo Lam** influenced his work. Alfonzo left the island in 1980 via Key West, Florida (see **Mariel Boatlift**). In 1981 he moved to Miami where he took permanent residence. In recognition of his aesthetic focus, the U.S. National Endowment for the Arts awarded him a fellowship in 1984. The following year he received a second fellowship from the Cintas Foundation to create a mural for the Miami-Dade Public Library System in Florida. Throughout his career he had numerous exhibitions in Spain, Cuba, and the United States. The exhibition that brought him national attention was the *Hispanic Art in the United States: Thirty Contemporary Painters and Sculptors* (1987), developed by the Corcoran Gallery in Washington, D.C., in partnership with the Houston Museum of Art in Texas. Alfonzo remained a painter throughout his life, exploring new abstract forms until his death from **AIDS** in 1991. *See also* Mariel Generation

Further Readings

Fuentes-Pérez, Ileana, Graciella Cruz-Taura, and Ricardo Pau-Llosa, eds. *Outside Cuba: Contemporary Cuban Visual Artists*. New Brunswick, NJ: Rutgers University Press, 1989.

Sullivan, Edward J. *Latin American Art in the 20th Century*. London: Phaidon Press Limited, 1996.

Viso, Olga, et al. *Triumph of the Spirit: Carlos Alfonzo, a Survey, 1975–1991*. Miami: Miami Art Museum, 1998.

Isabel Nazario

Architecture (Colonial Era)

The pre-Columbian antecedents of Cuba's colonial architecture were the board and palm-thatched houses used by the island's **indigenous inhabitants**. The two main variants of these houses were the circular *caney* used by chiefs and other members of the native elite and the rectangular *bohíos* of the common folk. Beginning in the 1500s, Spanish architectural elements, with strong Moorish influence, were imported by colonists and adapted and transcultured according to local **climate**, geographic conditions, and available building materials.

Students of Cuba's architectural history have periodized it into three chronological phases: a formative period (sixteenth and seventeenth centuries); a period of development of its essential characteristics (eighteenth century); and a classic period (nineteenth century), during which the so-called tropical architecture took root in **housing** structures as well as in industrial buildings (e.g., cigar factories) and military structures.

First in **Baracoa** and later in the island's other **early colonial settlements**, Spanish colonists laid out the basic elements of urbanization, namely the central town square and the urban gridiron. The first cathedral was erected in **Santiago de Cuba**, see of the island's bishopric. The cathedral buildings at this site have been destroyed repeatedly by fires and other disasters, so the current cathedral of Santi-

ago is of much more recent construction. Fortifications fashioned after Renaissance castles were also erected early on at strategic locations on or near the first villages.

As Havana gained preeminence within the colonial enterprise as the island's capital and major port, fortifications were built to protect it from foreign aggression (see **Corsairs Attacks** and **Fortifications of Havana**). These included the Castle of la Real Fuerza (1582) and the Tres Reyes del **Morro Castle** and San Salvador de la Punta Fort, the latter two completed in 1610. Church edifices such as parish churches and convents of the religious orders were also built at the time in Havana, Santiago, and Puerto Príncipe (**Camagüey**). These religious orders' buildings regularly consisted of thick rock walls with few outside windows that were crowned with intricate wood-beam ceilings, called *alfarjes,* and ceramic-tile roofs. Convents were built with atriums that were surrounded by covered galleries sustained by columned arches. Those typical indoor galleries were transplanted outdoors in later buildings, and beginning in the mid-nineteenth century they became one of the most emblematic architectural features of Havana and other Cuban cities; thus, Havana has been dubbed "la ciudad de la columnas" (city of columns).

Because of its protagonist role within the colony, Havana developed a unique style of architecture and urban design. As the coveted point of convergence of trade convoys (see **Trade and Navigation [1500s–1800s]**), Havana required an effective defensive network consisting of forts, fortified towers, and a defensive wall (completed in 1740). A host of distinguished military engineers labored over centuries to provide Havana with the necessary fortifications. Among these were the Italian Juan Bautista Antonelli, the Spaniards Juan de Ciscara and Francisco de Calona, and the Creoles Francisco de Calona (son) and Francisco Pérez.

During the first half of the eighteenth century, Havana's famed shipyards were built next to the bay and not far from the city walls. Other notable manifestations of the period's industrial architecture were the Real Factoría de Tabacos (Royal Cigar Factory) and the building complexes of the **sugar plantations** that increasingly dotted the hinterland. Resulting from the accumulation of agricultural and commercial wealth, an affluent class emerged with newly purchased titles of nobility, built palatial homes, and adorned them with coats of arms, frescoed walls and ceilings, and lavish furnishings. Typically, such mansions consisted of a lower level with storage spaces, carriage garages, and an interior patio with cisterns surrounded by a colonnaded gallery. An intermediate level included office space as well as the quarters of domestic servants, many of them slaves. The upper level included the living quarters of the mansion's owners and areas for socializing and entertaining. Among the notable examples of such seignorial homes were those of the counts of Jaruco and Casa Bayona.

Originally intended to serve as the church of the neighboring Jesuit San Carlos Seminary, the **Cathedral of Havana** is considered the island's most important baroque building. The **Palace of the Captains-General** and the Palace of el Segundo Cabo, flanking the nearby Plaza de Armas, are the finest examples of baroque public buildings of the eighteenth century.

The dramatic social, political, and economic changes of the nineteenth century were reflected in Cuba's urban and architectural development. Cities were modernized and further attention was paid to planning and sanitation and public works. Urban facades renounced the earlier heavy baroque ornamentation as simpler neoclassical lines began to predominate. As Havana's **population** pushed into the suburbs, new spacious homes were built in El Cerro, Marianao, and El Vedado. In 1863 demolition work began on Havana's confining walls. The old Espada Cemetery exemplified new standards of public hygiene. Its successor, Cementerio Cristóbal Colón (**Columbus Cemetery**), built between 1871 and 1886 to accommodate increasing demographic pressures, stood out as Havana's most monumental public work of the period. A new aqueduct to meet increasing water consumption levels was completed under the direction of Francisco Fernández de Albear in 1893. He was the first to employ concrete in Cuban architecture, mixing it with cement imported from the United States. New terminals were built for **railroads** and horse-drawn buses, and new markets were erected with prefabricated iron components that were imported or locally manufactured. Beginning in 1878 stricter building codes were implemented that aligned the facades of new urban constructions. These measures were greatly influenced by the Catalan urban planner Ildefons Cerdá. At the time, the architectural profession was separated from that of civil and military engineering, and the Professional School of Contractors and Surveyors began in 1871.

The austerity of nineteenth-century neoclassical architecture manifested itself primarily on exteriors. The interiors of the new mansions, meanwhile, were enriched by interior and lateral patios surrounded by columned galleries, as exemplified in the **Palace of Aldama** and the mansion of de Count of Moré. The mansions of the period reflect their adaptation to local light and climate through the use of a multitude of architectural features: high ceilings (between 4.5 and 5 meters); *celosías* (intricate lattice-work screens) for balconies and the use of door-windows providing extra protection from heavy rains and storms; *mediopuntos* (semicircular tinted-glass *vitrales*); *mámparas* (movable wooden screens); forged-iron gates for security; and the *zaguanes* (covered vestibules). Havana's humblest residents, meanwhile,

Interior patio of the Convent of los Escolapios, Guanabacoa. Photograph by Jorge B. Figueroa. Courtesy of La Galería del Medio, Miami.

inhabited the *solares* (crowded tenements), which followed the general format of the slaves' *barracones*. The finest example of the neoclassical style in a religious building was **El Templete**, built on the Plaza de Armas to commemorate Havana's first Catholic Mass.

Much of Cuba's, particularly Havana's, colonial architectural legacy remains standing thanks to ongoing preservation efforts led by the Office of the City Historian (see **Eusebio Leal Spengler**). In recognition of its valuable architectural heritage, Havana has been declared Humanity's Heritage Site by the United Nations Educational Scientific and Cultural Organization.

Further Readings

Carley, Rachel, and Andrea Brizzi (photographer). *Cuba: Four Hundred Years of Architectural Heritage*. New York: Whiteny Library of Design, 2000.
Carpentier, Alejo. *La ciudad de las columnas*. Havana: Editorial Letras Cubanas, 1982.
Weiss, Joaquín E. *La arquitectura colonial cubana (siglos XVI al XIX)*. Havana and Sevilla: Instituto Cubano del Libro and Junta de Andalucía, 1996.

Lohania J. Aruca Alonso

Architecture (Twentieth Century)

The evolution of Cuba's architecture during the twentieth century is usually divided into two chronological periods: the Republican Era (1902–1958) and the Revolutionary Era (1959–   ).

A military decree of April 1900 during the U.S. occupation of Cuba established the School of Engineering and Architecture of the **University of Havana**. Among the distinguished architects and engineers associated with that school and with the Academy of Arts and Letters were architects Félix Cabarroca Ayala, Eugenio Dediot, Evelio Govantes Fuertes, Pedro Martínez Inclán, Leonardo Morales y Pedroso, and Joaquín Weiss y Sánchez (the first historian of Cuban architecture), and civil engineers Enrique J. Montolieu y de la Torre and Juan A. Cosculluela y Barreras, to name but a few. Cuban architecture during the Republican era, Havana's in particular, was increasingly influenced by developments in U.S. architecture and engineering, something that was already evident during the colonial era.

Architectural eclecticism dominated Cuban architecture during the first decades of the twentieth century. Among the most notable public buildings that are examples of this style are the **Capitol Building** (1928; now building of the Academy of Sciences); the Centro Asturiano (1927), designed by Spanish architect Manuel del Busto and erected by the U.S. firm Purdy and Henderson; and the Art Deco skyscrapers, Bacardí Building (1930) (see **Bacardí Family**), López Serrano apartment building (1932), and the América Building, all designed by Cuban architects. Later hotel buildings reflective of the new international style were represented by the Habana Hilton (1955–1958; today Habana Libre) and the Habana Riviera (1957–1958), both built by U.S. architectural firms but incorporating artistic and technical features by Cuban artists **Amelia Peláez** and **René Portocarrero** (see **Tourism**).

Housing architecture during the Republican era reflected Cuba's social stratification, as it spanned the range from the palatial homes of the Condesa de Revilla Amargo (today Museum of Decorative Arts), the del Valle Palace in **Cienfuegos**, and the award-winning house of Cueto de la Noval, to middle-class apartment buildings and suburban homes, to working-class developments such as Lutgardita, Barrio Obrero, and Pogolotti, to the poorer classes' urban *solares* (tenements), improvised slums, and rural *bohíos*. Among the salient developments in housing architecture during the 1940s and 1950s were several notable condominiums or apartment buildings, such as SolyMar (1944) by Manuel Copado and the FOCSA building designed by Ernesto Gómez Sampera.

Among the period's significant educational buildings are the University of Havana, with its famous stairway built in 1927 and its Library Building designed by Weiss y Sánchez (1936-1937), and the Catholic University of Santo Tomás de Villanueva in Miramar, whose laboratory facilities were the island's first prefabricated concrete structure. Hospital buildings were also concentrated in and around Havana, among them the **Carlos J. Finlay** Military Hospital in Marianao (1943) by the architect José A. Pérez Benitoa. Other notable hospital Art Deco structures were the América Arias Maternity Hospital, the Workers' Maternity Hospital in Marianao, and the Municipal Children's Hospital (today Pedro Barras) in El Vedado.

Recreational architecture had among its salient manifestations the social beach clubs of Marianao, such as the Havana Yacht Club; Havana's many movie houses; the innovative architectural elements of the **Tropicana Nightclub**, emblematic of the Havana of the 1950s; and the Coliseum of Ciudad Deportiva (1952–1956).

The triumph of the **Revolution** in 1959 brought both new challenges and new priorities that shifted the course of Cuba's architecture; affordable housing became a pressing issue in a context marked by the sudden exile most of Cuba's architects and the imposition of a **trade embargo** by the United States. Thus, the training of new architects and civil engineers became a pressing educational concern (see **Educational System**). A new generation of architects and engineers was soon trained at the new Colegio Universitario **José Antonio Echeverría** (CUJAE). Meanwhile, some formerly exiled architects, such as Ricardo Porro, returned to Cuba and were joined by foreign architects who arrived on the island after the Revolution, such as Walter Betancourt (North American), Sergio Baroni and Roberto Gottardi (Italians), and Roberto Segre (Argentine). Other prominent architects of the early years of the Revolution were Antonio Quintana, Joaquín Galván, Mario Girona, Mario González Sedeño, and Raúl González Romero.

Since 1959 Cuban architecture has responded to state planning and has been carried out by collective work units. It has made extensive use of prefabricated systems and standardized models to fill social demand for rural homes, schools and universities, rural hospitals, clinics, and factories. Some of the most notable architectural results of the 1960s were small rural housing developments like Las Terrazas in Cayajabo, designed by Osmany Cienfuegos, and the Ciudad Escolar **Camilo Cienfuegos** in the **Sierra Maestra**. In Havana, meanwhile, a huge complex of high-rise apartment buildings known as La Habana del Este exemplified the use of simple forms and small spaces in harmony

View from el Malecón, Havana 1958, including FOCSA, Somellán, and López Serrano buildings and the *Maine* Monument in the foreground. Photograph by Alfredo Rey. Courtesy of La Galería del Medio, Miami.

with local climatic conditions. This massive project brought together the expertise of Roberto Carranza, Reynaldo Estévez, Eduardo Rodríguez, Mercedes Álvarez, Mario González, and Hugo Dacosta. The expansion of school building architecture during the 1970s was tied to the government's desire to link educational and productive endeavors and was heavily influenced by the former German Democratic Republic's Bauhaus de Weimar. Prominent in these efforts were the Cuban architects and urban planners Elmer López, Segio Ferro, Enrique Fornés, Modesto Campos, Josefina Rebellón, Mario Coyula Cowley, Gina Rey, Enrique Fernández, and Edmundo Azze.

The fall of the Soviet Union and Europe's socialist governments and the ad-

vent of the **Special Period** in Cuba in the early 1990s stimulated a shift in architectural and construction efforts toward the tourist industry. Previous works of tourist architecture, like the Hotel Santiago in **Santiago de Cuba** by José Antonio Choy, had successfully combined postmodern volumetric forms and bright primary colors, gleaming under eastern Cuba's intense sun. Also related to the growth in the tourist industry were projects like the Terminal Three of the **José Martí** International Airport, restaurant facilities, marketplaces, and numerous luxury hotels, like Havana's Cohiba and others in the capital city, in Varadero Beach, and on the island's surrounding **keys**.

Presently, efforts continue for the integral development of Cuban architecture, including its manifold economic, scientific, and cultural goals and reflecting the need for optimal use of space as well as human and **energy** resources.

Further Readings

Carley, Rachel and Andrea Brizzi (photographer). *Cuba: Four Hundred Years of Architectural Heritage*. New York: Whitney Library of Design, 1997.

Carpentier, Alejo. *La ciudad de las columnas*. Havana: Editorial Letras Cubanas, 1982.

Segre, Roberto. *La vivienda en Cuba en el siglo XX: República y Revolución*. Mexico City: Editorial Concepto, 1980.

Segre, Roberto, Eliana Cárdenas, and Lohania Aruca. *Historia de la arquitectura y del urbanismo: América Latina y Cuba*. Havana: Editorial EMPES, 1981.

Lohania J. Aruca Alonso

Ayón Manso, Belkis (1967–1999)

Born in Havana, **Afro-Cuban** artist Belkis Ayón Manso studied at the **San Alejandro Academy of Fine Arts** (1982–1986) and the Instituto Superior de Arte (ISA) in Havana. Although she graduated in 1991, Ayón took part in many international exhibitions as early as 1986. She was the only artist to concentrate on the Afro-Cuban **Sociedad de Abakuá**, and she remained faithful to this theme throughout her artistic career. She researched the topic very thoroughly and invented her own iconography to reinterpret the mythological origins, characters, symbols, and rituals of the society. Her artistic discourse related in a personal way with Sikán, the female figure associated with the origins of the society, and she utilized her own body as the model for Sikán in highly intricate and complex compositions to reflect her personal vision and sense of identity. Ayón's name became synonymous with engraving, as a pioneering and exceptional printmaker who created a unique and innovative technique in the form of large-scale polychrome collographs. These were composed of alternative engraving materials that Ayón utilized due to the severe shortages of traditional printmaking materials available in Cuba. Her specific printing technique and the use of multifarious visual devices and syncretic Abakuá and Christian religious iconography also helped her achieve a sense of mysteriousness that is intimately associated with the Abakuá society itself. At the time of her tragic suicide in September 1999 in Havana, Ayón was the head of the division of the visual arts at the **Unión de Escritores y Artistas de Cuba (UNEAC)** and a highly respected professor of printmaking at San Alejandro and the ISA.

Further Readings

Mateo, David. In *Siempre vuelvo. Grabados de Belkis Ayón*. Havana: Centro Provincial. de Artes Plásticas y Diseño, November 1993.

Mosquera, Gerardo. "Elegguá at the (Post?) Modern Crossroads." In *Santería Aesthetics in Contemporary Latin American Art*, ed. A. Lindsay. Washington, DC: Smithsonian Institution Press, 1996. 225–258.

Valdés Figueroa, Eugenio. *Belkis Ayón: The Revelation of a Secret*. Havana: Centro Wifredo Lam, 1991.

Jo-Ann Van Eyck

Bedía, José (1959–)

José Bedía is one of the leading and most influential contemporary Cuban artists and was an integral figure in the groundbreaking "First 1980s generation," taking part in the *Volumen 1* exhibition (1981) and many other important group and solo exhibitions. Born in Havana, of white, working-class origin, he attended the **San Alejandro Academy of Fine Arts** and the Instituto Superior de Arte (ISA) in Havana, graduating in 1981. He became a professor at the ISA after graduating, working with important future artists and art generations. Bedía has an interest in primitive cultures and has drawn on Cuba's transcultural heritage of Afro-Cuban,

Amerindian, and African traditions in his creative projects. His art production reflects the development from his ethnographic approach in the early 1980s to a more personalized expression of Afro-Cuban and Amerindian cosmologies and traditions. He was initiated into **Palo Monte** in 1984, and his art is based on the beliefs and practices of Palo Monte, **Santería**, and Sioux religiosity. His is a conceptual and analytical approach, based in ritual and the power and narratives of these cultures, especially *palero* myths. In a complex codification of everyday materials and techniques, Bedía articulates his own discourse through his trademark pictographic style that includes stylized and silhouetted figures, as in his 1989 installation, *¿Qué te han hecho Mama Kalunga?* His work has evolved from two-dimensional works and drawings to mixed-media installations, and he was a prizewinner at the Havana *Salón Paisaje '82* (1982) and the *2nd Havana Biennial* (1986). He has resided in Miami since 1991. *See also* Afro-Cubans; Indigenous Inhabitants

Further Readings

Lippard, Lucy R. "Made in the U.S.A.: Art from Cuba." *Art in America* (April 1986): 27–35.

Murphy, Jay. "The Young and the Restless in Habana." *Third Text* 20 (Autumn 1992): 115–132.

Sánchez, Osvaldo. "José Bedía: Restoring Our Otherness." *Third Text* 13 (Winter 1991): 63–72.

Jo-Ann Van Eyck

Bermúdez, Cundo (1914–)

Cundo Bermúdez, a painter and graphic artist, is one of the outstanding second-generation (1940s) Cuban modernist artists, known for his strongly chromatic representation of everyday scenes and of musicians. His formal artistic education was minimal; Bermúdez attended Havana's **San Alejandro Academy of Fine Arts** for one year in 1927 and took drawing courses in Mexico City for another year in 1938. In the next decade, Bermú-dez developed his "naive" figurative style of contour lines, extraordinarily high-pitch color, and idyllic view of ordinary life, as seen in *La barbería* and *El billar*, both of 1943. In the 1950s and 1960s, he concentrated on the theme of popular music expressed in a more abstract visual language, such as *Trío* (1960). He moved to San Juan, Puerto Rico, in 1968, and since the 1970s Bermúdez has pushed his style further toward decorative and colorful figurative compositions. Besides easel painting, he has designed murals in Havana (1958), San Juan (1970), Washington, D.C. (1983), and Miami (2000). He is also known for his graphic work in serigraphy, which he began to practice in 1970. Bermúdez began to exhibit regularly in Havana in 1937 and since the mid-1940s has exhibited throughout the Americas, including the São Paulo Biennial of 1956. That year he was also awarded first prize at the Caribbean International Exhibition, held in the Museum of Fine Arts of Houston, Texas. Bermúdez's paintings are found in private and public collections in Cuba and the United States, including the **National Museum of Fine Arts** in Havana and the Museum of Modern Art in New York. *See also* Puerto Rico, Cubans in

Further Readings

Gómez Sicre, José. "On Cundo's Barbershop." *Magazine of Arts* (February 1944).

Luis, Carlos M. *Cundo Bermúdez. Un homenaje.* Miami: Cuban Museum of Art and Culture, 1987. Bilingual exhibition catalog.

Pau-Llosa, Ricardo. *Cundo Bermúdez. Obras recientes.* Caracas: Galería Durban, 1991. Bilingual exhibition catalog.

Juan A. Martínez

Cabrera Moreno, Servando (1923–1981)

An eclectic painter in matters of style, Servando Cabrera Moreno was nevertheless a technical virtuoso within the history of contemporary Cuban painting. Born in Havana to a middle-class family, Cabrera Moreno attended and graduated from the **San Alejandro Academy of Fine Arts**, where he was among the last generation of artists to receive instruction from the painter **Leopoldo Romañach**. After graduating from the academy, he traveled to New York City, where he continued his studies at the Art Students League of New York. Throughout the late 1940s Cabrera Moreno traveled in Europe, residing in Spain for a number of years. His paintings from the late 1940s reflect a concern with a volumetric depiction of the figure, together with a preference for *chiaroscuro* reminiscent of the work of **Fidelio Ponce**. By the late 1950s his work was stylistically divided between the influence of Picasso (*Los héroes bajo el sol, Las damas de Buenavista*) and a series of grotesque nudes influenced by the paintings of Willem de Kooning and Jean Dubuffett. Starting in 1943, Cabrera Moreno had solo exhibitions at the Galerie La Rue in Paris, the Pan American Union in Washington, D.C., and the Lyceum in Havana. Cabrera Moreno's paintings represented Cuba at the 4th, 5th, and 6th São Paulo Biennials, and he received the silver medal at the Joan Miró International Drawing Exhibition in Barcelona. By the early 1960s Cabrera Moreno had found his mature style—a synthesis of sculptural, monumental drawing with a deep and vibrant color scheme consisting of layers of glazes of color. He would work in this manner until his death. Cabrera Moreno's favored subjects for his paintings were **guajiros**, *milicianos* (militia men), and *guerilleros* (guerilla fighters), as well as homoerotic fantasy. In the early 1970s he was fired from his teaching position at Cubanacán (Instituto Superior de Artes) due to his homosexual orientation (see **Gays and Lesbians**). By the mid-1970s, due to the support of Cuba's foreign minister **Raúl Roa**, who was a collector of Cabrera Moreno's work, the artist was rehabilitated in official circles. After this rehabilitation,

Cabrera Moreno enjoyed governmental support until his death from heart failure in 1981.

Further Reading

Mosquera, Gerardo. "Servando Cabrera Moreno: toda la pintura." *Revolución y Cultura*, no. 59 (July 1977): 44–59.

Alejandro Anreus

Capitol Building (Capitolio, El)

The Capitol Building (Capitolio) is one of the most recognized buildings in the urban landscape of Havana. It was built on the site of the former Villanueva train station in what was previously known as the "Ring" of Havana. The Capitol sits on a strip of land that once contained a rampart of the old city's walls. Construction on the Capitol was a long and painful process, typified by delays and numerous modifications. When construction began in 1910 it was to be the **presidential palace**. It was not completed until 1929 as part of a beautification project for Havana promoted by President **Gerardo Machado** and Public Works Secretary Carlos Miguel de Céspedes. Among the architects who took part in the project were Raúl Otero, Evelio Govantes, Félix Cabarrocas, Eugenio Rayneri Piedra, and José María Bens Árrarte. The gardens were designed by French landscape artist Jean Claude Nicolas Forestier.

The Capitol Building consists of a central portion crowned by a cupola more than 90 meters (295 feet) in height. Two horizontal wings jut out from the building's center, one side containing the Senate chamber and the other the chamber for the House of Representatives. Among the most remarkable features are the Salón de los Pasos Perdidos (Hall of Lost Steps) and a statue of the Republic, created by Angelo Zanelli. On the marble floor of the Capitol, below the cupola, is embedded a large Tiffany diamond symbolically representing "mile marker zero" for all the nation's roads. The Capitol was inaugurated on May 20, 1929. In 1939–1940, it served as the venue where the **Constitution of 1940** was drawn up. After the **Revolution**, the Capitol ceased to serve its previous legislative roles, becoming the site of the **Academy of Sciences**. Please see color insert in Volume I for photograph. *See also* Architecture (Twentieth Century); Fortifications of Havana

Further Reading

Rodríguez, Eduardo Luis. *La Habana. Arquitectura del siglo XX*. Barcelona: Blume, 1998.

Emma Álvarez-Tabío Albo

Cárdenas, Agustín (1927–2001)

An organic Surrealist, Agustín Cárdenas was one of Cuba's leading sculptors. An Afro-Cuban born in **Matanzas**, Cárdenas studied and graduated from the **San Alejandro Academy of Fine Arts**. At the academy he worked under the sculptor **Juan José Sicre**. In the early 1950s Cárdenas was a member of Los Once, a group of artists who opposed formal art training and favored an Abstract Expressionist aesthetic. Both the paintings of **Wifredo Lam** and the sculpture of Jean Arp influenced Cárdenas's early work. In 1955 Cárdenas settled in Paris. Throughout the 1950s Cárdenas's sculptures consisted of vertical and angular totems inspired by the forms of African art, particularly Dogon sculpture. In Paris, Cárdenas associated with André Breton and the surviving Surrealists. He exhibited with the Réalités Nouvelles group from the late 1950s to 1965. Throughout the 1960s Cárdenas focused on large carved sculptures in the media of stone and wood. Thematically these sculptures made reference to Afro-Cuban culture, **Santería** in particular (see **Afro-Cubans**). In 1963 he began to spend summers in Carrara, Italy. Cárdenas vis-

ited Cuba in 1967, and in 1968 he moved his studio and home from Paris to Meudon, France. The Museo de Bellas Artes in Venezuela presented a retrospective exhibition of his work in 1982. From 1996, when he was diagnosed with Alzheimer's, Cárdenas lived in a sanatorium on the outskirts of Havana till his death in 2001.

Further Reading

Museo de Bellas Artes. *Agustín Cárdenas: esculturas 1957–1981*. Caracas: Museo de Bellas Artes, 1982.

Alejandro Anreus

Carreño, Mario (1913–2000)

Painter Mario Carreño is one of the outstanding artists of the 1940s generation, known for his prolific production and stylistic variations. He began his artistic career as an illustrator in Havana and Madrid in the early 1930s, when he signed "Karreño," to express his leftist political ideology. In 1936 he turned his full attention to painting, while living in Mexico City and under the influence of the Mexican Muralist movement. Later in Paris (1938–1939) and New York (1940), Carreño developed a Neoclassical style adapted from Renaissance sources to represent American subject matter, such as *El nacimiento de las naciones americanas*. Carreño emerged as a mature artist in the 1940s, when he divided his time between New York and Havana. He moved away from Neoclassicism and toward Expressionism as a more suitable language to express Cuban themes, such as *Ciclón* of 1941 and *Patio colonial* of 1943. In the 1950s, Carreño leaped into hard-edge abstraction with emphasis on minimal geometric forms and pulsating rhythms. He moved to Santiago de Chile in 1957, where he spent the rest of his life, continuing to develop new subjects and artistic languages. In the 1980s and 1990s he returned to Caribbean subjects depicted in elegant reductive forms, such as *Noche de cocodrilos* of

1985. Carreño played a significant role in the development of Cuban modern art as well as Chilean contemporary art and is today recognized as a transcendent figure in twentieth-century Latin American painting. His paintings are found in numerous private and public collections in Cuba, the United States, and Chile, including the **National Museum of Fine Arts** in Havana and the Museum of Modern Art in New York.

Further Readings

Carreño, Mario. *Cronología del recuerdo.* Santiago de Chile: Ed. Antártica, S.A., 1991.

Ellena, Emilio. *Mario Carreño: 80 dibujos.* Santiago de Chile: Corporación Cultural de Los Condes, 1993. Exhibition catalog.

Gómez Sicre, José. *Cuadernos de la plástica cubana I—Carreño.* Havana: Ediciones Galería del Prado, 1943.

Juan A. Martínez

Cathedral of Havana (Catedral de La Habana)

Cathedral of Havana, built between 1748 and 1777. Photograph by Celestino Martínez Lindín.

The Cathedral of Havana is the most significant example of Cuban baroque architecture and a symbol of the colonial period. The facade of the Cathedral incorporates many elements of the baroque school in surprising fashion. The undulating wall, the uneven cornices, and the magnification of certain decorative motifs are among the elements that provide the facade with complexity and charm. The delicate design, attributed to Pedro de Medina, stands out because the facade is framed by two austere towers of different widths.

Situated on one side of the ancient Plaza de la Ciénaga, construction on the Cathedral began in 1748. It was originally to be the church of the Jesuits. However, construction was interrupted in 1767 because of the religious order's expulsion from the Spanish colonies. Construction resumed by royal order in 1772, with the goal of converting it into the city's primary church. Finally completed in 1777, it was designated a cathedral in 1788 with the establishment of the Diocese of Havana.

In the nineteenth century the interior of the Cathedral was greatly modified with the idea of incorporating Neoclassical elements, which predominated during that period. In the central nave a funerary monument was constructed to hold the ashes of **Christopher Columbus**. The ashes were brought to Havana in 1796 from Santo Domingo and later transferred to Seville in 1898. *See also* Catholicism; Architecture (Colonial Era)

Further Reading

Weiss, Joaquín E. *La arquitectura colonial cubana (siglos XVI al XIX).* Havana-Seville: Instituto Cubano del Libro–Junta de Andalucía, 1996.

Emma Álvarez-Tabío Albo

Cerra Herrera, Mirta (1908–1988)

Mirta Cerra, is one of the salient women artists of the Cuban modernist movement. She was a painter with a long artistic trajectory (1940s to 1980s) and a considerable body of paintings, ranging from social realism to abstraction. Cerra graduated from Havana's **San Alejandro Academy of Fine Arts** in 1934 and thereafter received a scholarship to study at the Art Students League in New York, where she took up graphics and sculpture. After traveling in Europe and experimenting with various media, she returned to Cuba and settled for painting, having her first one-person show in 1943 at Havana's Lyceum. In the 1940s she developed her own personal vision of social realism, characterized by dignified and somber peasant figures painted in earth tones, as seen in *El entierro*. In the 1950s and thereafter she turned to a more personal and abstract language to represent the narrow streets of **La Habana Vieja (Old Havana)**, boats in Havana Bay, and still lives. During her long artistic career, Cerra participated in numerous national and international exhibitions, winning many awards. In 1979, Cuba's **National Museum of Fine Arts** mounted a retrospective of her work with over 100 paintings. Cerra's paintings are found in private and public collections in Cuba and a few in the United States, including the Museum of Arts and Sciences of Daytona Beach, Florida.

Further Reading

LaDuke, Betty. *Compañeras: Women, Art, and Social Change in Latin America*. San Francisco: City Lights Book, 1985.

Juan A. Martínez

Columbus Cemetery (Cementerio Colón)

A virtual miniature city, Havana's Cementerio de Colón contains artworks by some of the most significant Cuban artists of the nineteenth and twentieth centuries. The original concept was suggested by Calixto de Loira, who had the dubious honor of inaugurating, with his interment, one of the oldest parts of the cemetery, the Galería de Tobías, shortly after the funerary monuments works were started in 1871. Eugenio Rayneri Sorrentino carried out the monumental neo-Roman entrance, after Loira's plans. A sculpture by José Vilalta de Saavedra of the three virtues, faith, hope and charity, adorns the cemetery entrance.

Two principal axes divide the cemetery, and at their intersection sits the Capilla Central (Central Chapel), an octagonal structure. The ceilings of the chapel were decorated by Miguel Melero. Along the cemetery's principal avenues lie the necropolis's most notable monuments, including the monument to the eight medical students executed by the Spanish on November 27, 1871, created by Vilalta de Saavedra, and the monument to the firemen killed at the Isasí iron foundry on May 17, 1890, by Julio Zapata and Agustín Querol. Among the most remarkable twentieth-century funerary monuments are the tomb of Catalina Lasa and Juan Pedro Baró, created by René Lalique; the tomb of the Falla Bonet family, with sculptures by Mariano Benlliure; the Aguilera family tomb, with a *Pieta* by **Rita Longa**; the Núñez family mausoleum, designed by Max Borges with the collaboration of the Mexican engineer Félix Candela; and the tomb of Raúl de Zárraga, designed by Eugenio Batista and with a mural by **René Portocarrero**. *See also* Architecture (Colonial Era); Architecture (Twentieth Century)

Further Readings

Aruca, Lohania, "The Cristóbal Colón Cemetery in Havana." *Journal of Decorative and Propaganda Arts* 22 (1996): 34–54.

Roig de Leuchsenring, Emilio. *La Habana. Apuntes históricos*. Havana: Oficina del Historiador de la Ciudad, 1964.

Weiss, Joaquín E. *La arquitectura colonial cubana (siglos XVI al XIX)*. Havana-Seville: Instituto Cubano del Libro–Junta de Andalucía, 1996.

Emma Álvarez-Tabío Albo

Consuegra, Hugo (1929–   )

Together with **Guido Llinás**, Hugo Consuegra through his paintings introduced the Abstract Expressionist aesthetic into Cuban art. Born in Havana, Consuegra studied painting at the **San Alejandro Academy of Fine Arts** (1943–1944) and graduated with a degree in architecture from the **University of Havana** (1955). A founding member of Los Once, Consuegra, in his paintings, writings, and activism, was an advocate of a gestural, non-objective abstraction. In 1953 and 1955 he had solo exhibitions at the Lyceum in Havana, and in 1956 the leading art critic and curator José Gómez Sicre invited Consuegra to exhibit his paintings at the Pan American Union in Washington, D.C. Consuegra's paintings of the late 1950s and early 1960s evoke a landscape reference (*La huella, La última herida*). From 1959 to the mid-1960s, Consuegra was the director of Visual Arts in the Department of Public Works in Havana. In 1967 Consuegra went into exile, settling in New York. His paintings from the 1970s on are not as gestural as his earlier works but are rather orderly areas of colors and shapes that reflect his architectural training.

Further Reading

Gómez Sicre, José. *Art of Cuba in Exile*. Miami: Editora Munder, 1987.

Alejandro Anreus

Cruz Azaceta, Luis (1942–   )

Luis Cruz Azaceta's paintings, drawings, and prints represent a highly original adaptation of the Neo-Expressionist aesthetic to a Cuban exile ethos. Born in Marianao, Havana, to a middle-class family, Cruz Azaceta attended accounting school until the prospect of military conscription forced him into exile at the age of eighteen. He went to live with distant relatives in Hoboken, New Jersey, and three years later he settled in New York City (see **New Jersey, Cubans in**). At about this time he started to draw and paint, eventually attending the School of Visual Arts in Manhattan. At the school he studied with Leon Golub, a painter known for monumental figurative paintings charged with political content. Cruz Azaceta graduated from the School of Visual Arts in 1969 and earned his living teaching at various art schools throughout the East Coast. He has been the recipient of two Cintas fellowships (1972, 1975), as well as a Guggenheim fellowship (1985).

Stylistically, Cruz Azaceta's early work reflected a colorful, pop art–like tendency in depicting everyday environments. By the early 1980s he had consolidated his mature pictorial style—a colorful and harsh figuration where his self-portrait served not as a narcissistic statement but rather as a stand-in for everyman. Cruz Azaceta has always had a preference for working in series such as *The AIDS Epidemic* (1987–1989), *The Balseros* (1990s), and most recently multimedia pieces reflecting urban squalor. In the 1990s Cruz Azaceta settled in New Orleans, Louisiana, where he continues to live and work.

Further Readings

Fuentes-Pérez, Ileana, Graciella Cruz Taura and Ricardo Pau-Llosa, eds. *Outside Cuba: Contemporary Cuban Artists*. New Brunswick, NJ: Rutgers University Press, 1989.

Gómez Sicre, José. *Art of Cuba in Exile*. Miami: Editorial Munder, 1987.

Torruella Leval, Susana. *Luis Cruz Azaceta: The AIDS Epidemic Series*. New York: Queens Museum of Art, 1990.

Alejandro Anreus

Darié, Sandú (1908–1991)

One of the leading abstract artists worldwide, Sandú Darié was born in Romania in 1908. His style was dominated by geo-

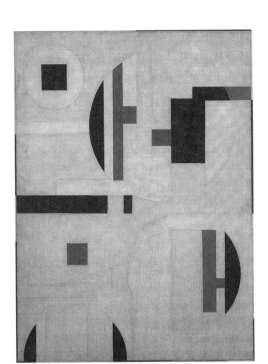

Multivisión espacial (*Spatial Multivision*) by Sandú Darié (1955) oil on canvas. Courtesy of the Museo Nacional de Bellas Artes, Havana.

metric abstractions. He studied law in France where he published antifascist political cartoons. He joined the French army in 1940. The following year he went to Cuba and became a citizen of Cuba in 1945. His first exposition at the Lyceum in Havana drew much attention. In 1952 he cofounded and coedited the Cuban magazine *Noticias de Arte* along with **Luis Martínez Pedro** and **Mario Carreño**. In 1964 he created a short film documentary entitled *Cosmorama*, the first of several cinematographic endeavors (see **Cinema**). In 1975 he took part in a special exhibition at the Cuban pavilion in Okinawa, Japan. His sculptures, murals, and other works can be found throughout Cuba. In 1983 he received the **Alejo Carpentier** Medal. Other distinctions include membership in Holland's Academy of Fine Arts and the International Association of Plastic Artists.

Further Reading

Sandú Darié: Exposición antológica. Havana: Ministerio de Cultura, 1988.

Luis González

Diago, Roberto (1920–1955)

Roberto Diago, a painter, is one of the most original artists of the 1940s generation, known for his meteoric artistic trajectory and expressive treatment of Afro-Cuban subjects (see **Afro-Cubans**). He graduated in 1941 from Havana's **San Alejandro Academy of Fine Arts** and produced a considerable body of paintings before his untimely death in 1955. In paintings such as *Abanico* of 1945, *Caridad del Cobre* of 1946, and *El oráculo* of 1949, he explored aspects of Afro-Cuban popular culture in a nascent personal style. In the 1940s he traveled and exhibited in Mexico City, New York, and Port-au-Prince, as well as having solo shows in Havana. He also taught at the School of Fine Arts in the city of **Matanzas**. Diago's work remains mostly in private collections in Cuba and the United States. He is well represented in the **National Museum of Fine Arts** in Havana.

Further Reading

Hernández, Orlando. *Roberto Diago*. Havana: Fondo Cubano de Bienes Culturales, 1989.

Juan A. Martínez

Eiriz, Antonia (1929–1995)

Antonia Eiriz was one of the major painters of the 1960s generation. She was known for her uncompromising Expressionist style and as an excellent teacher of fine arts and crafts. She graduated in 1958 from Havana's **San Alejandro Academy of Fine Arts** and began to create large explosive paintings with a sharp existentialist view of the human condition. Eiriz had her first one-person show in 1964, at La Habana Gallery in Havana, which opened the most productive period of her interrupted painting career: Havana, 1958–1969, and Miami, ca. 1991–1995. Her most recognized paintings include *Ni muertos* (n/d), *Cristo saliendo de Juanelo* (1964), and *La anunciación* (1964), all awesome images of human despair. One of her more recent paintings, *Entre líneas* (1993), was included in the Rings: Five Passions in World Art exhibition, held in Atlanta in 1996 as part of the Olympic Games and curated by James Carter Brown, director of the National Gallery of Art in Washington, D.C. In 1961, she received an Honorable mention at the VI São Paulo Biennial, and in 1994 she received the John S. Guggenheim Fellowship in Painting. Eiriz participated in solo and collective exhibitions throughout the Americas and Europe; her work is represented in numerous private collections, as well as in the **National Museum of Fine Arts** in Havana and the Museum of Art in Ft. Lauderdale, Florida.

El Combate (*The Combat*) by Carlos Enríquez (1941) oil on canvas. Courtesy of the Museo Nacional de Bellas Artes, Havana.

Further Readings

Blanc, Giulio V. "Antonia Eiriz, una apreciación." *Art Nexus* (July-September 1994): 44–46.

Eligio (Tonel), Antonio. "Antonia Eiriz en la pintura cubana." *Revolución y Cultura* (March 1987): 39–45.

Martínez, Juan A. *Antonia Eiriz: Tribute to a Legend*. Ft. Lauderdale, FL: Museum of Art, 1995. Exhibition catalog.

Juan A. Martínez

Enríquez, Carlos (1900–1957)

Carlos Enríquez, a painter and novelist, is one of the pioneers of the modernist movement in Cuban art and the foremost exponent of *criollismo* (Cuban rural vernacular culture) in painting. He had little formal artistic training but was well educated and traveled. Enríquez's formative years date from 1925 to 1933, when he lived in Havana, New York, Paris, and Madrid and developed a highly personal style from his encounter with Futurism, Expressionism, and Surrealism. His art reached full maturity from the mid-1930s to the late 1940s, when it became known for its visual language of fluid lines, overlapping transparent forms, and dynamic figure compositions representing the Cuban countryside, its light and color, inhabitants, history, and folklore. Enríquez called his production of that time *romancero guajiro*, or Creole ballads, and its main contribution to Cuban culture is the symbolization of a national identity based on an affirmative view of the rural vernacular. Enríquez's late period, circa 1950 to 1957, was productive but uneven due to sickness. He began to exhibit in Havana in 1925 and won purchase awards at the National

Exhibitions of Painting and Sculpture of 1935, 1938, and 1946, for *El rey de los campos de Cuba* (1934), *Rapto de las mulatas* (1938), and *La arlequina* (ca. 1945), respectively. He collaborated with the magazine *Revista de Avance* (1927–1930), illustrated books, notably Alberto Riera's collection of poems *Canto al Caribe* (1936), and executed a number of frescos in Havana. Enríquez's paintings are found in private and public collections in Cuba and the United States, including the **National Museum of Fine Arts** in Havana and the Museum of Modern Art in New York. *See also* Literary Journals

Further Readings

Luis, Carlos M. *Carlos Enríquez*. Miami: Museo Cubano de Arte y Cultura, 1986. Exhibition catalog.

Martínez, Juan A. *Cuban Art and National Identity: The Vanguardia Painters, 1927–1950*. Gainesville: University Press of Florida, 1994.

Sánchez, Juan. *Carlos Enríquez*. Havana: Editorial Letras Cubanas, 1996.

Juan A. Martínez

Esson, Tomás (1963–   )

The censorship surrounding Tomás Esson's solo exhibit *A Tarro Partido II* (1988) in Havana led him to become a cause célèbre in the Cuban art world, and it marked the beginning of a period of increasing restriction and censorship. A mulatto, born in Havana, he studied at the **San Alejandro Academy of Fine Arts** and the Instituto Superior de Arte (ISA), graduating in 1987. Like his late 1980s contemporaries, Esson's art is characterized by an ideological criticism of many aspects of Cuban life, including national issues and the institution of art itself. This generation of artists recodified symbols and patriotic slogans, and they demonstrated an ideological radicalism free of thematic limits and taboos. In his socially critical and explicit art, Esson's manner of painting incorporates violent, sexual, and scatological subjects, as well as exaggerated forms, grotesque creatures, written words, and Cuban national heroes. Esson is considered the most "painterly" of his generation and was influenced by Expressionism, Symbolism, and Cuban artists such as **Manuel Mendive** and Santiago Armada (Chago). In one of his censored images, *Mi homenaje al Che* (1987), he depicted distorted copulating animals in front of a portrait of a mulatto version of **Ernesto Che Guevara**. Esson identified himself with Che in this image, and this work also referred to the hypocrisy of some Cuban citizens and bureaucrats who leave Cuba. He traveled to the United States as part of *The Nearest Edge of the World: Art and Cuba Now* (1991) exhibit, and he has remained there since. He currently lives in Miami.

Further Readings

Camnitzer, Luis. *New Art of Cuba*. Austin: University of Texas Press, 1994.

Fernández, Antonio Eligio. "70, 80, 90 . . . Perhaps 100 Impressions of Art in Cuba." In *Cuba siglo XX: modernidad y sincretismo*. Las Palmas de Gran Canaria: Centro Atlántico de Arte Moderno, 1996: 413–422.

Murphy, Jay. "The Young and the Restless in Habana." *Third Text* 20 (Autumn 1992): 115–132.

Jo-Ann Van Eyck

Estopiñán, Roberto (1921–   )

Roberto Estopiñán's contribution to Cuban sculpture has been a commitment to the human figure within a humanist ethos. Born in Havana, Estopiñán received his first drawing lessons as a child at the Centro Asturiano. At the age of fourteen he received a special permission from the painter **Armando Menocal**, former director of the **San Alejandro Academy of Fine Arts**, so that he could enroll at the academy as a full-time student. At the academy, he was first a protégé of the landscape painter Antonio Rodríguez Morey, and eventually he became a student and protégé of the modernist sculptor **Juan José Sicre**. Estopiñán would be Sicre's studio assistant throughout the late 1940s and 1950s. After graduating from the academy, Estopiñán visited Mexico to study Pre-Columbian sculpture (1948). While in Mexico, he befriended the sculptor Francisco Zúñiga. It was at Zúñiga's studio where he executed a series of figurative ceramic sculptures reflective of Pre-Columbian forms. Estopiñán exhibited these sculptures at his first solo exhibition at the Lyceum in Havana (1949). In 1949 together with **Carlos Franqui**, **Guillermo Cabrera Infante**, **Néstor Almendros**, and others, he helped found the cultural group Nuestro Tiempo. The group's agenda was a synthesis of existentialism and critical Marxism. Later in the same year, Estopiñán traveled to Europe for the first time, visiting France and Italy and meeting the sculptor Marino Marini.

During the 1950s Estopiñán's sculpture experimented with both figurative and abstract elements, using native Cuban woods, plaster, and welded metals. His sculptures received first prizes at the Salón Nacional of 1951, 1952, 1953, and 1957. In 1953 he was the only finalist from the Spanish-speaking Americas at the international competition for the Monument for the Unknown Political Prisoner, sponsored by the Tate Gallery in London. In 1954, Estopiñán was appointed professor of drawing at the Escuela de Ceiba del Agua in Havana. Also in 1954 he began experimenting with printmaking, a medium in which he would produce a large body of work during the rest of his career. After **Fulgencio Batista**'s **coup of 1952**, Estopiñán became active in the urban guerrilla movement (see **Batista, Struggle against**). In 1959, the new revolutionary regime rewarded Estopiñán with diplomatic posts, first in Egypt and later in China. In 1961 Estopiñán went into exile in the United States, and since 1967 he has resided in New York. Throughout the 1960s his work,

Captive Torso, bronze sculpture (1951). Courtesy of Roberto Estopiñán.

in the media of sculpture, drawing, and printmaking, focused on Expressionist depictions of political prisoners, fallen warriors, and crucifixions. In the 1970s the work became less political, synthesizing animal and human forms into an organic figuration. Since the late 1980s, Estopiñán has been exploring the female torso in a minimalist manner.

Further Readings

Anreus, Alejandro. *Roberto Estopiñán, 5 Decades of Prints.* Jersey City, NJ: Jersey City Museum, 1996.

Nodarse Chao, Olga, ed. *Estopiñán, Sculpture and Related Drawings.* Birmingham, MI: Schweyer-Galdo Editions, 1983.

Alejandro Anreus

Fernández, Agustín (1928–   )

Agustín Fernández is an internationally acclaimed abstract expressionist. Born in 1928 in Havana, he left Cuba during the onset of the **Revolution** in 1959 through Paris. In the early 1970s he resided in Puerto Rico and Paris. By the late 1980s he had settled permanently in New York City. His work is in numerous international museums and galleries such as the Museum of Modern Art in New York City, the Victoria and Albert Museum in London, Yale University Art Galley in New Haven, Connecticut, and the Círculo de Bellas Artes in Maracaibo, Venezuela. Fernández began to study art at the age of twenty-four at the **San Alejandro Academy of Fine Arts**. At twenty-nine he began to get recognition in Latin America. He received in 1957 Honorable Mention at the IV Bienal de São Paulo, Brazil. Four years later, in 1961, he was invited to participate in his first group show in Paris at the Salon de Mai.

In 1974, the University of Puerto Rico, Río Piedras, organized the first retrospective of his work. Then in 1976 the Giumel and Weitzanhoffer Gallery in New York City organized a second retrospective that traveled to the Metropolitan Museum and Art Center in Miami, Florida. His work consists of very large paintings depicting abstracted sexually charged images. His aesthetic concern is with volume and the oscillation between what he calls the "exact" and "inexact." He sees his abstract forms as metaphysical entities relating to Georgia O'Keeffe's erotic abstract forms and to Roberto Matta's paintings. Fernández's paintings are a precursor to Roberto Mapplethorpe's erotic images, but unlike Mapplethorpe, his paintings are not considered controversial. Fernández continues to paint in New York City.

Further Readings

Blanc, Giulio V., and Juan A. Martínez. *Agustín Fernández: A Retrospective.* Miami: Art Museum at FIU, 1992.

Fuentes-Pérez, Ileana, Graciella Cruz-Taura, and Ricardo Pau-Llosa, eds. *Outside Cuba: Contemporary Cuban Visual Artists.* New Brunswick, NJ: Rutgers University Press, 1989.

Isabel Nazario

Fernández, Arístides (1904–1934)

A painter and author, Arístides Fernández enrolled in the **San Alejandro Academy of Fine Arts** in 1924 and left a year later. He painted and wrote short stories for about a decade, before his premature death. Working in relative isolation, with little artistic education and without the benefit of travel abroad, he developed a remarkable personal version of expressionism. His limited production consisted of portraits and rural and urban scenes executed in watercolors and oils. Most of his works are undated; it appears as if the portraits of his mother were painted in the 1920s and that his genre scenes were finished in the 1930s.

Fernández's portraits present intimate and subtly psychological representations of the subjects. Many of his later works offer a critical view of the dismal social conditions in the countryside, as seen in *La familia se retrata* (Family Portrait, n.d.) and *Batey* (n.d.). These paintings stand out for their prominent and strong depiction of women.

Fernández never exhibited his paintings or published his short stories during his lifetime. The Lyceum in Havana gave him a posthumous exhibition in 1934. In 1950 an exhibition of his paintings took place in the **Capitol Building** and the following year the Directory of Culture published a monograph by **José Lezama Lima** on him. Most of Fernández's paintings are in the collection of the **National Museum of Fine Arts** in Cuba. One of his most ambitious paintings, *El entierro* (The Entombment, n.d.), is in the church of El Espíritu Santo in **Havana Vieja (Old Havana)**. A few of his paintings and many of his watercolors are in private collections in Cuba and the United States.

Further Reading

Martínez, Juan A. *Cuban Art and National Identity: The Vanguardia Painters, 1927–1950*. Gainesville: Florida University Press, 1994.

Juan A. Martínez

Figueroa, Jorge B. (1917–)

Jorge B. Figueroa is considered by many to be one of Cuba's best photographers of the prerevolutionary era. Born in Havana in 1917, he began taking pictures as a teenager with a fifty-seven-cent Norton camera; he was essentially a self-taught photographer. Figueroa won his first photography award, the Concurso del Arte prize, in 1932. He went on to exhibit his work in many important photographic exhibitions and to win several awards, among them the Inter American Photographic Salon exhibition (1941), an Honor Diploma from the Photography Club of Bordeaux, France (1958), and a Four Star Diploma from the American Photography Society (1960). In Cuba he won the award by the Club Fotográfico de Cuba on four different occasions.

Shortly after the triumph of the Revolution, Figueroa resettled in New Jersey, where he continued his career as a photographer. In 1961 he joined New York's Modern Age Labs, where he worked as master printer until 1982, when he retired to Miami. While at Modern Age he printed photographs for numerous photography exhibitions, photography books, and magazines such as *Life* and *Look.* His own photographs have been published in the *New York Times, La Prensa* of Argentina, and numerous other venues. He was also an active member of the Photographic Club of New York, with which he exhibited and taught regularly.

Figueroa's black-and-white work has focused on landscapes, particularly architectural photography. During the post-1959 era he also experimented with abstract photography in color. One of his photographs appears as the illustration for this encyclopedia's entry for **Architecture (Colonial Era)**.

Further Reading

Márquez García, Sandra. "Photos Evoke Longing," *Miami Herald*, Nov. 29, 2000.

Luis Martínez-Fernández

Fortifications of Havana

Havana's urban landscape is graced by the remains of the hemisphere's finest and most extensive system of colonial fortifications. These fortifications attest to Havana's strategic location and the importance of its port within the Spanish empire's **trade and navigation** routes.

The oldest of Havana's forts is la Real Fuerza. Originally ordered built by Governor Hernando de Soto, it was completed in 1577. Half a century later its imposing tower was added, and it was crowned with *La Giraldilla,* the statue that went on to become one of the city's most enduring symbols. Following the completion of la Real Fuerza, construction began on two new forts, one on each side of the narrow mouth of the bay of Havana: **El Morro Castle** on the east and the smaller fort of La Punta on the west. In the 1630s two smaller coastal forts were built a few miles east and west of Havana, one in Cojímar, the other in La Chorrera. Later in the century, construction began on the walls that eventually surrounded Havana. It took over a century for the project to be finished. The walls stretched over a perimeter of nearly 5 kilometers (3.1 miles), averaging 10 meters (32.8 feet) in height and 1.4 meters (4.6 feet) in thickness. The demolition of the walls began in 1863, and only a few traces of them remain standing. Following the **British occupation of Havana** in 1762, Spanish authorities embarked on a number of defensive projects that supplemented the existing military infrastructure. New batteries were added to El Morro, and the new fortifications were built on the periphery of the walled city. The largest of these, San Carlos de la Cabaña, was in fact the largest in the Americas, measuring 10 hectares (24.7 acres). The other two forts were the Castle of Atarés, near the bay, and the Castle of El Príncipe, west of **Habana Vieja (Old Havana)**. The forts of Cojímar, El Príncipe, and Atarés are still used for military or police purposes, while those of La Cabaña, la Real Fuerza, La Punta, and El Morro are open as tourist attractions (see **Tourism**). Please see color insert in Volume I for photograph. *See also* Architecture (Colonial Era)

Further Readings

Fernández Núñez, José Manuel. *La Habana colonial: ciudad fortificada de América*. Havana: Editorial José Martí, 1998.

Préstamo y Hernández, Felipe J. ed. *Cuba: arquitectura y urbanismo*. Miami: Ediciones Universal, 1995.

Weiss, Joaquín E. *La arquitectura colonial cubana*. Havana-Seville: Instituto Cubano del Libro–Junta de Andalucía, 1996.

Luis Martínez-Fernández

Self-Portrait of Antonio Gattorno with nude models (Paris, 1926) from Ernest Hemingway, *Gattorno* (Havana, 1935).

Gattorno Águila, Antonio (1904–1980)

A key figure in Cuba's modernist movement, Antonio Gattorno was born in 1904. He began his formal studies at the **San Alejandro Academy of Fine Arts** in Havana while still in his teens. He studied under **Leopoldo Romañach**. At the age of sixteen, he was awarded a five-year scholarship to study in Europe. While in Europe, Gattorno developed a style that many in Cuba considered overly modern. Gattorno returned to Cuba in 1927 (two years later than planned). He soon joined **Grupo Minorista**, a Left-leaning anti-imperialist political group. Gattorno's artwork reflected his political views, often depicting people working the land.

In 1932, Gattorno met Ernest Hemingway. The two remained close friends until Hemingway's death in 1961. Hemingway even published a book featuring thirty-eight reproductions of Gattorno's work (see **Hemingway in Cuba, Ernest**). In 1936, with the help of Hemingway and writer John Dos Passos, Gattorno mounted an exhibit at New York's Passedoit Gallery. That same year, *Esquire* magazine featured a spread of his work.

Around 1939, Gattorno began to change his style, moving toward Surrealism. Works reflecting his new style include *La siesta* and a series of paintings he called *The Dream of the Fisherman.*

In 1963, Gattorno took a ten-year break from painting. In 1978, Southeastern Massachusetts University (now University of Massachusetts, Dartmouth) exhibited many of his works, spanning from his days as a student through his more recent works.

Further Reading

Hemingway, Ernest. *Gattorno*. Havana: Úcar, García y Cía., 1935.

Luis González

Giraldilla, La

In the tower of the Castillo de la Real Fuerza stands *La Giraldilla*, a small bronze statue of a female form that has come to symbolize the City of Havana. It is said that if you have not seen the statue, you have not seen the city.

Legend has it that *La Giraldilla* represents **Isabel de Bobadilla**, wife of famous explorer Hernando de Soto, who in 1530 was named captain-general of Cuba and governor of Florida. In 1539, de Soto, ambitious and eager for **conquest**, left Cuba to colonize Florida and search for the mythical fountain of youth, but he died in the exploration. *La Giraldilla*, which also served as a weathervane, is said to represent his wife, who would go to the tower every day searching in all directions for sight of her husband's returning ship. Bobadilla's story of love and loyalty inspired the sculptor Gerónimo Martín Pinzón (1607–1649) to create the statue, which is now on display at the Museum of the City of Havana in the former **Palace of the**

Original statue of *La Giraldilla*, housed in the Museum of the City of Havana. A replica stands atop the Castillo de la Real Fuerza. Photograph by Luis Martínez-Fernández.

Captains-General, while a replica stands in the tower.

The statue stands atop a cylindrical structure in the southeastern bulwark of the fort. At one time, bells hung from four holes in the structure and were used to alert residents and the militia to the approach of enemy forces. *La Giraldilla* appears to be in motion, almost appearing to dance. In her right hand she holds a palm leaf, while her left hand rests on a flagstaff. On top of her head rests a crown, and from her neck hangs a necklace with the name of the sculptor written on it. Although a remnant of the colonial era, the statue has become a powerful symbol of the Cuban nation. Some argue the statue represents the victory of the Cuban people, while others see the statue as a representation of the natives that populated the island before the arrival of the Spaniards. The likeness of *La Giraldilla* is represented on the label of Cuba's most famous **rum**: Havana Club. *See also* Fortifications of Havana; Habana Vieja (Old Havana), La

Further Readings

Iznaga, Alcides. "*La Giraldilla*, estatua que gira." *Bohemia*, September 15, 1972, 4–5.
"*La Giraldilla*." *Bohemia*, March 9, 1990, 73.

Araceli García Carranza

Gutiérrez Solano, Carlos (1947–)

Carlos Gutiérrez Solano is a distinguished installation/performance artist, a curator, and an arts administrator. He has won numerous awards for his work including the Bessie Award in 1991, two Art Matters Citations in 1988 and 1995, and a Cintas Foundation Fellowship to develop a project with the Institute of International Education in New York City. He was born in Havana in 1947 and currently resides in New York City. In 1961 he left Cuba to live in Miami, Florida. He studied art at the Kansas City Art Institute in 1970, where he earned a Bachelor of Fine Arts. Gutiérrez Solano completed his studies in 1972, earning a Master's of Arts at the University of California, Berkeley. The intellectual and aesthetic focus of his work is informed by an interest in vestigial performance, pondering the nature of media and representation as well as biographical narration as it relates to **AIDS** activism and biculturalism.

As a curator Gutiérrez Solano has developed over fifteen exhibitions in major institutions, including, among others, the Newark Museum in New Jersey, Asia Society in New York City, and the Munson Williams Proctor Institute–Museum of Art in Utica, New York. He was chief curator at the Queens Museum of Art from 1979 to 1981 in New York. Currently, he is the deputy director of the New York Transit Museum in Brooklyn. Gutiérrez Solano played a significant role in facilitating exhibitions and support for individual artists for ten years (1981–1991) as a director of the Visual Arts Program at the New York State Council on the Arts. In addition, he is known for his leadership in the gay community in New York, lecturing, leading fund-raising benefits, and producing programs that examine the sociopolitical concerns as experienced by the gay community. One such program was the AIDS Forum held in 1996 at the Tish School of the Arts, at New York University, where he lectured on "Fear, Rage, Love, Compassion, Tolerance, and Loss." Gutiérrez Solano remains active as a performance artist and continues his work as an AIDS activist in New York City.

Further Readings

Fuentes-Pérez, Ileana, Graciella Cruz-Taura, and Ricardo Pau-Llosa, eds. *Outside Cuba: Contemporary Cuban Visual Artists*. New Brunswick, NJ: Rutgers University Press, 1989.
Sullivan, Edward J. *Latin American Art in the 20th Century*. London: Phaiden Press Limited, 1996.

Isabel Nazario

Herrera, Carmen (1915–)

Within Cuban painting, Carmen Herrera stands as a pioneer practitioner of geometric abstraction. Born in Havana, as a child Herrera attended the Montessori School, which provided a solid primary education for women of her generation. In 1930–1931 she attended Marymount College in Paris, and in the late 1930s she was a student at the **San Alejandro Academy of Fine Arts**. Herrera studied architecture at the **University of Havana** in 1937–1938. At this time and into the 1940s, she was primarily interested in sculpture. In 1939 Herrera married Jesse Lowenthal and settled in New York City. In New York she befriended abstract painters Barnett Newman and Leon Polk Smith and continued her art studies at the Art Students League of New York (1943–1947). All throughout this period, Herrera continued to travel to Cuba to visit her family and maintained friendships with painters **Fidelio Ponce, Cundo Bermúdez**, and José Mijares, the sculptor **Alfredo Lozano**, and art critic José Gómez Sicre. Herrera's earliest work was eclectic in style and in the medium of sculpture. Sometime in the 1940s she abandoned sculpture and focused entirely on painting. After World War II Herrera lived in Paris again and was there at the time of the Salon des Réalités Nouvelles exhibition. This exhibition was a revelation for her; she was moved by the paintings of Josef Albers, and she was able to see more work by other Bauhaus artists. By 1954 Herrera had found her mature visual vocabulary: a rigorous synthesis of geometric and colorist concerns, one that is too sensual to be minimal, and a sense of color that, for all its intensity, is never allowed to overtake the classical structure of her pictures. Among Herrera's best-known works are the series *Days of the Week* (1970s) and *The Black and White Paintings* (1951–1989). Her first solo exhibition took place in the Lyceum in Havana. In 1998 New York's El Museo del Barrio exhibited her series *The Black and White Paintings*.

Further Readings

Fuentes-Pérez, Ileana, Graciella Cruz-Taura and Ricardo Pau-Llosa, eds. *Outside Cuba: Contemporary Cuban Visual Artists*. New Brunswick, NJ: Rutgers University Press, 1989.

Ponce de León, Carolina, and Alejandro Anreus. *Carmen Herrera, the Black and White Paintings, 1951–1989*. New York: El Museo del Barrio, 1998.

Alejandro Anreus

Korda (Díaz Gutiérrez), Alberto (1928–2001)

Alberto Korda, born Alberto Díaz Gutiérrez, is the Cuban photographer who took the famous picture of **Ernesto "Che" Guevara**, one of the world's most widely reproduced and famous images.

Born in 1928, Korda earned a living as a photographer before 1959. After the triumph of the **Revolution**, he joined the staff of the newspaper *Revolución*. He later served as **Fidel Castro**'s personal photographer.

Korda took the photograph of El Che on March 5, 1960, during the funeral services for the victims of the *La Coubre*, a Belgian weapons-laden French ship that exploded in the Bay of Havana, apparently the result of sabotage. The **Columbus Cemetery** funeral not only produced the famous photograph but served as the context where Fidel Castro first uttered the enduring slogan "¡Patria o Muerte!" (Homeland or Death!). The photograph captured a stunning image of a pensive Che crowned by long curly hair and a beret. In the full negative of the picture, El Che is flanked by the profile of an unidentified bystander and the leaves of a palm tree. The widely recognized version of the photograph was cropped to include only its subject's head and shoulders.

The photograph was initially published in Havana but forgotten until an Italian journalist discovered it and began to produce posters of it after El Che's death in 1967. Since then the photograph has been widely reproduced throughout the world on posters, t-shirts, postcards, pins, book covers, and murals. A giant metal sculpture based on the photograph hangs on the facade of a building in the **Revolution's Square**, a building that housed the Industries Ministry that El Che headed in the early years of the Revolution. The image captured by Korda's lenses has become an icon of revolutionary ideals and in some instances a fashionable emblem. A Cuban documentary traces the trajectory of the photograph.

Korda did not profit from his famous picture, allowing it to be reproduced around the world without demanding

Alberto Korda's famous photograph of "Che" Guevara (1960). Illustration is of the rarely seen full negative of the photograph.

copyright royalties. In 2000, however, he sued an advertising company that had used a distorted version of the photo for a liquor ad. The defendants settled and Korda donated the compensation money to Cuba's **health-care system**. Korda produced many other memorable photographs during his career, including those of victorious rebels arriving in Havana and other images of the Revolution. He died at seventy-two while visiting Paris in May 2001.

Further Readings

Chaskel, Pedro. *Una foto recorre el mundo* [Photo That Goes around the World]. Video recording. 2000.
Haya, María E. *Cuba, la fotografía de los años 60*. Havana: Fototeca de Cuba, 1988.

Luis Martínez-Fernández

Lam, Wifredo (1902–1982)

Wifredo Lam, a painter, printmaker, and ceramicist, is internationally acclaimed as one of the pioneers of Latin American modern art and the foremost exponent of Afro-Cuban culture in the visual arts (see **Afro-Cubans**). Lam studied at Havana's **San Alejandro Academy of Fine Arts** from 1918 to 1923, when he left for Madrid to continue his academic training. He remained in Spain until 1938, living for periods of time in Cuenca, León, and Barcelona, while painting portraits, landscapes, city scenes, and interiors in styles that ranged from Realism to Cubism and Surrealism. The turmoil of the Civil War in Spain, in which he participated on the Republican side, drove him to Paris. There he met Pablo Picasso and through him the major figures of the School of Paris, including Pierre Loeb, who arranged his first one-person show in 1939. When the Nazis entered Paris in 1940, he took refuge in Marseilles, where he developed close ties with a group of Surrealists, including their leader, André Breton. Lam's illustrations for Breton's poem *Fata Morgana*, done

A young Wifredo Lam in his studio. Courtesy of Instituto Cubano del Arte e Industria Cinematográficos, Havana.

while in Marseilles, signaled the end of a long formative phase. Lam developed his mature style soon after his return to Cuba in 1941, consisting in a personal synthesis of Picasso's Cubism, West African sculpture, and Surrealist concepts, used to express his reencounter with Cuba's tropical vegetation and African heritage. Among his best-known paintings of that period are *La jungla* of 1943 and the *Eternal Presence* of 1945. Between 1947 and 1952 he lived in Havana, New York, Paris, and Albisola, settling thereafter in Paris. During the rest of his long and productive career, his style evolved toward greater abstraction of form, empty backgrounds, and a darker palette, as seen in *El Tercer Mundo* (1965). In the last decade of his life, his art turned decorative. From the late 1950s on, he dedicated increasing attention to

graphics and ceramics. Lam has been the subject of numerous monographs and retrospective exhibitions in Europe, the Americas, and Asia. His work is found in private and public collections all over the world, including the **National Museum of Fine Arts** in Havana and the Museum of Modern Art in New York.

Further Readings

Fouchet, Max-Pol. *Wifredo Lam*. Barcelona: Ediciones Polígrafa, 1976.

Sims, Lowery Stokes. *Wifredo Lam and the International Avant-Gande, 1923–1982.* Austin: University of Texas Press, 2001.

Wifredo Lam. By various authors. Madrid: Museo Nacional Centro de Arte Reina Sofía, 1993. Exhibition catalog.

Wifredo Lam and His Contemporaries, 1938–1952. By various authors. New York: Studio Museum in Harlem, 1992. Exhibition catalog.

Juan A. Martínez

Llinás, Guido (1923–   )

Painter and printmaker Guido Llinás is one of the leading figures of the 1950s generation of Cuban artists. He is known as a founding member of the group Los Once (1953–1955) and as a premier abstract painter. After taking basic art courses in his native **Pinar del Río Province**, Llinás moved to Havana in the late 1940s, where he emerged as a mature artist in the next decade, practicing a highly personal version of the New York School's Abstract Expressionism. In line with the aim of Los Once, and international artistic trends in the 1950s, he was interested in an art of universal, rather than national, expression. He moved to Paris in 1963, where he still resides. Llinás has remained faithful to abstract expressionism throughout his artistic career and since the 1960s has expanded his production to wood engraving, in which field he has received international recognition. Llinás began to exhibit regularly in Havana in the 1950s and internationally since the 1960s. He was the subject of a retrospective exhibition in 1997 at the Art Museum of Florida International University, and his paintings and prints are in numerous private and public collections in Cuba, France, and the United States, including the **National Museum of Fine Arts** in Havana and the Museum of Arts and Sciences of Daytona Beach, Florida.

Further Readings

Desnoes, Edmundo. "1952–1962 en la pintura cubana." In *Pintores cubanos*. Havana: Ediciones R, 1962.
Singler, Cristoph. "Black Painting, the Art of Counterpoint." In *Guido Llinás and Los Once*. Miami: The Art Museum, 1997.

Juan A. Martínez

Longa, Rita (1912–2000)

Rita Longa was a renowned sculptor. Her work, first exhibited in 1932, transcended many different styles from the salon piece to urban landscape. A powerful advocate for sculpture in all its forms, in 1937 she joined the Estudio Libre de Pintura y Escultura. In 1960, she established the Guama Studio. From 1980 to 2000 she presided over a commission (Comisión para el Desarrollo de la Escultura Monumentaria y Ambiental) dedicated to the promotion of sculpture throughout the island.

Her public sculptures have influenced the collective imagination of the Cuban people. Among her best-known public works are the *Ballerina* (1950), the symbol of the **Tropicana nightclub**, and the head of **Hatuey** (1955), which appears on the label of a popular Cuban beer by the same name. Her works adorn many of Cuba's most significant and vital public places, such as *Grupo familiar* (1947), in Havana's zoological park; the *Virgen del Camino* (1948) at the crossroads of San Miguel del Padrón; and *Forma, espacio y luz* (1953), at the entrance to the **National Museum of Fine Arts**. Longa's works are not limited to Havana but can be found elsewhere on the island, including *Aldea taína* (1964), at the Zapata swamps; *Bosque de los héroes* (1973), at Santiago, and *Fuente de las Antillas* (1977), in **Las Tunas**.

Her most recent works have included *Clepsidra* (1997), for the vestibule of the Habana Libre Hotel, and *Resurrección* (1999), for the Banco Financiero Internacional. In 1995, she received the National award of Plastic Arts, and in 1997 she was awarded an honorary doctorate from the **University of Havana**.

Further Readings

Alonso, Alejandro G. *La obra escultórica de Rita Longa*. Havana: Editorial Letras Cubanas, 1998.
Alonso, Alejandro G. *Rita Longa, exposición homenaje*. Havana: Museo Nacional de Bellas Artes, 1992.

Emma Álvarez-Tabío Albo

Lozano, Alfredo (1913–1997)

Alfredo Lozano was one of Cuba's most distinguished twentieth-century abstract sculptors. Born in 1913 in Havana, Lozano studied studio art at the **San Alejandro Academy of Fine Arts**. He also studied sculpture at the San Carlos Academy in Mexico, at the Free School of Mexico, and at the Sculpture Center in New York City. He left Cuba at the age of fifty-four to reside in Miami, Florida, and years later, he moved to Puerto Rico.

Lozano won numerous awards throughout his career. Three times he was awarded the Premio Nacional de Escultura—1938, 1950, and 1951. Among others, in 1982 he was also awarded the Cintas Foundation Fellowship in the United States. Lozano's sculptures consist of geometric and organic forms made from clay, iron, and marble. Besides Cuba and Puerto Rico, his work was exhibited throughout Latin America and the United States. His largest exhibit was held in 1978 at the Museum of Modern Art of Latin America, **Organization of American States**, in Washington, D.C. Among others museums, his work is exhibited in the following collections: the Cintas Foundation in New York, **National Museum of Fine Arts** in Cuba, and the Miami-Dade Public Library System in Florida.

Further Readings

Fuentes-Pérez, Ileana, Graciella Cruz-Taura, and Ricardo Pau-Llosa, eds. *Outside Cuba: Contemporary Cuban Visual Artists*. New Brunswick, NJ: Rutgers University Press, 1989.

Sullivan, Edward J. *Latin American Art in the 20th Century*. London: Phaiden Press Limited, 1996.

Isabel Nazario

Malecón, el

The Malecón is part of Cuba's national architectural patrimony and one of Havana's most representative sights. The seawall, which runs for more than 7 kilometers (4.35 miles), from the Castillo de la Punta,

View of el Malecón from the top of the FOCSA Building. Photograph by Luis Martínez-Fernández.

at the mouth of Havana Bay, to the Almendares River, west of the city, is a symbol of the city and its relationship with the sea. It is both monument and meeting place for Havana residents. Its construction proposed as far back as 1874, work on the Malecón began only in 1901 under the architectural firm of Mead and Whitney. Most of the construction was completed under President **Gerardo Machado** in the period between 1925 and 1933. The last section between the Avenida de los Presidentes and the Almendares River was finished between 1952 and 1954. Jean Forestier, an urban planner and landscape painter, also oversaw work on the project. The scenes of waves crashing over the Malecón as young lovers walk hand in hand are part of what makes Havana uniquely Havana. El Malecón is oftentimes referred to as the "Portal to Havana" and the island's longest seat. *See also* Architecture (Twentieth Century); Fortifications of Havana

Further Reading

Hernández, Orlando. *La isla grande: cien viejas postales de Cuba.* Italy: Oltre L'Orizzonte, 1998.

Julio Domínguez García

Manuel García, Víctor (1897–1969)

Born Manuel García, the painter Víctor Manuel is one of the precursors of the modernist movement in Cuban art and its most ardent proselytizer. He studied at Havana's **San Alejandro Academy of Fine Arts** from 1910 to the early 1920s, continuing his artistic training, informally but most productive, in Paris between 1925 and 1927. There he began to develop his personal style adapted from the art of Paul Cézanne and Paul Gauguin and started to sign his work Víctor Manuel. His 1927 one-person show in Havana, exhibiting his Parisian production, was one of the events

Gitana tropical (1929) by Víctor Manuel. Courtesy of the Museo Nacional de Bellas Artes, Havana.

that launched the modernist movement in Cuban art. He turned against academic art, became a strong defender of French modernism, and attracted a following of young art students. Víctor Manuel's style is characterized by a simplified naturalism, colorful after 1940, focused on melancholic female figures and tranquil yet populated landscapes and cityscapes. His paintings represent a major contribution to the long tradition that views Cuba as an attractive, sensual, serene island. He began to exhibit regularly in Havana in 1917 and won purchase awards at the National Exhibitions of Painting and Sculpture of 1935 and 1938 for *Figuras y paisaje* (n.d.) and *Gitana tropical* (1929), respectively. He received a retrospective exhibition in Havana in 1969 and a smaller one in 1997. His work was also the subject of a major exhibition in Miami in 1982. His paintings are included in numerous private and public collections in Cuba and the United States, including the **National Museum of**

Fine Arts in Havana and the Museum of Arts and Sciences of Daytona Beach, Florida.

Further Readings

Martínez, Juan A. *Cuban Art and National Identity: The Vanguardia Painters, 1927–1950*. Gainesville: University Press of Florida, 1994.
Rigol, Jorge. *Víctor Manuel*. Havana: Editorial Letras Cubanas, 1990.

Juan A. Martínez

Martínez, Raúl (1927–1995)

Raúl Martínez, a painter and graphic artist, is one of the leading figures of the 1950s generation of Cuban artists. He is known as a pioneer in Cuba of abstract expressionism in the 1950s and of pop art in the 1960s. Martínez studied art at Havana's **San Alejandro Academy of Fine Arts** (1946–1948) and at the Institute of Design in Chicago (1952). In 1953 he joined the group of abstract artists known as Los Once (1953–1955), developing a personal version of abstract expressionism, which he practiced until the early 1960s. Following that, he worked in a variety of artistic fields as magazine director, design professor, graphic artist, stage designer, and easel and mural painter. By 1966 he had developed a personal adaptation of pop art to depict popular subjects and historical icons, such as *José Martí* (1966) and *Fénix* (about **Che Guevara**) (1968). This phase of his artistic career culminated with the series entitled *Isla* of 1970. In the last year of his life he returned to a light version of abstract expressionism. From 1948 Martínez exhibited regularly in Havana, including numerous one-person shows, and exhibited extensively in Latin America and Europe. His works are included in private and public collections, including the **National Museum of Fine Arts** in Havana and the Lowe Art Museum in Coral Gables, Florida.

Further Readings

Camnitzer, Luiz. *New Art of Cuba*. Austin: University of Texas Press, 1994.
Mosquera, Gerardo. *Nosotros: exposición antólogica de Raúl Martínez*. Havana: Museo Nacional, 1988.

Juan A. Martínez

Martínez Pedro, Luis (1910–1990)

An internationally renowned artist, Luis Martínez Pedro gained notice for his drawings of mythological creatures. Born in Havana on December 19, 1910, he attended the School of Architecture at the **University of Havana** in 1929. The following year he enrolled at Tulane University in New Orleans. Martínez Pedro had left Cuba due to differences with the government of **Gerardo Machado**. He returned to Cuba in 1933, following the end of Machado's rule.

In 1943 Martínez Pedro had his first one-man show at the Lyceum Gallery in Havana. The show featured the now-famous mythological drawings. From 1945 to 1947 he held an exhibition at New York's Perls Galleries. The following year he founded an advertising agency serving Latin America. In 1953, he took first place in UNESCO's (United Nations Educational, Scientific, and Cultural Organization) biennial competition in São Palo, Brazil. That same year, he founded *Noticias de Arte* in Cuba.

In 1956, Martínez Pedro attended the Massachusetts Institute of Technology, studying form and technique under Arshile, Gorky, Gyorgy Kepes, and Phillypowski. In the early 1960s, he resided in New York City. During those years, he taught at the School of Art Instructors and designed costumes and scenery for the Experimental Dance Theater. In 1973 Martínez Pedro illustrated the book *The Silent World* by Jacques Cousteau. Throughout the 1970s, he traveled much throughout Latin America and Europe. He had several exhibitions throughout Eastern Europe.

In 1981 Martínez Pedro was awarded the order of "**Félix Varela**" First Class by the Ministry of Culture of Cuba. He passed away in Havana in 1990.

Further Reading

Martínez, Juan A. *Cuban Art and National Identity: The Vanguardia Painters*. Gainesville: University Press of Florida, 1994.

Luis González

Mendieta, Ana (1948–1985)

Ana Mendieta's art production has left a lasting mark on contemporary art history, and she became an influential force and symbol for many artists. Her large corpus of work was the result of her experimentation with the new exploratory media in the 1970s, her feminist consciousness, her displacement, and the search for her personal identity. Born in Havana, she was sent with her sister to the United States in 1961 and spent several years in an orphanage (see **Pedro Pan [Peter Pan] Operation**). She earned an M.A. in 1972 and an M.F.A. degree in multimedia and video in 1977, both from the University of Iowa. Perhaps her best-known work is the long-running *Silueta* series of "earth-body sculptures" that began in 1973. The female form was the primary focus of her work, and she sought to establish a connection between herself, Cuban culture, the earth, and universal energy powers. She was interested in Afro-Cuban and indigenous ritual and beliefs, and after her initial return to Cuba in 1980, she carved her *Rupestrian* sculptures (1981) in the cave walls of the Escalera de Jaruco, on an ancient indigenous site. During subsequent trips to Cuba, she had an important influence on the 1980s generation artists, providing them with "outside" information, criticism, and moral support. She traveled

Silueta Works in Mexico, 1973–1974. Courtesy of Estate of Ana Mendieta and Galerie Lelong, New York.

and worked internationally and received a number of prestigious awards, including a Guggenheim Fellowship (1980). She married U.S. sculptor Carl Andre in 1985 but died tragically later that year in New York City. Andre was subsequently tried and acquitted of her murder in 1988; however, controversy remains around her death. *See also* Afro-Cubans; Indigenous Inhabitants

Further Readings

Blocker, Jane. *Where Is Ana Mendieta? Identity, Performativity, and Exile*. Durham, NC: Duke University Press, 1999.

Camnitzer, Luis. "Ana Mendieta." *Third Text* 7 (Summer 1989): 47–52.

Jacob, Mary Jane. "*Ashé* in the Art of Ana Mendieta." In *Santería Aesthetics in Contemporary Latin American Art*, ed. A. Lindsay. Washington, DC: Smithsonian Institution Press, 1996. 189–200.

Jo-Ann Van Eyck

Mendive Hoyo, Manuel (1944–)

The art of Manuel Mendive represents the first direct expression ever produced of an Afro-Cuban from within his own religious-cultural space, one based on his own experiences and knowledge as an initiate of **Santería**. Born in Havana to a mulatto family with a tradition in Santería, he won a UNESCO (United Nations Educational, Scientific, and Cultural Organization) prize for painting (1955) and graduated from the **San Alejandro Academy of Fine Arts** in 1963. His art is quintessentially Afro-Cuban, although he produces contemporary artworks, not religious objects. He has internalized Afro-Cuban myths as an artistic strategy, yet his vision extends beyond the narrative aspects of the myth to reflect on universal concerns, life, and humanity. The 1960s were the highpoint of his career, his "dark period" when he fused painting, sculpture, and natural materials to create profound artworks based on real Afro-Cuban mythological objects. He lost his right foot in an accident in the late 1960s, and he claimed that the sight of so much blood changed his concept of color. Throughout the 1970s, his art became more decorative and brightly colored, his "light period," depicting historic events, politics, and daily life. He began to include African-derived fantastic creatures of his own imagination by the 1980s, and he produced cloth designs for Telarte. Since 1986, he has focused on interdisciplinary projects, and he won an award at the 2nd Biennial of Havana (1986) for his choreography based on African Yoruba rituals and painted dancers' bodies. He lives in Santa María del Rosario near Havana.

Further Readings
Camnitzer, Luis. *New Art of Cuba*. Austin: University of Texas Press, 1994.
Mosquera, Gerardo. "Elegguá at the (Post?) Modern Crossroads Cuba." In *Santería Aesthetics in Contemporary Latin American Art*, ed. A. Lindsay. Washington, DC: Smithsonian Institution Press, 1996. 225–258.
Mosquera, Gerardo. "Strokes of Magical Realism in Manuel Mendive." In *Afrocuba: An Anthology of Cuban Writing on Race, Politics and Culture*, ed. Pedro Pérez Sarduy and Jean Stubbs. Melbourne, Australia: Ocean Press, 1993. 146–154.
Mosquera, Gerardo. "Towards a Different Post-Modernity: Africa in Cuban Art." In *Cuba siglo XX: modernidad y sincretismo*. Las Palmas de Gran Canaria: Centro Atlántico de Arte Moderno, 1996: 229–252.

Jo-Ann Van Eyck

Menocal, Armando (1861–1942)

Armando Menocal's contribution to the Cuban painting of his time is a synthesis of academic and Impressionist tendencies into a realist style. Born in Havana to a distinguished family, Menocal was a cousin of General **Mario García Menocal**, Cuba's president from 1913 to 1921. Menocal graduated from the **San Alejandro Academy of Fine Arts** in 1878 at the age of seventeen. At the academy he had been a student and protégé of its first Cuban-born director, Miguel Melero. Founded in Havana in 1818 by Jean Baptiste Vermay, the academy's program of study was based on both the French (École des Beaux-Arts) and Spanish (Academia de San Fernando) models. Menocal would be connected to the academy his whole life, first as a student and later as a professor and director (1927–1930). In 1880 Menocal traveled to Madrid, where he continued his studies under Francisco Jover y Casanova. For ten years Menocal lived in Europe, residing between Madrid and Paris. In Paris he encountered the work of Jean-Baptiste-Camille Corot, Gustave Courbet, and Edouard Manet, painters who would influence his use of light and understanding of realism.

Menocal returned to Cuba in 1890 and spent the next five years painting his native landscape and ambitious history compositions, such as *Reembarque de Colón por Bobadilla* (1893). In 1891 Menocal was appointed professor of landscape painting at the San Alejandro Academy. In 1895 he joined the Cuban liberation army, where he served, first under General **Máximo Gómez**, and later under General **Antonio Maceo** (see **War of Independence**). During this period, he kept sketchbooks, where he documented battles, landscapes, and individual portraits, usually executed in pencil or pen and ink. In 1902, after the establishment of the Republic, Menocal rejoined the faculty of the academy, once again teaching landscape painting. He executed a number of landscapes of the Cuban countryside (1890–1895, 1910s), where there is a real understanding of the burning quality of tropical light, as well as the lushness of the *campiña*. As a painter of contemporary history, Menocal executed important works such as *Muerte de Maceo* (1906) and *La batalla de Mal Tiempo*. His best portraits combine an Impressionistic sense of color with a rigorous academic drawing (*Retrato de Lily, Autoretrato*). In talent and technical skill, Menocal was the equal of his Puerto Rican contemporary Francisco Oller. Please see color insert in Volume I for artwork.

Further Reading

Valderrama, Esteban. *La pintura y la escultura en Cuba*. Havana: Editorial Lex, 1953.

Alejandro Anreus

Morro Castle (El Morro)

The castle of the Tres Reyes del Morro (Three Kings of the Morro) typifies the system of harbor fortifications built in the colonial period in Havana. Its spectacular and conspicuous location at the entrance of Havana harbor makes it a powerful symbol of city and country. El Morro sits on a

El Morro Castle is one of Havana's most enduring and recognizable symbols. Photograph by Luis Martínez-Fernández.

promontory, and part of the fortress is organically incorporated with the solid rock.

Construction on El Morro began in 1589 as part of an elaborate defense plan approved by King Philip II of Spain. The massive construction project was directed by Bautista Antonelli, who was later succeeded by Cristóbal de Roda. The fort was completed in 1630 at the same time as the castle of La Punta, on the other side of the bay's entrance. El Morro was severely damaged by the English during their successful attempt to capture Havana in 1762. Efforts to rebuild El Morro, after the city returned to Spanish hands, commenced in 1763 and continued through 1767 under the supervision of Silvestre Abarca and Agustín Crame. The lighthouse, which stands 30 meters (98.4 feet) high, was built in 1844, under the rule of Captain-General Leopoldo O'Donnell.

A witness to the political evolution of the island, the flags of several competing nations have flown from its mast. Between 1762 and 1763, the British flag replaced the Spanish. In 1899, the U.S. flag flew from El Morro, replaced on May 20, 1902, by the Cuban **national flag**. *See also* Architecture (Colonial Era); British Occupation of Havana; Fortifications of Havana

Further Readings

Blanes Martín, Tamara. *El Castillo de los Tres Reyes del Morro*. Havana: Editorial Letras Cubanas, 1998.

Roig de Leuchsenring, Emilio. *La Habana. Apuntes históricos*. Havana: Oficina del Historiador de la Ciudad, 1964.

Weiss, Joaquín E. *La arquitectura colonial Cubana (siglos XVI al XIX)*. Havana and Seville: Instituto Cubano. del Libro–Junta de Andalucía, 1996.

Emma Álvarez-Tabío Albo

National Museum of Fine Arts (Museo Nacional de Bellas Artes)

The National Museum of Fine Arts was established by government decree on February 23, 1918. Initially it was a general museum with sections devoted to archaeology, ethnography, history, painting, and sculpture. It was moved to its present location in the mid-1950s. After the **Revolution** the museum was reorganized into a museum of fine arts consisting of three departments: Cuban, Western European, and Ancient Art. The National Museum of Fine Arts houses a conference hall, a special library, a gallery devoted to contemporary Cuban art, and a department whose prime function is to popularize the fine arts throughout the island. The collection includes Western European paintings representing various national schools beginning in the fifteenth and sixteenth centuries. In addition, the museum exhibits seventeenth-century Flemish painting, Italian Renaissance art, eighteenth-century

English portraits, and Venetian and French painting. The Cuban painting collection includes works by some of the island's master twentieth-century artists. Included are **Eduardo Abela**, **Carlos Enríquez**, **Antonio Gattorno**, **Amelia Peláez**, **Arístides Fernández**, **Fidelio Ponce de León**, Jorge Arche, **René Portocarrero**, **Luis Martínez Pedro**, **Mariano Rodríguez**, **Wifredo Lam**, **Raúl Martínez**, **Antonia Eiriz**, **Servando Cabrera Moreno**, and **Ángel Acosta León**.

In the mid-1990s, the museum underwent restoration. It is now located in two buildings, with the Cuban collection remaining in the older building and the European and Ancient collections now housed at the grand building of the former Centro Asturiano.

Further Reading

Museo Nacional de Bellas Artes. *La Habana: salas del Museo Nacional de Cuba, Palacio de Bellas Artes*. Havana: Museo Nacional de Bellas Artes, 1990.

Isabel Nazario

Palace of Aldama (Palacio de Aldama)

The most imposing and impressive Cuban private residence of the nineteenth century, the Aldama Palace typifies colonial architecture of the period with its strong neoclassical influences. Situated on one side of the old Campo de Marte, (Mars Camp), it was constructed in 1844 under the direction of Manuel José Carrera. Its monumental size is offset by the sobriety and elegance of the facades, which envelop what in reality were two homes: that of Domingo Aldama and the home of his daughter Rosa and son-in-law **Domingo del Monte**. The interior design, with its two inner courtyards, conforms to the standard model for wealthy Havana families of the period, although the refinement of some of the finishing touches is incomparable.

Nineteenth-century print of the Plaza of the Palace of the Captains-General (Plaza de Armas). Print by Federico Mialhe from B. May, *Album pintoresco de la Isla de Cuba*.

The palace was sacked on January 24, 1869, by an angry mob of Spanish volunteers (see **Voluntarios Cuerpo de [Volunteer Corps]**), when **Miguel Aldama**, son of the property owner, was linked to Cuba's growing independence movement. The residence was converted into a cigar factory in 1926, and enormous modifications were made to the building. It was scheduled for demolition in 1946, but efforts by the citizenry to save the building were successful. Shortly thereafter it was declared a national monument. Efforts to restore the palace were completed in 1948 under the direction of José María Bens Árrarte. Presently the building houses the offices of the Instituto de Historia. *See also* Architecture (Colonial Era)

Further Reading

Weiss, Joaquín E. *La arquitectura colonial cubana (siglos XVI al XIX)*. Havana and Seville: Instituto Cubano del Libro–Junta de Andalucía, 1996.

Emma Álvarez-Tabío Albo

Palace of the Captains-General (Palacio de los Capitanes Generales)

The Palace of the Captains-General was the most important public building in eighteenth-century Havana and the best example of colonial Cuban **architecture**. Constructed on the site of the original city church, it sits at one side of the Plaza de Armas.

The Marquis de la Torre proposed construction of the palace to the Cabildo (City Council) in 1773. As proposed, the building included the residence of the captains-general, the "Casas Capitulares," and the jail. Work on the palace began in 1776, under the direction of Antonio Fernández Trevejos. It was inaugurated in 1791 with the dedication of the Central Hall (Sala Capitular), but it was not completed until 1835 under the direction of Manuel Pastor. Its present appearance is due to restoration efforts in 1930 carried out by Evelio Govantes and Félix Cabarrocas. The goal of the restoration was to expose the stone by removing paint and mortar. The project restored the courtyard to its current state, a beautiful remnant of the colonial era.

The palace was used extensively by the republican governments that followed the colonial period. It was the setting for the transfer of power from Spain to the United States in 1899. Three years later there was another ceremony at the palace to transfer power from the United States to the newly independent Republic of Cuba. The Cuban **national flag** first flew from the palace on May 20, 1902. Currently, the building houses the Museum of the City and the offices of the Historian of the City of Havana (see **Leal Spengler, Eusebio**). *See also* Architecture (Colonial Era); Colonial Institutions; Habana Vieja (Old Havana) (Municipality), La

Peces (Fishes) by Amelia Peláez del Casal (1943) oil on canvas. Courtesy of the Museum of Modern Art, New York. Inter-American Fund. Photograph © 2000 The Museum of Modern Art, New York.

Further Readings

Roig de Leuchsenring, Emilio. *La Habana. Apuntes históricos*. Havana: Oficina del Historiador de la Ciudad, 1964.

Weiss, Joaquín E. *La arquitectura colonial cubana (siglos XVI al XIX)*. Havana and Seville: Instituto Cubano del Libro–Junta de Andalucía, 1996.

Emma Álvarez-Tabío Albo

Peláez del Casal, Amelia (1896–1968)

Amelia Peláez, a painter and ceramicist, is one of the originators of the modernist movement and of abstraction in Cuban art. She graduated from Havana's **San Alejandro Academy of Fine Arts** in 1924, continued her studies at New York's Art Students League, and from 1927 to 1934, studied in various ateliers of Paris, most significantly with the Russian Constructivist artist Alexandra Exter. She culminated her European formative phase with a 1933 solo exhibition at the Galerie Zak, which was very well received in the Parisian press. Peláez developed her mature style in the late 1930s and 1940s, consisting of a synthesis of Cubism, Henri Matisse's decorative style of the 1920s, and Cuban nineteenth-century architectural ornamentation, which visual language she used to interpret still lives of "Cuban" fruits and flowers set in Creole domestic interiors. In form and content, her mature paintings contributed to the symbolization of a national identity emphasizing the Spanish side of the Cuban cultural heritage, Cuba's tropical **flora**, and domesticity. Two major paintings from the 1940s in North American museums are *Hibiscus* (1943), in the collection of the Museum of the **Organization of American States (OAS)** in Washington, D.C., and *Fishes* (1943), in the Museum of Modern Art in New York. In the 1950s, she dedicated most of her creative energies to ceramics and murals, as her visual language became more abstract and simplified. Peláez returned to easel painting and to her 1940s style in the last decade of her life. She began to exhibit regularly in Havana in 1918 and won awards at the National Exhibition of Painting and Sculpture of 1935, 1938, 1956, and 1959. She has been the subject of several major retrospective exhibitions: Havana, 1968 and 1996; Miami, 1988; Caracas, 1991; and Spain (various cities), 1998. Her paintings are in numerous private and public collections, including the **National Museum of Fine Arts** in Havana and the Museum of Modern Art in New York.

Further Readings

Blanc, Giulio V. *Amelia Peláez*. Miami: Cuban Museum of Art and Culture, 1988. Exhibition catalog.

Vázquez, Ramón. *Amelia Peláez: 1929–1964*. Salamanca: Caja Duero, 1998. Exhibition catalog.

Juan A. Martínez

Pérez Bravo, Marta María (1959–   )

Born in Havana of white-working class origin, Marta María Pérez Bravo studied at the **San Alejandro Academy of Fine Arts** (1975–1979) and the Instituto Superior de Arte (ISA) (1979–1984). Since her ISA studies, she has worked exclusively in the medium of black and white photography and with African-derived religious and popular Cuban cultural elements in a highly personalized artistic enterprise. Although not a religious practitioner, Pérez has a profound respect for many religious traditions, and the artist draws upon her cultural heritage to utilize African and Afro-Cuban beliefs, rituals, and iconography in polysemic images to reflect more generic and universal spiritual and existential concerns. She was the first artist to treat the Afro-American presence using her own body and in relation to her feminine experience, and her personal maternity was a key experience in the direction her artistic enterprise took. The use of her body is a consistent feature in her photographs, and she uses the correct religious elements in powerful images to transform her body into ritual and cultural objects. Her aim is to present images that suggest concepts, symbols, and metaphors that reach beyond the reference materials they are derived from. She married fellow Cuban artist Flavio Garcíandia, and they have twin daughters, born in 1986. Like many of her 1980s contemporaries, she has exhibited extensively overseas. She lived in Germany in the early 1990s and currently resides in Monterrey, Mexico. Pérez returns to Cuba on a regular basis to visit family and to exhibit there, as well as internationally. *See also* Afro-Cubans; Santería

Further Readings

Martínez, Rosa. "Marta María Pérez Bravo in Conversation with Rosa Martínez." In *Cuba: Maps of Desire*. Wien: Folio, 1999.

Mosquera, Gerardo. "Towards a Different Post-Modernity: Africa in Cuban Art," In *Cuba siglo XX: modernidad y sincretismo*. Las Palmas de Gran Canaria: Centro Atlántico de Artè Moderno, 1996.

Jo-Ann Van Eyck

Plaza de la Revolución (Revolution's [Civic] Square)

Previously called the Plaza Cívica or Civic Square, the Plaza de la Revolución is situated in the geographic heart of Havana. Known simply as la Plaza, it is surrounded by numerous and diverse government and cultural buildings and structures of which the monument to **José Martí** is the most impressive. The monument, called Memorial José Martí, sits atop a hill. Its base is in the shape of a five-point star. From this base springs upward a marble obelisk. In front of the obelisk, there is a giant statue, sculpted by **Juan José Sicre** in white marble, of the poet and patriot José Martí. In front of the statue stands a marble platform and podium from where officials watch the parades and massive rallies convened by the government.

Behind the monument is the former Palace of Justice, erected in 1957. This structure was meant to house the Supreme Court and "Fiscalía de la República." Today, it is the headquarters for the national government, housing offices for the Central Committee of the **Communist Party**, the State Council, Executive Committee of the Council of Ministries and **Fidel Castro**'s offices.

Placed in front of Memorial José Martí is the former "Tribunal de Cuentas," designed by the architects A. Capablanca and A. Santana and constructed in 1957. Since 1961, this building has served initially as the Ministry of Industries, originally directed by **Ernesto Che Guevara**, and it is now the **Ministry of the Interior**. Next to the Martí Memorial is a skyscraper where the Ministry of Armed Forces is located (see **Revolutionary Armed Forces [Fuerzas Armadas Revolucionarias, FAR]**). Prior to this ministry, the building housed offices for Havana's City Hall, and then it was headquarters for the National Institute for Agrarian Reform (INRA) (see **Agrarian Reform Acts**). During the first years of the **Revolution**, it was from this building that the major national and political changes were administered.

Near the monument stands the original site for the National Lottery, which was converted first into the now-defunct National Institute for Savings and Housing, in 1959, and then the Central Planning Board. Currently, the Ministry of Economics and Planning occupies the site. In close proximity is an elegant and functional building, designed by M. Gastón in 1954, which initially headquartered the Ministry of Communications but now houses the Ministry of Information and Communications. Nearby stands the Ministry of Construction (originally the Ministry of Public Works), erected in 1969, and the National Theatre (see **Theaters**). The latter structure contrasts sharply with the buildings in the Plaza. Finished at the end of the 1980s, the building for the National Theater, the creation of architects N. Arroy and G. Menéndez, is a modern structure that uses glass and crystal instead of white, hygienic marble. Visible from the Plaza is the **Biblioteca Nacional José Martí**. Please see color insert in Volume I for photograph. *See also* Architecture (Twentieth Century)

Further Readings

Dávalos, Fernando. *Mi Habana querida*. Seville, Spain: Editorial SI-MARSA, 1999.

Roig de Leuchsenring, Emilio. *La Habana: Apuntes históricos*. Havana: Oficina del historiador de la Ciudad de La Habana, 1963.

Armando H. Portela

Ponce de León, Fidelio (1895–1949)

Born Alfredo Fuentes Pons, Fidelio Ponce was a painter and one of the most unique forerunners of the modernist movement in Cuban art. He attended Havana's **San Alejandro Academy of Fine Arts** irregularly in the 1910s, traveled about **La Habana Province** doing commercial art in the 1920s, and established himself as a leading modernist artist in the 1930s. Unlike most of his contemporaries, he never traveled abroad. During his short mature period, from 1934 to 1949, Ponce developed a highly personal brand of Expressionism with concentration on the human figure, mysteriously revealed by a dramatic use of *chiaroscuro*. His ghostly figures, an assortment of characters—pious old women, bourgeois ladies, children, the sick, and Christ—appear compressed in an interior space or surrounded by a desolate landscape. He also painted landscapes and still life. In all cases, his paintings do not share the interest in "typical" Cuban color and themes of his contemporaries; instead, he depicted a harsh and desolate place and the desire to transcend it. Despite a life of extreme poverty and alcoholism, he produced a substantial body of work, which received national and international recognition in his lifetime. Ponce began to exhibit regularly in Havana in 1934 and received purchase awards at the National Exhibition of Painting and Sculpture of 1935 and 1938 for *Beatas* (1934) and *Niños* (1938). He was the subject of a retrospective exhibition in Havana in 1995 and a major exhibition in Miami in 1992. His paintings and drawings are in numerous private and public collections, including the **National Museum of Fine Arts** in Havana and the Museum of Modern Art in New York.

Further Readings

Luis, Carlos M. *Fidelio Ponce and His Time*. Miami: Cuban Museum of Art and Culture, 1992. Exhibition catalog.

Merino Acosta, Luz, et al. *Fidelio Ponce de León*. Havana: Museo Nacional, 1995. Exhibition catalog.

Sánchez, Juan. *Fidelio Ponce*. Havana: Editorial Letras Cubanas, 1985.

Juan A. Martínez

Portocarrero Villiers, René (1912–1986)

In his paintings, drawings, and prints, René Portocarrero reflected the Cuban Creole baroque sensibility. Born in the once-aristocratic Havana suburb of El Cerro, whose domestic interiors and architecture would be a lifelong subject in his art, Portocarrero was something of a child prodigy. Essentially self-taught, Portocarrero attended the **San Alejandro Academy of Fine Arts** for a brief period. He taught himself to paint by studying the work of other artists such as the Mexicans Jesús Guerrero Galván and Manuel Rod-

ríguez Lozano, as well as the Cubans **Eduardo Abela** and **Amelia Peláez**. Portocarrero's earliest efforts in painting were everyday scenes of Cuban peasants, in a monumental style reminiscent of the Mexican artists. In 1940 he met the New York Expressionist painter George McNeil, who was living in Cuba at the time. McNeil influenced Portocarrero as a colorist, and as a former Hans Hoffman student, he taught the Cuban about the "push and pull" of a painting's surface. Portocarrero was appointed drawing teacher at the Havana Penitentiary in 1940, an experience he claimed was an important influence. Early on, Portocarrero met the painter Raúl Milián (1914–1986), who would be his lifelong companion. In the 1940s Portocarrero, together with painter **Mariano Rodríguez** and sculptor **Alfredo Lozano**, would be a member of the intellectual group centered on the magazine *Orígenes* (1944–1956). His ink and pencil drawings served as illustrations for the magazine. By the mid-1940s Portocarrero was painting in a mature, yet still eclectic style. His ink and watercolor drawings depicted angels and mortals in mystical, Surrealistic compositions. His thickly painted and colorful oil paintings focused on baroque interiors, still lives, and the urban architecture of **Habana Vieva (Old Havana)**. Yet throughout the 1950s, Portocarrero produced semiabstract paintings that stressed color and geometry. Portocarrero had his first solo exhibition at the Lyceum in 1942. His work was included in the important 1944 exhibition *Cuban Painting of Today* at New York's Museum of Modern Art. Portocarrero's series of *Catedrales* and *Paisajes de La Habana* won him the first prize for painting at the 1956 Salón Nacional de Pintura y Escultura. Throughout the 1950s and 1960s, Portocarrero worked with ceramics, executed stage designs, and illustrated books for **José Lezama Lima** and other Cuban authors. After the triumph of the 1959 **Revolution**,

Portocarrero became a sort of official Cuban artist; he was the favorite of **Celia Sánchez**, his paintings were given as gifts to visiting dignitaries, and in 1968 he created a ceramic mural for the Palacio de la Revolución in Havana (see **Presidential Palace**). At the São Paulo Biennial of 1963, he exhibited more than fifty works in many media (ink, watercolor, and oil) and won the international prize. Please see color insert in Volume I for artwork.

Further Readings
Gómez Sicre, José. *Pintura cubana de hoy*. Havana: María Luisa Gómez Mena, 1944.
Ministerio de Cultura. *René Portocarrero*. Madrid: Museo Español de Arte Contemporáneo, 1984.

Alejandro Anreus

Presidential Palace (Museum of the Revolution)

The Presidential Palace was the residence for **presidents** of the Cuban Republic from 1920 to 1959. The building takes up nearly a square block and is located in **La Habana Vieja**. The palace was inaugurated in January 1920 by President **Mario García Menocal**, who was the first to occupy it. In 1959, **Fidel Castro** refused to use it for his official residence.

The palace, sitting atop square, chiseled, and massive white cinderblocks, and culminating in a majestic cupola, is rich in architectonic, artistic, and historic details. It was the work of the Cuban architect Carlos Maruri and the Belgian Jean Beleau. It evokes German architecture of the twentieth century as well as influences from Spanish military and civil construction. But the structure stands above any architectural eclecticism and merges well with its surroundings, becoming an essential element in the heart of the old colonial section of Havana. Tiffany was hired as the interior decorator, and the resulting Hall of Mirrors is one of the most beautiful rooms in the palace. The steps were built with Carrara marble. The ring that encircles the cupola is encrusted with sheets of 18 karat gold.

In March 1957, university students who were plotting to overthrow dictator **Fulgencio Batista**, who was in the building, attacked the palace. The violence resulted in dozens of deaths. Currently, the palace houses the Museum of the Revolution. The museum displays artifacts from Castro's revolutionary struggle. It also features artwork from Cuba's best artists and designers from the period. Please see color insert in Volume I for photograph. *See also* Architecture (Twentieth Century); Echeverría, José Antonio

Further Readings
Cuba en la mano, enciclopedia popular ilustrada. Havana: Impreta Úcar, García y Cía, 1940.
Roig de Leuchsenring, Emilio. *La Habana. Apuntes históricos*. Havana: Oficina del Historiador de la Ciudad de La Habana, 1963.

Armando H. Portela

Rodríguez Álvarez, Mariano (1912–1990)

A second-generation modernist, Mariano Rodríguez was perhaps the leading Cuban painter of the 1940s. Born in Havana, and known by his first name Mariano, Rodríguez was basically a self-taught artist. What little training he received was at La Esmeralda art school (1936) in Mexico City, where he studied drawing and oil painting with Manuel Rodríguez Lozano and fresco with Pablo O'Higgins. In 1937 Rodríguez returned to Cuba, where the painter **Eduardo Abela** invited him to teach at the short-lived Escuela Libre de Pintura y Escultura. At this time Rodríguez joined the Communist Party, known then as the **Partido Socialista Popular**. He would remain a party member until his death. His 1938 painting *Unidad* showed the stylistic influence of the Mexicans, as well as the evocation of the communist ideology in the depiction of a solidarious couple. This work received a prize in the Salón Nacional of that year. In the 1940s Rodríguez emerged as an important painter—his mature style was a combination of a tropical use of color with a highly structured yet modern sense of drawing, which owed much to both Cézanne and Matisse. In the 1940s he started painting the Cuban rooster, which became an icon within his painting. In Mariano Rodríguez's hands, the Cuban rooster became a colorful celebration of national identity, as well as a celebratory depiction of **machismo**. With **René Portocarrero** and **Alfredo Lozano**, he was an active member of the cultural group Orígenes. Rodríguez's oil paintings, watercolors, and ink drawings were included in New York's Museum of Modern Art's 1944 exhibition *Cuban Painting of Today*. After the 1959 **Revolution**, Rodríguez held a diplomatic post in India. When he returned to Cuba, he was an official of the artists' union, as well as head of the visual arts section at the **Casa de las Américas** in Havana. During the late 1950s and early 1960s, Rodríguez went through a brief yet very interesting abstract phase in his work. See also *Orígenes*

Further Readings

Casa de las Américas. *Mariano Rodríguez, 1912–90*. Havana: Galería Haydée Santamaría, 1998.

Museo Nacional. *Mariano: uno y múltiple*. Santa Cruz de Tenerife: Sala de Exposiciones Centro Cultural Cajacanarias, 1988.

Alejandro Anreus

Romañach, Leopoldo (1862–1951)

Leopoldo Romañach was Cuba's academic version of an Impressionist painter. Romañach was also a liberal teacher who influenced the first generation of Cuban modernists. Born in Sierra Morena, old province of Las Villas, Romañach studied at the **San Alejandro Academy of Fine Arts** in Havana. After studying at the academy, he traveled to Rome, where he continued his studies (1889–1895). While in Italy he studied the work of the Florentine painters Domenico Morelli and Antonio Mancini, who painted in dabs and patches, and worked outdoors. In 1895, with the help of his patron **Marta Abreu**, Romañach established a studio in New York City, where he earned a living as a portrait painter. He returned to Cuba in 1900, and he was immediately appointed professor of *colorido* (advanced oil painting) at the San Alejandro Academy. He was director of the academy from 1932 to 1936. In 1904 Romañach received the gold medal at the Saint Louis Exposition with his painting *La convaleciente* (the work was lost on the return trip to Cuba). Stylistically, Romañach's paintings are academic interpretations of Impressionism. At his worst, he painted sentimental portraits and genre scenes, with occasional moments of authenticity and freshness (*La niña de las cañas*). Perhaps his best paintings were the seascapes he produced during the last two decades of his life—these are direct and spontaneous landscapes of the coastal town of Caibarién. As a liberal teacher, Romañach nurtured the talents of the first generation of Cuban modernists—painters like **Víctor Manuel, Amelia Peláez, Eduardo Abela, Antonio Gattorno**, and **Fidelio Ponce** were among his students.

Further Reading

Valderrama, Esteban. *La pintura y la escultura en Cuba*. Havana: Editorial Lex, 1953.

Alejandro Anreus

Saavedra, Lázaro (1964–)

Lázaro Saavedra's multimedia works represent a synthesis of Dada concerns and irreverent Cuban humor, used to narrate an acute critique of Cuba's past and present and the roles of the artist within it. Born in Havana during the fourth year of the

Cuban **Revolution**, Saavedra received his undergraduate artistic education at the **San Alejandro Academy of Fine Arts** (1979–1983) and his graduate degree at the Instituto Superior de Arte (1983–1988), where he currently teaches. With four other artists Saavedra founded the artists' collective Grupo Puré in 1986, which favored the assimilation of international styles to visually narrate everyday life in Cuba. Starting in the late 1980s Saavedra began producing a series of small, cartoonlike drawings executed with a ballpoint pen on scraps of paper; these were everyman hominoids that questioned universal, even metaphysical issues, as well as day-to-day problems in **Fidel Castro**'s Cuba. His series of acrylic/collages depicting Cuban and Western icons (Marx, La Caridad del Cobre, The Sacred Heart of Jesus) mix irreverent humor with great skill in reproducing popular illustrations. Saavedra's most recent work has been in the media of installation and photography. Please see color insert in Volume I for artwork. *See also* Virgen de la Caridad del Cobre (Our Lady of Charity of El Cobre)

Further Readings

Camnitzer, Luis. *New Art of Cuba*. Austin: University of Texas Press, 1994.

Vives Gutiérrez, Cristina. *From the Negative*. Minneapolis: Photographic Arts, 2000.

Alejandro Anreus

San Alejandro Academy of Fine Arts (Academia San Alejandro de Bellas Artes)

The Free School of Drawing and Painting, later known as the San Alejandro Academy of Fine Arts, was founded in 1818, patronized by the progressive **Sociedad Económica de Amigos del País**, with the idea of raising the aesthetic level of the dominant Creole class. Its first director, the French neoclassical painter Jean Baptiste Vermay, emphasized the teaching of drawing as artistic discipline and for its industrial applications. The academy became better organized and expanded its curriculum under the directorship of Francisco Cisneros (1859–1878) and Miguel Melero (1878–1907). Melero, its first Cuban director, introduced progressive measures, such as opening the academy to women students. The outstanding artists-teachers associated with it in the twentieth century were the painters **Armando Menocal** (1860–1942) and **Leopoldo Romañach** (1862–1951), as well as the sculptor **Juan José Sicre** (1898–1974). San Alejandro remained Cuba's main official art school until 1962, and it is still in existence. In the 1920s its most promising students rejected the academy's conservative teachings and went on to form a separate modernist movement. Since then the best-known Cuban artists have followed a similar path.

Further Readings

Merino, Luz. "Academia de San Alejandro (1818–1900)." In *Selección de lecturas de arte. Cuba colonia*. Havana: Universidad de La Habana, 1991. 437–460.

Valderrama, Esteban. *La pintura y escultura en Cuba*. Havana: Editorial Lex, 1952.

Juan A. Martínez

Sánchez, Tomás (1948–   )

Tomás Sánchez is recognized as a multitalented artist, known for his paintings, drawings, engravings, and designs. Sánchez was born in Aguada de Pasajeros **Cienfuegos**. He completed studies at the **San Alejandro Academy of Fine Arts** and later went on to the Cubanacán school of art. In 1980, he won first place in the 19th International Joan Miró Prize of Drawing in Barcelona, Spain. He has had several personal exhibitions in Cuba, Spain, Greece, Austria, and elsewhere. His surreal style is known for its precise detail as well as spiritual themes. His work, *Culto a la caida de las aguas* (which features a waterfall), earned more than $100,000 at auction in 1996. Sánchez presently lives and works in Florida and Costa Rica.

Further Reading
"Pasaje de Peligro." *Juventud Rebelde* 1988.

Luis González

Serra-Badué, Daniel (1914–)

Daniel Serra-Badué is a Surrealist painter whose work is influenced by the European masters of Surrealism including Salvador Dalí, René Magritte, and Giorgio de Chirico. Serra-Badué is an internationally recognized second-generation modernist. Born in 1914 in **Santiago de Cuba**, Serra-Badué came of age as an artist in Havana, where he studied art in 1943 at the **San Alejandro Academy of Fine Arts**. He completed his studies in 1948, earning a doctorate at the **University of Havana**. Throughout his career he traveled back and forth between Cuba and Spain. In 1936, he studied in Spain at the School of Fine Arts in Barcelona, where he became familiar with European Modernism. In 1962, at the age of forty-eight, he left Cuba via Jamaica to settle in New York City. There he studied printmaking in 1964 at the Pratt Institute Graphic Center.

Serra-Badué's work is in numerous international museums including, among others, the Metropolitan Museum of Art in New York City, the Museum of Modern Art of Latin America in Washington, D.C., Museo de Arte Contemporáneo in Ibiza, Spain, and the Museum of Modern Art in New York City. His aesthetic focus was similar to that of the Parisian Surrealists. He was interested in the complexities of the unconscious, including the dream state as a fleeting temporal moment. The search for a national identity was also a concern for Serra-Badué, as it was for other Cubans of his generation. He expressed this through his paintings of colonial scenes of his hometown of Santiago. His paintings combined hard-edge analytical abstraction with representational metaphoric symbolism. Throughout his career in the United States his work received great praise from major art institutions. As early as 1938–1939, he was awarded a Guggenheim Foundation Fellowship. In 1963 and 1964, he received the Cintas Foundation Fellowship. In 1968 the National Academy of Design awarded him a Certificate of Merit in Graphics.

Further Readings
Fuentes-Pérez, Ileana, Graciella Cruz-Taura, and Ricardo Pau-Llosa, eds. *Outside Cuba: Contemporary Cuban Visual Artists*. New Brunswick, NJ: Rutgers University Press, 1989.
Sullivan, Edward J. *Latin American Art in the 20th Century*. London: Phaiden Press Limited, 1996.

Isabel Nazario

Sicre, Juan José (1898–1974)

Juan José Sicre introduced the ideals of modern sculpture to Cuban art. He did this not only through his own body of work but also through his many years of teaching at the **San Alejandro Academy of Fine Arts**. Sicre was born in the sugar mill town of Carlos Rojas in **Matanzas Province**. He received his artistic education at the Academia Villate (1916) in **Matanzas**, San Alejandro Academy in Havana (1918), and the Academia San Fernando in Madrid (1921–1922). In Spain Sicre became aware of the work of the Spanish sculptors Victorio Macho and Manolo Hugué. Sicre continued his studies in Paris at the Académie de la Grande Chaumière (1923), where he studied modeling with Antoine Bourdelle and direct carving with José de Creeft. Through Bourdelle, Sicre discovered the work of Auguste Rodin as well as archaic Greek sculpture. In the years 1924–1925, Sicre traveled throughout Italy, studying in Florence with the sculptor Domenico Trentacoste. In 1926 Sicre settled in Paris, where he befriended fellow Cuban artists like **Víctor Manuel** and **Antonio Gattorno** and Latin American writers like César Vallejo and Miguel Ángel Asturias. He sculpted portrait busts of all four. In 1927 Sicre returned to Cuba and was appointed a professor of sculpture at the San Alejandro Academy. In 1928 Sicre modeled the head of his future wife Sylvia Descoubet—in its simplicity and elegance this portrait brings to mind classical Greek sculpture. At the academy Sicre introduced the teaching of direct carving, which he had learned from de Creeft. Among his many students were the sculptors **Roberto Estopiñán** and **Agustín Cárdenas**. Sicre was a very prolific sculptor of public monuments. Among his best-known public sculptures are *Fuente de las Antillas, Monumento a Finlay*, and his best known work, the *Monumento a Martí* in the **Plaza de la Revolución**. Sicre went into exile in the United States in 1962. Once in exile, through the patronage of his cousin, art critic José Gómez Sicre, who headed the visual arts section at the Pan American Union in Washington, D.C., Sicre executed busts of John F. Kennedy and Rubén Darío. Sicre died in Cleveland, Ohio, where he lived with his son, a cellist for the Cleveland Symphony.

Further Readings

Museum of Modern Art of Latin America. *Selections from the Permanent Collection*. Washington, DC: Organization of American States, 1985.

Valderrama, Esteban. *La pintura y la escultura en Cuba*. Havana: Editorial Lex, 1953.

Alejandro Anreus

Soriano, Rafael (1920–   )

Rafael Soriano is an abstract painter who was born in 1920 in Cidro, **Matanzas Province**. He studied painting in 1942 at the **San Alejandro School of Fine Arts**. He was later founder and director for thirteen years of the first art school in the province of his birthplace. Soriano was one of the members of the abstract artists'

group "Diez Artistas Concretos" (1957–1959), which introduced the concept and practice of concrete art into Cuban art. At the age of forty-two Soriano left Cuba to reside in Miami.

Soriano is one of the principal figures in the Latin American painting tradition of Luminist paintings with a rich color that creates an overall light rendered through abstraction. He uses color to create a translucent light that he interprets as a symbol of energy and spirit. Over the years he has had numerous solo exhibitions including, among others, a one-man show in 1983 at the Centre Editart in Geneva, Switzerland. His work is in numerous collections including the Museum of Modern Art of Latin America in Washington, D.C., the Arthur M. Huntington Art Gallery at the University of Texas in Austin, and the Museo de Arte Zea, in Medellín, Colombia. Soriano remains an active painter in Miami.

Further Reading

Pau-Llosa, Ricardo. *Rafael Soriano and the Poetics of Light*. Coral Gables: Ediciones Habana Vieja, 1998.

Isabel Nazario

Templete, El

The Templete is the first Neoclassical structure built in Havana. Although small in size, it exerted an enormous influence on Cuban architecture in the nineteenth century. The design signaled a break with eighteenth-century baroque architecture, which dominated the city at the time. The emphasis on Neoclassical design underpinned a striving for modernity.

Located on one side of the Plaza de Armas, the Templete was built, according to tradition, on the site where Havana's first Mass and first city council meeting were held in 1519 under the shade of a ceiba tree. The monument was inaugurated on March 19, 1828, with a solemn mass

El Templete was built on the site where Havana's first Catholic mass is believed to have taken place. Photograph by Luis Martínez-Fernández.

officiated by Bishop Juan José Díaz de Espada y Landa and attended by the authorities of the island, including Captain-General Francisco Dionisio Vives.

The Templete was designed by Antonio María de la Torre, who incorporated into the structure the commemorative column erected in 1754 by Captain-General Francisco Cagigal de la Vega. In the building's interior, two murals by French painter Jean Baptiste Vermay celebrate the city's founding. A third mural by the same painter commemorating the dedication of the Templete was added at a later date. Vermay's ashes are interred in the building in a marble urn. The monument was restored in 1927 by Evelio Govantes and Félix Cabarrocas. *See also* Architecture (Colonial Era); La Havana Vieja (Old Havana)

Further Readings

Roig de Leuchsenring, Emilio. *La Habana. Apuntes históricos*. Havana: Oficina del Historiador de la Ciudad, 1964.

Weiss, Joaquín E. *La arquitectura colonial cubana (siglos XVI al XIX)*. Havana and Seville: Instituto Cubano del Libro–Junta de Andalucía, 1996.

Emma Álvarez-Tabío Albo

10

Popular Culture and Religion

Abakuá, Sociedad de

The Sociedad de Abakuá is an Afro-Cuban religious secret society, also known as the Ñáñigos, that is an important thread in Afro-Cuban identity and has contributed to the larger Cuban culture. The exclusively male group is thought to be a creation of slaves from eastern Nigeria and Cameroon who were known as Carabalí in Cuba (see **Afro-Cubans**; **Slavery**).

Like other African-based religious systems, masquerade is an important element of the Abakuás's rituals. The central rite, *el plante*, bears a resemblance to Ekpe and Egba rituals of West Africa. Community relationships are a central feature of the group, and they span the gap between the living and the dead. It is through ritual that ties between members and between the living and the dead are reaffirmed and maintained.

Dance and drumming, as part of the ritual complex, have extended the reach of the group beyond its small circle. Its distinctive rhythms have influenced the music world and can be heard in groups such as the **Matanzas**-based Los Muñequitos.

Historically Abakuá practice was referred to as *ñañiguismo*. It was feared and suppressed by the colonial government and sugar planters. This was in reaction to the "criminal" records of some members and the belief that the meetings were preludes to rebellions. In spite of official sanctions Abakuá survived.

Members have maintained Abakuá as a secret society, which has helped to strengthen the society as a cultural stronghold and reinforced its mystique. The group remains a vibrant part of Cuban culture. *See also* Palo Monte; Santería

Further Readings
Duany, Jorge. "After the Revolution: The Search for Roots in Afro-Cuban Culture." *Latin American Research Review* 23, no. 1 (1988): 244–255.
Quiñones, Tato. *Ecorie Abakuá: cuatro ensayos sobre los ñáñigos cubanos*. Havana: Ediciones Unión, 1994.

William Van Norman, Jr.

Bodegas

Bodegas is the name popularly given to grocery stores that not only sell food but also a wide variety of items. Until 1959, the word was typically associated with Spanish immigrants (frequently referred to as *gallegos*), who owned and operated most of these stores. The stores frequently were open long hours, starting from 6 A.M. until late at night. In 1910, legislation limiting working hours (Ley de Cierre) to ten

Poorly stocked bodega in Havana. Photograph by Celestino Martínez Lindín.

hours a day was adopted. The legislation had little impact on bodegas, however, because after the designated closing hour, bodega workers continued to transact business in the rear of the store. In the 1930s and 1940s, additional legislation was passed regulating working hours, time off from the job, and vacations. Bodega workers were typically young immigrants from Spain who worked and lived in the stores. Makeshift beds were set up in the stores to accommodate the workers. The poor living conditions and unsanitary conditions became the subject of many jokes and theatrical productions. The bodega, in slightly altered form, continues in Cuba today. It is where Cubans go to present their ration books (*libretas*) and pick up foodstuffs. There is a bodega on nearly every block that sells goods to those registered as living on the corresponding block. Since the **Revolution**, the term *bodega* is applied to the so-called Tiendas del Pueblo, which sell basic items on the ration system. *See also* Immigration (Twentieth Century); Nutrition and Food Rationing

Further Readings

Loveira, Carlos. *Generales y doctores*. Havana: Editorial Letras Cubanas, 2001.

Méndez Capote, Renée. *Historia de una cubanita que nació con el siglo*. Barcelona: Argos Vergara, 1985.

Meza, Ramón. *Mi tío el empleado*. Havana: Editorial Letras Cubanas, 2001.

Consuelo Naranjo Orovio

Botánicas

Botánicas are specialty shops that sell herbs and implements used by practitioners of **Santería** as well as home and herbal remedies. The shops are usually divided in two. The front is arranged like a store. Herbal lotions, candles, beads, and statues of saints are displayed and sold to the public. In the back of the shop is the consultation room. In this room, a faithful who needs help with emotional or family problems or who is suffering from an ailment meets with a *santero*. The santero will diagnose the condition and will proceed to help or cure the afflicted. The room also serves as a meeting place for the santeros to conduct their religious rituals. An altar is usually set up for the particular saint worshiped by the santero who owns or runs the botánica.

In Cuba, botánicas were usually located in poor neighborhoods. The botánicas were not advertised, and only the faithful knew about their existence and location. In the United States, botánicas gained notoriety beyond the Cuban and Latino communities when the Dade County Court, in Florida, attempted to close one shop in 1991, claiming that the store was selling animals for sacrifice. This incident was part of a larger legal battle to determine whether or not Santería was a legitimate religion. The state of Florida eventually lost the case.

The first botánicas were established in the United States when Cuban exiles settled in Florida, New Jersey, and New York in the early 1960s. The popularity of the stores, and the growth of Santería, spread to other Spanish-speaking groups. Today, there are botánicas in California, Illinois, and other states with large Latino communities. Many of the botánicas are now owned or managed by Puerto Ricans and Dominicans. In New Orleans, there are botánicas, but these shops serve practitioners of Voodoo and other traditions from Haiti.

As cultural icons of the Cuban experience, botánicas are portrayed in many literary works. The two most recent examples where the protagonist visits a botánica are in the novels *Dreaming in Cuban* (1992), by **Cristina García**, and *Going Under* (1996), by **Virgil Suárez**. *See also* Religion under Castro; San Lázaro (Saint Lazarus)

Further Reading

Matibag, Eugenio. *Afro-Cuban Religious Experience*. Gainesville: University Press of Florida, 1996.

D.H. Figueredo

Caballero de París (José María López Lledín), El (1899–1985)

El Caballero de París was a legendary figure from pre-**Revolution** Cuba. He was a distinguished-looking homeless man who roamed the streets of Havana. Of a gentle disposition, the Caballero de París did not beg for money. When a passer-by offered him a coin or a "peso," the Caballero would accept the gift but only after handing the passer-by a pencil or a postcard. Cuban American poet Pablo Medina described him thus: "He had matted shoulder-length white hair yellowed at the edges and a beard that radiated outward over his chest. Somewhere between his cheeks, a set of darkened teeth smiled at me." He wore a long white robe.

The Caballero's real name was José María López Lledín. He was born in Spain into a wealthy family. As a youth, he was falsely accused of having killed a man and was sent to prison. By the time he was released, he had lost his mental faculties. The name he eventually received was probably an allusion to a French film, *Monsieur de Paris*, from the late 1930s.

The Caballero was regularly caricatured in newspapers and magazines. In 1955, he was featured in a popular television program. After the triumph of the Revolution, the Caballero was interned in Mazorra Psychiatric Hospital where he was shaven and briefly treated; according to a rumor, he was released at **Fidel Castro**'s request. For Cubans in exile, the Caballero is a nostalgic symbol of a pre-Castro Cuba. In 2001 a statue was unveiled to commemorate his tragic life.

El Caballero de París. Courtesy of La Galería del Medio, Miami.

Further Reading

Medina, Pablo. *Exiled Memories*. Austin: University of Texas Press, 1990.

D.H. Figueredo

Carnivals

Carnivals in Cuba celebrate either a religious or a political festivity. Originally, carnivals were expressions of African and Catholic traditions that evolved out of a practice of singing praises to a deity (see **Afro-Cubans**; **Catholicism** and **Santería**).

During colonial times, Spanish authorities allowed slaves to celebrate Epiphany Day, also known as the **Three Kings' Day**, on January 6. The slaves would parade before their masters in a dancing procession called *comparsa*. The slaves would sing and play drums and trumpets. Over the years this public celebtration turned into carnivals which then spilled out of the rural areas and **sugar plantations** into cities and towns. The carnivals in Havana and **Santiago de Cuba**, lasting nearly a week, became the most popular.

The carnival in Havana took place in January. Large floats made their way through wide boulevards, followed by streams of flamboyantly dressed comparsa dancers. Audiences watched the procession from bleachers or balconies decorated with banners, streamers, and balloons. In **Santiago de Cuba**, located in the old province of Oriente (present-day **Santiago de Cuba Province**), there were two carnivals. One was scheduled before Lent and was meant to attract white Cubans. The second, and most popular, took place in July to celebrate the end of the sugar harvest (see **Sugar Industry**). For this carnival, not only did the comparsa dancers take to the streets but also the general public, dancing for hours along a designated road that crossed the width of the city. A popular song paid tribute to the carnival in Santiago: "I'm going to the Carnival in Oriente, That's the one carnival where I can have the most fun."

It was at the end of the July carnival in Santiago in 1953 that **Fidel Castro** launched the attack on the **Moncada Army Barracks**, hoping that most soldiers would be on leave and dancing at the carnival. For that reason after 1959 the carnival in Santiago has also been regarded as a celebration of the **Revolution**. Today, the carnival in Havana is also celebrated during the summer, from July 28 to August 10.

La Conga de Santiago. Photograph by Oronzo Leva.

Further Readings

Luis, William. *Culture and Customs of Cuba*. Westport, CT: Greenwood Press, 2001.

Williams, Stephen. *Cuba: The Land, the History, the People, the Culture*. Philadelphia: Running Press, 1994.

D.H. Figueredo

Catholicism

Roman Catholicism came to Cuba with the Spanish colonization in 1511, and since then, it has been an important spiritual and social force on the island. Presently, about 40 percent of Cubans claim to be Catholic. Early Catholic religiosity in Cuba was a product of a theology shaped by the zeal of the crusades against Moors and the fervor of the Catholic Counterreformation. Early in the Iberian expansion, the Spanish crown reached an agreement with the Vatican (*Patronato Real*), which gave the Spanish rulers control over ecclesiastical appointments and facilitated the frequent fusion of religious and government interests in Cuba (see **Colonial Institutions**).

The Church's agenda ranged from combating immorality to fighting the buccaneers. During much of the colonial era Church authorities created and administered all the schools and institutions of higher learning and sponsored many cultural events. With such a broad scope of concerns, and exclusive control over the celebration and registration of baptisms, marriages and funerals, it was virtually impossible to avoid the impact of the Church in daily life. The authority of bishops was often comparable to that of the island's highest civilian and military authorities.

However, radical initiatives also came from the Church ranks in Cuba. Father **Bartolomé de las Casas** labored beginning in the 1510s for better treatment for the **indigenous inhabitants**. Religious orders like the Jesuits and Augustinians often fought for the rights of the slaves and other oppressed Cubans. Ordinary individuals, meanwhile, appropriated the official religion in a popular religiosity corresponding to lifestyles of humbler classes. The **Virgen de la Caridad del Cobre** (Virgin of Charity of El Cobre) became popular among the general population. Devotion to the virgin started around 1600 when she appeared to two Indians and one black slave sailor wrestling a storm (later versions of the story claim that it was a black, a white, and an Indian sailor). After centuries of veneration, Pope Benedict XV declared the Virgin of Charity patron of Cuba in 1916.

The first diocesan synod of 1680 and the tenure of Bishop Diego Evelino de Compostela (1685–1704) marked the beginning of the Catholic Church's golden age in Cuba, which lasted until 1832. Some distinctive features of this period were the multiplication of church buildings and seminaries, the increase of the native clergy, and a powerful influence in culture and politics. As in Spain, the official Cuban Church after 1832 was on the defensive against liberal forces and becoming increasingly reactionary, pro-Spain, and elitist. In the midst of increasing secularization and dissatisfaction with **Spanish colonialism**, the Church leadership decided to support colonial rule.

After the U.S. invasion in 1898 and the **Constitution of 1901**, the Church was no longer under state patronage. Despite lacking government protection or exclusive rights, the Catholic Church adapted quickly to the new political realities. New lay organizations like the Knights of Columbus, the Catholic Knights, and the Isabelline Ladies became increasingly important in Republican Cuba. Although early in the Republic the Church acted timidly, by the end of **Fulgencio Batista**'s regime, it was again active in politics. According to a 1954 poll, 72.5 percent of Cubans claimed to be Catholic but less than a quarter attended church regularly.

Following an initial period of excitement about the advent of the **Revolution**, support quickly turned into disappointment. The first clashes between the Church hierarchy and the **Fidel Castro** regime occurred over new education legislation in 1959. By the time all Catholic schools and Catholic charitable organizations and their properties were confiscated in 1961, relations had soured. Within the first two years of the Revolution, furthermore, 70 percent of all priests and 90 percent of all nuns left Cuba either voluntarily or through deportation. During the balance of the 1960s the Catholic Church in Cuba continued on the defensive and assumed a posture of silence vis-à-vis the regime's atheistic and anti-clerical policies. The 1970s witnessed minimal improvements in the Church's standing. Significantly, however, while the Constitution of 1976 proclaimed scientific materialism as the philosophical foundation of the Cuban state, it provided for a degree of restricted religious freedom. By the 1980s, both the Church and the government had made concessions, and they had established a constructive dialogue. In September 1993, Cuba's bishops issued a stern pastoral letter in which they denounced the moral crisis of Cuban society and the regime. **Pope John Paul II's visit to Cuba** in February 1998 marked a high point in Cuba's Catholic Church history since the end of Spanish colonialism. The pope arrived by Castro's personal invitation, and about 500,000 Cubans attended his public masses. Although the Catholic Church in Cuba is still below its pre-1959 strength, there are indications of a growing Catholic spiritual revival. The Church, moreover, is playing an increasingly important charitable role in the context of the lingering **Special Period**. *See also* Religion under Castro

Further Readings

Kirk, John M. *Between God and the Party: Religion and Politics in Revolutionary Cuba.* Tampa: University of South Florida Press, 1989.

Maza Miquel, Manuel. *Esclavos, patriotas y poetas a la sombra de la cruz: cinco ensayos sobre catolicismo e historia en Cuba.* Santo Domingo: Centro de Estudios Sociales Padre Juan Montalvo, 1999.

Peritore, Patrick N. *Catholicism and Socialism in Cuba.* Indianapolis: Universities Field Staff International, 1989.

Dennis R. Hidalgo

Choteo

Choteo (mockery) is a particular brand of Cuban humor that goes hand in hand with quick wit, improvisation, and irrespectability. It is impressionistic, giving quick biting glances at reality. The choteo's comic peculiarity is that it targets authority in any form, with the purpose of undermining hierarchy, order, honor, and regulation. The choteo deauthorizes authority by debunking it, constituting a form of rebellion. It is undisciplined, unserious, even if the business at hand is of the utmost importance. Choteo reflects contempt for and cynicism about higher-ups and the institutions of society. One of the purposes of choteo is to privatize social relations, at least momentarily, by bringing the people and the institutions that stand above them down to the level of the popular, of the streets, of "us." This is choteo's equalizing effect. The choteo breeds jocular contempt for impersonal norms, the hallmark of modernity, as well as for ordinary people and leaders. The space of the choteo is social and public, for it always requires an audience of sympathetic ears who will understand the punch line and the sociocultural references. Above all, the choteo is an expression of disenchantment. Those who engage in it realize that nothing is totally sacred, believable, or honorable. The romantic idealism of Cuban culture finds a counterpoint in the choteo. Whether the choteo is the cause or effect of public disappointment is not clear; it is probably a bit of both. While the political history of the island provides adequate material for which the choteo can craft its peculiar humor, the choteo contributes to the erosion of legitimacy of institutions and leaders. It renders social relations relaxed but guarded at the same time, because anyone can *chotear* (mock) as readily as they can be *choteado* (mocked). The classic examination of choteo is **Jorge Mañach**'s *Indagación del choteo*. Anthropologist **Fernando Ortiz** traced choteo as one of the cultural contributions of black Cubans (see **Afro-Cubans**).

Further Readings

Ibarra, Jorge. *Un análisis psicosocial del cubano: 1898–1925*. Havana: Editorial de Ciencias Sociales, 1985.

Mañach, Jorge. *Indagación del choteo*. Miami: Mnemosyne, 1969.

Damián J. Fernández

Cigars and Cigar Making

European explorers first encountered tobacco cigars and cigar making in Cuba during **Christopher Columbus**'s first voyage to the Americas in 1492. Over the course of the next five hundred years, Cuba would become as famous for the quality of its tobacco cigars as for the way they are manufactured (see **Tobacco Industry**).

Cuba's **indigenous inhabitants** cultivated and smoked tobacco using a number of tubular instruments for ceremonial and medicinal purposes for centuries before the arrival of Spanish colonizers in the sixteenth century. Spanish colonists cultivated tobacco and began to popularize the cigar as the preferred method of smoking tobacco leaf early in the colonial enterprise. By the mid-sixteenth century, as demand for cigars featuring Cuban tobacco leaf increased in Europe, Cuba's tobacco production rose sharply. By the end of the seventeenth century, tobacco and cigar exports dominated Cuban commerce (see **Trade and Navigation [1500s–1800s]**).

Cigar making is a complicated process that begins with the sowing of tobacco seedbeds in early September. After a more than month-long period of gestation, seedlings are transferred to a field where they will come to maturity. When the tobacco plant blooms it is topped-off, forcing sprouts on the sides of the main stem. These sprouts are then removed and the leaf is picked. Once picked, the leaves are placed on poles and carried to curing barns, where they undergo a process of drying and fermentation. From here the leaf is placed in bulk stacks, where it undergoes a process of grading and continued fermentation. Once the second process of fermentation is complete, the leaves are sorted into two groups, called *tripa* (filler) and *capa* (wrapper). Now sorted into these two groups, the leaf is again baled and sent to a warehouse for a final stage of fermentation. Before being sent off to be rolled into cigars, the leaves are graded one last time by a *rezagador*, who ranks each piece according to size, color, and aroma.

Cigar making in Cuba has traditionally been an artisanal craft done in small *fábricas*. The *torcedor* (cigarmaker) has typically apprenticed in the trade for a few years before joining a workshop. Using a *chaveta* (a sort of knife), the cigarmaker cuts the leaf to form. He then creates a tubular filler of tobacco leaf and wraps a larger leaf around the filler, creating a cylinder that, while tight enough to maintain its shape, allows for a sufficient amount of air to work its way through the cigar, ensuring a consistent burn. The cigarmaker accomplishes this using a tool called a *cepo* which measures both the length and the diameter of each cigar. The quality of each individual cigar is judged on three factors: strength, aroma, and burn. Cigars are ready for market after they have been sorted, sized, labeled, and placed in cedar boxes, typically bearing the name, logo, and design of the individual workshop that manufactured the product.

Tobacco production in Cuba is traditionally divided into five regions, based on the quality of the leaf produced in each area. The finest leaves, and consequently the most prized cigars in the island, come from the western Vuelta Abajo region in modern-day **Pinar del Río Province**. Other regions include the semi vuelta, de partido, Remedios, and Oriente.

In the late nineteenth and early twentieth century, facing increased competition from foreign tobacco producers, Cuban cigarmakers created national standards for the manufacture of the island's famed habano cigars. These standards, which were codified through a series of legislative acts in the early twentieth century, guaranteed that, among other things, genuine habanos could only be manufactured by hand, in Cuba, using exclusively Cuban leaf.

Cuban cigars still maintain a place of prestige among cigar aficionados. Despite competition from a flourishing cigar industry in places like the Dominican Republic, Cuban cigars still command high prices on the international market and are part of a lively illicit trade between the island and the United States. Please see color insert in Volume I for photograph.

Further Readings

Cabrera Infante, Guillermo. *Holy Smoke*. New York: Harper and Row, 1985.

García Galló, Gaspar Jorge. *Biografía del tabaco habano*. Santa Clara, Cuba: Universidad Central de Las Villas, 1959.

Ortiz, Fernando. *Cuban Counterpoint: Tobacco and Sugar*. Trans. Harriet de Onís. Durham, NC: Duke University Press, 1995.

Perdomo, José E. *Léxico tabacalero cubano*. 1st ed. Havana: N.P., 1940.

John A. Gutiérrez

Cockfighting

Cockfighting (*peleas de gallos*) is a popular, if brutal, traditional Cuban sport where two roosters are prodded into fighting each other. The roosters are placed in a circular pit, called *la valla*. There is no exit out of the pit, and usually a wire fence tops the pit, thus making it impossible for the birds to fly away. The roosters' spurs have been sharpened; often, steel projections, similar to hooks or small knives, are placed over the natural spurs. The fight is over when one rooster disables or kills the other. Usually, the loser is tossed into the backyard. As chicks, the roosters are trained to fight against other chicks, often placing the bird in front of a mirror and prodding it to attack its own reflection.

Cockfighting dates back to Roman times from where the sport spread throughout Europe. It is believed that Spanish colonizers from southern Spain brought the practice to Cuba though there are some who maintain that the British introduced the sport during the **British occupation of Havana** in 1762. Regardless of how it came to the island, cockfighting became a favorite activity shared by all the social classes. It was common for aristocrats and peasants to attend the same event and sit in proximity of one another.

Cockfighting also attracted the attention of foreigners. During and after the Cuban **War of Independence**, U.S. troops often watched a game while they were on leave; this was also true of many diplomats visiting Cuba. Toward the end of the nineteenth century, the Spanish had outlawed the sport. After Cuba gained independence in 1902, however, the Cuban government legalized and regulated the sport. **Presidents** and other members of high society were ardent fans of the sport. President **Gerardo Machado**, for example, owned several fighting roosters.

Cockfighting permeated Cuban culture. Postcards depicting the event were common. Tobacco labels and boxes often portrayed roosters fighting each other. In the 1940s, matches between champion roosters were as eagerly anticipated as boxing encounters between famous boxers. A popular expression was *pelea como un gallito*, meaning "fight like a rooster," an allusion to the bravery displayed by the birds in the valla.

Today, the sport is illegal in Cuba, thought the event still takes place in the countryside. There are breeders working on the island who take pride in nurturing roosters known for their fighting spirit. **Raúl Castro** is said to be an ardent aficionado of the game. In recent years in Florida, authorities have closed down pits owned by Cuban Americans.

Further Readings

Fox, Mary Virginia. *Cuba*. San Diego, CA: Lucent Books, 1999.

Luis, William. *Culture and Customs of Cuba*. Westport, CT: Greenwood Press, 2001.

D.H. Figueredo

Coppelia Ice Cream Parlor

The giant Coppelia ice cream factory and parlor opened in Havana on June 4, 1966. A metallic cupola, surrounded by profuse leafy vegetation, dominates the entrance to the building by architect Mario Girona. On the first floor of this national institution there are three serving areas where one can purchase any of twenty-five flavors. There are also three open-air salons that comfortably accommodate more than 1,000 patrons. Coppelia sits on the site of the former "Reina Mercedes" Hospital, which was founded in 1597 and originally called "Felipe el Real" (Phillip the King). The hospital was demolished in 1959. Coppelia is a favored meeting place for *Habaneros*. The giant ice cream parlor was featured prominently in opening and closing scenes of the film *Fresa y chocolate* (1993). *See also* Celia Sánchez

Further Reading

"Abierta al público la heladería 'Coppelia.'" *Granma*, June 5, 1966, 3.

Araceli García Carranza

Cuban Spanish (Language)

Cuban Spanish is the variety of the Spanish language currently spoken by some 11 million inhabitants of the island and some 1.25 million Cubans and Cuban Americans in the United States and elsewhere. It shows a range of peculiarly Cuban features, as well as many characteristics common to Caribbean Spanish, common, indeed, to the lowland coastal regions of Spanish America more generally.

Cuba's linguistic influences began with the **indigenous inhabitants** (Taínos) and others native groups, virtually annihilated by the mid-sixteenth century. Spanish immigration began with the voyages of discovery and **conquest** and continued throughout colonial times; southern Spain (Andalusía) established itself as the biggest Iberian source alongside a strong, continuous immigration of Canary Islanders. Spanish influence persisted strongly even after 1825, when all of mainland Spanish America had gained independence, but Cuba (like Puerto Rico) remained a colony. Africans, particularly West Africans (of Yoruba, Kikongo, and as many as twenty other ethnolinguistic origins), arrived beginning in the sixteenth century via the **slave trade**, but only some 100,000 reached Cuba before 1790 (see **Afro-Cubans**). Thereafter, well over half a million were brought by the nineteenth-century **sugar plantation** boom; in all, over 700,000 Africans arrived on Cuban shores. Renewed Spanish emigration in the late nineteenth and early twentieth centuries drew heavily from Galicia and the Canaries (see **Colonization and Population [Nineteenth Century]** and **Immigration [Twentieth Century]**). Two other demographic infusions deserve mention: some 125,000 **Asian contract laborers** in the third quarter of the nineteenth century, then some 30,000 more in the 1920s, and tens of thousands of African-descent laborers from elsewhere in the Caribbean in the early twentieth century (see **Caribbean Immigration**). Lastly, though not realized through large-scale immigration, the influence of British and (later) U.S. English was considerable, beginning in the late eighteenth century.

In its phonology, Cuban Spanish presents a cluster of recognizable characteristics, most of them largely shared with the Puerto Rican and Dominican varieties. Three are most readily noted: (1) *s* at the end of a word is often aspirated or eliminated (*los amigos* is pronounced *loh amigo*); (2) *n* at the end of a syllable is velarized, that is, articulated toward the back of the mouth, at the uvula, and resembling the last sound in the English *king* (*con alegría* is pronounced *cong alegría; entre* as *engtre*); and (3) in the context of some general confusion of *r* and *l*, *r* at the end of a word shifts for some speakers to an *l* sound (*cantar* is pronounced *cantal*). Other features of the sound system include (4) devoicing of *rr* as in *rápido*, a trait that carries some stigma of low socioeconomic status; (5) less frequently, and usually in the humblest social strata and the rural center and east, velarization of *rr* to resemble standard French *r*; (6) faint aspiration of *x*, rendered as *h*, instead of the standard sound akin to the Scottish *ch* in *Loch Ness* (thus, *bajo* is pronounced *baho*); (7) *yeismo*, that is, pronunciation of *ll* as Spanish *y*; and (8) pronunciation of initial *y* as an affricative, that is, like the initial sound in English *juice*. A notable feature of rural, working-class, and less-educated speech generally, shifts *r* at the end of a syllable or word to *y*, thus rendering *comer* as *comey* and reducing *compadre* to *compay*.

Morphologically—that is, in word formation—Cuba is *tú* territory for informal address, but faint traces of an old *voseo* tradition survived well into the twentieth century; verb forms such as *coméi* and *hablái* are vestiges of that tradition. Cubans tend to favor diminutives ending in *-ico*, instead of the more standard *-ito* (thus, *chiquitico, momentico*). A rustic plural form survives in *manises*, **mambises**, and so on. Pronouns also tend to be retained where standard Spanish would elide them: *Yo no entiendo esa canción* instead of *No entiendo esa canción*.

Most recognizably Cuban in syntax—how phrases and sentences are formed—is probably the interrogative form retaining pronoun and verb without inversion: *¿Qué tú quieres?* instead of the standard *¿Qué quieres [tú]?* Notable too is the relative absence of subjunctives in constructions, such as: *¿Qué me sugieres para yo llegar a tiempo?* Also typical is the initial *más* in negative combinations such as *más nada* and *más nunca*.

The Cuban lexicon is heavily stocked with words of Spanish, particularly Andalusian and Canary origin; indigenous terms, mainly from Taíno; and Africanisms. English influence has grown steadily, beginning in the mid-eighteenth century; Chinese loan words are relatively few.

Within the spoken sentence, a marked rise in intonation, leading to a sustained, moderately high pitch, followed by a rather sudden fall—often devoiced—at the end, characterizes the informal spoken language. Cubans tended to be regarded as among the most rapid speakers of Spanish; the general term of address *chico* is often taken as emblematic of Cuban speech, in much the manner of *che* in the Río de la Plata. Cuban Spanish can fairly be said to show fondness for word-play, diminutives, metaphor, and comical euphemism (see **Choteo**).

Cuban Spanish has challenged generations of scholars. Beginning with his path-breaking *Los negros brujos* (1906), **Fernando Ortiz** campaigned nobly for recognition and respect for Cuba's Afro roots but was sometimes too quick to assert African etymologies without adequate documentation. The Dominican writer

Max Henríquez Ureña fought for decades against facile readings of Cuban Spanish as a transposition from Andalusía. Certainly there are many Andalusianisms, but some are hard to disentangle from West African and other sources. The *r–l* confusion and the "disappearing" *s* exemplify features of possible West African, Canary Island, or Andalusian provenance—or a combination? The intriguing puzzle of the noninverted question (*¿Cómo tú estás?*) has been ascribed to factors ranging from English syntactic "contamination" to internal linguistic dynamics of Spanish; Germán de Granda has made a serious, plausible case for West African origin embodied in a now-defunct Spanish-African Creole. Of course, some Afro-Cuban traits appear on closer study to be social-class, not race, based. Overall, though, Cuban-Spanish linguistic study appears to be taking West African influences increasingly seriously.

The notion that Cuban Spanish is meaningfully related to a Caribbean pattern retains much credibility. Indeed, many students of the language continue to find useful and compelling Ramón Menéndez Pidal's larger contrast of a relatively dynamic, Andalusía-influenced "trade-route Spanish" comprising the Caribbean and other lowland, coastal areas with the relatively static "viceregal Spanish" of Mexico, Peru, and other interior highlands.

The rise of a large Cuban-origin population on the North American mainland raises the question of whether Cuban Spanish there has evolved into a new language variety (see **United States, Cuban Migrations to the**). Certainly mainland Cubans are far from socially (and linguistically) uniform: The largely professional, middle-class, white influx of the early 1960s was joined two decades later by a smaller but considerable contingent, poorer and more ethnoracially mixed, from the **Mariel boatlift**. Young Cuban Ameri-

cans of the second post-1959 generation are tending toward English-dominant bilingualism, but densely settled Spanish-speaking ethnic enclaves make this process slower than for other Latin American immigrant groups. Some indices show significant differences between island and mainland; the weakening of the *n* consonant through velarization (the *ng* sound), for instance, is more marked in Miami than in Havana). But the overall evidence is far from conclusive. And relative relaxation in U.S.-Cuban relations in the 1990s led to renewed island-mainland contact, evoking the far from implausible prospect of a coming, large-scale reencounter—linguistic and otherwise—between the two great segments of *cubanidad*.

Further Readings

Canfield, D. Lincoln. *Spanish Pronunciation in the Americas*. Chicago: University of Chicago Press, 1981.

De Granda, Germán. *Español de América, español de África y hablas criollas hispánicas*. Madrid: Editorial Gredos, 1994.

Lipski, John M. *Latin American Spanish*. London: Longman, 1994.

Menéndez Pidal, Ramón. "Sevilla frente a Madrid." In *A Andrés Martinet: estructuralismo e historia*. La Laguna, Canary Islands: Universidad de la Laguna, 1957–1958: 3:99–165. Cited by D. Lincoln Canfield. *Spanish Pronunciation in the Americas*. Chicago: University of Chicago Press, 1981, 42.

Ortiz, Fernando. *Nuevo Catauro de cubanismos*. Havana: Editorial de Ciencias Sociales, 1974.

Perl, Matthias, and Armin Schwegler, eds. *América negra: panorámica actual de los estudios lingüísticos sobre variedades hispanas, portuguesas y criollas*. Madrid: Iberoamericana, 1998.

Santiesteban, Argelio. *El habla popular cubana de hoy*. Havana: Editorial de Ciencias Sociales, 1985.

Pablo Julián Davis

Cuisine

Cuban cuisine made its way from the countryside and the peasants' table to Cuban society at large. It is the blend of African, Amerindian, and Spanish cookery with Arabic and Chinese influences. Though the sea surrounds Cuba, fish is seldom used in cooking; instead, meat is the favored food. Soup, white rice, beans, maize, and rooted vegetables make up the traditional Cuban diet. Desserts are milk and/or fruit based with lots of sugar. Tropical fruit juices are favored drinks. Cubans like their meals hot, even sandwiches, and usually finish off eating with a cup of strong coffee.

The *ajiaco* is Cuba's national dish. It appeared early in Cuban history, combining native ingredients with those imported by Spanish colonizers and African slaves. In the sixteenth century, a Spanish colonizer described it as "the union of fresh meats cut up in small pieces that stew with diverse root vegetables that are stimulated by means of a caustic pepper called 'ají-ají,' that they give color with a seed called 'vija.'" In essence, ajiaco was a stew made first by Cuba's **indigenous inhabitants**, then the Creole peasants, and later on by slaves. It consisted of stewing anything that was available at the moment. Though it was regarded as a food for the lower classes, ajiaco became popular throughout the island among all classes. Today, a typical recipe includes several types of meat (salt-dried beef, flank steak, ribs) and a variety of tropical rooted vegetables (*ñame*, yucca, sweet potato) and green plantain.

The second most popular dish is the *congrí oriental* and its western variant, *moros y cristianos*; both recipes call for white rice and beans. Rice was first introduced by the colonizers from southern Spain, used by African slaves from West Africa (see **Slavery**), and popularized by **Asian contract laborers**; beans were used by Amerindians and Africans alike. Congrí oriental is prepared in the eastern provinces, and it uses red beans; moros y cristianos is from the western side of the island, and it uses black beans. In both cases, the rice and the beans are cooked together and served with some meat dish. For the **Noche Buena** meal (Christmas Eve dinner) these were favorite dishes, served with pork, which was roasted outdoors over a grill. The name moros y cristianos alludes to Spanish and Moorish culture on the Iberian Peninsula before the Reconquest of Spain, finalized in the 1490s.

Other popular dishes include *guiso de quimbombó*, a stew with pork, green plantain, and okra, which was introduced by African slaves; *potaje*, a bean-based soup; *fufú*, mashed green plantains with garlic; *picadillo*, ground beef seasoned with garlic, onions, and peppers; and *ropa vieja*, spicy shredded beef with sauce served over steaming white rice.

All of these meals created a cuisine different from that eaten by the Spanish in Europe. By the nineteenth century, it was evident that Cuban cookery had come into its own, a fact acknowledged in 1857 with the publication of the book *Nuevo manual de la cocinera catalana y cubana*.

In the 1900s, American presence on the island influenced Cuban cuisine. Sandwiches gained popularity. Cuba developed its own version of the hamburger, the *frita*, as well as the *media noche*, a roast pork, boiled ham, and cheese sandwich, served on soft egg buns and slightly toasted. The name "midnight" alluded to the practice of eating this sandwich late at night, usually after attending a theatrical performance or seeing a movie. The cuban sandwich is similar to the midnight sandwich but uses Cuban or Italian bread.

Cubans love sweets, the legacy of the dominance of the **sugar industry**. The most popular milk-based desserts are *flan* and *natilla*, custard puddings; *arroz con leche*, rice pudding; and *dulce de leche*, milk boiled with sugar into tiny brown crusts. Fruit-based desserts are the *boniatillo*, a confection made with sweet potato and sugar and particularly popular in the countryside; *dulce de coco*, shredded coconut with cinnamon; coconut, guava, orange, and papaya marmalade. Cubans are fond of guava paste with cheese. The guava is sliced into a piece about half an inch wide and served over a slice of cream or white cheese.

Cuba yields a great variety of tropical fruits. Some of the favorite drinks are guava, mango, and papaya juices, to name a few. *Zambumbia* was a sugarcane juice that emerged in the 1840s. A version of this juice is still popular today, called *guarapo*. Cuba also manufactured two local soft drinks: Ironbeer, similar to root beer, and Materva. Malta is another favorite Cuban drink; it is a nonalcoholic malt-based beverage.

Cuban coffee is strong, dark, and sweet. The cup of coffee that accompanies the meal is usually served in demitasse cups. *Café con leche* is usually drunk early in the morning; it is similar to the French *café au lait*.

Cuban recipes were collected in 1959 in a book, *Cocina al minuto*, written by television gourmet **Nitza Villapol**. For many, this is the best volume on the subject.

Further Readings
González, Reynaldo, and José A. Figueroa. *Échale salsita*. Havana: Editorial Casa de las Américas, 2000.

Luis, William. *Culture and Customs of Cuba*. Westport, CT: Greenwood Press, 2001.

Urrutia Randelman, Mary, and Joan Schwartz. *Memories of a Cuban Kitchen*. New York: Simon and Schuster, 1992.

Villapol, Nitza. *Cocina al minuto*. Havana: Orbe, 1959.

D.H. Figueredo

Dominoes

The game of dominoes rivals **baseball** as the national pastime of the Cuban people. Predominantly played by older Cuban males, this form of entertainment is an important vehicle of social cohesion and camaraderie. It is usually accompanied by drinking, cigar smoking, and joking (see **Choteo**).

Dominoes are believed to be a Chinese invention. Others hold that they originated in Ancient Egypt. The game made its way to Europe in the early eighteenth century, from where Spanish colonists most likely brought it to Cuba.

Dominoes can be played by two to four players, either individually or in teams. The dominoes themselves are rectangular pieces (twenty-eight pieces in all) made of wood, bone, ivory, or plastic. Each piece has dots on the front and is blank on the back. The face (the side with the dots) has a horizontal division across the middle, and each half has anywhere from zero to six dots. Cubans developed an expanded variation of the game using 55 pieces (0 to 9 dots).

The game starts with the players placing all the dominoes face down on the table and turning and mixing them (such as to shuffle them). Players are then dealt an equal number of dominoes. A player then places one of his dominoes on the center of the table. The next player must place a piece with a matching number of dots on one or the other half, next to the previous piece. For instance, if the first player opens with a domino that has three dots on one end and, say, two on the other, the next player may play a domino with three dots on one end (and some other number on the other) or a domino with two dots on one end (and some other number on the other). In one version, if a player does not have a piece with the necessary number of dots, he must draw from the pile until he does. As the dominoes are placed on the table, they form a "skeleton." Dominoes are always placed at one or another end of the skeleton. The person who plays all of his dominoes first is the winner. In each round of play, the winner is awarded points according to the number of dots on the remaining players' pieces. The first player to

Young *Habaneros* spend an afternoon playing dominoes in la Plaza Vieja in Havana. Photograph by Luis Martínez-Fernandez.

reach 200 points is the overall winner. Cuban exiles settling in **Little Havana** brought the game with them and established the famous Máximo Gómez Domino Park off la Calle Ocho (8th Street).

Further Reading

Pérez Firmat, Custavo. *Next Year in Cuba: A Cuban's Coming of Age in America*. New York: Doubleday, 1996.

Luis González

Freemasonry

The origins of Masonry in Cuba date back to the eighteenth century and the **British occupation of Havana** in 1762. One of the earliest lodges, known as San Juan #218, dates back to that period and was made up of military men. Later on, there were lodges composed of French immigrants fleeing Haiti. Another of the earliest lodges in Cuba was the "Templo de las Virtudes Teologales," the formation of which was sanctioned by the Grand Lodge of Pennsylvania. Later on, other groups, such as the Grand Lodge of Louisiana, also established lodges on the island.

In 1822, the Gran Logia Española del Rito de York (Grand Spanish York Rite Lodge) was established and lasted until 1828. The Masonic movement spread throughout the island, despite official efforts in the nineteenth century to discourage membership. The Fraternidad and Perseverancia lodges were formed in **Santiago de Cuba** in 1857. The San Andrés Lodge merged with the others in 1859 to form the Gran Logia de Colón (Grand Lodge of Columbus). In 1859, Andrés Cassard, delegate of the Supreme Council in Charleston, founded the Supreme Council of Columbus for Cuba and the other islands of the West Indies. The establishment of the Gran Oriente of Cuba and the Antilles in 1862 by Antonio Vicente de Castro provoked a crisis in the Masonry movement. In 1880, the Gran Logia de la Isla de Cuba (Grand Lodge of the Island of Cuba) and the Gran Logia de Colón (Grand Lodge of Columbus) decided to merge and form the Gran Logia Unida de Colón e Isla de Cuba (United Grand Lodge of Columbus and the Island of Cuba). Antonio Govín became the first grand master of the lodge, which consisted of forty-four different branches and more than 2,000 members. The Spanish orders of the movement, including the lodges Grande Oriente de España, Gran Oriente Nacional de España, and Gran Oriente Español, were established in the 1870s. The Masonic movement remains active in Cuba today, represented by the Gran Logia de Cuba (Grand Lodge of Cuba), recognized internationally.

Throughout Cuba's history Freemasons have played important political roles. They were prominent in the Águila Negra conspiracy of the mid-1820s and later in the annexationist movements of the 1840s and 1850s and the separatist wars of the last third of the nineteenth century. Since 1959 the membership and activities of Masonic lodges have been drastically reduced. *See also* Annexationism; National Flag; López de Uriolaz, Narciso

Further Readings

Castellano, José M. *La Masonería Española en Cuba*. Tenerife, Canary Islands: Centro de la Cultura Popular Canaria, 1996.

Fernández Callejas, R. *Historia de la Francmasonería en Cuba*. Havana: Orientación Masónica, 1944.

Manuel de Paz Sánchez

Guajiros

Guajiros is an affectionate nickname applied to Cuba's rural dwellers, typically of white complexion and consisting primarily of immigrants from the Canary Islands. The people of Oriente often use the term *montuno* instead of guajiro. The guajiros are people traditionally identified with **agriculture** and cultivation, whether they owned the land or had access to it through some other arrangement. The image of the guajiro is one of a small farmer working the land next to one or two slaves, cultivating vegetables, and raising animals on the outskirts of a city or town.

With the increase of tobacco farming in the seventeenth century, guajiros expanded into new areas, particularly in **La Habana Province**. Small tobacco farmers, known as *vegueros*, emerged to challenge the interests of the Spanish crown and the state tobacco monopoly. The disputes led to open rebellion between 1717 and 1723 against the monopoly (see **Vegeros' Revolts**). The small tobacco farmers were eventually displaced from their lands by the sugar planters and forced to relocate to more remote areas, including Vuelta Abajo, Las Villas, and **Holguín**. There they grew crops for internal markets. The life of the guajiro/veguero was a difficult one and compared by Cuban Scholar **Enrique José Varona** to that of the slave (see **Slavery**). By 1862, they made up 15 percent of the population but produced more than 25 percent of the agrarian goods. In the twentieth century, new immigrants flowed into Cuba and expanded into regions in the central part of the island.

The predominance of guajiros in tobacco growing areas explains their unique contribution to tobacco culture (see **Tobacco Industry**). Unlike other immigrant groups, Canary Islanders (also known as *isleños*) migrated as family units, with an equal percentage of women, a trend dating back to the seventeenth century. The maintenance of the family structure created the conditions under which strong cultural traditions were passed from one generation to the next. This accounts for the emergence of a body of folklore that can be traced back to the Canary Islands. Unique musical instruments such as the *timple* or *tiple* and the *güiro* are still popular. These instruments are used during large reunions in which dancing and storytelling, with a strong emphasis on irony and satire, take center stage (see **Choteo**). The guajiro and his proclivities are synonymous with Cuban rural life, including the image of the quarreling gambler losing his money on **cockfights**, or the sleeping farmer laying on a hammock with his machete hanging from his belt. Another popular image of the guajiro is of a stubborn, robust farmer proud and protective of his independence. Even his typical clothes, the striped trousers, straw hat, and Moorish shoes, have become symbols of Cuban identity. Please see color insert in Volume I for photograph. *See also* Immigration (Twentieth Century)

Further Readings

Galán, Natalio. *Cuba y sus sones*. Madrid: Pretextos, 1997.

Ortiz, Fernado. *Cuban Counterpoint: Tobacco and Sugar*. Durham, NC: Duke University Press, 1995.

Manuel Hernández González

Guayaberas

Widely considered a typical Cuban garment, the *guayabera* is an elegant but convenient warm weather shirt, worn outside the pants. It has become a classic expression of Cuban identity and tropical practicality. Decorated with pockets, pleats, and a profusion of buttons, and often embroidery in two rows down the front, the

Traditional *guayabera* shirt. Sketch by Luis Alberto Martínez.

that the shirt's original name was *yayabera*, for the Yayabo River. Its name may also derive from the fruit guayaba, as its pockets are wide enough to hold a number of the fruits. The guayabera comes in a wide range of styles. Originally white and made of linen or light cotton, today guayaberas may be seen in all colors, highly decorated or plain, and with matching or contrasting embroidery or pleats. The number of pockets also may vary from the usual four. The guayabera allows for decorous attire in a sunny and humid climate without a cumbersome and uncomfortable tie or jacket and furthermore expresses *cubanía*, a proud sense of "Cubanness." The stylish Cuban president **Carlos Prío Socarrás** wore guayaberas in the **presidential palace** and thus helped popularize them in the late 1940s and early 1950s.

Further Readings

Calasibetta, Charlotte M. *Fairchild's Dictionary of Fashion*. New York: Fairchild Publications, 1988. 493–494.

Molinet, María E. "La guayabera." *Cuba Travel Magazine* 2, no. 2 (2000): 24.

David C. Carlson

Judaism

The presence of Jews in Cuba dates to the early years of the Spanish **conquest**. Later colonial history shows that from 1500 to the late 1800s crypto-Jews participated directly in the sugarcane culture and industry and in commerce and the **contraband trade**. Jews also collaborated during the **War of Independence**. During the Spanish-Cuban-American War (1898), some 3,500 Jewish soldiers and officers from the United States volunteered in the war, and they later founded the first synagogue and cemetery in 1906. In 1914, the first Sephardic society was founded during the inflow of thousands of immigrants from Turkey and the Balkans. B'nai B'rith Lodge was founded in 1943,

guayabera is a distinctive garment for men. A longer, women's version of the guayabera was, and is still, used by female shop clerks. Guayaberas are worn long or short sleeved throughout Latin America and the Caribbean for both formal and informal occasions. While stories of the shirt's origins in both coastal Mexico and Cuba abound, the guayabera is strongly associated with Cuba.

It is thought that the guayabera originated in **Sancti Spíritus** two centuries ago, where it was used by the region's rural population (see **Guajiros**). With splits on both sides, guayaberas allowed for machetes to be carried on belts. Some believe and later the Adath Israel Religious Society in **Habana Vieja**. In 1952, there were 12,000 Jews in Cuba (of these, 7,200 were Ashkenazic).

After the **Revolution**, about 94 percent of the 15,000 Jews of Cuba left the country, including 500 children alone brought out by the HIAS (Hebrew Immigrant Aid Society) to the United States (see **Pedro Pan [Peter Pan], Operation**). The remaining community survived despite its isolation, depletion, and assimilation into the Cuban culture and the legal restrictions (until 1991) on religious practice in Cuba. Although **Fidel Castro**'s foreign policy remained strongly anti-Zionist and anti-Israel, Cuban Jews enjoyed a relative freedom of worship and respect; all synagogues have remained open, and despite migratory waves to Israel and other countries, some 600 Jews keep their religion and traditions in Havana and other Cuban cities. *See also* Immigration (Twentieth Century); Religion under Castro; *St. Louis* Affair

Further Readings

Asís, Moisés. *Judaism in Cuba, 1959–1999*. Miami: University of Miami Institute for Cuban and Cuban-American Studies, 2000.

Bettinger-López, Caroline and Ruth Behar. *Cuban-Jewish Journeys: Searching for Identity, Home, and History in Miami*. Knoxville: University of Tennessee Press, 2000.

Levine, Robert M. *Tropical Diaspora: The Jewish Experience in Cuba*. Gainesville: University Press of Florida, 1993.

Moisés Asís

New Year's Day (Primero de Enero; Día de Año Nuevo)

New Year's Day is a traditional Cuban holiday, also known since 1959 as Liberation Day. It celebrates the advent of the new year and the triumph of the Cuban **Revolution**. On January 1, 1959, dictator **Fulgencio Batista** resigned from his post

and left Cuba along with his family and a few close associates. As the news spread throughout the island, **Fidel Castro** ordered **Ernesto Che Guevara** and **Camilo Cienfuegos** to march to Havana and take over the capital city's military garrisons. In the meantime, hundreds of rebels were guarding the streets of Havana, trying to keep order. A few days later, Castro arrived in Havana, taking over the government (see **Batista, Struggle against**).

Prior to the Revolution, families and friends gathered together on the evening before New Year's Day. Just before midnight, they toasted with Spanish cider and ate twelve grapes—one grape for each toll announcing midnight; and then, especially in Havana, some poured buckets of water onto the street to signify getting rid of the old and bringing in the new. Since 1959, New Year's Day is celebrated with marches and parades. Thousands of Cubans gather at the **Plaza de la Revolución**, or other historic sites on the island, to hear Castro address the nation.

As the Revolution became institutionalized in the early 1960s and imposed its atheistic dogma, New Year's Day replaced the traditional Christmas festivities held on December 24 and 25 and on January 6. Many families exchange gifts on New Year's Day.

Further Reading

Moses, Catherine. *Real Life in Castro's Cuba*. Wilmington, DE: Scholarly Resources, 2000.

D.H. Figueredo

Noche Buena (Christmas Eve)

During the 1950s, a popular Cuban song asked "¿Cuándo llegará la Noche Buena?" (When will Christmas Eve Arrive?). The song yearned for the advent of Cuba's most popular holiday, Noche Buena.

Falling on December 24, Noche Buena, especially before the **Revolution**, was a major holiday in Cuba in its own right, and not secondary to the celebration of Christmas Day. The holiday celebrated the birth of Christ and the gathering of peasants and shepherds around the newborn.

On Noche Buena, family, friends, and relatives gathered together for a big meal. The meal traditionally consisted of roast pork, white rice with beans, either black or red, depending on the region, and fried plantains (see **Cuisine**). For dessert, there was *flan* and *turrones* (nougats) from Spain. Just before midnight, families went to church to attend the *misa del gallo*, the rooster's mass. Throughout the day, radio stations played Christmas and religious music. The following day, Christmas Day, was a day for rest. Gifts were exchanged twelve days later on January 6, on **Three Kings' Day** (Epiphany Day).

The revolutionary government officially suspended Noche Buena in 1962. In the 1990s, there was talk of restoring the holiday. This took place finally in 1997, when **Fidel Castro** announced that families were free to celebrate Christmas and Noche Buena.

In the United States, Cubans and Cuban Americans celebrate Noche Buena as well as Christmas Day. In places like Miami, Tampa, and Union City, New Jersey, some families order a leg of roasted pork for the Noche Buena supper. *See also* Catholicism

Further Readings

Cabrera, Cloe. "The Ultimate Feast." *Tampa Tribune*, December 13, 2000, 1.

Luis, William. *Culture and Customs of Cuba*. Westport, CT: Greenwood Press, 2001.

D.H. Figueredo

Ortega y Alamino, Jaime Lucas (1936–   )

A soft-spoken and thoughtful critic of the revolutionary government, Cardinal Jaime Lucas Ortega y Alamino was primarily re-

Cardinal Jaime Ortega, Cuba's highest prelate.

sponsible for negotiating the conditions under which Pope John Paul II traveled to Cuba in 1998 (see **Pope John Paul II's Visit to Cuba**). To pave the way for the pope's visit, Cardinal Ortega appeared on Cuban television just days before to give a carefully worded statement intended to allay the concerns of the government, while at the same time seeking to create an environment of greater freedom for the Roman Catholic Church. Vatican insiders consider him a strong candidate for the papacy (see **Catholicism**).

The son of a sugar worker and a housewife, Ortega was born in Jaguey Grande in **Matanzas Province**. He attended seminary in Quebec, Canada, at St. Albertus Magnus under the direction of the Mission Fathers and was ordained a priest in 1964 in the Cathedral of **Matanzas**. After serving two years as a parish priest, Ortega was imprisoned in a worker reeducation camp where he began ministering to his fellow inmates (see **Religion under Castro**). In 1967, after a year at the camp, he was released and allowed to continue his parish duties. He was later reassigned to the Cathedral of Matanzas. In 1978, Ortega was named to the position of bishop of **Pinar del Río Province** where he served for two years before his installation as archbishop of Havana, where he presides over the **Cathedral of Havana**. Pope John Paul II elevated him to cardinal in 1994.

Throughout his pastoral career, Ortega has walked a fine line between overt criticism of the revolutionary government and silence. On several occasions, Ortega has directly criticized the government and come under fire by the state-run media. At times, his decisions to grant interviews to dissident journalists or attack the **Revolution**'s **human rights** record have angered the government. Some elements of the Cuban exile community criticize Ortega for being far too gentle in his criticisms of the government and **Fidel Castro**. For his work, Ortega has received a number of honorary degrees, including several in the United States. *See also* Dissent and Defections (1959–   )

Further Reading

"College of Cardinals Collection." *Daily Catholic*, vol. 10, no. 162, August 27–29, 1999, section 3, p. 1.

Frank Argote-Freyre

Palo Monte

Palo Monte, or *Mayombe*, is a religious system widely practiced throughout Cuba that originated on the island among slaves from Dahomey and among Bantu speakers. Slaves known as Congos practiced Palo Monte as a form of solidarity and as a means of resistance and cultural survival under a repressive slave system. Among its several variations are a mixture of practices from Dahomey and ideas adopted from Oyo and from the Congo region. In addition, practitioners integrated elements of **Catholicism** and, later, European **Spiritism**.

Core elements of Palo Monte are the *mpungus*, or nonhuman persons, divination, symbolic signs, and ritual, including the use of pots, music, and dancing. The mpungus are spiritual figures similar to the *orishas* of **Santería**. Some are associated with natural phenomena, while others are the spirits of ancestors. In some instances, they overlap with Santería. Such is the case with Changó, who is known as Munalungo among the *paleros*.

Historically, Palo Monte has been viewed as a form of witchcraft. Practitioners used natural substances in rituals, placing sticks, herbs, leavings, and other objects in a pot to influence the mpungus and people for their own ends. This was perceived as malevolent and in fact sometimes was done with intent to cause harm or as a form of revenge. Although these practices have continued, the religion also has another side. Practitioners perform rituals to influence people positively or to create conditions of reconciliation. Like other African-derived religious systems there is an emphasis on community, interdependence, and a focus on the pragmatics of everyday life. *See also* Afro-Cubans; Slavery

Further Readings

Cabrera, Lydia. *Reglas de Congo: Palo Monte Mayombe*. Miami: Peninsular Print, 1979.

Fernández Robaina, Tomás. *Hablen paleros y santeros*. Havana: Editorial de Ciencias Sociales, 1994.

Maitbag, Eugenio. *Afro-Cuban Religious Experience*. Gainesville: University Press of Florida, 1996.

William Van Norman, Jr.

Pope John Paul II's Visit to Cuba

More than any other pope before him, John Paul II has traveled far and wide. Few of his visits, however, captured the imagination as much as his visit to Cuba, a country that at the time of his visit in January 1998 had been under the communist rule of **Fidel Castro** for thirty-nine years. The international drama of the pope's visit was played out alongside many personal dramas of family reunification. Many Cubans who left the island as exiles, or the children of exiles, returned to Cuba—some for the first time—to experience this dramatic event on Cuban soil. Cubans prepared a warm welcome for the pope. All over the city posters of the pope against a true blue sky were pasted on the walls. They read: "John Paul II, ¡Te Esperamos! (We Await You!)" or "¡Bendícenos! (Bless Us!)." When he arrived, the response of the Cuban people was nothing less than joyful. Thousands and thousands of people on the streets and at the masses waved flags and chanted their support for the pope in unison.

The pope's visit to Cuba coincided with the so-called **Special Period**—the worst crisis in the island's history—and with a concomitant resurgence in spirituality, particularly **Catholicism** and **Protestantism**. The pope arrived a few weeks after Cubans were allowed to openly celebrate Christmas for the first time since 1962 and when the churches were full, also the result of the work of a new generation of young Cuban priests that are a source of tangible help to the people and present Cubans with an alternative vision of society, a social message of justice with mercy. The pope's visit affirmed and strengthened this new church.

In his five-day visit, from January 21 to 25, 1998, the pope offered four masses: the first one in **Santa Clara**, the second one in **Camagüey**, the third in **Santiago de Cuba**, and the last one in Havana, at the **Plaza de la Revolución**. In addition, the pope held numerous meetings, such as with many of Cuba's foremost intellectuals at the **University of Havana**, with representatives of Cuba's youth, with Cuba's *el mundo del dolor* (world of sorrow), the lepers at the Sanctuary of Saint Lazarus

(see **San Lázaro**), popularly known as el Rincón. Posters, banners, cheers, flags, and songs welcomed the pope in rhyme and unison wherever he went. People waved the Vatican and Cuban flags together with enormous joy. And Cubans who came out to the masses in support of the pope were of all social classes, all races, all ages—truly *el pueblo* (the people).

The mass in Santiago de Cuba was particularly moving in a number of ways. The archbishop of Santiago, Pedro Meurice, spoke loudly and boldly in defense of **human rights** when he underscored that the Cuban nation lives both on the island and in the diaspora, and Cubans "suffer, live, and hope both here and there." The Church's commitment, as affirmed in Puebla, Mexico, is, indeed, with the poorest of the poor; and, he added, the poorest among us are those who lack liberty.

Moreover, since Santiago de Cuba is very near El Cobre, the shrine where Cuba's patron saint, **la Virgen de la Caridad del Cobre (Our Lady of Charity)** resides, at the Santiago de Cuba mass the pope symbolically crowned her. Our Lady of Charity has long been a symbol of identity and nationhood in Cuban society. The importance of this devotion in Cuba today can be seen in the way Cubans express their present plight in Cuba in paintings that depict Our Lady of Charity herself in the traditional manner yet substitute the **balseros** of the 1990s—the thousands of Cubans who desperately put out to sea on anything that floats—for the rowing boat with the three fishermen she traditionally stands over. When Pope John Paul II crowned her, in the mass at Santiago de Cuba, the Cuban people accompanied him in song, a deeply moving *rencuentro* of the Cuban people with themselves—a newly found tradition.

By the time the last mass took place in Havana, Cubans came out very massively—running to the **Plaza de la Revol-**

Juan
Pablo II

¡Bendícenos!
21 al 25 de
Enero de 1998

Poster celebrating Pope John Paul II's visit to
Cuba in 1998. Luis Martínez-Fernández Collection.

ución, where it was held. In the middle of
the mass, repeated shouts of "Liberty"
could be heard. The pope's visit was a
meld of religious and political purposes.
As he has for many years, the pope both
critiqued the **U. S. trade embargo** of Cuba
as a form of violence against a poor country that hurts the poorest there the most, as
well as Castro's human rights violations as
a denial of individual human dignity.
Throughout, he called for Cubans to assume their protagonist role within their
own history—not to seek their liberty elsewhere by leaving the island but to seek it
within.

The pope's visit holds various meanings for Cubans. One is that which John
Paul II himself intended, as expressed in
one of his homilies: to defend a larger
space for the Church, and along with it a
larger space of liberty for all Cubans—part
of the process of the return of civil society.
Second, since in his farewell address the
pope called "for Cuba to open itself to the
world, and for the world to open itself up
to Cuba," within the United States it
helped to reopen the debate and controversy over the U.S. embargo of Cuba and
sparked efforts at humanitarian assistance
of food and medicine. Third, Cubans on
the island came out clearly and massively
in support of the alternative values the
pope articulated regarding the central importance of the family, the school, the
church, as independent social institutions
that need to play leading roles in society
not totally usurped by government—a call
for change. And for many Cubans, the
pope's visit prompted family reunion and
reconciliation. *See also* Noche Buena
(Christmas Eve); Ortega y Alamino, Jaime
Lucas; Religion under Castro

Further Readings

Calabuig, Ignacio. *El Papa en Cuba: la paloma de
    la libertad*. Madrid: Agualarga, 1998.
Pablo II, Juan. *Mensajero de la paz y la esperanza:
    visita de su Santidad Juan Pablo II a Cuba*.
    Miami: Ediciones Universal, 1998.

Silvia Pedraza

Protestantism

From the early sixteenth century until the
late nineteenth century Roman **Catholicism** was the official and only legal religion on the island. In 1741, British forces
commanded by Edward Vernon occupied
a portion of the island and celebrated the
first Anglican services in Cuba. This was
just a preamble to the **British occupation
of Havana** in 1762, when British authorities enforced freedom of worship and
even utilized some Catholic churches for
Protestant services.

The nineteenth century brought a series of events in the Atlantic world that
catapulted Cuba to a more prominent position within the dwindling Spanish empire and within the international markets.
Motivated by these changes and by new

immigration laws, foreigners from Protestant nations started arriving on Cuban soil to engage in commerce, diplomacy, and for some, the struggle to abolish **slavery** (see **Abolition and Emancipation**). Most, however, came because of the booming **sugar industry** and settled in Havana, **Matanzas**, and other cities. The growing foreign colony included Anglicans from Great Britain, Episcopalians from the United States, Presbyterians, Congregationalists, Baptists, Methodists, and German Lutherans. Protestants living in Cuba accommodated in different ways to the rigid colonial regime, but their religious experience was always a sour point of contention between their beliefs and the religious rules of the land. The obstacles against performing Protestant services were many, and Protestant Christians even had problems finding ground for burials.

In 1869 the declaration of religious tolerance, motivated by a brief period of political reform in Spain, at first produced just subtle changes in Cuba. The first Protestant minister to perform religious duties with the consent of the colonial government was Reverend Edward Kenney. An Episcopalian from the United States, Kenney arrived in Havana in 1871 to organize the first Episcopalian mission, but his labor was limited to Protestant foreigners, as he was forbidden to proselytize Cubans. Despite the limitations imposed by the colonial authorities, Kenney expanded his ministry considerably to include all the foreigners he could find, even some Cubans.

During the wars of independence several tens of thousands of Cubans sought exile in the United States. (See **Political Exile [Nineteenth Century]**). Some converted to Protestantism while in exile, and those who did not often brought back with them an appreciation for religious pluralism. Many of these Protestant Cubans or sympathizers of Protestantism were also linked to the revolutionary movement. In 1883 returnees like Alberto J. Díaz and Pedro Duarte established Reformed and Episcopal churches in Havana and Matanzas, respectively.

In 1898 North American intervention brought full religious lawful equality to Cuba (see **U.S. Interventions**). The arrival of large numbers of returning Cuban exiles and foreign missionaries also contributed to a growing number of Protestant churches. The years following the U.S. intervention were years of sway for the North American Mission Boards in Cuba. Adventist, Baptist, Congregationalist, Disciples of Christ, Episcopal, Methodist, Presbyterian, Pentecostal, and Quaker, missionary organizations energetically expanded their efforts in Cuba. Their activities were not limited to organizing churches, but many also invested in founding schools and hospitals. The large U.S. missionary presence in Cuba to a certain point eclipsed the original native missionary efforts, and tensions between foreign and local leaders occurred in virtually every Protestant denomination. The Catholic Church responded to the growing number of Protestant converts with attacks on the institution and a revival of its own.

In 1929 the most important convention to date of Latin American Protestant leaders took place in Havana: the Hispano-American Congress of Havana. This gathering, the first with a majority of native Latin Americans, was an important step toward making Cuban Protestantism more indigenous. From the early 1930s to the late 1950s, Protestant groups experienced a renewed enthusiasm among Cubans, particularly among the working classes. North American mission boards began yielding control to local leaders, and new denominations began challenging traditional Protestant organizations. All this was in part prompted by the growing number of Cuban ministers graduated from seminaries founded during the early years of the century. Still, the majority of the population on the island remained nominally Catholic, and the hierarchy of the Catholic Church continued to strongly oppose the Protestant challenge.

After the **Revolution** circumstances deteriorated drastically for Protestants and Catholics alike. The new government perceived organized religion as a threat to its revolutionary program. In the first half of the 1960s about 70 percent of all Catholic priests, 90 percent of the nuns, some Protestant clergy, and all rabbis left the country either voluntarily, under social pressure, or through deportation. Protestant churches lost their schools, hospitals, and other types of institutions that supported their ministries on the island. Pressure from **Fidel Castro**'s government started to lessen by the end of the 1960s; the **Constitution of 1976** proclaimed scientific materialism as the basis of the state and education but granted religious freedom, although with limitations. By the 1980s both Protestant churches and the government had made some concessions and approximated harmonious relations. In response to increased religious freedoms dating from the early 1990s, Protestant churches in Cuba have grown faster than any other religion. Some 300,000 Cubans belong to Protestant churches. It is estimated that 1,666 Protestant churches of over fifty denominations currently operate on the island. The Baptists are the single largest denomination. *See also* Religion under Castro

Further Readings

Hageman, Alice L., comp. *Religion in Cuba Today: A New Church in a New Society*. New York: Association Press, 1982.

Martínez-Fernández, Luis. *Protestantism and Political Conflict in the Nineteenth-Century Hispanic Caribbean*. New Brunswick, NJ: Rutgers University Press, 2002.

Ramos, Marcos A. *Protestantism and Revolution in Cuba*. Coral Gables, FL: Research Institute for Cuban Studies, 1989.

Yaremko, Jason M. *U.S. Protestant Missions in Cuba: From Independence to Castro*. Gainesville: University Press of Florida, 2000.

Dennis R. Hidalgo

Quince, los

Los quince is a coming-of-age celebration that signals the transition from girlhood into young womanhood. A combination of debutante ball and a bas mitzvah, los quince is a lavish affair that, in many ways, resembles a wedding reception.

The celebration might begin with a mass at Church. The guests then gather at a ballroom where the *quinceañera*, the girl who is turning fifteen, is introduced to the gathering. A waltz is played, and after the father has the first dance, the girl waltzes with her dance partner. Soon, fourteen other couples join in the waltz. The waltz might be simple or an intricate choreography. Some parents hire a consultant who selects the music with the young girl and teaches the couples how to dance. Halfway through the night, a large, decorated cake is wheeled out onto the floor, and all the guests sing "Happy Birthday."

In the past, the girl's dancing partner was her sweetheart, and the party was a way to acknowledge that the girl could now be officially courted. The celebrations allowed the parents to show their social conditions and affluence. The wealthier the parents, the more lavish the quinces.

In the United States, the quinces are still part of the coming of age of Cuban American girls. Even families who cannot afford elaborate celebrations may borrow money to stage a memorable spectacle. In Cuba, the revolutionary government discourages the practice, though many families—with enormous sacrifices—still hold a scaled-down version of the quince celebration.

Girl celebrating her fifteenth birthday in Los Palacios, Pinar del Río. Photograph by Luis Martínez-Fernández.

Further Reading

King, Elizabeth. *Quinceañera: Celebrating Fifteen.* New York: Dullon's Childrens Books, 1998.

D.H. Figueredo

Religion under Castro

The Cuban people have always manifested a preoccupation with the spiritual and transcendental. Eighty percent of Cubans considered themselves Catholic in 1959. While **Catholicism** was the largest religion on the island, religious life was by no means dominated by the Catholic Church. Catholicism coexisted and was practiced syncretically with several other religions: **Protestantism** (around 6 percent of the population), **Santería** (Afro-Cuban religions), *Espiritismo* (a type of animism), *Brujería* (witchcraft), and "superstitions." A 1954 survey conducted by an organization of Catholic university students revealed that although 96.5 percent of the Catholics polled believed in the existence of God, only 17 percent attended religious services regularly. For the majority of the population religion was personal rather than institutional, and syncretic rather than purist. There are fifty-three Christian denominations in Cuba today in addition to the Catholic Church. There are also at least four Afro-Cuban religious practices, **Spir-**

itism (in three varieties), and other less popular religions (see **Afro-Cubans**). Despite growing interest and participation in traditional forms of worship, the most widespread manifestation of religion is popular religion, an informal religiosity that is syncretic, flexible, poorly defined, and not formally institutionalized.

Since 1959 the revolutionary regime has emphasized the values, symbols, and myths associated with noninstitutional and popular religious style. Popular religiosity has been married with revolutionary myths and symbols in order to strengthen individual's identification with the state and, during the early stages of the **Revolution**, to confront the challenges posed by conservative elements of the Catholic Church.

The official campaign against the Catholic Church began in late 1960. By late 1961, the year Castro embraced Marxism-Leninism as the official ideology of the Revolution, the Church was a crippled institution. By 1964 the Church had resigned itself to live within the parameters set by the state, to accept the Revolution, and to pursue ecclesiastical activities as best it could. Church-state relations improved in Cuba after 1968. In 1975, the First Congress of the **Cuban Communist Party** (PCC) recognized the right of Cubans to practice any religion, but in practice, believers were discriminated against if not persecuted (i.e., the case of Jehovah's Witnesses, who endured persecutions for refusing to participate in government activities). Since the late 1980s, as Cuba weathered economic and social crisis, a reemergence of interest and participation in traditional religions has been apparent. In 1992 religious believers were allowed to join the Party. By the 1990s and especially with **Pope John Paul II's visit** (in 1998), the Catholic Church demonstrated its newly found vigor on the island, as well as its commitment and ability to secure a greater presence in the society. By 2000, despite limitations, the Church is the only truly national institution that is independent from the communist government. Since the 1980s Protestantism and Afro-Cuban religious practices have grown as well, and it is the latter that probably is the most influential at the grassroots.

Further Readings

Castro, Fidel. *Fidel y la religión: conversaciones con Frei Betto*. Santo Domingo: Alfa & Omega, 1985.

Crahan, Margaret. *Religion and Revolution: Cuba and Nicaragua*. Washington, DC: Latin America Program, Wilson Center, 1987.

Kirk, John M. *Between God and the Party: Religion and Politics in Revolutionary Cuba*. Tampa: University of South Florida Press, 1989.

Damián J. Fernández

Rum

Distilled from sugarcane molasses, Cuban rum has historically been one of the most widely recognized and renowned liquors in the world. Rum was first distilled in the seventeenth century in the Caribbean as a by-product of sugar production. Molasses, the thick syrup remaining after sugarcane juice has been crystallized by boiling, is usually used as the basis for rum, although the juice itself, or other sugarcane residues, can also be used. The molasses are allowed to ferment and later are distilled to produce a clear liquid that is aged in oaken casks. The golden color of some rums results from the absorption of substances from the oak.

Of the many corporations that have produced and manufactured Cuban rum, Bacardí and Company has been at the forefront of the rum industry since in the nineteenth century (see **Bacardí Family**; **Bacardí Moreau, Emilío**). A wine merchant named Don Facundo Bacardí Massó emigrated from Catalonia to **Santiago de Cuba**. At the time of his arrival, rum was cheaply made and reserved for the consumption of poorer individuals, not by the polite of society. Bacardí began to experiment with the process of rum creation and was able to mellow the rum through charcoal filtration to remove impurities, a technique never used before. On February 4, 1862, Bacardí y Compañía was established. On the island, various brands of rum continue to be produced for export and the local market. The most popular is Havana Club, currently produced by a joint French and Cuban company.

Cuban rum is central to many of the island's most popular cocktails. Rum and Coke is said to have been invented during the Cuban **War of Independence** by a troop of soldiers who were sitting around and concocted the drink, naming it "Cuba Libre," or "free Cuba," in honor of the struggle for freedom. In the exile community, the drink is nicknamed "Menti-rita," which means "little lie," a reference to the belief that Cuba since 1959 has not been free. The "Mojito," which is composed of Cuban rum, seltzer water, sugar, lime, and mint leaves, has also come to be recognized globally. Also popular is the daiquirí, made with crushed ice, lime juice, rum, and sugar. *See also* Sugar Industry

Further Reading

Campoamor, Fernando G. *Coctelería cubana, cien recetas con ron*. Havana: Editorial Científico-Técnica, 2000.

Nilo Jorge Barredo

San Lázaro (Saint Lazarus)

San Lázaro is one of the most widely recognized and venerated saints among the Cuban people. The rites surrounding San Lázaro provide an opportunity to observe the convergence of multiple aspects of Cuban culture.

Those who practice African-derived religions consider San Lázaro to be a representation of Babalú Ayé. This powerful African spiritual figure most likely originated among the Ewe-Fon, or Arará as they were known in Cuba. Practitioners of **Santería** incorporated knowledge of Babalú Ayé into their religious system, contributing to the spread of his rites throughout the island. Babalú Ayé is considered primarily the *orisha* of the disempowered and the sick and traditionally has power over serious diseases such as smallpox and leprosy. Like practitioners of Santería and Arará, Catholics honor San Lázaro as a healer of the sick.

A significant aspect of the rites surrounding San Lázaro/Babalú Ayé is the annual pilgrimage to the Church of San Lázaro at Rincón on the outskirts of Havana. Many Catholics and followers of African-derived religions alike make the trip to secure a blessing, a healing, or to fulfill a vow. The throngs who descend on Rincón every December 17 reflect the racial and spiritual diversity of Cuba. The use of San Lázaro among diverse elements of the Cuban population also reveals the ability of Cubans to allow for differing interpretations of symbols and events. Devotion to San Lázaro has been carried over to the United States by Cubans settling there after the **Revolution**. *See also* Catholicism

Further Readings

Bolívar Aróstegui, Natalia. *Los orishas en Cuba.* Havana: Ediciones Unión, 1990.

Lachatañeré, Rómulo. *El sistema religioso de los Afrocubanos.* Havana: Editorial de Ciencias Sociales, 1992.

William Van Norman, Jr.

Santería

Santería is a religious practice that originated among enslaved people in Cuba known as Lucumí (see **Slavery**). This religious expression, through ritual, dance, music, and food, informed Cuban culture and is important in understanding not only **Afro-Cubans** but also Cuban history and culture in general.

In Cuba, diverse peoples of western Nigeria found commonalities in uniting against slavery's oppression. As a way of resistance and cultural survival, they constructed Santería out of memories from Africa and combined them with elements of **Catholicism**. Central to the practice of Santería are *orishas*, ritual, and divination. The Orishas, powerful nonhuman persons associated with specific Catholic saints, are possibly the most identifiable aspect. Some popular orishas include Changó/Santa Bárbara, Ochún/La **Virgen de la Caridad del Cobre**, and Babalú Ayé/**San Lázaro**.

Regular practice of Santería involves ritually establishing and maintaining relationships between individuals, an orisha, and other practitioners. These associations define the community-based pragmatic characteristic of the religion. An individual develops an interdependent relationship with an orisha through maintaining a stone thought to hold the essence of the orisha. Also important are divination and consultation with a religious specialist or *santero/a*.

Public ritual is also significant. Typically, a Santero keeps a private house where groups celebrate rituals such as the *bembé*. These occasions are marked by food, music, and dance.

Santería's emphasis on community and interdependence influence many aspects of the daily lives of Cubans. Continued practice has spread Santería beyond the shores of Cuba and its distinctive rhythms onto the stages of musical venues around the world. *See also* Botánicas; Religion under Castro

Further Readings

Brandon, George. *Santería from Africa to the New World: The Dead Sell Memories.* Bloomington: Indiana University Press, 1993.

Matibag, Eugenio. *Afro-Cuban Religious Experience: Cultural Reflections in Narrative.* Gainesville: University Press of Florida, 1996.

William Van Norman, Jr.

Spiritism

Spiritism, a body of religious practices that seek communication with spirits, has influenced popular religious practices in Cuba. Allan Kardec's books, such as *The Spirits' Book,* first published in 1856, made their way from France to Cuba through Freemasons (see **Freemasonry**). Kardec, considered the creator of modern Spiritism, illustrated in his books a hidden but powerful spiritual world and explained how the spirits communicate with the living. According to Kardec, the spirits would lift and tilt tables during séances to answer people's questions through a series of raps, or knocks, similar to someone knocking on a door.

With his unprecedented explanation of the spirits' world, Kardec appeared to vindicate Cuban popular religiosity like **Santería**. Santería, "the way of the saints" or "Regla de Ocha," despite its obvious Catholic imagery, is closer to Kardec's spiritualist cosmology. At the turn of the twentieth century, Kardecian Spiritism blended with Santería. Examples of Spiritism within Santería are the offering of masses, séances, and white table ceremonies in which mediums convey messages from the spirit world.

The popularity of spiritist religions like Santería in Cuba has been strong among the poor in rural areas since colonial times. The unpopularity of official **Catholicism** during the wars for independence at the end of the nineteenth century aided the spread of Spiritism to cities and other social classes. Later, **Fidel Castro**'s revolutionary government would perceive institutionalized religion more threatening to the **Revolution** than Spiritism, and this has strengthened its position in Cuban society.

Further Reading
Moreno Vega, Marta. *The Altar of My Soul: The Living Traditions of Santería.* New York: One World, 2000.

Dennis R. Hidalgo

Three Kings' Day (Día de Reyes)

The Three Kings' Day falls on January 6, Epiphany Day. Before the **Revolution**, children wrote letters to the Three Kings asking for toys and gifts. In the city of Havana, many children visited the Reyes Magos store where they talked to the kings. At dawn on January 6, the Three Kings brought gifts to Cuban children, placing the packages near the Christmas tree.

The Three Kings' Day combined Afro-Cuban and Catholic traditions (see **Afro-Cubans**; **Catholicism**). Within the Catholic Church, Epiphany Day was a celebration of the birth of Jesus; traditionally, it was on this day that the Three Kings visited the holy infant, bringing him gifts. Within Afro-Cuban customs, it was on Epiphany Day, during the Spanish colonial era, that slaves were allowed to be free for one day: they did not have to work and could feast, dance, and play music. The slaves used the occasion to render tribute to their African gods (see **Slavery**).

In the early 1960s, the Cuban government abolished the Three Kings' Day and transplanted all celebrations to January 1, the anniversary of **Fidel Castro**'s triumph over the **Fulgencio Batista** regime. Around 1995, Cuban families restored, privately, Three Kings' Day. In 2000, the government allowed visitors from a church in Puerto Rico to tour Cuban churches dressed up as the Three Kings. Parents were encouraged, however, to tell their children not to ask for toys but for spiritual gifts. *See also* New Year's Day (Primero de Enero; Día de Año Nuevos); Noche Buena (Christmas Eve)

Further Reading
Luis, William. *Culture and Customs of Cuba.* Westport, CT: Greenwood Press, 2001.

D.H. Figueredo

Twenty-Sixth (26th) of July (Holiday)

The Twenty-sixth of July (Veintiseis de julio) is Cuba's most important holiday since the triumph of the **Revolution**. The holiday commemorates the attack by **Fidel Castro** and a few dozen of his associates on the **Moncada Army Barracks** in **Santiago de Cuba** on July 26, 1953. Although the attack failed and led to the imprisonment of Castro and other revolutionaries, it marked the beginning of the **struggle against Batista** and gave its name to the **26th of July Movement**, the leading force against the dictatorship of **Fulgencio Batista**.

Coinciding with the date of the traditional **carnivals** and with the end of the sugar harvest, the Twenty-six of July holiday is observed throughout the island and serves as an opportunity to organize massive rallies in which dictator Fidel Castro and other leaders address the Cuban people. Each year a city is selected to host the central celebrations, and other gatherings take place at Havana's **Plaza de la Revolución** and other venues. Since the advent of the economic crisis of the so-called **Special Period**, celebrations have been toned down a bit. Still, each year the citizenry expects the availability of a chicken per household or some other special item at the **bodegas** to mark the celebrations with a special meal.

Further Reading
Luis, William. *Culture and Customs of Cuba*. Westport, CT: Greenwood Press, 2001.

Luis Martínez-Fernández

Villapol Andiarenas, Nitza (1923–1998)

A nutritionist and gourmet cook, Nitza Villapol was born in New York City but lived most of her life in Havana. Regarded as the "guru" of Cuban cuisine, she became an expert on home economics during World War II while studying in London. Beginning in 1951, she hosted a cooking program on Cuban television. Called *Cocina al minuto*, (Minute Cooking), the program, which instructed how to prepare national dishes in a fast and economical manner, was broadcast over a period of thirty-five years. Through the show, Villapol promoted Cuban **cuisine** and emphasized the importance of a healthy diet and eating properly; she also maintained that cooking was an artistic and cultural expression of a given people or country. She disliked mayonnaise, which she described as a North American invention designed to spoil food.

Villapol seasoned her dishes as she cooked on live television. Her imaginative recipes and ability to improvise allowed her to develop creative recipes that reflected the food shortages experienced in Cuba after **Fidel Castro** rose to power in 1959 (see **Nutrition and Food Rationing**).

Her books *Cocina criolla* (1954) and *Cocina al minuto* (1958) became international bestsellers and were even published in the United States without the author's permission. Today, those two titles are regarded as "bibles" for Cuban cookery. In 1983, the documentary *Con pura magia satisfechos*, about her culinary labor, was produced in Cuba. She died in 1998.

Further Reading
Villapol, Nitza. *Cuban Cuisine* Havana: Editorial José Martí, 1997.

Wilfredo Cancio Isla

Virgen de la Caridad del Cobre (Our Lady of Charity of El Cobre)

The Virgen de la Caridad del Cobre is the spiritual patron of Cuba. The Madonna is widely venerated and is believed to heal and to perform miracles. Our Lady of Charity is enshrined in a basilica in the town of El Cobre, near **Santiago de Cuba** on the eastern end of the island. The fifteen-inch-tall wooden Madonna is usually draped in an elaborate cloth gown. She holds the infant Jesus in her left arm, and in her right, a gold cross. Because the figure is carved from dark wood, the Virgen de la Caridad is often referred to as being mulatto.

According to legend, the Virgin first appeared to three fishermen in 1628 in the Gulf of Nipe when they were caught in a storm and feared for their lives. The Madonna came to them on the water, floating on planks inscribed with the phrase *Yo soy la Virgen de la Caridad*. The fishermen believed the Virgin had miraculously saved them from death. Shortly after the figure was encountered, she was placed in a shrine at El Cobre. Through the years, there have been reported appearances of the Virgin Mary in the copper mines near the shrine.

The Virgen de la Caridad del Cobre is a spiritual focal point in Cuba. Cuban patriots venerated her during the wars of independence, while their enemies prayed to the "Spanish" Virgen de la Covadonga. Recognizing the importance of la Caridad del Cobre to the Cuban people, Pope Benedict XV declared her to be the spiritual patron of Cuba in 1916. In 1998, Pope John Paul II made a much-celebrated visit to El Cobre in which he crowned an image of the venerated Caridad del Cobre. The day of la Virgen de la Caridad del Cobre is celebrated each year on September 8.

The Virgen de la Caridad del Cobre is sacred not only to followers of the Catholic faith but also to adherents of Afro-Cuban religions, such as **Santería**. In the syncretic tradition of Santería, Caridad del Cobre symbolizes Ochún, the deity who governs femininity and rivers.

The shrine at El Cobre is a pilgrimage site. Many Cubans who believe in the

La Virgen de la Caridad del Cobre, Cuba's Patron (from a poster promoting a Miami HMO). Courtesy of the Cuban Heritage Collection of the Otto G. Richter Library of the University of Miami.

power of the Virgen de la Caridad have not only visited the shrine but have given gifts to Caridad, including letters, photos, jewelry, medals, and more poignant objects like crutches and braces that are no longer needed. Cubans in Miami have erected their own sanctuary in honor of la Caridad del Cobre. *See also* Pope John Paul II's Visit to Cuba; Ten Years' War; War of Independence

Further Readings

Díaz, María Elena. *The Virgin, the King, and the Royal Slaves of El Cobre: Negotiating Freedom in Colonial Cuba*. Stanford, CA: Stanford University Press, 2001.

Portuondo Zúñiga, Olga. *La Virgen de la Caridad del Cobre: símbolo de cubanía*. Santiago de Cuba: Editorial Oriente, 2001.

Catherine Moses

11

Sports

Acosta Fernández, Baldomero Pedro (1896–1963)

Baldomero Acosta was born on May 19, 1896, in Bauta, **La Habana Province**. In Cuba, Acosta played with the Monjes Grises and later with los Tigres de Marianao. He also played with the La Habana club. In the **U.S. Major Leagues**, Acosta played outfielder with the Washington Senators between 1913 and 1916. He also played with the Philadelphia A's. Following his stint with the A's, in 1918 he was sent to the Minor Leagues, where he played with Atlanta. His Major League career statistics were 111 hits in 436 at bats, for a .255 average. He concluded his career with Louisville in 1928. Acosta was inducted into the Cuban Exile Baseball Hall of Fame in 1965. He passed away on November 17, 1963, in Miami.

Further Reading

Torres, Ángel. *La leyenda del béisbol cubano, 1878–1997*. Miami: Review Printers, 1997.

Nilo Jorge Barredo

Arocha, René (1966–)

René Arocha was the first Cuban **baseball** player to defect in the 1990s (see **Dissent and Defections** [1959—]). A pitcher

for the Cuban National Team, he left the team during a stopover in Miami in July before the 1991 Pan American Games in Havana. Manuel Hurtado, a former Cuban pitching coach who had defected years earlier, arranged his defection and had a car waiting for him. Tryouts had already been set up. Eight teams were interested in Arocha, so a lottery was held. He pitched for the Louisville Redbirds (a AAA team for the St. Louis Cardinals) for two seasons. His first season in Triple A, Arocha went 12-7 with a 2.70 ERA (earned run average) in 25 starts. Arocha later pitched for the St. Louis Cardinals from 1993 to 1995, and the San Francisco Giants from 1996 to 1997. In the Majors he won 18 games and lost 17, with an ERA of 4.11 and 190 strikeouts. *See also* Major Leagues, Cubans in the U.S.

Further Reading

"Cuban Defector Gets Tryouts." *USA Today Baseball Weekly*, September 27, 1991, 31.

Paula J. Pettavino

Baseball

Introduced to Cuba from the United States in the mid-nineteenth century, baseball became well established on the island by the first decade of the twentieth century and a national passion by the 1920s. By the mid-twentieth century, Cuba had become the sport's greatest single influence—and source of talent—outside the United States. The **Revolution** severed much of Cuban baseball's connection to its own past and to the baseball world, though the sport continued to flourish and produce fine players for decades.

The Cuban history of the sport North Americans call their "National Pastime" is deep, almost as old on the island as in its birthplace. The first game ever played in Cuba with local participants is believed to have occurred in 1866, the first between strictly local teams in 1868, and the first Cuban ballpark, at Palmar del Junco, **Matanzas**, was inaugurated in 1874.

The Cuban professional league, born in 1878–1879, would endure nearly uninterrupted for eight decades. The Cuban League typically fielded four teams in a December-to-March season of about fifty games, with mostly Cuban and African American players and a limited number of U.S. Major Leaguers. The lion's share of success went to the "eternal rivals," La Habana and Almendares. Between them they won fifty-three of the League's seventy-four completed championships; no other club won more than five. Most years, the League was composed of the quartet of Almendares, La Habana, **Cienfuegos**, and Marianao. Establishing viable third and fourth teams posed endless difficulties, owing to the capital city's concentration of population and disposable income. Even **Santa Clara**'s 1923–1924 club, celebrated as the greatest in League history, drew fans scantily and failed to sustain its on-the-field success.

Cuba's voracious appetite for the sport permitted several parallel realms of baseball to survive and even flourish; along with the professional league, there was sugarmill ball, company leagues, and amateur baseball. Gritty sugarmill competition furnished black professional players, par-ticularly, extra opportunities to hone their game and supplement their earnings (see **Sugar Industry**). The amateur game, at times rivaling the professionals in popularity, enjoyed glory days from the 1920s through the 1940s; it excluded blacks until 1959. The international amateur tournament, launched in England in 1938, moved to the Caribbean; Cuba hosted five straight tournaments during the 1940s and won eleven of eighteen championships between 1940 and 1972.

Cubans began to play in the **U.S. Major Leagues** just before World War I, but only those light-skinned enough to be considered white by U.S. standards were given the chance. Thus, as with U.S. black players, some of the greatest talents ever to don spikes were excluded from the sport's summit.

A legendary trio of early-twentieth-century players forced to ply their trade outside the Majors helps illustrate what was lost. **José de la Caridad Méndez** (1887–1928), "The Black Diamond," one-hit the Cincinnati Reds for Almendares in November 1908; pitched 7 shutout innings against them two weeks later; and followed that up with a 5-hit, 8-strikeout shutout—25 consecutive shutout innings that made him a national hero and drew the notice of all baseball. Méndez compiled a Cuban career record of 74-25 and pitched successfully in the **U.S. Negro Leagues** (including a 20-4 stretch with the Kansas City Monarchs in the 1920s). Possibly the greatest power hitter Cuba ever produced, **Cristóbal Torriente** (1895–c. 1938) compiled a .352 lifetime average (third-highest in Cuban League history), .339 in the U.S. Negro Leagues, and .311 against U.S. Major League pitchers. In 1916, at age twenty, he batted .402 and led the Cuban League in triples, home runs, and steals. He became a legend in 1920 by slugging three home runs in a game against a barnstorming New York Giants club that included Babe Ruth. Then there was **Martín**

Dihigo, "El Inmortal," celebrated as the greatest player in Cuban history, brilliant on the pitcher's mound and every other position, too, a member of three national Halls of Fame.

Cubans played a big role in the U.S. Negro Leagues. By World War I, Cuban baseball was so prestigious that team names such as Cuban Giants, Cubans, and Authentic Cubans became commonplace. The most famous of these clubs (most of which featured a combination of Cubans and U.S. blacks) was the New York Cuban Giants, winners of the 1947 Negro Leagues championship. However, the exploits of Cuban stars in the Negro Leagues received scant attention on the island. Not so the storied encounters of Cubans with U.S. Major Leaguers: During their winter, U.S. teams routinely visited Cuba to play individual clubs or all-star squads.

In the late 1930s, Cuban professional baseball was reorganized under government auspices; a Hall of Fame was established in 1936. In 1947, U.S. Organized Baseball's growing taste for Cuban talent (nurtured during the war), coupled with fear of the Mexican League's challenge to control of players, led to creation of a new, institutionalized relationship with the Cuban League. The Minor Leagues were another link to the United States: Havana was home to the AAA-level International League's Sugar Kings, a Cincinnati Reds affiliate from 1954 on. The B-level Havana Cubans were another successful franchise, winning the Florida International League's 1947 title.

The annual Caribbean Series (Serie del Caribe) showcased the region's top professional clubs. Between 1949 and 1960, the Series matched the Cuban, Panamanian, Puerto Rican, and Venezuelan leagues' pennant winners; Cuba won more than half of these tournaments, including five straight from 1956 through 1960.

After 1959, the Revolution severed much of Cuban baseball's connection to the baseball world and to its own past. The Sugar Kings were moved Stateside, and the 1960–1961 season was the Cuban League's last, as exclusive amateurism was imposed. The regime had to create a domestic sporting-goods industry. The immortal Dihigo returned from exile to run Cuban baseball in this strange new era. Cuba truly dominated international amateur competition throughout the last third of the twentieth century, including the Pan American Games and **Olympics**, though the playing field between its own amateurs and those of other countries was never remotely level. As the long Cold War between Havana and Washington rolled on through the decades, initiatives to reopen baseball ties included George Steinbrenner's maneuverings in the 1980s and a two-game, "home-and-home" series between the Baltimore Orioles and the Cuban national team in 1999.

By the end of the twentieth century, however, Cuban baseball appeared to be in decline. While still fielding strongly competitive teams in international play, the country was losing more and more players to defection (see **Dissent and Defections [1959–]**). While the Stateside successes of such expatriates as Rey Ordóñez and **Orlando Hernández** vindicated Cuban baseball, in the eyes of many, a contrary awareness was also taking root. Cuban fans, enormously knowledgeable and brutally objective about their beloved sport (nationalist pride notwithstanding), increasingly sensed that the island's game was no longer being legitimately tested against baseball's best, as had once been the case.

Still, the island's achievement has been immense. By the end of the twentieth century, Cuba had produced more than 150 Major League players, including two members of the Hall of Fame (Dihigo and **Atanasio "Tany" Pérez**) and numerous other stars. In its first century and a third,

Club Habana of the 1950s. Courtesy of La Galería del Medio, Miami.

Cuban baseball had become a major act of cultural creation and a significant contribution to the forging of a national identity. *See also* Sports in Revolutionary Cuba

Further Readings

González Echevarría, Roberto. *The Pride of Havana: A History of Cuban Baseball*. New York: Oxford University Press, 1999.

Jamail, Milton H., and Larry Dierker. *Full Count: Inside Cuban Baseball*. Carbondale: Southern Illinois University Press, 2000.

Torres, Ángel. *La leyenda del béisbol cubano, 1878–1997*. Miami: Review Printers, 1997.

Pablo Julián Davis

Boxing

Along with **baseball**, boxing was one of the most popular sports in pre-Revolutionary Cuba. For the lower classes, both sports constituted a possible ticket out of poverty, as well as steady, reliable entertainment.

The first professional match was held in Havana in 1909. In 1910, a Chilean named John Budinich established the first boxing academy in Havana. Two years later, boxing was suspended by the government because of its brutality and to stop the violence that occurred when blacks fought whites. The sport merely moved underground, where it spread rapidly throughout the island. By 1921, the Cuban government relented and legitimized boxing with the establishment of the National Commission on Boxing and Wrestling. Years later a national boxing academy was established to train talented athletes.

By 1959, Cuba had six professional world champions, including **"Kid Gavilán," "Kid Chocolate,"** and Benny Paret.

Stamp commemorating Cuban boxing during the 1980 Moscow Olympics. Luis Martínez-Fernández Collection.

Despite the sport's promise of riches, Cuban boxers—even those who earned tremendous money in the ring—almost invariably died penniless. Some also developed connections with the Mafia and other sources of corruption (see **Organized Crime**). Cuba's boxing reputation also drew foreign boxers as well, such as Jack Dempsey, Jess Willard, Joe Louis, and Sugar Ray Robinson.

In 1961, along with other sports, the Revolutionary government banned professional boxing. However, Cuba has remained the dominant boxing power in amateur sports. At the 1962 Central American and Caribbean Games, Cuba won first place in boxing. By the 1980s, Cuban boxers were dominant in all major international amateur competitions, including the **Olympics**. From 1968 in Mexico City to Sydney in 2000, Cuban boxers have participated in seven Olympic tournaments, winning twenty-seven gold medals, thirteen silver, and seven bronze, for a total of forty-seven, a number unmatched by any other country. Cuba is also the only country that can boast of two three-time Olympic champions: **Teófilo Stevenson** and Félix Savón.

Boxing, like baseball, is also a sport with great depth in Cuba. By 1992, there were over 16,000 boxers on the island. Across Cuba today, there are 494 boxing coaches and 185 facilities. Of the 99,000 athletes in Cuba, 19,300 are boxers, including 81 of Olympic caliber, even though only 12 make the Olympic team. *See also* Sports in Revolutionary Cuba

Further Readings

Alfonso, Jorge. *Puños dorados: apuntes para la historia del boxeo en Cuba*. Santiago de Cuba: Editorial Oriente, 1988.

Crespo, Rolando. *Cuba en el boxeo olímpico*. Havana: Editorial Científico-Técnica, 1998.

Grasso, John. *The Olympic Games Boxing Record Book*. Guilford, NY: International Boxing Research Organization, 1984.

Pettavino, Paula J., and Geralyn Pye. *Sport in Cuba: The Diamond in the Rough*. Pittsburgh: University of Pittsburgh Press, 1994.

Paula J. Pettavino

Campaneris Blanco, Dagoberto "Bert" (1942–)

Dagoberto Campaneris was a brilliant-fielding shortstop whose glove, bat work, and base-stealing prowess became a key component of the Oakland Athletics dynasty of the early 1970s.

Born in Pueblo Nuevo, **Matanzas** (also the birthplace of "El Inmortal" **Martín Dihigo**), Campaneris belonged to the first ball-playing generation to come to maturity after the Cuban League's demise. Of his twenty Major League seasons, the thirteen spent wearing the Athletics' green and gold (1964 through 1976) brought glory as infield anchor, offensive sparkplug, and destabilizing force on the basepaths for three consecutive World Series championships (1972–1974). Campaneris's durability was another virtue: Playing the most difficult infield position, and despite a slender frame (five feet ten inches, 160 pounds), he appeared in 134 or more games for thirteen consecutive seasons beginning in 1965. On the basepaths he achieved even longer, a fourteen-season streak of 20 or more steals; in one extraordinary six-year span, also beginning in 1965, he had at least 50 steals per season and increased his total each year. In his career, he amassed 649 steals, with a 76 percent success rate. At the end of his last full-time season, 1977, he ranked ninth all-time in that category. He scored 80-plus runs seven times and was selected an All-Star six times. *See also* Baseball; Major Leagues, Cubans in the U.S.

Further Readings

González Echevarría, Roberto. *The Pride of Havana: A History of Cuban Baseball*. New York: Oxford University Press, 1999.

Torres, Ángel. *La leyenda del béisbol cubano, 1878–1997*. Miami: Review Printers, 1997.

Pablo Julián Davis

Canseco Capas, José (1964–   )

Inspiring fear as perhaps no Major League Cuban slugger had ever done before, José Canseco showed glimpses of an almost unparalleled combination of power and speed until injuries brought him back to earth.

Canseco was born in Regla, **La Habana Province** (along with twin brother Osvaldo); within a year, the family moved to Miami to stay. Scouted by Camilo Pascual, Canseco signed with the Athletics and debuted with them in 1985. Right away, he matched a Herculean physique with eye-popping home-run blasts that became the talk of **baseball**. Before his third full-time season, 1988, Canseco announced an unprecedented goal: 40 home runs and 40 steals. He achieved it and more: 42 homers, 40 steals, 120 runs, 124 RBIs (runs batted in), and unanimous selection as Most Valuable Player. He and teammate Mark McGwire were dubbed "The Bash Brothers" for their slugging and their habit (which became baseball fashion) of smashing forearms together in

celebration; the A's went to three World Series. Canseco also became something of a matinee idol, with endorsements, magazine covers, and even a telephone line marketed to adolescent girls. His high-impact playing style was costly, though; injuries dogged him from 1989 on. Traded to Texas in 1992, he moved from team to team, seemingly doomed by injuries to an increasingly one-dimensional, part-time role—though when healthy, he remained fearsome. Acquired by the Yankees in mid-2000 to keep him from rival Boston, Canseco displayed eye-popping power when he played but got only one postseason at-bat; he still sought health and the right outlet for his prodigious abilities. Canseco announced his retirement in 2002. His Major League career numbers were 462 home runs, 1,407 runs batted in and .266 batting average. *See also* Major Leagues, Cubans in the U.S.

Further Readings

Aaseng, Nathan. *José Canseco: Baseball's 40-40 Man*. Rev. ed. Minneapolis: Lerner Publications, 1993.

González Echevarría, Roberto. *The Pride of Havana: A History of Cuban Baseball*. New York: Oxford University Press, 1999.

Shea, John. *Magic by the Bay: How the Oakland Athletics and the San Francisco Giants Captured the Baseball World*. Berkeley, CA: North Atlantic Books, 1990.

Torres, Ángel. *La leyenda del béisbol cubano, 1878–1997*. Miami: Review Printers, 1997.

Pablo Julián Davis

Capablanca, José Raúl (1888–1942)

José Raúl Capablanca was a stellar child prodigy who grew up to become a world chess champion whose elegance, charm, and brilliance contributed mightily to the game's popularity.

Born in Havana, Capablanca grew up in a fertile environment: The Club de Ajedrez de La Habana dated back to 1886,

World chess champion José Raúl Capablanca. Photograph courtesy of the Biblioteca Nacional José Martí, Havana.

and many masters visited the island to compete. He became Cuban champion in 1901, at age twelve, defeating Juan Corzo in a set match. He attended Columbia University in New York in 1906–1907 for engineering, but chess increasingly absorbed his energies. In 1909, at age twenty, he administered a sensational beating (eight wins, one loss, fourteen draws) to U.S. champion Frank Marshall and followed this feat two years later with victory against a powerful field at San Sebastián, Spain. In 1913 he obtained an appointment to Cuba's diplomatic corps, which was, in effect, a chess scholarship and travel grant. At St. Petersburg (1913), against the strongest opponents yet, he barely lost to Emanuel Lasker, champion since 1893, proving himself of championship caliber. By 1915, he was the object of unprecedented hero-worship (chess would not witness its like

until U.S. prodigy Bobby Fischer a half-century later). From 1916 to 1924 he lost not a single game in tournaments or match play. The year 1926 saw his greatest triumph, in the New York "sextangular tournament." He lost his title unexpectedly in 1927 to Alexander Alekhine of Russia; for the rest of his life Capablanca struggled fruitlessly to obtain a well-deserved return match. He died in 1942, in New York, of a cerebral hemorrhage. President **Fulgencio Batista** took personal charge of the funeral arrangements.

Capablanca's body of work is one of chess's mightiest. In 584 lifetime games, he lost only 36. His legacy is in that sustained brilliance; the beauty and artistic elegance of his play; and a major contribution through his play, personality, lectures, and writing to chess's growth worldwide. In Cuba he was a national hero alongside such contemporaries as boxer **Kid Chocolate** and **baseball** players **Adolfo Luque**, **Cristóbal Torriente**, and others. He raised the classical style, with its emphasis on the relentless development of small material advantages into invincible positions, to its highest perfection but also its exhaustion, as a less cautious, more dynamically attacking school of play arose in the mid-twentieth century.

Further Readings

Capablanca, José Raúl. *Last Lectures*. New York: Simon & Schuster, 1966.

Capablanca, José Raúl. *My Chess Career*. Corsicana: Grandmaster Publishing, 1994.

Chernev, Irving. *Capablanca's Best Chess Endings: 60 Complete Games*. New York: Dover Publications, 1982.

Euwe, Max. *Meet the Masters: The Modern Chess Champions and Their Most Characteristic Games*. London: Sir Isaac Pitman & Sons, Ltd., 1940.

Reinfeld, Fred. *The Immortal Games of Capablanca*. New York: Horowitz & Harkness, 1942.

Pablo Julián Davis

Colón, María Caridad (1958–   )

María Caridad Colón was the first Latin American woman to win gold in the **Olympics**. She placed first in the Javelin in the 1980 Olympics in Moscow with 68.40 meters. She reached her longest throw ever in Havana in 1986 (70.14 meters). She is one of the many Cuban national athletes who received top-level training in the system of specialized sports schools run by the Cuban government. Her talent was discovered at the School Games that are held throughout the country. Retired from competition, Colón now heads up the Recreational Activities Department of INDER (National Institute for Sports, Physical Education, and Recreation). *See also* Sports in Revolutionary Cuba

Further Reading
Pettavino, Paula J., and Geralyn Pye. *Sport in Cuba: The Diamond in the Rough*. Pittsburgh: University of Pittsburgh Press, 1994.

Paula J. Pettavino

Cuéllar Santana, Miguel "Mike" (1937–   )

One of the dominant left-handed pitchers of his generation, Miguel Cuéllar was a mainstay of one of the best pitching staffs in **baseball** history, the 1969 American League champion Baltimore Orioles.

Cuéllar's career began with Almendares, where he played the final five Cuban League seasons beginning 1956–1957. He entered U.S. Organized Baseball with the AAA Cuban Sugar Kings in 1957. His Major League star began to shine with Houston, where he became a starter, registering a 16-11 record in 1967 and the first of four All-Star selections. Mastery of the forkball put him on the path to greatness, which he achieved in Baltimore beginning in 1969. That year he won 23 games and

the Cy Young award (shared with Denny McLain), as part of only the second pitching staff in Major League history with four 20-game winners. A paragon of consistency and durability, the warhorse exceeded 225 innings in a season nine times; from 1969 to 1971, he pitched 290-1/3, 297-2/3, and 292-1/3 innings, respectively (his won-lost totals were 23-11, 24-8, and 23-9). Tested repeatedly in the postseason crucible, he compiled only a 4-4 won-lost mark but always pitched superbly under pressure, with a 2.68 earned run average in 41-1/3 World Series innings and 2.99 for his postseason career. He pitched three scoreless All-Star innings. All told, he won 185 and lost 130 (an outstanding .587 winning percentage); his 3.14 earned run average was fifteenth best in his era. As did many Cubans before him, Cuéllar played in Mexico after his U.S. retirement. *See also* Major Leagues, Cubans in the U.S.

Further Readings
González Echevarría, Roberto. *The Pride of Havana: A History of Cuban Baseball*. New York: Oxford University Press, 1999.
Torres, Ángel. *La leyenda del béisbol cubano, 1878–1997*. Miami: Review Printers, 1997.

Pablo Julián Davis

Dihigo Llanos, Martín (1905–1971)

Regarded by some as baseball's finest player, Martín Dihigo was the first Cuban inducted into the U.S. **baseball** Hall of Fame, despite his exclusion from the Major Leagues due to his color.

Born in Pueblo Nuevo, **Matanzas**, he debuted at age seventeen in the Cuban and **U.S. Negro Leagues**. Dihigo played every position with consummate skill and grace; off the field, his elegance and poise were striking. Four times the Cuban League's leading pitcher (including a 14-2 mark in 1938–1939), Dihigo's stunning versatility shone in 1935–1936: He won the batting title with a .358 average, tied for the home-run crown, and led pitchers with 11 wins and 2 defeats, while managing Santa Clara to the championship. He managed the Kansas City Monarchs to two U.S. Negro League championships. During one incredibly stellar season in Mexico, 1938, he led pitchers with an 18-2 record and 0.90 earned run average, while hitting .387 to win the batting championship. At the end of the twentieth century, Dihigo remained the only player to have been inducted into the Cuban (1951), Mexican (1954), and U.S. (1977) Halls of Fame. He wedded skill and versatility extraordinarily; only Babe Ruth could possibly compare. Baseball luminaries who considered him the most complete of players included John McGraw, Satchel Paige, Buck Leonard, Al Campanis, and Johnny Mize. Dihigo's support for the **struggle against Batista** led to his exile; after Cuba's post-1961 rupture with Organized Baseball, Dihigo returned to help reestablish the sport in Cuba. He died in Cruces, **Santa Clara**. *See also* Sports in Revolutionary Cuba

Further Readings

González Echevarría, Roberto. *The Pride of Havana: A History of Cuban Baseball*. New York: Oxford University Press, 1999.

Holway, John B. *Blackball Stars: Negro League Pioneers*. Westport, CT: Meckler Books, 1988.

Torres, Ángel. *La leyenda del béisbol cubano, 1878–1997*. Miami: Review Printers, 1997.

Pablo Julián Davis

Estalella, Roberto "Bobby" (1911–1991)

Born in **Cárdenas** on April 25, 1911, Roberto Estalella was the second Cuban-born **baseball** player to play in the **U.S. Major Leagues**. Nicknamed "Tarzán" due to his imposing physique, Estalella played third base and outfield.

After a stint playing as an amateur in Cárdenas, Estalella began to play profes-sionally in 1931 with Habana. Estalella later played with numerous other baseball clubs in Cuba, including Almendares and Marianao.

Estalella first played organized North American baseball with Albany in 1934. The following year, he moved on to the Major Leagues, playing for two years with the Washington Senators of the American League. Between 1937 and 1938, he played in the Piedmont Leagues, where he distinguished himself as a league leader in runs batted in, home runs, doubles, triples, and stolen bases with the Charlotte club. Between 1940 and 1941, Estalella played for four different minor league teams: Harrisburg, Minneapolis, Toledo, and San Antonio. In 1941 he played for a brief stint with the St. Louis Browns, then returning once again with the Senators in 1942. During the next two years he played with the Philadelphia A's under Connie Mack.

After playing for the A's, Estalella went to play in Mexico, first for Veracruz in 1946, then with San Luis de Potosí in 1947. He returned briefly to the A's in 1949, his last Major League intervention. During his Major League career, Estalella played in 680 games, achieving a .282 batting average, hitting 44 home runs, and batting in 308 runs.

In 1950, Estalella began to play with the Havana Cubans in the Florida Leagues, where he finished his career. He was inducted into the Cuban Exile Baseball Hall of Fame in 1968. He died on January 7, 1991, in Hialeah, Florida.

Further Reading

Torres, Ángel. *La leyenda del béisbol cubano, 1878–1997*. Miami: Review Printers, 1997.

Nilo Jorge Barredo

Fonst, Ramón (1883–1959)

Fencing champion Ramón Fonst is one of Cuba's all-time sports greatest. He was the first Latin American, in fact, to win a gold

Olympic medalist fencer Ramón Fonst. Photograph courtesy of the Biblioteca Nacional José Martí, Havana.

medal in Olympic competitions (see **Olympics, Cuba in the**). At the tender age of sixteen, in 1899, he became a world champion. A year later, the imposingly tall Fonst challenged Europe's master fencers on their own turf, earning the gold medal for individual épée and the silver medal for open épée during the Paris Olympic Games of 1900. Four years later, during the St. Louis Olympiads, Fonst expanded on his earlier feat, winning gold medals in individual épée, individual foil, and foil team. One of his medal-winning teammates was Manuel Díaz, also Cuban.

Also a master of French boxing and marksmanship, Fonst remained active in international fencing competition for many decades until the Central American and Caribbean Games of 1938. He won three individual gold medals in the Central American and Caribbean Games of 1926 (Mexico City) and two more during the Central American and Caribbean Games

of 1930 (Havana). He died in 1959. Since the mid-1960s the Fonst Memorial International Tournament is hosted by Cuba's Fencing Federation. On the other side of the Florida Straits, meanwhile, a Miami fencing academy bears the name of the Cuban champion.

Further Readings

Forbes, Irene. *As de espada*. Havana: Editorial Letras Cubanas, 2000.
Forbes, Irene. *Soles sin Manchas: muerte en Barbados*. Havana: Editorial Orbe, 1981.

Luis Martínez-Fernández

García, Silvio (1914–1978)

Widely regarded as the greatest shortstop Cuba ever produced, Silvio García nearly became the first black Major League player of modern times.

Born in Limonar, **Matanzas Province**, the cradle of black Cuban ballplayers, García debuted in the Cuban League in 1931–1932 with Habana but played seven seasons with **Cienfuegos** and nineteen overall. He won batting championships in 1940–1941 and 1950–1951. With a powerful throwing arm and outstanding speed, he won the stolen-base title in 1950–1951. García also competed in the **U.S. Negro Leagues** (he was a shortstop for the mighty New York Cubans, 1947 Negro World Series champions, with teammates including Rafael Noble, Luis Tiant, Sr., and young **Orestes Miñoso**) and played seven outstanding seasons in Mexico. When, in the mid-1940s, Brooklyn Dodgers executive Branch Rickey undertook to introduce black players to U.S. Major League **baseball**, thereby breaking the "color line" of racial exclusion, García was one of the men considered. Baseball lore brims with speculation on why García was passed up. One explanation holds his nationality and limited English responsible; another, that background checks revealed avoidance of military service. The most striking version holds that when Rickey asked how he would react to a white player's attacking him with racist invective, he responded, "I kill him." In the event, time worked against him: In 1947, García was already thirty-three. In photographs of the epoch, his ebullient, charismatic smile fairly leaps from the page. Silvio García is remembered for his greatness on the diamond and for what might have been. *See also* Major Leagues, Cubans in the U.S.

Further Readings

Bretón, Marcos, and José Luis Villegas. *Away Games: The Life and Times of a Latin Baseball Player*. New York: Simon and Schuster, 1999.

González Echevarría, Roberto. *The Pride of Havana: A History of Cuban Baseball*. New York: Oxford University Press, 1999.

Torres, Ángel. *La leyenda del béisbol cubano, 1878–1997*. Miami: Review Printers, 1997.

Pablo Julián Davis

Gómez, Pedro "Preston" (1923–   )

Preston Gómez, a catcher, was signed to the **U.S. Major Leagues** by Joe Cambria, the famous scout for the Washington Senators who signed 400 Cubans to U.S. organized **baseball**. He played eight games for the Senators during wartime (1944) and also for the New York Dodgers. After retiring from active play, he served at various times as a manager of the Triple A Havana Sugar Kings, as a manager in Major League baseball, and as an executive with the California Angels. He managed the San Diego Padres during 1969–1972, the Houston Astros during 1974–1975, and the Chicago Cubs for a brief time in 1980. As a Major League manager, his teams won 346 games and lost 529.

Further Reading

Murphy, Jack. "Gómez's Visit to Cuba Includes Chat with Castro." *Sporting News*, February 21, 1970, 33.

Paula J. Pettavino

González, Driulis (1973–   )

Considered one of the world's best women judo fighters, Driulis González has amassed an impressive number of medals in international competition. Born in 1973, she has competed in the lightweight division of the sport. Besides several gold medals in world championship competitions and Pan American Games, she won the bronze medal in the 1992 **Olympics**, the gold medal four years later in Atlanta, and the silver medal in the Sydney Olympiads of 2000. González was voted among Cuba's top 100 athletes of the twentieth century. *See also* Sports in Revolutionary Cuba

Further Reading

Pettavino, Paula J. and Geralyn Pye. *Sport in Cuba: The Diamond in the Rough*. Pittsburgh: University of Pittsburgh Press, 1994.

Luis Martínez-Fernández

Driulis González holding gold medal won during 1999 World Judo Championship. AP /Wide World Photos. Photograph by Findlay Kember.

González Cordero, Miguel Ángel "Mike" (1890–1977)

Baseball player Miguel Ángel González was one of the earliest Cubans, and Latin Americans, in the **U.S. Major Leagues** and the most successful manager in the history of the Cuban League.

González played eighteen Major League seasons for five different National League teams, mostly as a catcher, where he appeared in 880 contests. At six feet one inch and 200 pounds, he was a big ballplayer for the epoch and was famed for his defensive skill and knowledge of the game. At the helm of Habana, he won his first Cuban championship as a player in 1914–1915 and his last in 1952–1953, as a manager; there were thirteen championships in all, including separate stretches of three consecutive titles in the 1920s and the 1950s. His longtime nemesis was **Adolfo Luque** manager of "eternal rival" Almendares. In 1944 he became part owner of Habana and principal owner by 1947; considerable wealth followed.

In 1934 González became the first Cuban to coach in the Major Leagues; he held that position with St. Louis of the National League for thirteen years; he also scouted for the club and twice served as interim manager. His incisive baseball judgment (and imperfect command of English) led him to contribute a phrase inadvertently to the baseball lexicon, when he once cabled to management this assessment of a prospective player: "Good field, no hit." On one of the most famous plays in baseball history, when Enos Slaughter scored all the way from first base to win the 1946 World Series, González was the third-base coach urging him on.

Further Readings

González Echevarría, Roberto. *The Pride of Havana: A History of Cuban Baseball*. New York: Oxford University Press, 1999.

Torres, Ángel. *La leyenda del béisbol cubano, 1878–1997*. Miami: Review Printers, 1997.

Pablo Julián Davis

Guerra Romero, Fermín "Mike" (1912–1992)

Fermín Guerra played **baseball** ten years in the **U.S. Major Leagues** and had a successful career as player and manager in the Cuban League.

Born in Havana, he was known to his compatriots as "Isleño" in allusion to the Canary Island birthplace of his parents. The toughness and hard work associated with that immigrant group in Cuba certainly applied to Guerra (see **Guajiros**). His Major League debut came in 1937; five of his ten years in the Majors were with the club then most closely associated with Cuba, the Washington Senators. At the demanding position of catcher, Guerra never achieved a starting role but did appear in ninety-five games for the Philadelphia Athletics in 1949, and seventy-eight the next year. In the latter season, he was at his most effective, recording a .990 fielding percentage on only three errors (he had achieved the same notable percentage in 1945 with Washington). In Cuba, he played mostly with Almendares, where he competed thirteen seasons and also managed the club to consecutive championships in 1948–1949 and 1949–1950. In 1949, he piloted Almendares to victory in the first Caribbean Series. Guerra's greatest baseball glory came in Nicaragua, where he managed the Boer club to consecutive championships two separate times. His most cherished moment on the baseball diamond came in a game against Cleveland's Bob Feller when, with the bases loaded, he hit a triple against the future Hall of Famer. He died in Miami Beach, two days short of his eightieth birthday.

Further Readings

González Echevarría, Roberto. *The Pride of Havana: A History of Cuban Baseball*. New York: Oxford University Press, 1999.

Torres, Ángel. *La leyenda del béisbol cubano, 1878–1997*. Miami: Review Printers, 1997.

Pablo Julián Davis

Hernández, Liván (1975–   )

Liván Hernández, pitching hero of the 1997 Florida Marlins championship club, became the first Major League star among defectors from postrevolutionary Cuban **baseball**.

Hernández left the Cuban national team in Monterrey, México, in 1995, part of a wave of defections begun with **René Arocha** (1991) (see **Dissent and Defections [1959–   ]**). The **Santa Clara** native's professional debut came with the Dominican Republic's Escogido Leones. Hernández burst onto the Major League stage in 1997, leading the pitching staff of the Florida Marlins to the Major League championship in only the club's fifth year of existence. At age twenty-two, he made seventeen starts and recorded a lost-won mark of 9-3 (including a stretch of nine consecutive victories) to accompany a 3.18 earned run average, outstanding in a hitting-dominating epoch. Under playoff pressure, Hernández was superb: He struck out fifteen Atlanta Braves in a National League championship game, then won two games and Most Valuable Player honors in Florida's scintillating, seven-game World Series triumph over Cleveland. His star faded somewhat in succeeding seasons, as he struggled with earned run averages well over 4.00; Marlins management, in a cost-cutting frenzy, proceeded to dismantle the championship team; and in 1998 Hernández found himself overshadowed by the performance of his elder half brother **Orlando Hernández** with the New York Yankees. From the depleted Marlins, Hernández moved West late in the 1999 season to join the San Francisco Giants rotation. The 2000 season saw him recapture at last his rookie-year form, as his pitching helped the Giants to the West Division title. By the end of the 2001 Season, Hernández's Career totals stood at 57 wins/53 losses with an earned run average of 4.43 and 683 strikeouts. *See also* Major Leagues, Cubans in the U.S.

Further Readings

González Echevarría, Roberto. *The Pride of Havana: A History of Cuban Baseball*. New York: Oxford University Press, 1999.
Torres, Ángel. *La leyenda del béisbol cubano, 1878–1997*. Miami: Review Printers, 1997.

Pablo Julián Davis

Hernández, Orlando "El Duque" (1965–   )

Orlando Hernández, one of Cuba's best postrevolutionary pitchers, left the island in 1997 and became a brilliant star for the New York Yankees.

In eleven seasons with the Havana Industriales he was 129-47 (.743) and excelled in international competition. Cuban authorities, wary after half brother Liván's departure, suspended him in 1996. In late 1997, with agent Joe Cuba's guidance, he left via Costa Rica, thereby gaining free agency. He signed with the Yankees, whose physicians termed him the best-conditioned athlete they had ever seen. His sensational account of journeying in a makeshift craft across shark-swarming waters and survival on a desert island, his strange exercise routines combining gymnastic athleticism with meditation, and his uncertain age and aristocratic nickname all surrounded him with a legendary aura. Details of the Caribbean survival tale soon came under question but not his ability and competitiveness. He became a linchpin of the 1998 Yankee rotation, helped the club reach **baseball**'s pinnacle with 114 victories, and utterly mastered postseason pressure; his game-four road victory against Cleveland (New York had trailed the league championship series 2-1) saved the season. Even better the next year, he helped the Yankees to consecutive championships. His poise and intelligence were remarkable; once, fielding an awkward infield ball that became caught in the glove's webbing, he threw ball and glove together to first base for the out. In his first two postseasons, he was 5-0 with a 1.02 ERA (earned run average); in 2000 he ran the record to 8-0 before losing to the Mets in the World Series. Hernández's totals at the end of the 2001 season stood at 45 wins/33 losses and a 4.13 earned run average. *See also* Hernández, Liván; Major Leagues, Cubans in the U.S.

Further Readings

Fainaru, Steve, and Ray Sánchez. *The Duke of Havana: Baseball, Cuba, and the Search for the American Dream*. New York: Villard Books, 2001.

González Echevarría, Roberto. *The Pride of Havana: A History of Cuban Baseball*. New York: Oxford University Press, 1999.

King, George. *Unbeatable: The Historic Season of the 1998 World Champion New York Yankees*. New York: HarperCollins, 1998.

Pablo Julián Davis

Juantorena, Alberto (1950–   )

Alberto Juantorena is most well known for winning gold medals at the 1976 Olympic Games in Montreal in both the 400- and 800-meter races. He burst onto the scene of international competitive athletics and became known as El Caballo, the horse. He remains the only man to have won Olympic gold medals in those two events.

The career of Juantorena epitomizes the Cuban athlete-student. During his active athletic career, he studied postgraduate economics at the **University of Havana** on a schedule that allowed him to train and to compete.

Juantorena began his athletic career playing basketball. In 1971, two of his trainers convinced him that if he could run the 400 meters in fifty-one seconds in basketball shoes, he might do well to try his hand at track. In 1973 he won the gold for

Orlando "El Duque" Hernández pitching for the New York Yankees in 1998, a few months after defecting from Cuba. AP/Wide World Photos. Photograph by John Lehmann.

Runner Alberto Juantorena beats U.S. opponent in 800-meter event at the Montreal Olympics of 1976. AP/Wide World Photos.

400 meters in the university world competitions in Moscow, a feat he repeated the following year during the Central American and Caribbean Games. The highest point of his career was during the 1976 Montreal **Olympics**, when he took home two gold medals and was later voted the Athlete of the Year. His last major medal was the gold for the 400-meter relay during the 1982 Central American and Caribbean Games. His athletic career ended with a series of injuries to his Achilles tendon in the 1980s.

Juantorena has remained active in the sports arena as a vice president with INDER, the National Institute for Sports, Physical Education, and Recreation. He is also the president of Cuba's Athletic Federation and vice president of the island's Olympic Committee. In addition, he was appointed to the Central Committee of the **Cuban Communist Party** in 1991. *See also* Sports in Revolutionary Cuba

Further Reading

Pettavino, Paula J., and Geralyn Pye. *Sport in Cuba: The Diamond in the Rough*. Pittsburgh: University of Pittsburgh Press, 1994.

Paula J. Pettavino

Kid Chocolate (Eligio Sardinias Montalbo) (1910–1988)

Eligio Sardinias Montalbo, better known as "Kid Chocolate," is the first in a long line of prominent Cuban boxers (see **Boxing**). Sardinias was born on January 6, 1910, in the Havana working-class district of El Cerro. Growing up, Sardinias sold newspapers. It has been said that Sardinias picked up his fighting skills from having to defend his corner from other kids. Sardinias entered a boxing tournament sponsored by the newspaper he sold. He won easily, despite having no formal training. Sardinias's performance caught the atten-

"Kid Chocolate," one of Cuba's all-time greatest fighters. Photograph courtesy of *Bohemia*.

tion of the newspaper's sports editor, Luis Gutiérrez, who encouraged Sardinias to pursue boxing and became his mentor. As an amateur, Sardinias won 113 fights and had no defeats.

Sardinias turned pro as a Bantamweight. His first professional bout was on December 8, 1927, when he defeated Johnny Cruz in six rounds. He won his first twenty-one bouts in Cuba (all by knockout). He then went to New York and continued his winning streak for two and a half years.

On August 7, 1930, Sardinias fought Jackie "Kid" Berg, the Junior Welterweight champion at the time, at the Polo Grounds in New York in a nontitle bout. Sardinias suffered his first loss. Four months later he lost to Christopher Battalino in the fight for the World Featherweight championship. Sardinias took six months off to recuperate.

On July 15, 1931, Sardinias took his first championship, claiming the title of Junior Lightweight champion from Benny "The Fish" Bass in Philadelphia. Sardinias later attempted to take the Lightweight and Junior Welterweight championship from Tony Canzoneri, who held both belts, but

Welterweight world champion "Kid Gavilán." Luis Martínez-Fernández Collection.

failed. Sardinias thereafter decided to stick to lower weight classes.

Sardinias mounted an impressive career in the years that followed, showcasing his talent in New York, Havana, Philadelphia, Madrid, Paris, and other venues. Sardinias's last fight ended in a draw against Nicky Jerome on December 18, 1938. His professional record was impressive: 135 wins, 9 losses, and 6 draws. Sardinias retired to Cuba, becoming a trainer. He passed away in Cuba on August 8, 1988 and was inducted into the International Boxing Hall of Fame in 1991.

Further Readings

Alfonso, Jorge. *Puños dorados: Apuntes para la historia del boxeo en Cuba.* Santiago de Cuba: Editorial Oriente, 1988.

New York Times, August 21, 1988, 28.

The Sporting News, May 23, 1983, 53.

Luis González

Kid Gavilán (Gerardo González) (1926–)

A popular boxer and world champion, Kid Gavilán invented the "bolo" punch, which consisted of a looping uppercut with a half cut. Also known as the Cuban Hawk, he was one of the first pugilists whose fights were broadcast on television. Gavilán was a fast boxer with a lot of energy and staying power.

Born Gerardo González in 1926 in **Camagüey**, Kid Gavilán was a worker on a sugarcane plantation. He said that he developed the "bolo" punch by spending years cutting cane. At the age of twelve, he competed in amateur bouts and was recruited by professional **boxing** managers from Havana. He began his professional career in 1943, boxing in Cuba, Mexico, and Puerto Rico. His managers encouraged him to move to New York City where he could command larger pursues. By the late 1940s, Kid Gavilán was regarded as a top contender for the Welterweight crown. In 1949, he tried to take the title away from Sugar Ray Robinson but lost. Two years later, however, Gavilán fought for the world title again, and this time he won.

Kid Gavilán successfully defended his title against several contenders. In 1954, he moved up to the Middleweight division but was not as successful. That same year, he lost by a judicial decision to boxer Johnny Saxton. Most experts believe that this fight was fixed and the only way for Gavilán to win was through a knockout. A few years later, Gavilán retired with an impressive 107 victories (28 by knockout), 30 losses, and 6 ties. He lives in a nursing home in Miami.

Omar Linares, left, and Orestes Kindelán wear their gold medals during ceremonies at the Centennial Olympic Games in Atlanta in 1996. AP/Wide World Photos. Photograph by Al Behrman.

Further Reading

Alfonso, Jorge. *Puños dorados: apuntes para la historia del boxeo en Cuba.* Santiago de Cuba: Editorial Oriente, 1988.

D. H. Figueredo

Kindelán, Orestes (1964–   )

Orestes Kindelán is a left fielder on the Cuban National **Baseball** team and a consistent power hitter along with **Omar Linares**. Kindelán was born in Palma Soriano, **Santiago de Cuba Province**, in 1964. Ranking among the top all-time home run hitters of the Cuban League, he holds the record for the most home runs in a single Olympiad (nine in Atlanta, 1996) and shares with Linares the record for most home runs in the **Olympics**: twelve. In the Atlanta games he hit a monstrous homer that measured 521 feet. He was part of the Cuban teams that won gold medals in Barcelona (1992) and Atlanta (1996) and the silver in Sydney (2000). Kindelán was a featured player during the Cuba-Baltimore Orioles series in 1999. *See also* Sports in Revolutionary Cuba

Further Readings

Jamail, Milton H. and Larry Dierker. *Full Count: Inside Cuban Baseball.* Carbonale: Southern Illinois University Press, 2000.
Price, S.L. *Pitching Around Fidel: A Journey into the Heart of Cuban Sports.* New York: Ecco Press/HarperCollins, 2000.

Paula J. Pettavino

Linares, Omar (1967–   )

Omar "The Kid" Linares, from San Juan y Martínez in the **Province of Pinar del Río**, is the third baseman for the Cuban National **Baseball** team. He was the youngest ever to make the national team, at the age of seventeen in 1985. That same year, at a tournament in Edmonton, the Toronto Blue Jays offered him a contract that would have allowed him to play only home games, thereby not having to travel to the United States. He turned them down. The New York Yankees later offered him a contract for $1 million, to which he reportedly replied: "I would rather play for 11 million people than for $11 million." Japanese teams also have offered millions for him to play in Japan.

Linares was a member of the Cuban Olympic teams that won gold in Barcelona (1992) and Atlanta (1996) and silver in Sydney (2000). He is tied with **Orestes Kindelán** with the most homers in Olympic competitions: twelve. As is the case with other top Cuban athletes, Linares has been elected to the **National Assembly of People's Power**, earns significant bonuses on top of his meager salary, and receives a car from the Cuban government. He was a featured player for the 1999 Cuba–Baltimore Orioles series. *See also* Major Leagues, Cubans in the U.S.; Olympics, Cuba in the; Sports in Revolutionary Cuba

Further Readings

Jamail, Milton H., and Larry Dierker. *Full Count: Inside Cuban Baseball.* Carbonale: Southern Illinois University Press, 2000.

Price, S.L. *Pitching Around Fidel: A Journey into the Heart of Cuban Sports.* New York: Ecco Press/HarperCollins, 2000.

Paula J. Pettavino

Luis, Mireya (1967–   )

Winner of several Olympic gold medals and a host of other awards, Mireya Luis was one of the world's leading figures in women's volleyball. Luis was born in **Camagüey** on August 28, 1967, the youngest of nine children. She earned the first of her gold medals at the World Cup in 1989, a feat repeated in 1991. She then went on to win a gold medal at the 1992 **Olympics** in Barcelona. Luis earned Olympic gold again in Atlanta in 1996 and Sydney in 2000. Measuring 1.75 meters (5 feet 9 inches), she is renowned for her ability to jump very high when blocking and spiking. Between 1990 and 1995 she was selected as Cuba's best athlete in team sports. She retired from competition in 2001. *See also* Sports in Revolutionary Cuba

Further Reading

Pettavino, Paula J. and Geralyn Pye. *Sport in Cuba: The Diamond in the Rough.* Pittsburgh: University of Pittsburgh Press, 1994.

Luis González

Luque Guzmán, Adolfo Domingo (1890–1957)

A brilliant **baseball** pitcher and manager of legendary toughness, Adolfo Luque was the first Cuban, and Latin American, star in the **U.S. Major Leagues**.

He played twenty seasons in the Majors, winning 194 games against 179 defeats, with a 3.24 earned run average. (In twenty-three Cuban League seasons, he won 93 and lost 62). In 1923, with Cincinnati, he achieved one of the greatest seasons ever by a starting pitcher: 27 wins, 8 defeats, and a 1.93 earned run average; from World War I to the end of the twentieth century, only seven pitchers won more in a season. Luque led the National League three times in shutouts, twice in earned run average, and three times in batting average allowed. In two World Series (1919 with Cincinnati, 1933 with New York Giants), he pitched 9-1/3 innings, allowing zero earned runs with eleven strikeouts; he ended the 1933 Series with a strikeout. After his playing career, Luque stayed in baseball; he coached nine seasons for the Giants. As manager, he won eight Cuban championships from 1919–1920 to 1946–1947, all but one with Almendares. His frequent nemesis was **Miguel Ángel González**, manager of archrival Habana. Luque's ferocious competitiveness and pugnacious strut were reminiscent of John McGraw or Leo Durocher; anecdotes of his fiery temper abounded, including some involving firearms. Though white, he was known and celebrated as "Papá Montero," after the legendary Afro-Cuban **rumba** dancer remembered in a **Nicolás Guillén** poem. He died in Havana, his native city, in relative poverty.

Further Readings

González Echevarría, Roberto. *The Pride of Havana: A History of Cuban Baseball*. New York: Oxford University Press, 1999.

Torres, Ángel. *La leyenda del béisbol cubano, 1878–1997*. Miami: Review Printers, 1997.

Pablo Julián Davis

Major Leagues, Cubans in the U.S.

While the first Cuban to play U.S. professional **baseball** was Esteban Bellán, with the National Association's Troy Haymakers (1871–1873), Cubans began to make their mark forty years later: seventeen debuted from 1911 to 1920, including **Adolfo Luque** and **Miguel Ángel González**. But due to the "color line," only those fair-skinned enough to qualify as white could compete (though Spanish-sounding names or accents "redeemed" somewhat darker complexions). The sport thus excluded some of its greatest talents: **José de la Caridad Méndez, Martín Dihigo**, "Perucho" Formental, and Alejandro Crespo, among many others.

Certain clubs developed Cuban connections. The Cincinnati Reds signed Luque and Rafael Almeida in the 1910s. In the 1930s, Washington Senators scout "Papa Joe" Cambria began systematic recruiting in Cuba. The St. Louis Cardinals (González's longtime club) and the Brooklyn (later Los Angeles) Dodgers also had Cuban ties.

Twenty-three Cubans entered the Majors during the 1940s, as the war created opportunities. Then, in 1949, **Orestes Miñoso**, an outfielder from **Matanzas**, became the first Afro-Cuban Major Leaguer (see **Afro-Cubans**). His brilliant career opened doors for others; apartheid dismantled, the Cuban stars now tended to be blacks.

A cherished moment came in the 1955 World Series, when left fielder Edmundo "Sandy" Amorós's sensational catch helped Brooklyn beat the Yankees and finally win a championship. But the 1965 American League Champion Minnesota Twins marked the Cuban "arrival": **Zoilo Versalles** won Most Valuable Player honors (the first Cuban, and Latin American, so recognized); teammate **Pedro "Tony" Oliva** finished second; Camilo Pascual, a dominating right-hander since the late 1950s, helped lead the pitching staff.

The talent nurtured in the hothouse of 1950s Cuba flowered in the 1960s and 1970s: pitchers Pascual, **Miguel Cuéllar**, and **Luis Tiant, Jr.**; first baseman **Atanasio "Tany" Pérez**; middle infielders Versalles, Octavio "Cookie" Rojas, Tony Taylor, and **Dagoberto Campaneris**; and outfielders Oliva and José Cardenal. The U.S.-Cuban rupture, though, weighed heavily on Cubans who, unlike other Latin Americans, could no longer return home in the winter. Moreover, coaching and managing opportunities were scarce.

After about 1985, Cuba's Major League presence consisted of U.S.-raised sons of expatriates (notably, **José Canseco** and **Rafael Palmeiro**); U.S.-born offspring of Cubans (Eduardo Pérez, Danilo Tartabull, Roberto Estalella, and others, several being sons of ex–Major Leaguers); and expatriates (such as Rey Ordóñez, **Liván Hernández, Orlando Hernández**, and Osvaldo Fernández). Inevitably, all three groups were distanced from the fountainhead of Cuban baseball traditions.

Through the end of the twentieth century, more than 150 Cubans had played in the U.S. Major Leagues.

Further Readings

Bretón, Marcos, and José Luis Villegas. *Away Games: The Life and Times of a Latin Baseball Player*. New York: Simon and Schuster, 1999.

González Echevarría, Roberto. *The Pride of Havana: A History of Cuban Baseball*. New York: Oxford University Press, 1999.

Torres, Ángel. *La leyenda del béisbol cubano, 1878–1997*. Miami: Review Printers, 1997.

Pablo Julián Davis

Marrero, Conrado "Connie" (1911–   )

Conrado "Connie" Marrero played Minor League ball with the Havana Cubans. In 1950, he joined the pitching staff of the Washington Senators until 1954. He had a Major League career record of 39 wins and 40 losses, with a 3.67 ERA (earned run average). Marrero was a stylistic favorite with his Cuban fans, as he performed head-bobbing gyrations before he ever released the pitch. He once received a standing ovation for his windup. He threw out the ceremonial first pitch to Brady Anderson in the first game of the Cuban–Baltimore Oriole's series in 1999. *See also* Baseball; Major Leagues, Cubans in the U.S.

Further Readings
Nieto Fernández, Severo. *Conrado Marrero: el Premier.* Havana: Instituto Cubano del Libro, 2000.

Paula J. Pettavino

Méndez, José de la Caridad (1889–1926)

José de la Caridad Méndez was a star right-handed pitcher in both the Cuban and **U.S. Negro Leagues**. He is one of the great Cuban players who never played Major League ball. He was known for his rising fast ball and sharp-breaking curve. Nicknamed "El Diamante Negro," the Black Diamond, Méndez had a 62-17 pitching record in Cuba by 1914; after thirteen seasons in Cuba he won 74 games and lost 25 for a .747 record. In 1909, while with the Cuban Stars, he won 44 games and lost only 2. He became a regular in the Negro Leagues, with the Kansas City Monarchs and the Cuban Stars. In four years of barnstorming against all-white Major League teams, Méndez picked up 8 of 32 victories. He took a no-hitter into the ninth inning the first time he faced the Cin-

cinnati Reds and defeated the Philadelphia Phillies several times. As a manager-player with the Monarchs, he led his team to three consecutive Negro Leagues' championships: 1923, 1924, 1925.

Forced by arm trouble to switch to shortstop and outfield, Méndez also played for the Detroit Stars and the Chicago American Giants. He became so popular in Cuba that when he entered a restaurant, he received a standing ovation. He died in 1926 after a brief illness.

Méndez was inducted into the Cuban Baseball Hall of Fame when it was established in 1939. *See also* Major Leagues, Cubans in the U.S.

Further Reading
Torres, Ángel. *La leyenda del béisbol cubano, 1878–1997.* Miami: Review Printers, 1997.

Paula J. Pettavino

Miñoso, Orestes "Minnie" (1925–   )

Born Saturnino Orestes Arrieta Armas, Minnie Miñoso became the first Major League star from Cuba since **Adolfo Luque**. Miñoso was a superb player, honored in U.S. **baseball** lore mainly for matters extraneous to his considerable abilities and achievements.

Born in Perico, **Matanzas Province**, Miñoso was of the last generation directly affected by the apartheid of "the color line." The year 1946 saw his Cuban League debut, with Marianao, and the first of three seasons with the New York Cubans including the 1947 powerhouse, winner of the **U.S. Negro Leagues** World Series. After a brief turn in 1949, his real Major League debut came in 1951 with Cleveland (and a trade to the Chicago White Sox). He slammed a home run against the Yankees in his first at-bat, had a superb season (league leader in steals and triples, second in batting average and runs), and won *The Sporting News'*

Orestes "Minnie" Miñoso wearing Washington Senators' uniform. Courtesy of the National Baseball Hall of Fame Library, Cooperstown, New York.

recognition as top rookie; and for over a decade, it was full speed ahead.

Miñoso's talent and accomplishments were enormous. He had blazing speed (three times league leader in triples and steals), got on base (eight times exceeding .300 batting average, nine times 90-plus runs), had power (four times 20-plus homers, five times 90-plus RBIs [runs batted in], career slugging average .460), and played outstanding left field (three Gold Glove awards). Fearless at the plate, he was hit by pitches 189 times, setting a record that stood more than twenty years. Three times Miñoso finished among the top four in Most Valuable Player balloting and hit .300 in seven All-Star Games. A 1962 outfield injury (including a skull fracture) truncated his career (at thirty-nine, he had a lifetime average of .304), though he revived it with seven fine seasons in Mexico. In Cuba, he contributed over a decade of memorable work and set a number of records; the Cuban Baseball

Hall of Fame in exile inducted him in 1983.

Miñoso was not a showy player, but he was exciting. Not for nothing was he the subject of a dance hit, Enrique Jorrín's 1955 **cha-cha-chá** "Miñoso al bate." Unfortunately, but rather typically for Latin American players, he is remembered more for "showmanship" (famous photographs in his Cadillac convertible; donning bullfighter's regalia; brief Major League appearances in 1976 and 1980, at advanced age, making him a "five decade player," and a Minor League appearance in 1996 to make it six) than as a superlative ballplayer and precursor to Rickey Henderson and others whose fusion of speed and power later revolutionized baseball. Miñoso remains active with the White Sox organization, employed by its community relations department. *See also* Major Leagues, Cubans in the U.S.

Further Readings

González Echevarría, Roberto. *The Pride of Havana: A History of Cuban Baseball*. New York: Oxford University Press, 1999.

Miñoso, Orestes. *Just Call Me Minnie: My Six Decades in Baseball*. Champaign, IL: Sagamore Publishing, 1994.

Torres, Ángel. *La leyenda del béisbol cubano, 1878–1997*. Miami: Review Printers, 1997.

Vanderberg, Bob. *Minnie and the Mick: The Go-Go White Sox Challenge the Fabled Yankee Dynasty, 1951 to 1964*. South Bend, IN: Diamond Communications, 1996.

Pablo Julián Davis

Morales, Pablo (1964–   )

Born in Chicago, Illinois, of Cuban parents, Pablo Morales is a three-time Olympic Gold medallist swimmer. Morales won a relay gold and two silver medals for the United States at the 1984 **Olympics** in Los Angeles. While attending Stanford University, he helped his team attain three consecutive National Collegiate Athletic Association (NCAA) titles (1985–1987). He also set world and U.S. records in butterfly and individual medley. Morales is the winningest swimmer in NCAA history, capturing eleven national titles. In 1988 he was co-winner of the Stanford A-1 Masters Award, the university's highest honor for athletic performance, leadership, and academic excellence.

In 1992 Morales returned to the Olympics (held that year in Barcelona) as captain of the U.S. swim team, capturing the individual gold in the 100-meter butterfly (the first American Olympic champion in the event since 1976) and another in the 400-meter relay.

Following Stanford, Morales earned his law degree from Cornell University. However, he has opted to coach rather than practice law.

Further Reading
Bay Area Sports Hall of Fame (bashof.org).

Luis González

Moreno González, Julio (1921–1987)

Julio Moreno was one of the most recognized players of Cuban **baseball**. He was born in Havana on January 28, 1921. Nicknamed "Jiqui" for his strong arm and fast pitches, Moreno began playing the game with the Stars of Pancho in Güines. Between the years of 1939 and 1944, he pitched for San Antonio de los Baños, in the National Amateur Leagues. In 1944, playing for Marianao, he finished off with a record of 26 wins and 3 losses. The following year he was victorious in twenty more games. His feats included pitching a no-hitter on March 19, 1944.

In 1945 Moreno pitched for Veracruz in the Mexican Leagues, where he had 14 wins and 10 losses. He would once again play in Veracruz eleven years later. During his tenure in the Mexican Leagues, Moreno also played for Yucatán, Nuevo Laredo, and Puebla. His overall record in Mexico was 124 wins and 99 losses.

He also pitched for **Cienfuegos** and Habana between 1948 and 1956. His best year was 1952, when he helped Habana win the championship. Jiqui pitched the final championship played in Cuba (1960–1962).

Moreno played for four years, between the years of 1946 and 1950, with the Havana Cubans in the Florida International Leagues, before signing with the Washington Senators in 1950, where he played until 1953. Toward the end of his career, he practiced as a pitcher with the Detroit Tigers when they won the World Series in 1968. In the majors he had 50 wins and 53 losses and a 4.25 earned run average.

Moreno passed away on January 2, 1987, in Miami, Florida. *See also* Major Leagues, Cubans in the U.S.

Further Reading
Torres, Ángel. *La leyenda del beisbol Cubano, 1878–1997*. Miami: Review Printers, 1997

Nilo Jorge Barredo

Negro Leagues, Cubans in the U.S.

The largest contingent from the Spanish-speaking Americas to enter U.S. professional **baseball** during its segregated period (1880s to 1947), Cubans started participating in the black baseball circuits in the early 1900s. For the majority of Cuban players, the Negro Leagues represented their sole U.S. professional option due to the **U.S. Major Leagues'** practice of excluding nonwhite players. A combination of phenotypical features and racial perceptions thus forestalled the Major League aspirations of a host of Cubans that included **José de la Caridad Méndez, Cristóbal Torriente**, and **Martín Dihigo**.

North Americans developed awareness of Cuban players mainly through tours that began in 1879 while the island was still a Spanish colony. Tours by U.S. professional teams became more regular

after the U.S. military occupation following the War of 1898 (see **War of Independence**). The success Cubans enjoyed
compelled Major League and Negro
League organizations to sign Cuban players. Their inclusion in the U.S. segregated
leagues challenged the effective policing
of racial lines where anything from a
player's hair to skin color to facial features
that indicated possible African ancestry
had resulted in exclusion from the Major
Leagues. After Cubans appeared in the
Major Leagues in 1911, segregationists
who defended the color line grew concerned not just that blacks might "pass" as
white but also that they would possibly
pass as "Spanish" or "Cuban."

Aware of the available market for Cuban participants in the United States, en-
terprising men like Agustín Molina, Abél
Linares, and Alejandro Pompez emerged
as the vanguard of Cuban baseball.
Throughout the first half of the 1900s
these men organized and financed Cuban
teams that competed in exhibition games
against Minor League, Major League, and
black baseball teams in the northeastern,
midwestern, and southern regions of the
United States. In the following decades
they were also instrumental in the formation of the All Cubans, the Cuban Stars,
and the New York Cubans that participated
in the black baseball circuits.

Formal organization of the Negro National League in 1920 provided Cubans
viewed as racially ineligible for the Major
Leagues their sole opportunity to pursue a
professional career in the United States.
Cubans participated in different capacities
in the organized league. A handful of ex-
ceptionally talented players like Martín
Dihigo, José de la Caridad Méndez, and
Cristóbal Torriente, however, starred on
Negro Leagues teams featuring African
American and Latino talent. A few Cubans
worked in executive positions as team
owners or serving on the leagues' executive boards. Operating primarily out of

Chicago since 1907, Agustín Molina's Cuban Stars team joined the Negro National
League as a charter member. Based in New
York, and bearing the same name, Alejandro Pompez's Cuban Stars operated as an
independent club from 1916 to 1922 before
participating in the Eastern Colored League
from 1923 to 1929. During this initial period of Negro Leagues baseball (1920–
1933), most Cuban players performed on
teams composed entirely of Latinos, such
as the Cuban Stars. In fact, Pompez often
received criticism from black newspapers
for not including African American players
on his team; he would change tactics when
black baseball entered a new era following
the Great Depression.

After a brief disruption, the Negro
Leagues resumed operation in 1935 featuring two leagues with four teams each.
Unlike the Major Leagues, which suffered
declining attendance, World War II proved
an economic boon for the Negro Leagues.
Wartime travel restrictions and greater employment rates for African American and
Latino laborers boosted attendance at Negro Leagues games. The war effort, however, depleted the leagues' U.S.-born talent
pool as some were called into military service or to work in defense industry plants.
In response, Negro Leagues teams increasingly signed players from the Spanish-
speaking Americas.

The 1940s featured the highest level of
Cuban participation in U.S. professional
baseball during the Jim Crow era. Greater
entry into the structure of the Major
Leagues during the war years foreshadowed
the end of segregationist practices. New
York Cubans owner Alejandro Pompez la-
mented the immediate impact this had on
Negro Leagues clubs; it forced them to
continually locate new players. Thus, Pompez redoubled scouting efforts, signing new
players like **Orestes "Minnie" Miñoso** and
Edmundo "Sandy" Amorós, who contributed to the New York Cubans' 1947 Negro
Leagues championship. Negro Leagues tal-

ent was further depleted by the advent of Major League integration in 1947. With its more talented players departing and the Major Leagues making no overture toward incorporating the Negro Leagues into "organized baseball," Negro League team owners quickly lost the battle of economic viability. After the 1948 season, the Negro American League folded, and the New York Cubans ceased operations; Negro League baseball would never again play at the "big league" level it had performed for so long. However, dozens of Cubans like Miñoso and Amorós who enjoyed their initial U.S. professional playing experience in the Negro Leagues became part of the first generation of players of African ancestry appearing in the Major Leagues.

Further Readings

Burgos, Adrian, Jr. "The Latins from Manhattan: Confronting Race and Building Community in Jim Crow Baseball, 1906–1950." In *Mambo Montage*, ed. Agustín Lao-Montes et al. New York: Columbia University Press, 2001. 71–93.

Clark, Dick, and Larry Lester. *The Negro Leagues Book*. Cleveland, OH: Society of American Baseball Researchers, 1994.

González Echevarría, Roberto. *The Pride of Havana: A History of Cuban Baseball*. New York: Oxford University Press, 1999.

Riley, James A. *The Biographical Encyclopedia of Negro Baseball Leagues*. New York: Carroll & Graf, 1994.

Adrian Burgos, Jr.

Oliva López, Pedro "Tony" (1940–   )

Tony Oliva was a magnificent left-handed hitter for the Minnesota Twins whose career was plagued by debilitating injuries but who still created an outstanding body of work.

Born in **Pinar del Río**, he grew up among **sugar plantations**. He was the last Major League Cuban star to have played in the Cuban League and one of the last discoveries by Washington scout "Papa Joe" Cambria. Using his brother Antonio's

passport to enter the United States for a tryout, he became known as "Tony." In his 1964 debut, Oliva took **baseball** by storm: In 161 games with Minnesota (the ex-Washington Senators), he batted .323 to lead the league, set a league rookie record with 217 hits, plus 109 runs, 32 homers, and 94 RBI's (runs batted in)—all good for near-unanimous Rookie of the Year honors. Showing immunity to baseball's feared "sophomore jinx," Oliva penned a sidereal second act, becoming the only player in baseball's first 150 years to win batting titles his first two seasons. With Minnesota (his only Major-League team) he led a powerful attack alongside compatriots **Zolio Versalles**, Camilo Pascual, **Luis Tiant, Jr.**, and Leo Cárdenas, and Rod Carew of Panama, winning the 1965 pennant and two division titles (batting .314 in the postseason). His outfield work won him a Gold Glove (1966). After a 1971 injury and five knee operations, though, he was never the same, though he extended his career four years via the new "designated hitter" rule. Oliva's .304 lifetime average trailed only Carew, Roberto Clemente, Mateo Alou, Ralph Garr, and Hank Aaron during that pitching-dominated era. *See also* Major Leagues, Cubans in the U.S.

Further Readings

Gillette, Gary. *Total Twins 2000: The History and Lore of the Minnesota Twins*. (Kingston, NY: Total Sports, 2000).

González Echevarría, Roberto. *The Pride of Havana: A History of Cuban Baseball*. New York: Oxford University Press, 1999.

Torres, Ángel. *La leyenda del béisbol cubano, 1878–1997*. Miami: Review Printers, 1997.

Pablo Julián Davis

Olympics, Cuba in the

For a country of its size—a little over 11 million inhabitants—Cuba has developed scores of world-class athletes that have made the island nation a major Olympic contender that rivals the United States, Russia, China, Germany, and other sports powerhouses. While sports—and world-class athletes—did not arrive in Cuba with the **Revolution**, the emphasis of the **Fidel Castro** regime has produced dramatic results in the island's recent Olympic history.

Cuba did not participate in the first modern Olympiads held in Athens in 1896; it was still a colony, and Cuban separatists were staging an all-out **war of independence** against Spain. Cuba's first Olympic athlete was fencer **Ramón Fonst** who in the 1900 Paris Olympic games won the gold medal for épée individual and the silver for épée for amateurs and masters. These were the first Olympic medals earned by a Latin American athlete. In the following Olympic games, St. Louis, 1904, Fonst expanded on his earlier feat, earning gold medals in foil individual and épée individual; his teammate and compatriot Manuel Díaz won gold for saber individual, while teammates Albertson van zo Post and Charles Tatham won another gold medal, two silvers, and three bronzes, for a team total of nine individual medals. Cuba did not send representatives to the next five scheduled Olympic games: London, 1908; Stockholm, 1912; Berlin, 1916 (canceled); Antwerp, 1920; and Paris, 1924. The quarter-century lull in Cuban Olympic competition ended in 1928 when Cuba sent a single representative to the 1928 games in Amsterdam: sprinter José Barrientos. Nicknamed "Relámpago de la Pista" (Track's Lightning), Barrientos competed in the 100 meters event. Cuba, once again, failed to participate in the 1932 Los Angeles Olympics and the controversial Berlin games of 1936. Because of World War II, the 1940 and 1944 games were not held. Cuba participated in the 1948 London Olympics with a sizable delegation of fifty-four athletes, including twelve basketball players. On that occasion Carlos de Cárdenas, Sr. and Jr., won the silver medal in yachting on the sailboat

Kurush IV. The Cuban athletic delegations to the next three Olympiads (Helsinki, 1952; Melbourne, 1956, and Rome, 1960) failed to gain medals. In the 1956 games the first Cuban woman, Berta Díaz, competed in track and field.

With the advent of the Revolution, Cuba experienced a boom in sports participation and excellence that the government used to project a positive image in the international arena. As the government poured resources into the field of sports and imported coaches from the Soviet Union and Eastern Europe, Cuba's presence in the Olympics increased, and medal totals mounted, particularly in **boxing** and track and field. Unlike amateurs in capitalist nations, Cuban athletes devoted full time to training while being generously supported by the Cuban state. In the 1964 Tokyo Olympics, sprinter Enrique Figarola won silver in the 100-meter race—Cuba's first medal since 1948. The island's performance in Mexico in 1968 was the best to date with a total of four silver medals: men's and women's 100 meter relays and boxing in the welterweight and middleweight categories. Medal totals doubled during the Munich games of 1972 with three gold, one silver, and four bronze. Five of the eight medals and all three of the gold ones were in boxing, including that of heavyweight **Teófilo Stevenson**. Another of the 1972 Olympic medals was won by Silvia Chivás—the first individual medal by a Cuban woman. That year Cuba's basketball team also won bronze, after beating Italy's squad. During the next Olympics, Montreal, 1976, Cuba's medal total rose to thirteen, the number of gold medals doubling to six. During the Montreal games attention focused on Cuban track star **Alberto Juantorena**, who won the 400- and 800-meter races, setting a record on the latter. Another Cuban athlete, Silvio Leonard, was a hopeful winner in the 100-meter race, but an injury affected his performance. Boxing, once

Cuba s Olympic Medals*				
Olympiad	Gold	Silver	Bronze	Total
1900, Paris	1	1	0	2
1904, St. Louis	4	2	3	9
1928, Amsterdam	0	0	0	0
1948, London	0	1	0	1
1952, Helsinki	0	0	0	0
1956, Melbourne	0	0	0	0
1960, Rome	0	0	0	0
1964, Tokyo	0	1	0	1
1968, Mexico City	0	4	0	4
1972, Munich	3	1	4	8
1976, Montreal	6	4	3	13
1980, Moscow	8	7	5	20
1984, Los Angeles	Joined Soviet Boycott.			
1988, Seoul	Boycotted with Ethiopia and North Korea.			
1992, Barcelona	14	6	11	31
1996, Atlanta	9	8	8	25
2000, Sydney	11	11	7	29
Totals	56	46	41	143

*Includes only Olympiads in which Cuba competed.

again, was Cuba's medal factory. Cuban fighters earned four gold, two silver, and two bronze medals, including a repeat victory by Stevenson.

Cuba's medal count jumped yet again in the Moscow games of 1980, competitions marked by the boycott of the United States and many other countries that were protesting the Soviet invasion of Afghanistan. On that occasion, Cuba earned a total of twenty medals: eight gold, seven silver, five bronze. This included the dominant performance of Cuban boxers; ten of the eleven fighters won medals, including six gold medals, among them Stevenson's third straight in Olympic competition. That year **María Caridad Colón** became the first Cuban and Latin American woman to win a gold medal when she established a new Olympic record in javelin. Cuba then skipped the Olympic games of 1984 in Los Angeles and 1988 in Seoul, joining the Soviet boycott of the former and in solidarity with North Korea in the latter.

Cuba reappeared in Olympic competitions in 1992 in Barcelona, where its athletes gained a total of thirty-one medals, fourteen of them gold. This total ranked Cuba fifth among the nations of the world. Cuba far outranked all other Latin American nations, their combined total of medals that year reaching only thirteen, two of them gold. Cuba's 1992 medals included gold for high jumper **Javier Sotomayor** and gold for discus thrower Maritza Marten. Seven boxers won gold and another two won silver, reasserting Cuba's dominance in that sport. Women's judo and men's Greco-Roman wrestling brought Cuba four and three medals, respectively. Perhaps the most anticipated gold medal was the one gained by Cuba's **baseball** team. This was the first time that baseball was an official Olympic sport, and Cuba won first place after defeating the U.S. team twice. In 1996 Cuba's trajectory of growing numbers of medals was reversed for the first time in its revolutionary history, doubtless the effect of the crisis of the so-called **Special Period** and the consequent falling morale among athletes, several of whom defected. During the Atlanta Olympics Cuba won a total of twenty-five medals, its ranking falling to number eight; on a per capita basis Cuba ranked fifth. Among the notable medals of 1996 were a repeat gold medal by the Cuban baseball team; seven boxing medals, among them a repeat gold medal by heavyweight Félix Savón; gold medal in women's volleyball with **Mireya Luis** at the helm; and five medals in women's judo, among them the gold for lightweight **Driulis González**. Much attention was paid to **Ana Fidelia Quirot**, who won silver in the 800-meter race after recuperating from a serious burn accident three years before. Cuba's Olympic delegation achieved a total of twenty-nine medals in the 2000 Sydney games, eleven gold, eleven silver, seven bronze. While the number of medals increased a bit, the island's ranking fell to ninth and, on a per capita basis, to sixth. In terms of gold medals per capita, however, Cuba ranked third both in 1996 and 2000. Some of the salient Cuban medal winners of 2000 were the baseball team (silver); women's volleyball team (gold); six boxing medals, including Savón's third straight heavyweight gold; four women's judo medals; long jump gold for Iván Pedroso; and high jump silver for Sotomayor.

In sum, Cuba has had a remarkable Olympic trajectory, particularly since the 1960s. Overall, its athletes have accumulated a total of 146 medals, 56 of them gold. Since 1976, Cuba has averaged 24 medals per Olympiad. *See also* Sports in Revolutionary Cuba

Further Reading
Ruiz Vinageras, Fabio. *Un siglo de deporte olímpico: Cuba y América Latina, 1896–1996*. Havana: Editorial Deportes, 1998.

Luis Martínez-Fernández

Oms, Alejandro "El Caballero" (1895–1946)

Considered by many to be the best batter of all times in Cuban **baseball**, Alejandro Oms was born in **Santa Clara** in 1895.

His family was very poor, and Oms worked as a child in an iron foundry. He began playing organized baseball in 1910 and from 1921 to 1935 played in the Negro National League on the Cuban Stars and the New York Cubans while playing in Cuba during the winter. His lifetime batting average in the **U.S. Negro Leagues** was .325.

While playing for the Santa Clara team Oms had a .436 batting average during the 1922–1923 season. He went on to become batting champion in Cuba three times: 1924–1925 (.393), 1928–1929 (.432), and 1929–1930 (.380). His lifetime batting average in the Cuban League was .351. During the 1940s he played in the Venezuela League. He became famous for his flamboyant behind-the-back fly ball catches.

Further Reading
Torres, Ángel. *La leyenda del béisbol cubano, 1878–1997*. Miami: Review Printers, 1997.

Luis González

Palmeiro Corrales, Rafael (1964–)

Cuban-born, U.S.-raised Rafael Palmeiro challenged **"Tany" Pérez**'s legacy as Cuba's greatest Major League first baseman with his quietly consistent but devastating slugging beginning in the mid-1980s.

Along with **José Canseco**, most famously, Palmeiro was part of a generation of Cuban ballplayers born on the island but whose formation, careers, and **baseball** memories all unfolded in the United States. He played college ball at Mississippi State, performing brilliantly in 1984 and making his Major League debut just two years later with the National League's Chicago Cubs. After three seasons there, he was acquired by the Texas Rangers and began a long rampage against American League pitchers. Palmeiro seemed to improve with age, first reaching 30 home runs in a season at age twenty-nine. At age thirty-five, in 1999, having returned to Texas from Baltimore, his performance probably bested Pérez's of 1970 and Canseco's of 1988 as the best season yet by a Cuban hitter in the Majors: 47 homers, 148 RBIs (runs batted in), 96 runs, .324 average, and .630 slugging. Despite his prodigious bat work, the limelight seemed to elude Palmeiro; in part, this may have been due to his relatively frequent changes of uniform (four clubs in his first twelve seasons) and to the long shadows thrown by other, stellar first basemen of his era, such as Keith Hernández, Don Mattingly, and Mark McGwire. At age 37, Palmeiro showed no signs of slowing down, having amassed 447 home runs, 1,470 RBIs, and seven consecutive 100-plus RBI campaigns through the 2001 season. *See also* Major Leagues, Cubans in the U.S.

Further Readings

Brandt, Ed, and Banbana J. Marvis. *Rafael Palmeiro: Living the American Dream*. Elkton, MD: Mitchell Lane Publishers, 1997.

González Echevarría, Roberto. *The Pride of Havana: A History of Cuban Baseball*. New York: Oxford University Press, 1999.

Torres, Ángel. *La leyenda del béisbol cubano, 1878–1997*. Miami: Review Printers, 1997.

Pablo Julián Davis

Pérez Rigal, Atanasio "Tany" (1942–)

Hall of Famer Tany (Tony) Pérez played first base for the legendary Big Red Machine (Cincinnati Reds) between 1964 and 1976. AP/Wide World Photos.

First baseman Atanasio "Tany" Pérez wielded a mighty bat on the Cincinnati Reds of the 1970s and was one of the greatest run producers of his era.

Pérez grew up in Violeta, **Camagüey**, too young to have competed in the Cuban League. Promoted in 1964 to the Reds— "el Querido Cinci" to Cubans since the days of **Adolfo Luque**—Pérez played twenty-three seasons, a glorious thirteen in Cincinnati. In 1970, his .329 batting, 40 homers, 129 RBIs (runs batted in), 107 runs, .401 on-base average, and .589 slugging constituted a performance no Cuban had ever equaled in the Majors. He amassed twelve 90-plus RBI seasons; his 1,078 RBIs during 1967–1976 were the Majors' best; his 1,652 lifetime RBIs set the record for Latin Americans. He was in the century's top twenty in longevity (2,777 games). Pérez's fifteenth-inning home run won the 1967 All-Star game; for bigger stakes, his 3-run homer sealed Game 7, and a Reds championship, in the treasured 1975 World Series. Though he truly powered the "Big Red Machine," his modesty, limited English, and Latin American origin denied him the attention lavished on teammates Johnny Bench, Pete Rose, and Joe Morgan. He was never awarded Most Valuable Player. Cincinnati traded him to Montreal in 1976, to their later—and public—regret. Brought back to coach, he was named Reds manager in 1993 but fired after only 44 games. Since 1993 he has been with the Florida Marlins organization, serving in various capacities including managing the team during part of the 2001 season. Hall of Fame induction (July 2000) was thus particularly sweet. "I always played to win," he said characteristically at Cooperstown, "and never cared for numbers or records." *See also* Baseball; Major Leagues, Cubans in the U.S.

Further Readings

González Echevarría, Roberto. *The Pride of Havana: A History of Cuban Baseball*. New York: Oxford University Press, 1999.

Hertzel, Bob. *The Big Red Machine*. Englewood Cliffs, NJ: Prentice-Hall, 1976.

Torres, Ángel. *La leyenda del béisbol cubano, 1878–1997*. Miami: Review Printers, 1997.

Pablo Julián Davis

Quirot, Ana Fidelia (1963–)

Ana Fidelia Quirot was a leading figure during the late 1980s and 1990s in both 400- and 800-meter races; her speed earned her the nickname "Tormenta del Caribe" (Caribbean Storm).

Quirot was born in 1963 in the town of Palma Soriano in Oriente Province, today **Santiago de Cuba Province**. A school coach spotted her running barefoot at play and wondered how fast she could be with the proper equipment and the proper training. Eventually, she became a top competitor in athletics and ran all over the world for the Cuban national team. Her first major triumph came at the age of fifteen, when she received a gold medal as part of the 400-meter relay team during the 1978 Central American and Caribbean Games. She won all her races in 1989, including a gold medal in the Barcelona Athletic World Cup (800 meters in 1:54,44). That year the International Association of Athletics Federations (IAAF) named her Female Athlete of the Year. In the 1991 Pan American Games in Havana, she broke the Games' records in the 400 and 800 meters. She was a bronze medallist in the 800 meters at the 1992 **Olympics** in Barcelona.

In 1993, Quirot was severely burned when a kerosene cooker exploded in her kitchen. Thirty-eight percent of her body was covered with third-degree burns. **Fidel Castro** visited her in the hospital the night of the accident. Quirot had been married for eight years to former world champion wrestler Raúl Cascaret, whom she divorced in 1991. At the time of the accident, she was carrying a baby fathered by Cuba's world-record high jumper **Javier Sotomayor**. Her baby was born prematurely at seven months and died shortly after birth as a result of the accident. She recovered from her injuries in record time,

Ana Fidelia Quirot crosses finish line to win 800-meter race in Havana Pan Am Games (1991). AP/Wide World Photos. Photograph by David Longstreath.

training by running the stairs in the hospital. Quirot returned to competition and, in 1995, won the gold medal in the World Championships in Sweden. In 1996, she won the silver medal in 800 meters in the Olympics in Atlanta. Her last major victory came in 1997, when she earned a gold medal in the 1997 World Championships in Athens.

Quirot is one of the most popular athletes in Cuba today, and she remains an inspiration to Cubans everywhere. *See also* Sports in Revolutionary Cuba

Further Reading

Pettavino, Paula J., and Geralyn Pye. *Sport in Cuba: The Diamond in the Rough*. Pittsburgh: University of Pittsburgh Press, 1994.

Paula J. Pettavino

Rodríguez, Jennifer (1976–)

Cubans have gained a reputation for dominating several events of the Summer Olympic games. But few (if any) have been known for their talents in the Winter games. Jennifer Rodríguez is the exception, having been born and raised in Miami (where winters are mild) and taking home two bronze medals in speed skating at the 2002 Olympic Winter Games.

Rodríguez started out as a roller skater. She was a five-time world team member and finished second at the World Figure Rollerskating Championships in 1992. She won a silver medal at the 1995 Pan American Games. Rodríguez made the switch to ice skates in 1996. She made the team for the 1998 Winter Games and finished fourth overall. Rodríguez is married to teammate K.C. Boutiette. Her nickname is "Miami Ice."

Further Reading
"Ice Queen." *Latina*, January 2000, 58.

Luis González

Salazar, Alberto (1958–)

One of the world's most winning marathoners, Alberto Salazar was born in Havana on August 7, 1958. At the age of two he moved with his parents to south Florida eventually resettling in Connecticut. The family later moved to Wayland, Massachusettes, where Salazar was named high school all-American twice for his performance as a two- and three-mile runner.

In 1976 Salazar began his studies at the University of Oregon. Bill Dellinger, a former Olympian, was his coach. In 1978 he won the National Collegiate Athletic Association (NCAA) individual championship. In 1979 he set a U.S. road record of 22:13 for five miles. He qualified for the Olympic team, in 1980 but the United States boycotted the games in Moscow.

That same year Salazar won the prestigious New York City Marathon, setting a record for the fastest first marathon. He repeated his win the following year, this time setting a new world record of 2:08:13, and again in 1983, making it his third consecutive win. Salazar again qualified for the **Olympics** in 1984 but finished fifteenth overall in Los Angeles.

Between 1992 and 1996 he worked for Nike, and he continues to consult for them.

Further Reading
Salazar, Alberto. *Alberto Salazar's Guide to Running*. New York: McGraw Hill, 2001.

Luis González

Sports in Revolutionary Cuba

Although sports in Cuba have a long pre-Revolutionary history, since 1959 they have been thoroughly transformed by the values and objectives of the **Revolution**, and Cuba has become a consistent world power in international competitions. Within fifteen years of the Revolution, Cuba had transformed itself from a nation that had won only a handful of medals to one of the top ten medal-winning nations in the **Olympics**. On a per capita basis, Cuba is the world's top Olympic medal winner of the later decades of the twentieth century. Some of the success can be attributed to the technical support that Cuba received from the Socialist bloc; however, even more important is the emphasis placed on sports and nationwide participation by the revolutionary government.

In 1959 there were only thirteen state-owned sports arenas. Private clubs and centers were nationalized, and a program was launched to build new facilities. In 1961, the government institutionalized sports with the establishment of INDER, the Instituto Nacional de Deportes, Educación Física y Recreación. By 1965, Cuba had firmly established a domestic sports industry to manufacture its own athletic equipment. By 2000, there were more than 11,523 sports facilities across the island.

INDER is responsible for all matters connected with sports, from physical education to recreation to high-level competitive athletics. Ciudad Deportiva in Havana houses the central INDER offices, along with the Instituto Superior de Cultura Física (ISCF), the Instituto de Medicina Deportiva, the National Training Center, and the Industria Deportiva. INDER reports directly to the Cuban Olympic Committee.

The Cuban sports system maintains two major goals: the mass participation in sports of most Cuban citizens and the continual search for and development of top-level competitive athletes. In large part, Cubans have reached these goals. Supporting these efforts is a well-organized system of physical education and physical culture that is required by the **educational system**. In addition, these sports culminate in a series of competitions called the School Games, during which top-level athletic talent is scouted. Once these athletes are identified, they are then given the opportunity to further develop their talent in a system of specialized sports schools that are run by the state. In fact, this system of sports schools, although modeled after the system that existed in the former Soviet Union and East Germany, is in many ways uniquely Cuban. It is one of the more impressive institutional creations of the Revolution.

This system of sports schools follows the regular curriculum at the same time that they train top-level athletes for international competition. At the first level are fifteen Escuelas de Iniciación Deportivas Escolares (EIDEs). The next level contains fourteen Escuelas Superiores de Perfeccionamiento Atlético (ESPAs), 162 specialized sports academies, and at the top, two Centros de Alto Rendimiento

Souvenir philatelic sheet celebrates Cuba's national pastime and international sports competition. Luis Martínez-Fernández Collection.

(CEARs). Both of the CEARs are located in Havana at the facilities developed for the Pan American Games held in Havana in 1991. In September 2000, Cuba opened an Escuela Internacional de Educación Física.

The Cuban sports system is able to earn some hard **currency** by "renting out" teams, players, and trainers. There are 500 Cuban trainers and coaches in thirty-eight countries (see **World, Cubans around the**). These professionals return approximately 80 percent or more of their earnings to the Cuban government. Contracts are signed with the Cuban Sports Federation, which then gives some money to individual players as compensation.

One of the more significant recent developments in the Cuban sports system is the establishment of a marketing firm called Cuba Deportes, S.A. Requests by foreign journalists, for example, to interview athletes and other sports figures are referred by INDER to Cuba Deportes. Payment is required for setting up interviews.

Success in international athletic competition strengthens Cuban nationalism and contributes needed support to the government in a period of declining morale. Mass sports participation provides an outlet for the frustrations of young Cubans and is used by the government as a way to demonstrate its commitment to egalitarianism. The sports system has served the Revolution well. As it becomes even more of a moneymaker, it is likely to become even more important in the future. *See also* Baseball; Boxing

Further Readings

Pettavino, Paula J., and Geralyn Pye. *Sport in Cuba: The Diamond in the Rough.* Pittsburgh: University of Pittsburgh Press, 1994.
Price, S.L. *Pitching Around Fidel: A Journey into the Heart of Cuban Sports.* New York: Ecco Press, 2000.

Paula J. Pettavino

Sotomayor, Javier (1967–)

Javier Sotomayor has reached the highest jump on earth by the mere propulsion of his feet. Sotomayor holds world records in high jump: 2.45 meters in open-air competitions in Salamanca in 1993 and 2.43 meters in an indoor event in Budapest in 1989. He was the first to have cleared the eight feet (2.44 m) barrier. Only two other athletes have surpassed 2.40 meters. He is the high-jump athlete who has practiced these sports longest—for seventeen years.

Born in **Matanzas** on October 13, 1967, Sotomayor is the winner of three Pan American competitions, two Central American and Caribbean competitions, and seven other international competitions between the years of 1989 and 1997. He received the gold medal during the 1992 **Olympics** in Barcelona and was honored by King Juan Carlos of Spain with the Príncipe de Asturias de los Deportes award a year later.

In 1999, while attending a competition in Winnipeg, doctors spotted cocaine in his system during a routine examination. The International Association of Athletics Federation suspended him for two years but later reduced the sentence to twelve

months. In Cuba, the authorities denounced the suspension, and **Fidel Castro** claimed that the enemies of the Cuban **Revolution** had framed the athlete. In the year 2000, Sotomayor was able to attend the Sydney Olympics, where he earned a silver medal. In 2001, Sotomayor tested positive for a banned substance in Tenerife and later announced his retirement. In Cuba, he was chosen as one of the best 100 athletes of the twentieth century.

Further Reading

Velázquez Videaux, Juan. *Sotomayor, el Saltanubes.* Havana: Editora Política, 1997.

Wilfredo Cancio Isla

Stevenson, Teófilo (1952–)

A dominating heavyweight boxer, Teófilo Stevenson was the first fighter to win three Olympic gold medals in the same weight class and became a symbol of **Fidel Castro**'s Cuba.

A native of Puerto Padre, **Las Tunas Province**, he was physically imposing both in his size (six feet two inches, 195 pounds in his prime) and his sculpted, muscular build. He carried himself quietly and proudly—some said sullenly. He won gold medals in 1972 (Munich), 1976 (Montreal), and 1980 (Moscow). His first Olympic gold was a surprise, coming against highly rated U.S. fighter Duane Bobick to whom Stevenson had lost in the previous year's Pan American Games. Besides the **Olympics**, Stevenson also won three World Amateur **Boxing** titles, a distinction only one other boxer achieved in the twentieth century.

Though widely seen to be declining by the early 1980s, he was still a contender for the heavyweight gold in 1984, and just three months before the Games, he defeated Tyrell Biggs, a likely Olympic opponent. But Cuba joined the East bloc boycott of the Los Angeles Olympics, essentially in revenge for the West's boycott

Teófilo Stevenson after winning his third Olympic heavyweight medal (Moscow, 1980). AP/Wide World Photos.

of Moscow in 1980. Cold War politics thus deprived Stevenson of the chance at a fourth gold medal, though the boxer had always identified his career with a political stance. He boxed until 1987, retaining his amateur status despite offers to fight professionally. Stevenson's standing in the world of boxing was contradictory: He created a historic body of Olympic work, but in the professional heavyweight realm he was never tested; speculation on "what might have been" created an air of mystery around his career. Talk of a match with Muhammad Ali created a stir but came to nothing. In Cuba he enjoyed a privileged position and the standing of a legendary national hero—a reputation he thrived on and nourished. When offered $3 million for a fight in 1972, he was said to have asked rhetorically what money could possibly mean to him next to the love of 10 million Cubans. Always a vigorous supporter of the Castro government, he worked long past his fighting days as an official of the Cuban Boxing Federation. In 1999, after his arrest for allegedly head-butting an airport employee in Miami, who he claimed had maligned Cuba and Castro, he explained defiantly: "I do not permit insults to the Revolution, my people, nor to the Comandante."

Further Readings

Cabalé Ruiz, Manolo. *Teófilo Stevenson, grande entre los grandes*. Havana: Editorial Científico-Técnica, 1985.

Crespo, Rolando. *Cuba en el boxeo olímpico*. Havana: Editorial Científico-Técnica, 1998.

Grasso, John. *The Olympic Games Boxing Record Book*. Guilford, NY: International Boxing Research Organization, 1984.

Pablo Julián Davis

Tiant, Luis, Jr. (1940–   )

Known to his fans as "El Tiante," pitcher Luis Tiant, Jr. achieved notable success throughout his lengthy career in the **U.S. Major Leagues**. His father, Luis Tiant, Sr., had been a star in the **U.S. Negro Leagues** in the 1930s and 1940s, winning the Negro Leagues' World Series with the New York Cubans in 1947.

Tiant made his Major League debut with the Cleveland Indians in 1964. That first game, he led the Indians to victory over the New York Yankees. Tiant pitched for the Indians through the 1969 season. He won twenty-one games in 1968 and led the American League with an amazing 1.60 ERA (earned run average) and nine shutouts. He set a Major League record by striking out thirty-two batters over two consecutive games.

In 1969, he was traded to Minnesota as part of a six-player deal. He was in the Minor Leagues in 1971 when the Red Sox signed him. He played for the Sox until 1978. In 1972, he posted a 15-6 record and a league-leading 1.91. He had led the league in ERA in 1968 with 1.60. He also led the league in shootouts in 1966, 1968, and 1974. He won the Comeback Player of the Year Award that season. From 1972 to 1978, he averaged 17 wins per season and was named to the All-Star team twice. Tiant finished his career with two seasons with the Yankees (1979–1980), followed by one each in Pittsburgh and California. In nineteen years of Major League pitching he won 229 games, lost 172, and accumulated a 3.30 ERA and 2,416 strikeouts.

After serving as a Minor League pitching coach for the Los Angeles Dodgers and Minor League instructor for the Chicago White Sox, Tiant was named coach of the Savannah College of Art and Design's baseball team in 1998.

Further Reading

Torres, Ángel. *La leyenda del béisbol cubano, 1878–1997*. Miami: Review Printers, 1997.

Luis González

Torriente, Cristóbal (1895–1938)

Born in **Cienfuegos** in 1895, Cristóbal Torriente starred in the **U.S. Negro Leagues** (1913–1932) and Cuban **baseball**. Much like many of his Cuban contemporaries, Torriente was excluded from the **Major Leagues** where any indication of "African" ancestry (i.e., hair, skin color, facial features) resulted in exclusion until the Leagues' color line was broken in 1947. The hard-hitting outfielder exploits in the Negro Leagues, where he led the Chicago American Giants to consecutive championships (1920–1922), and in the Cuban League, where he compiled a lifetime batting average of .352, earned him induction into the Cuban Baseball Hall of Fame's initial class in 1939. Contemporary newspaper accounts and oral interviews conducted by baseball historian John Holway document the intrigue Torriente

sparked among Major League clubs. Negro League teammates and opponents alike attest to the impression Torriente made on Major League scouts who watched him perform in Cuba and in the Negro Leagues. These contemporaries also acknowledged what held them back: Torriente lacked the proper phenotypical features for a Major League team to attempt signing him.

Further Readings

Figueredo, Jorge. "November 4, 1920: The Day Torriente Outclassed Ruth." *Baseball Research Journal* (1982): 59–60.

Holway, John. *Blackball Stars: Negro League Pioneers*. 1988. Reprint, New York: Carroll & Graf, 1992.

Holway, John. *Voices from the Great Black Baseball Leagues*. New York: Da Capo Press, 1992.

Adrian Burgos, Jr.

Versalles Rodríguez, Zoilo "Zorro" (1939–1995)

The first Cuban and Latin American to win Most Valuable Player (MVP) honors, Zoilo Versalles was the defensive and offensive motor of the 1965 American League champion Minnesota Twins. That year he led the league with 126 runs, 45 doubles, and 12 triples.

A brilliant-fielding shortstop, Havana-born Versalles competed in the final four seasons of the Cuban League; his Major League debut came at age nineteen, in 1959, with the Washington Senators. This placed him in a long line of Cubans to wear the flannels of the "Nats" dating back to the scouting work of "Papa Joe" Cambria in the 1930s. In 1961, Versalles followed the club to Minnesota; he won Gold Glove awards for his shortstop work (1963, 1965). The latter season witnessed an astounding performance: He amassed 126 runs; 27 steals in 32 attempts; 45 doubles; 12 triples; 19 home runs; 77 RBIs (runs batted in); and a slugging average of .462—gaudy numbers for a shortstop of that era, particularly the slender, five-feet-nine-inch, 146-pound right-hander. Most important, he anchored the infield of a superb team (including four Cubans) that fought nobly to a seven-game World Series defeat against Los Angeles. Though the Twins could not overcome Sandy Koufax's brilliance, Versalles made the most of his one October in the limelight with 8 hits, 3 runs, and 4 RBIs; he was Minnesota's best hitter. Debilitating back injuries ended his playing career, though he resuscitated it briefly in the early 1970s in Mexico. Ill-ness and poverty forced him to part with his MVP and other trophies. He died of arteriosclerosis in Minnesota in 1995, a forgotten hero.

Further Readings

Bretón, Marcos, and José Luis Villegas. *Away Games: The Life and Times of a Latin Baseball Player*. New York: Simon and Schuster, 1999.

González Echevarría, Roberto. *The Pride of Havana: A History of Cuban Baseball*. New York: Oxford University Press, 1999.

Torres, Ángel. *La leyenda del béisbol cubano, 1878–1997*. Miami: Review Printers, 1997.

Pablo Julián Davis

12

Cuban Diaspora

Abdala, Agrupación

The Agrupación Abdala was an anti–**Fidel Castro** organization that was radically different from others within the Cuban exile community due to its youthful membership and Social Democratic ideology. Founded in New York in 1970 by a group of Cuban college students, the organization took its name from **José Martí**'s epic drama of the same title, about a young Greek prince who sacrifices himself for his enslaved nation. From the beginning Abdala identified itself as a Social Democrat organization, and as such its opposition to the Castro regime was from a leftist perspective. As Social Democrats Abdala members came in contact with and received the support of anticommunist socialists such as Bayard Rustin (United States), Mario Soares (Portugal), and Willy Brandt (West Germany).

Abdala was active on college campuses across the United States in counteracting the influence of pro-Castro elements. The organization published a monthly newspaper for a decade, had delegations in five major U.S. cities as well as in Puerto Rico and Mexico (see **Puerto Rico, Cubans in**), and met yearly for a four-day congress. The international awareness of **human rights** violations in Cuba was key to Abdala's anti-Castro strategy, and as part of this strategy, it launched campaigns demanding freedom for **political prisoners** such as **Huber Matos, Eloy Gutiérrez Menoyo, Armando Valladares**, Jorge Valls, and others. The traditional political elements within the Cuban exile community viewed Abdala with skepticism due to its youth and left-wing politics. As a Social Democrat organization Abdala supported the right of Puerto Rico to self-determination, and it also opposed the right-wing regimes of Anastasio Somoza, Alfredo Stroessner, and Augusto Pinochet. By the mid-1980s the organization had ceased to exist due to a crisis in leadership and dissolution of the Social Democrat ideology.

Further Readings

ABDALA newspaper, 1970-1980.

Blanco, Ray. *Black and White in Exile*. Plainfield, NJ: Cutting Edge Productions, 1997. Documentary.

Miguel Socarrás

Alpha 66

Alpha 66 is an exile, anti–**Fidel Castro** paramilitary organization founded in 1961 with Central Intelligence Agency (CIA) assistance after the failed counterrevolutionary **Bay of Pigs Invasion**. It initially integrated sixty-six members from various armed formations opposed to the increasingly Marxist-Leninist orientation of the Cuban **Revolution**—including veterans of Assault Brigade 2506—all without overt ties to the discredited **Fulgencio Batista** regime. Alpha 66 represented a U.S. and Cuban émigré attempt to create a viable united politicomilitary group to undertake renewed covert actions against the socialist revolutionary government in Cuba. The first Greek letter, "alpha," was chosen to indicate a new start for the anticommunist movement.

Under the direction of the anti-Castro accountant and CIA opperative Antonio Veciana Blanck, Alpha 66 began its activity in Puerto Rico and Miami training members in demolitions, explosives, sabotage, and tactics. The group staged several attacks from boats and infiltrated groups in Cuba during the CIA's Operation Mongoose, designed to disrupt and destabilize the revolutionary regime prior to its envisioned overthrow. By 1964, U.S. agencies attempted to rein in the campaign of terrorism and sabotage, but Alpha 66 and the **Segundo Frente del Escambray** continued unsuccessful efforts to reinitiate guerrilla warfare against the Cuban government as well as making intermittent attacks on Cubans coasts. Alpha 66 has remained intermittently active within the milieu of militant anti-Castro factions and organizations within the United States. *See also* Omega 7; Puerto Rico, Cubans in; United States, Cuba's Relations with the

Further Readings

Escalante, Fabián. *The Secret War: CIA Covert Operations against Cuba, 1959–1962*. Melbourne: Ocean Press, 1995.
Hinckle, Warren, and William Turner. *Deadly Secrets*. New York: Thunder's Mouth Press, 1993.
Wyden, Peter. *Bay of Pigs*. New York: Simon and Schuster, 1979.

David C. Carlson

Areíto

Areíto was a left-wing magazine, originally published as a quarterly in Miami, then in New York, and again irregularly in Miami, between 1974 and 1994. *Areíto*'s editors posited the Cuban **Revolution** as a necessary historical fact and proposed the reestablishment of diplomatic links between Cuba and the United States. These positions were advocated by a vocal minority of Cuban émigrés, mostly well-educated, middle-class youth. With an initial printing of 1,000 copies, the first issue of *Areíto* sold out quickly in 1974. In starting the magazine, its editors purported to create an alternative vehicle of expression for silenced political positions within the Cuban exile community. The magazine attempted to present a serious albeit nonacademic coverage of contemporary Cuba, ranging from economic and social policies to **cinema** and popular religion on the island. Later articles included other Latin American countries as well as Latinos in the United States. Most of *Areíto*'s founders and collaborators were young Cuban students and university professors living in the United States and Puerto Rico who had become disgruntled with the dominant ideology expressed in the leading publications of the Cuban exile community. Many of them were closely linked with the **Brigada Antonio Maceo**, founded in the 1970s to promote a rapprochement between Cubans on and off the island. *Areíto*'s major achievement was to initiate a dialogue between Cuban intellectuals in exile and at home. The publication of *Areíto*, as well as the emergence of several kindred organizations such as the Brigada Antonio Maceo, belied the apparent ideological uniformity of the Cuban community abroad, who were seen as politically conservative. *See also* Puerto Rico, Cubans in; United States, Cuba's Relations with the

Bacardí Rum plant in Cataño, Puerto Rico. Photograph by Celestino Martínez Lindín.

Further Readings

"Editorial." *Areíto* 1 (1974): 3.

García, María Cristina. "Hardliners v. 'Dialogueros': Cuban Exile Political Groups and United States–Cuba Policy." *Journal of American Ethnic History* 17, no. 4 (1998): 3–28.

Jorge Duany

Bacardí Family

The creator of what is arguably the best-known **rum** empire, Facundo Bacardí Massó was born in Stiges, Spain, in 1814. At age fifteen, Bacardí and his brothers emigrated to Cuba, settling in **Santiago de Cuba**. In 1843 Bacardí married Amalia Moreau. In 1862 he purchased a small distillery and founded Bacardí y Compañía. It is said that on the roof of the building lived a family of fruit bats. To this day, the bat is the symbol found on every Bacardí product. Bacardí came up with a number of innovations, including a light rum. In

1902, when Cuba won its independence, Facundo and Amalia's son, **Emilio Bacardí Moreau**, became the first democratically elected mayor of Santiago. Four years later, he was elected senator. Emilio's brother, Facundo M. Bacardí, meanwhile, continued to perfect his father's distilling methods.

In the 1910s, Facundo M. Bacardí's son-in-law, Henri Schueg, oversaw the opening of a bottling plant in Barcelona, Spain, and another in New York City. However, Prohibition later forced the closing of the New York plant. In the 1920s, the Bacardí family commissioned the construction of a building in Havana, noted for its art deco architecture (see **Architecture [Twentieth Century]**). A patron of the arts, Emilio Bacardí also founded the Academy of Fine Arts. He also established a number of libraries and schools. Emilio Bacardí passed away in 1922. In 1928, the Bacardí family opened up a museum in

Santiago, the first on the island. Part of the collection included a mummy Emilio Bacardí had purchased on a trip to Egypt a few years earlier.

In the 1930s, the Bacardí firm expanded outside of Cuba, including Puerto Rico and Mexico. In 1944 Bacardí Imports was opened in New York City, making the rum widely available in the United States. In 1949, Schueg's son-in-law Jose "Pepín" Bosch became Cuba's minister of the treasury. He later became president of Bacardí.

On October 14, 1960, the Cuban assets owned by Compañía Bacardí were nationalized by the **Fidel Castro** regime. Subsequently, the family fled the island. In 1966, Coca-Cola and Bacardí created Rum-n-Coke with an aggressive ad campaign. In the 1970s, Bosch's nephew, Edwin Nelson, became president of the firm, followed by Emilo Bacardí's great-grandson, Manuel Jorge Cutillas, in the 1980s.

In 1992, the company acquired Martini and Rossi, and other firms in 1999. Bacardí-Martini USA became one of the largest suppliers of alcoholic spirits in the world. Since 1862, six generations of Bacardí family members have led the company. In March of 2001, Fidel Castro announced that Cuba would be producing its own Bacardí rum. This is part of a long-standing trademark dispute with the Cuban-exile company now based in Bermuda. *See also* Manufacturing

Further Reading

Foster, Peter. *Family Spirits: The Bacardí Saga.* Toronto: MacFarlane Walter & Ross, 1990.

Luis González

Balseros

The term *balseros* refers to people who attempt to migrate from Cuba to the United States in rafts (*balsas*), small boats, and other makeshift vessels. Technically, balseros are undocumented migrants because they leave Cuba without proper authorization from the Cuban and U.S. governments. More than 63,000 Cuban rafters arrived in the United States between 1959 and 1994. However, balseros are most closely associated with the sudden and massive wave of unauthorized migration from Cuba to the United States in August and September of 1994. During this period, the number of Cuban immigrants broke all records since the Mariel exodus of 1980 (see **Mariel Boatlift**). The so-called balsero crisis involved about 36,000 Cubans interdicted at sea by the U.S. Coast Guard in the Florida Straits between August 13 and September 13, 1994. The crisis was temporarily solved with the renewal of a 1984 agreement between the Cuban and U.S. governments, allowing the migration of 20,000 Cubans per year, in addition to a special lottery for 5,000 new visa applications (see **Migration Accords**). The balsero crisis also led to a major shift in U.S. policy toward Cuban migrants. Since then, the U.S. government has treated Cubans leaving their country without visas as illegal aliens subject to deportation unless they manage to set foot on U.S. soil. Illegal exits became the primary means of migrating from Cuba to the United States during the so-called **Special Period** in Times of Peace, the official euphemism for the persistent economic crisis in Cuba. Migratory pressures accumulated rapidly, including broad sectors of the island's population. Material deprivation and family reunification became increasingly salient reasons for leaving Cuba, although ideological factors continued to be important. When interviewed in Cuba, balseros said they wanted to leave their country primarily for economic or personal reasons, especially to meet with family members already living abroad. Once on the **Guantánamo U.S. Naval Base** or in the United States, most rafters said that their chief motivation to migrate was the desire for freedom and

Balseros fleeing Cuba hoping to reach U.S. territory. Fidel Castro Photograph Collection, Manuscripts Division, Department of Rare Books and Special Collections, Princeton University Library.

release from state control. Demographically, balseros overrepresented the young, white, male, urban, and educated population of the island. Unlike earlier refugees, most were manual workers, especially in **transportation** and **communications**, although many were professionals, technicians, and administrators. A surprising 21 percent of a sample of balseros detained in Cuba belonged to the **Cuban Communist Party** or the **Communist Youth Union**. Not surprisingly, 29 percent were unemployed. Altogether, the balseros' profile reflects the deteriorating situation of the Cuban economy during the 1990s. Possibly the most famous *balsero* incident was the **Elián Gonzáles Case**: Six-year-old Elián was rescued from a raft in the sea, where his mother and others had died. *See also* Cuban Adjustment Act; United States, Cuban Migrations to the

Further Readings

Ackerman, Holly. *The Cuban Balseros: Voyage of Uncertainty.* Miami: Cuban American National Council, 1995.

Martínez, Milagros, et al. *Los balseros cubanos: un estudio a partir de las salidas ilegales.* Havana: Editorial de Ciencias Sociales, 1996.

Jorge Duany

Benes, Bernardo (1934–   )

A hero to some and outcast to others, Bernardo Benes was the lead *dialoguero* (dialoger) in a series of secret meetings that took place beginning in February of 1978 between prominent members of the Cuban exile community and the **Fidel Castro** government. Benes had been a high-profile banker in Miami and was director of United Way International.

While vacationing with his family in

Panama in 1977, Benes had been contacted by the Cuban government to negotiate the release of key **political prisoners**. President Jimmy Carter authorized the meetings, and Benes and other exiles met with Castro and his representatives on fourteen occasions. As a result of the meetings, exile travel back to the island opened up, **remittances** were allowed, and 3,600 political prisoners were released.

Benes's actions and their results enraged the right-wing elements within the exile community. He and other participants were seen as negotiating with, and benefiting, the enemy. The changes in policy provided Castro with millions of dollars in hard currency.

Benes's bank was bombed, as were the homes of other dialogueros. Given the onslaught of verbal and physical attacks, Benes had to withdraw from public view and has since lived a very private life.

Further Reading
Levine, Robert H., *Secret Missions to Cuba: Fidel Castro, Bernardo Benes, and Cuban Miami.* New York: Palgrave Macmillan, 2001.

Luis González

Botifoll, Luis J. (1912–)

Known as the "dean" of the Cuban exile community, Luis J. Botifoll has been at the forefront of numerous Cuban American organizations.

His many accomplishments and distinctions began before leaving Cuba in 1960. He had been a lawyer and adviser for the Cuban Commerce Department, as well as chief of maritime economic affairs at the Cuban Maritime Commission. Botifoll had also been editor of *El Mundo* (a leading newspaper) and president of Unión Radio.

Once in exile, Botifoll continued his role as community leader. In 1970 he became director of Republic National Bank, which helped many Cubans in the United States. In 1978 he was elected chairman of

the bank's board of directors. He retired in 1993 and was named chairman emeritus. Botifoll has served on the board of several Cuban American organizations, including the **Cuban American National Foundation**. An auditorium at the University of Miami was recently named in his honor.

Further Reading
González-Pando, Miguel. *The Cuban Americans.* Westport, CT: Greenwood Press, 1998.

Luis González

Brigada Antonio Maceo

The Brigada Antonio Maceo (Antonio Maceo Brigade) represented a small minority of radicalized young Cubans in the United States, Puerto Rico, Venezuela, Mexico, and Spain. Most members of this organization were born in Cuba but went into exile as children. In the 1970s, they were typically in their early twenties. Like other Cuban émigrés, they tended to come from middle-class families. Many were students or professionals, and most were college graduates. Many had participated in the U.S. civil rights and antiwar student movements of the late 1960s and early 1970s. Although they did not necessarily agree with the ideological principles of the Cuban **Revolution**, they strove to know it personally and advocated better relations between Cuba and the United States. Some became well-known scholars, especially in Cuban studies, and a few grew disenchanted with Cuban socialism during the 1990s. Since 1977, the Brigade's most important activity was to organize a "contingent" of exiles who traveled to Cuba for several weeks. Once in Cuba, participants performed voluntary agricultural or construction work, visited historical sites, attended lectures, and visited relatives. Their activities were well publicized by the Cuban media but were not well received by the general émigré community. The Brigade revealed the growing political pluralization of Cubans in exile. Its members were ideologically marginal to mainstream émigré communities and assumed positions considered subversive by right-wing exiles. The most important difference between the Brigade and other exile organizations was the former's support for a permanent dialogue between Cubans abroad and the Cuban government. *See also* Puerto Rico, Cubans in; Spain, Cuba's Relations with; United States, Cuba's Relations with the

Further Readings

Grupo Areíto. *Contra viento y marea: jovenes cubanos hablan desde su exilio en Estados Unidos*. Mexico City: Siglo XXI, 1978.
Torres, María de los Ángeles. *In the Land of the Mirrors: Cuban Exile Politics in the United States*. Ann Arbor: University of Michigan Press, 1999.

Jorge Duany

Cambio Cubano

Cambio Cubano (Cuban Change) was founded in Miami in 1992 by anti–**Fidel Castro**, exiled, ex-prisoner, and ex-guerrilla **Eloy Gutiérrez Menoyo** as a peaceful, democratic opposition alternative to the communist regime in Cuba. After breaking with Fidel Castro's totalitarian ways and going into exile, Menoyo returned to Cuba as a commando in 1964; he was subsequently captured and spent twenty-two years in prison under severe conditions (see **Political Prisoners**). Once released under international pressure in 1986 Menoyo shifted to a nonviolent form of opposition and, on January 20, 1992, at the Press Club in Washington, D.C., he announced the formation of Cambio Cubano. Cambio Cubano remains a minor organization with scarce support in Cuba or among the Cuban exile communities in the United States. Its goal has been to gain a political space inside Cuba through dialogue with Castro and other communist leaders. For years, Cambio Cubano has requested of Castro to be legalized as a posi-

tive opposition voice, to have an office in Havana, and to work with the regime in areas of agreement such as the end of the U.S. commercial and financial embargo toward Cuba, the abolition of the **Cuban Adjustment Act**, U.S. payment of reparations for losses caused by the embargo, among many other claims. Cambio Cubano is among the most conciliatory exile organization, and it is seen with distrust by many Cubans in exile, in Cuba, and elsewhere. *See also* U.S. Trade Embargo and Related Legislation

Further Reading

Vargas Llosa, Álvaro. *El exilio indomable: historia de la disidencia cubana en el destierro*. Madrid: Espasa, 1998.

Moisés Asís

Cuban Adjustment Act

The Cuban Adjustment Act, or Ley de Ajuste Cubano, is a generous and unique U.S. law signed by President Lyndon B. Johnson on November 2, 1966, to forbid deportation of any Cuban arrivals touching U.S. soil and to further grant rights to permanent resident status to them one year plus one day after entering U.S. territory. This law applies to Cuban-born or -naturalized individuals as well as to their spouses and minor children, regardless of nationality. For decades, hundreds of thousands of Cubans and their families have benefited from this law whose intention has been to provide protection to Cubans defecting or fleeing by illegal means from repression by the **Fidel Castro** regime. After the 1994 crisis of the **balseros** (rafters) that led to the admission to the United States of tens of thousands of rafters detained for months in camps at the **Guantánamo U.S. Naval Base**, and to immigration talks between the U.S. and Cuban governments, the Cuban Adjustment Act has been reinterpreted by the Immigration and Naturalization Service.

Accordingly, all rafters intercepted in U.S. and international maritime territory are being returned by U.S. Coast Guard vessels to Cabañas port in Cuba. Beginning in spring 2000, after successfully pressuring the Bill Clinton administration in the case of six-year-old **Elián González**, Castro has increasingly organized mass demonstrations and mobilized diplomatic, political, and propaganda resources to pressure the U.S. Congress to abrogate the Cuban Adjustment Act. *See also* Dissent and Defections (1959–); United States, Cuban Migrations to the; United States, Cuba's Relations with the Migration Accords

Further Reading

Masud-Piloto, Félix R. *With Open Arms: The Evolution of Cuban Migration to the U.S., 1959–1995*. New York: Rothman & Littlefield, 1998.

Moisés Asís

Cuban American National Foundation (Fundación Nacional Cubano Americana)

The Cuban American National Foundation (CANF, or Fundación Nacional Cubano Americana) is the most important and most powerful Cuban American organization in the United States. It seeks to provide the Cuban American community with a strong voice in Washington and to bring about the replacement of the current communist government in Cuba. It describes itself as "an independent, non-profit organization dedicated to the re-establishment of freedom and democracy in Cuba." The Foundation holds the principles of: "respect for human rights; freedom of thought and expression; freedom of religion; the right of the people to freely elect their government; the right to private property; free enterprise; and economic prosperity with social justice." It also has a political action committee called the Free Cuba PAC. The CANF's original founder was **Jorge Mas Canosa**,

a Cuban exile leader and enemy of **Fidel Castro**. In 1981, after many years of fruitless attempts by Cuban exiles to militarily overthrow Castro, Mas Canosa and a group of prominent Cuban Americans decided to establish a political lobby to influence and advise U.S. foreign policy makers on the Cuban case. The CANF was inspired by the very successful experience of the Israeli lobbies, whose strategies they followed. Some of the CANF's main achievements have been the passing of important pieces of legislation that have tightened the **U.S. trade embargo** on Cuba, such as the Torricelli bill (or Cuban Democracy Act) and the Helms-Burton Act (see **Appendix 13**). The CANF also lobbied successfully for the establishment of **Radio Martí** (and later, TV Martí), U.S. government-owned stations that beam their signals directly into Cuba, seeking to provide the Cuban people with an alternative source of information (see **Communications**). After the collapse of communism in the former Soviet Union and Eastern Europe, the CANF tried to convince the new Russian government to end its special economic relationship with Cuba. The CANF was also actively involved in lobbying for strong sanctions against the Castro administration after it downed two unarmed civilian planes off the coast of Cuba in 1996 (see **[Hermanos al Rescate] Brothers to the Rescue**).

The CANF has also been active in pressing its agenda in the U.S. media, and protests actively against those which they perceive as taking a biased stance against CANF. One very controversial undertaking was the 1992 CANF-led boycott against the *Miami Herald* newspaper, over disagreements with the *Herald*'s editorial policy regarding Cuba (see *Nuevo Herald, El*). The CANF owes its considerable political success to its organization, charismatic leadership, ample financial resources, and keen political strategies. After Mas Canosa's death in 1997, leadership of the

Jorge Mas Canosa and other members of the Cuban American National Foundation; Juanita Castro (Fidel's sister) is sitting next to U.S. flag (Miami, 1984). Courtesy Historical Museum of Southern Florida.

organization was assumed by his son, Jorge Mas Santos.

In what seems like a generational rift, about two dozen CANF board members resigned in August 2001 over Mas Santos's policies, accusing him of "softening" the CANF's traditional hard-line stance. Mas Santos, born and raised in the United States, has sought to establish closer bonds with the U.S. Democratic Party—particularly after the **Elián González case**—and instead of concentrating the CANF's efforts solely on the elimination of Fidel Castro's regime, he has argued that the organization should look beyond that to post-Castro scenarios for the re-establishment of liberal democracy in Cuba. *See also* United States, Cuba's Relations with the

Further Readings

García, María Cristina. *Havana USA: Cuban Exiles and Cuban Americans in South Florida, 1959–1994.* Berkeley: University of California Press, 1996.

Torres, María de los Ángeles. *In the Land of Mirrors: Cuban Exile Politics in the United States.* Ann Arbor: University of Michigan Press, 1999.

Vargas Llosa, Álvaro. *El exilio indomable: historia de la disidencia cubana en el destierro.* Madrid: Espasa, 1998.

Ernesto Sagás

Cuban Committee for Democracy (Comité Cubano por la Democracia)

The Cuban Committee for Democracy (CCD) is a nonprofit organization founded in 1993 by moderate Cuban Americans in the United States to counter the perception that the Cuban American community is a monolithic, uniformly conservative one. The CCD works to promote a peaceful transition to democracy in Cuba, to advocate for a revision in U.S. policies toward Cuba, and to promote the democratization of politics on the island as well as within the Cuban American communities in the United States.

Since its inception, the CCD has focused its work in the United States on two areas: Washington and Miami. In Washington, the CCD works to change U.S. policy toward Cuba and encourages dialogue between the two governments. While CCD members oppose the present political order in Cuba, they also oppose the U.S. trade embargo against the island as contrary to the interests of the Cuban people and as politically counterproductive. Such a policy of external hostility simply reinforces the claim of the Cuban government to represent national sovereignty and stifles the rising voices of opposition within the island. CCD members believe that knowledge and understanding will foster democratic thoughts and actions among Cubans. In Miami, the CCD has concentrated its efforts on opening space for political tolerance and opening dialogue within the Cuban community. To this end the CCD operates a daily **radio** program in Miami, distributes a monthly newspaper, and makes constant calls for change in the local media.

In Cuba, the CCD works with the government and dissidents (see **Dissent and Defections [1959–   ]**) alike in order to promote a culture of dialogue, respect, and understanding, with the aim of fostering the necessary conditions for a transition toward democracy.

The CCD is grounded in the community. Its membership includes prominent intellectuals, artists, academics, professionals, entrepreneurs, and working people dedicated to fostering a peaceful transition to democracy in Cuba and a diplomatic resolution to the long-standing conflict between Cuba and the United States. The CCD focuses its work within the Cuban American community by promoting political tolerance for all opinions within the community.

Further Reading

García, María Cristina. "Hardliners v. 'Dialogueros': Cuban Exile Political Groups and United States-Cuba Policy." *Journal of American Ethnic History* 17, no. 4 (1998): 3–28.

Alfredo Durán

Cuban Politics in the United States

Cubans are, after Mexicans and Puerto Ricans, the third largest Hispanic community in the United States and the only one composed largely of political refugees. As such, Cubans and Cuban Americans have had an active political life in their host country. Since the early days of the Cuban **Revolution** Cuban exiles in the United States began plotting to overthrow **Fidel Castro**. Since then, the main goal of Cuban politics in the United States has remained unaltered (though its strategies have changed): the downfall of Castro's socialist regime and its replacement by a capitalist-based, democratic government.

The first main strategy within Cuban politics in the United States was military action. Cuban exile leaders—and their supporters inside Cuba—plotted and carried out military attacks against the Castro government. This aggressive strategy was in line with the U.S. government's view that Castro could be overthrown through military means. That reasoning led to the ill-fated 1961 **Bay of Pigs Invasion**, in which hundreds of Cuban exiles—backed by the Central Intelligence Agency (CIA)—were quickly defeated and captured by Castro's army. The Bay of Pigs fiasco, coupled with an agreement with the Soviet Union after the 1962 **Missile Crisis**, led the United States to halt its military plans to overthrow Castro and forced Cuban exiles to seek other alternatives.

For years thereafter, Cuban politics in the United States concerned itself with issues that were dear to the Cuban exile community: **Cuban migration to the United States**, the denunciation of Castro's repression, and the fate of **political prisoners** serving long terms in Cuban jails. This **human rights**–oriented strategy lasted well into the 1970s. By then, many Cubans had begun to realize that Castro would be in power for the long term and that they were in fact becoming established residents of the United States. Slowly at first, but later more quickly and in large numbers, Cubans began to naturalize as U.S. citizens, to register, and to vote.

For geographical and historical reasons, Miami has been the heart of the Cuban exile community (see **Little Havana**). As Cubans naturalized in increasingly greater numbers, their demographic muscle and political solidarity gave them an edge in local politics. In 1973, for the first time two Cuban Americans were elected to public office in Miami: Manolo Reboso and Alfredo Durán. By 1985, Miami had its first Cuban American mayor: Xavier Suárez. In 1989, **Ileana Ros-Lehtinen** became the first Cuban American elected to the U.S. House of Representatives. A Republican from Miami, she was quickly joined by another southern Florida Republican, **Lincoln Díaz-Balart**, and by a New Jersey Democrat, **Robert "Bob" Menéndez**, thus bringing the total number of Cuban American representatives to three. In spite of their party differences the three representatives firmly oppose the Castro regime and have unanimously stood behind bills seeking to undermine it. There are now also several Cuban American mayors, city board members, and state legislators, particularly in southern Florida, where Cuban Americans constitute a majority among Hispanics.

During the 1980s Cuban politics in the United States shifted into a more diplomatic tack with the creation of the **Cuban American National Foundation** (CANF). This organization sought to influence U.S. foreign policy regarding Cuba and to overthrow Castro not by risky military operations but by lobbying the highest spheres of the U.S. government. Using tactics that had been very successful for the Israeli lobbies, the CANF made its presence felt in the White House (particularly during the Ronald Reagan and George Bush administrations), the Department of State, and—particularly—the U.S. Congress. So successful was the CANF in its efforts that it helped pass through Congress some very controversial bills, such as the one creating **Radio Martí** and the Helms-Burton Act (see **Appendix 13**). The CANF used to its advantage the anticommunism of many U.S. leaders during the final stages of the Cold War, as well as their desire to help a popular cause and get the votes and contributions of Cuban Americans. The CANF also helped change the perception that many U.S. policy makers had of the Cuban exile community. Instead of looking like bickering military adventurers, Cuban Americans were now perceived in a more positive, professional way as a valuable part of the U.S. political system.

Regarding U.S. national electoral politics, Cuban Americans are an anomalous case: While most other Hispanic groups have traditionally voted for the Democratic Party, Cuban Americans have mostly aligned themselves with the Republicans. Over 90 percent of Cuban Americans voted Republican during Ronald Reagan's election in 1980 (and his subsequent reelection in 1984), as well as George Bush's election in 1988. This trend has at least two main explanations. First, Cuban Americans sympathized with the anticommunist, "hard-line" Cold War rhetoric of Republican presidential candidates. And second, there has been a historical "rupture" between the foreign policies of Democratic presidents and Cuban American interests. For example, John F. Kennedy was accused of "treason" for the Bay of Pigs Invasion fiasco and for achieving a modus vivendi with the Soviet Union regarding Cuba. Similarly, Jimmy Carter was labeled as "soft" and "bland" on communism for not dealing forcefully with Castro during the **Mariel boatlift**. Finally,

Bill Clinton has also been labeled a "traitor" for engaging in migration talks with Cuban officials and changing the long-standing U.S. policy of accepting all Cuban **balseros** (rafters) as political refugees. The Clinton administration's handling of the **Elián González case** also fostered this negative perception. The few thousand Cubans who switched their support to the Republican Party after their unhappiness with the Elián González affair are said to have cost Al Gore the presidency in the close contest of 2000. At the state and local level, however, Cuban American communities vote both ways, with apparently only one caveat: The candidates' anticommunist, anti-Castro public credentials must be well established. There is, however, a certain proclivity for second-generation Cuban Americans to be less politically rigid than their elders who went through the bitter experience of political exile. The politics of the Cuban American community in the United States thus present a unique case in which foreign policy concerns often seep into and permeate local issues. Moreover, southern Florida Cuban Americans are a coveted voting bloc, since their electoral support is capable—as was the case in 2000—of tipping the scales one way or the other in a major state vital for presidential hopefuls.

In spite of its ups and downs, Cuban politics in the United States has been highly successful in at least one major aspect: It has managed to hold U.S. foreign policy toward Cuba unwavering in its containment of the Castro regime and in its refusal to normalize relations with the island's government—the hard-line position. Critics have called it the "hijacking" of U.S. foreign policy for its support for Cold War postures in spite of the fact that Cuba's potential threat has now been severely diminished by the collapse of the communist Eastern bloc and that Castro has weathered many political crises and is still firmly in power. Nevertheless, Cuban

politics in the United States shows what a highly motivated, closely aligned political community in the United States is capable of doing, in spite of its minority status. Cuban Americans represent one of the most influential ethnic minority groups in the United States, courted by U.S. politicians for their vital southern Florida votes. *See also* Migration Accords; United States, Cuba's Relations with the

Further Readings

García, María Cristina. *Havana USA: Cuban Exiles and Cuban Americans in South Florida, 1959–1994*. Berkeley: University of California Press, 1996.
Torres, María de los Ángeles. *In the Land of Mirrors: Cuban Exile Politics in the United States*. Ann Arbor: University of Michigan Press, 1999.

Ernesto Sagás

Diario Las Américas

One of the most influential publications in the Cuban American community, *Diario Las Américas* provides comprehensive coverage of Cuba and Latin America six days a week. The newspaper, with a circulation of 70,000, does not publish an edition on Mondays. Horacio Aguirre, a Nicaraguan lawyer, who still owns and manages it along with several other family members, founded the Miami-based newspaper in 1953. The afternoon newspaper also circulates in New York City and Washington, D.C. On Fridays, the newspaper publishes an entertainment magazine titled *La Revista del Diario*.

Diario Las Américas fiercely opposes the Cuban revolutionary government and the leadership of **Fidel Castro**. It dedicates much of its editorial page content to lambasting the regime and its poor record on **human rights**, the Marxist economic model, and foreign policy. It periodically publishes stories written by dissident journalists inside Cuba. A sympathetic voice for conservative political causes, the newspaper generally supports Republican Party candidates for national, state, and local office.

The format of *Diario Las Américas* comes directly out of the newspaper traditions of Latin America, and some of its features are reminiscent of the newspapers of prerevolutionary Cuba. It dedicates a substantial amount of space to society functions and often publishes several pages of photos of prominent Miami community leaders. On the front page of its regional section it publishes the names of the Roman Catholic saints for that day and the following day. Although its local coverage centers on the Cuban American community, in recent years the newspaper has dedicated more space to other Hispanic groups, including the large and growing Nicaraguan community in south Florida. Its multinational emphasis may be best captured by the motto on its masthead: "Por la Libertad, la Cultura y la Solidaridad Hemisférica" (For Hemispheric Liberty, Culture and Solidarity.) See also Dissent and Defections (1959–); Independent Journalists (Periodistas Independientes)

Further Reading
Soruco, Gonzalo R. *Cubans and the Mass Media in South Florida.* Gainesville: University Press of Florida, 1996.

Frank Argote-Freyre

Díaz-Balart, Lincoln (1954–)

Lincoln Díaz-Balart is heir to a politically influential Cuban family; his father Rafael served as an undersecretary in the cabinet of President **Fulgencio Batista**. Ironically, his aunt, Mirta, was briefly married to **Fidel Castro**, a man he has made a political career of reviling.

The Díaz-Balart family left Cuba in 1959, when he was four years old, after the triumph of the Cuban **Revolution**. He

Lincoln Díaz-Balart, member of the U.S. House of Representatives, Florida's 21st district since 1992. ©2000, Roldan Torres-Moure, Picture Works, Inc, Miami, Florida. Courtesy of the Office of Congressman Díaz-Balart.

attended elementary school in south Florida before receiving a high school diploma from the American School in Madrid. After college, he received a law degree from Case Western Reserve University, Cleveland, in 1979. Díaz-Balart practiced law in Dade County for several years before embarking on a political career in 1986, when he was elected to the Florida House of Representatives. He moved quickly through Republican political ranks, securing a State Senate seat in 1989 and election to Congress in 1992 for Florida's 21st District, which includes most of Hialeah and other parts of Dade County.

In Congress, Díaz-Balart, in alliance with fellow Cuban Americans, Republican **Ileana Ros-Lehtinen** (18th District—FL) and Democrat **Robert "Bob" Menéndez** (13th District—NJ), has led the fight to tighten the economic embargo on Cuba.

The strategy seeks to secure political concessions from the Castro government and a democratic transition by isolating the regime diplomatically and economically. He has attacked the Castro government as "one of the most brutal dictatorships in the world." In turn, the Cuban media has described him as a representative of the Cuban-American "mafia" in Miami. Critics within the United States argue that the embargo strengthens the Castro government because it justifies a state-of-siege mentality within Cuba. He lives in the Miami area with his wife and two sons. *See also* U.S. Trade Embargo and Related Legislation; Cuban Politics in the United States

Further Reading

Torres, María de los Ángeles. In the *Land of Mirrors: Cuban Exile Politics in the United States*. Ann Arbor: University of Michigan Press, 1999.

Frank Argote-Freyre

Fanjul Family

The Fanjuls are Cuban and Cuban American sugar growers in Cuba and the United States whose holdings made them among the largest sugar manufacturers in pre-Revolutionary Cuba and currently the largest sugarcane growers in the United States. The Fanjul family holdings were the product of the marriage of Alfonso Fanjul, Sr. (d. 1980) and Lillian Gómez-Mena in 1936. Fanjul, Sr., was heir to the Cuban Trading Company, a sugar concern formed in the early twentieth century by **Manuel Rionda y Polledo**. Gómez-Mena was the daughter of José "Pepe" Gómez-Mena, an owner of numerous sugar mills. During the Cuban **Revolution**, the Fanjul–Gómez-Mena businesses were seized, and the family fled to Florida (see **Agrarian Reform Acts**). By 1960, Fanjul, Sr., had rebuilt the family business, establishing the Osceola Mill near Lake Okeechobee.

By the mid-1980s, Fanjul, Sr.'s sons, Alfonso, Jr., José, Alexander, and Andrés, had turned their father's investment into the largest sugar concern in the United States, Florida Crystals. The Fanjul family holdings now extend to the Dominican Republic, and the company's products also include organic produce. In the 1990s, as concerns over the environmental impact of the Fanjul family's sugar operations on the Florida Everglades grew, Alfonso, Jr., and José became more involved in state and national politics. The Fanjuls have been the subject of attention and criticism for their role in preserving the U.S. government sugar subsidy. Most notably, in 1994, novelist Carl Hiaasen used the Fanjul brothers as the inspiration for the sugar baron Rojo brothers in the novel *Strip Tease*. *See also* Sugar Industry

Further Readings

Ayala, César J. *American Sugar Kingdom: The Plantation Economy of the Spanish Caribbean, 1898–1934*. Chapel Hill: University of North Carolina Press, 1999.

Dye, Alan. *Cuban Sugar in the Age of Mass Production: Technology and the Economics of the Sugar Central, 1899–1929*. Stanford: Stanford University Press, 1998.

García Álvarez, Alejandro. "Una saga azucarera entre dos siglos." In *Asturias y Cuba en torno al 98. Sociedad, economía, política y cultura en la crisis de entresiglos*, ed. Jorge Uría González. Barcelona: Editorial Labor, S.A., 1994. 43–55.

Hiaasen, Carl. *Strip Tease: A Novel*. New York: Knopf, 1993.

John A. Gutiérrez

Freedom Flights

Freedom Flights was the term given by the U.S. government to the airlift of Cuban immigrants between December 1965 and April 1973. The expression captures the Cold War ideological context in which the air bridge operated, as it explicitly associated Cuban socialism with tyranny and American capitalism with freedom. In

Some of the first exiles to leave Cuba arrive in Miami in 1960. AP/Wide World Photos.

view of its symbolic value, President Lyndon B. Johnson decided to provide federally funded transportation to carry persons from Cuba to the United States. The Cuban airlift became the largest airborne refugee operation in U.S. history. In conjunction with the Cuban Refugee Program, these twice-daily flights helped to transport and relocate hundreds of thousands of Cubans in the United States. Approximately 2,800 flights carried more than 302,000 Cubans to Miami, representing around 28 percent of all Cuban migrants to the United States between 1959 and 1996. Because of the sheer number of arrivals, this period became the most important stage of emigration since the triumph of the Cuban **Revolution**.

As a result of the Cuban **Missile Crisis** (October 1962), direct legal travel between Cuba and the United States was suspended until September 1965, when the Cuban government unilaterally opened the port of Camarioca, **Matanzas Province**, allowing some 5,000 persons to leave the country. Camarioca ushered in a new migration wave from Cuba to the United States. Diplomatic negotiations between Washington and Havana created a regular air bridge between Varadero (a town east of Havana) and Miami beginning on December 1, 1965. The so-called Freedom Flights took from 3,000 to 4,000 Cuban refugees per month to the United States.

On April 6, 1973, **Fidel Castro** unilaterally ended the Freedom Flights, reducing Cuban migration to a mere trickle until 1980, when the exodus of the **Mariel boatlift** began. As stipulated by the agreements between the U.S. and Cuban governments, most Freedom Flights exiles had close relatives already living in the United States. Kinship networks therefore played an important role in the process of migration and resettlement. This factor helps to account for the increasing concentration of Cuban immigrants in south Florida, northern New Jersey, and other traditional centers of the Cuban diaspora. Like their predecessors, the new immigrants settled primarily in the city of Miami, Hialeah, and other parts of Dade County, Florida, recreating their society of origin's heterogeneous class structure (see **Little Havana**).

The main destination of the new arrivals reaffirmed a trend that had become evident in the early 1960s: Miami had replaced New York City as the capital of Cuban America. Like earlier Cuban refugees, most of the air bridge migrants were white and urban, but they were predominantly female, older, and less skilled than the earlier wave, because of strict restrictions imposed by Castro's government. Although the Freedom Flights still overrepresented Cubans from higher socioeconomic strata, the refugee flux drew increasingly on lower-status groups. As the proportion of professionals and managers declined among the new refugees, the proportion of salespersons and manual workers correspondingly increased. Skilled and semiskilled workers, small business persons, and small farmers constituted the core of the migrants between 1965 and 1973. Compared to earlier exiles, this migrant wave was also more diverse with regard to income, education, and place of residence in Cuba. Moreover, economic motives loomed larger than political reasons during this stage of the Cuban exodus. In March–April 1968, for example, the so-called Revolutionary Offensive nationalized thousands of small businesses in Cuba, and it is likely that many displaced workers chose to move abroad rather than stay on the island. Thus, the Freedom Flights increased the socioeconomic complexity of the Cuban population in the United States. *See also* United States, Cuban Migrations to the; United States, Cuba's Relations with the

Further Readings

García, María Cristina. *Havana USA: Cuban Exiles and Cuban Americans in South Florida, 1959–1994.* Berkeley: University of California Press, 1996.

Pedraza, Silvia. "Cuba's Refugees: Manifold Migrations." In *Origins and Destinies: Immigration, Race, and Ethnicity in America*, ed. Silvia Pedraza and Ruben G. Rumbaut. Belmont, CA: Wadsworth, 1996. 263–279.

Pérez, Lisandro. "Cubans in the United States." *Annals of the American Academy of Political and Social Science* 487 (1986): 126–137.

Portes, Alejandro, Juan M. Clark, and Robert L. Bach. "The New Wave: A Statistical Profile of Recent Cuban Exiles to the United States." *Cuban Studies* 7 (1977): 1–32.

Jorge Duany

Goizueta, Roberto C. (1931–1997)

Roberto C. Goizueta was the Cuban leader of the Coca-Cola Company who was widely credited with ushering in the greatest period of growth in the company's history. Born in Havana to a family of Basque origin, Goizueta attended the Colegio de Belén, Cheshire Academy, and Yale University. In 1954 Goizueta joined Coca-Cola in Havana. With the Cuban **Revolution** of 1959, Goizueta moved his family to Miami and eventually Atlanta, where he redesigned the company's technical operations. In 1965, Goizueta became the company's youngest vice president and by 1981 was appointed chairman and chief executive officer. In 1982, he launched Diet Coke and increased the company's presence in the diet soft-drink market. Three years later, Goizueta changed Coca-Cola's formula and launched New Coke. After a public outcry against the change, he relaunched Coca Cola Classic to much fanfare and increased sales. Goizueta increased the company's market share outside of the United States by promoting sales in Eastern Europe and Latin America. In 1996, Goizueta established the Goizueta Foundation to support educational programs.

Further Reading

Greising, David. *I'd Like to Buy the World a Coke: The Life and Leadership of Roberto Goizueta.* New York: John Wiley & Sons, 1998.

John A. Gutiérrez

Hermanos Al Rescate (Brothers to the Rescue)

Hermanos al Rescate (Brothers to the Rescue) was born in Miami in 1991 as a volunteer organization formed by José J. Basulto, Billy Schuss, and thirty-five other volunteer pilots who regularly flew over the Florida Straits searching for fleeing Cuban **balseros** (rafters) who might otherwise have perished at sea. In 1991–1994 the Brothers launched hundreds of search-and-rescue missions that spotted balseros and proceeded to drop provisions of drinking water, food, lifesavers, and other equipment and then to alert the U.S. Coast Guard about their location. After the fall of 1994, when the U.S. and Cuban governments convened to repatriate all rafters found in U.S. territorial waters, the Brothers became very cautious, as once Cuban rafters were detected, alerting U.S. authorities meant repatriation to Cuba. In subsequent years, the organization became more political, and on July 13, 1995, they performed the first act of open defiance to the **Fidel Castro** regime by demonstrating in Cuban waters in commemoration of the martyrs of the "13 de Marzo" tugboat sunk by the Cuban military the previous year (see **Dissent and Defections [1959–]**). On January 9 and 13, 1996, two Brothers' planes dropped half a million leaflets on Havana. The most dramatic event came on February 24, 1996, when three Cessna bimotor planes went close to the Cuban coast in a search-and-rescue mission, and two of them were shot by MiG's 29 air-to-air missiles while flying over international space. Four young volunteer pilots were killed, and this led to President Bill Clinton's partial signing of the Helms-Burton Act, which included provisions that tightened the trade embargo, and U.S. courts ordered financial compensation to victims' relatives. *See also* Migration Accords; Appendix 13; United States, Cuba's Relations with; U.S. Trade Embargo and Related Legislation

Further Reading

Levine, Robert M., and Moisés Asís. *Cuban Miami.* New Brunswick, NJ: Rutgers University Press, 2000.

Moisés Asís

Little Havana

"Little Havana" is the name given since the early 1960s to a southwest Miami neighborhood formerly known as Riverside. This area extends from the Miami River, or Fourth Avenue, separating it from downtown, westward to Twenty-Seventh Avenue, or for some to Thirty-Sixth Avenue, and from West Flagler Street southward to Sixteenth Street. Its main attraction is the chain of stores and restaurants with Spanish signs along Southwest Eighth Street, best known as Calle Ocho. So many Cubans moved into Riverside that newspapers dubbed it "Little Havana." This Miami section sprouted not only repair shops and other small businesses but offices of accountants, physicians, dentists, and lawyers who catered to fellow Cubans. Also prominently visible throughout were dozens of Cuban restaurants and coffee counters and grocery stores that gave Little Havana the distinctive flavor it retains today. Many streets and avenues in Little Havana have names of exiled Cuban singers, **baseball** players, politicians, businessmen, lawyers, martyrs, and organizations. The names of stores and restaurants are similar to those that existed in Cuba, and in these establishments can be found Cuban brands of soft drinks, beers, preserves, coffee, crackers, and other products (see **Cuisine**). Supermarkets, bakeries, cafeterias, funeral homes, flower

Mural welcomes visitors to Cuban enclave in Miami. Photograph by Robert M. Levine.

shops, and other establishments were replicated and renamed after their Cuban predecessors. Cuban flags and signs or murals in Spanish everywhere remind the visitor of the dominant Cuban presence, although since the 1980s an increasing number of other Hispanics have moved to the neighborhood. The population of little Havana stands at about 92,000, 80 percent of whom are Cuban.

Further Reading

Levine, Robert M., and Moisés Asís. *Cuban Miami.* New Brunswick, NJ: Rutgers University Press, 2000.

Moisés Asís

Mariel Boatlift

The mass migration of Cubans from Mariel harbor west of Havana, to Key West, Florida, took place between April 21 and September 26, 1980. The sudden and dramatic exodus partly resulted from the visits of more than 100,000 exiles to Cuba in 1979, which renewed social contacts with relatives and familiarized them with economic opportunities in the United States. The immediate cause of the boatlift was the takeover of the Peruvian embassy in Havana by more than 10,800 Cubans who wanted to migrate. **Fidel Castro** resented that the Peruvian government failed to re-

turn 6 Cubans who had stormed the embassy requesting political asylum on March 28, 1980. In retaliation, Castro removed the embassy's police custody and encouraged all those wishing to leave the country to go to the compound. In a reprise of an earlier decision to open Camarioca in 1965 (see **Freedom Flights**), the Cuban government opened the port of Mariel, near Havana, for those who could be picked up by relatives living abroad. Thus began what became known in the United States as the "Freedom Flotilla." When the exiles arrived in Mariel aboard boats and ships, the Cuban government forced them to take unrelated persons, some of whom had been inmates at prisons or mental hospitals. The boatlift ended when Castro announced that Mariel harbor was closed for further emigration. More than 125,000 Cubans arrived in Key West during the Mariel exodus, representing about 12 percent of the entire migration between 1959 and 1996.

Most of the *Marielitos* (as they were pejoratively labeled) were young, single males; the majority were of working-class background and had less than a high school education. Approximately 13 percent of the Marielitos were classified as black or mulatto, compared to only 3 percent of the exiles in 1973 (see **Afro-Cubans; Racial Composition**). Many of the new migrants had grown to adulthood after 1959 and were strongly exposed to the socialist ideology of the Cuban **Revolution**. Because of their youth, most could not even remember the days of pre-revolutionary Cuba. Few had close relatives and friends who could support them in the United States. In Miami, Mariel refugees faced longer periods of unemployment, low-paid work, and welfare dependence than earlier migrants. Thus, the socioeconomic profile of the Mariel exodus differed significantly from that of previous waves of Cuban refugees in the United States, especially during the early 1960s.

Boats loaded with Cubans departing the island during the Mariel Boatlift of 1980. Courtesy of the Cuban Heritage Collection of the Otto G. Richter Library of the University of Miami.

The Mariel boatlift has been popularly cast in a negative light. The Cuban government as well as the U.S. mass media exaggerated the presence of criminals, homosexuals, mental patients, prostitutes, and other misfits among the new exiles (see **Crime**; **Gays and Lesbians**; **Prostitution**). Sensationalist stories and editorials about Marielitos' delinquent activities began to appear in the main U.S. newspapers. Brian De Palma's popular remake of the film *Scarface* (1983), which depicted Mariel exiles as vicious mobsters, pimps, and drug dealers, is one of the best-known unflattering portrayals. Another is *The Perez Family* (1995), an unsympathetic comedy about the marriage of convenience between a Cuban political prisoner and a former prostitute who come together

to the United States via Mariel. A 1981 Gallup poll showed that North Americans perceived Cubans to be the second least desirable group of neighbors after religious cult members. In November 1987, the media gave a wide coverage to prison riots involving Mariel refugees in Oakdale, Louisiana, and Atlanta, Georgia. As a result, U.S. public opinion toward Cuban immigrants became increasingly hostile. Contrary to widespread media reports, less than 2 percent of the Marielitos were serious criminals, although about 25 percent had been imprisoned for various reasons, including violating the Cuban law of *peligrosidad*, or "dangerous behavior," such as engaging in public homosexuality, vagrancy, and antisocial acts. Many of these "crimes" would not be penalized in the

United States, such as trading on the **black market**, and some were clearly expressions of political unconformity, such as distributing "propaganda" against the socialist regime. But the public image of the Marielito became tarnished with illegal and immoral connotations. In Havana, the Cuban government officially branded the refugees as *escoria* (scum) and *lumpen* because it considered them undesirable, antisocial, and counterrevolutionary elements. In Washington, federal government authorities became increasingly concerned about the negative impact of admitting thousands of Cubans with criminal records. In Miami, where most of the Marielitos eventually settled, rifts between "old" and "new" immigrants deepened. Date of departure from Cuba—before or after 1980—became a symbol of one's social status. The diminutive term *Marielito* itself reflected the public scorn accorded to the new immigrants, both in Cuba and the United States.

Nonetheless, the Mariel exodus had some salutary effects on the Cuban diaspora. Little public attention has been given to an important group of Cuban writers, artists, and other intellectuals who came to the United States via the Mariel boatlift or shortly thereafter (see **Mariel Generation**). Well-known authors like **Reinaldo Arenas** and **Heberto Padilla** and painters like **Carlos Alfonzo** and Andrés Valerio contributed to a renaissance of Cuban American literature and arts. The literary journals *Mariel*, first established in Miami and later in New York (1980–1988), and *Linden Lane Magazine*, based in Princeton since 1982, showcased the work of this new generation of exiles. From a broader perspective, the Mariel exodus renewed the sources of Cuban language and culture in the United States. **Santería**, the most popular Afro-Cuban cult, experienced a revival in Miami and elsewhere with the arrival of several priests and many believers. Other religious groups, such as Seventh-Day Adventists and Jehovah's Witnesses, were well represented in the Mariel exodus.

The Mariel boatlift also prompted a major reassessment of U.S. policy toward Cuban immigration. After 1980, the federal government did not automatically consider all Cubans arriving in the United States as refugees. Instead, Marielitos were classified as "entrants (status pending)," an ambiguous category that placed them in a legal limbo for an indefinite period and did not provide the special benefits accorded to those granted political asylum under the U.S. Refugee Act of 1980. To qualify as refugees, applicants had to prove political persecution in their home country.

However, ideological dissidence with Fidel Castro's policies was less overt among Mariel Cubans than among earlier waves. Only some groups of Cubans, such as former political prisoners, were eligible for refugee status. Most Marielitos were labor migrants, such as craft workers and factory operators, reflecting the socioeconomic composition of the Cuban population more accurately than ever before or since. The Mariel exodus transformed the Cuban community abroad, especially in Miami. The sudden influx of tens of thousands of immigrants in Miami increased housing, employment, education, welfare, crime, and other problems that stigmatized the entire Cuban population in the United States. The Cuban American community, once the darling of the U.S. mass media, lost its grip on U.S. public opinion and the federal government. The attitudes of the local Miami population toward Cuban exiles quickly deteriorated after the Mariel exodus. Furthermore, the Cuban American community became a wider cross section of the island's population. After Mariel, Cuban Miami was much more diverse racially, economically, generationally, and ideologically than before. Perhaps the most enduring consequence of the Mariel boatlift was forcing Cuban émigrés to organize politically to combat growing prejudice and discrimination in the United States. Since 1980, Cuban Americans have experienced a swift ideological transition from being political exiles primarily concerned with the fate of their homeland to becoming an ethnic group increasingly involved with domestic issues as well. *See also* United States, Cuban Migrations to the

Further Readings

Bach, Robert L. "Socialist Construction and Cuban Emigration: Explorations into Mariel." *Cuban Studies* 15 (1985): 19–36.

Clark, Juan M., and José I. Lasaga. *The 1980 Mariel Exodus: An Assessment and Prospect.* Washington, DC: Council for Inter-American Security, 1981.

Portes, Alejandro, Juan M. Clark, and Robert M. Manning. "After Mariel: A Survey of the Resettlement Experiences of 1980 Cuban Refugees in Miami." *Cuban Studies* 15 (1985): 37–59.

Jorge Duany

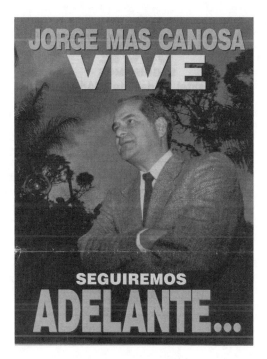

Poster celebrating Jorge Mas Canosa's legacy. Courtesy of the Cuban American National Foundation.

Mas Canosa, Jorge (1941–1997)

Jorge Mas Canosa was a Miami-based exile leader, lobbyist, and businessman, founder and chairman of the influential **Cuban American National Foundation** (CANF). Born in **Santiago de Cuba**, Mas Canosa was exiled twice in the United States: first in 1956 as a teenage student after commenting on a radio program against the **Fulgencio Batista** regime, then in 1960 as a member of the Democrat Christian Movement youth while conspiring against **Fidel Castro**'s regime. Once in Miami, he participated in the **Bay of Pigs Invasion**. Later he was elected as a board member of the Representación Cubana del Exilio (RECE), but the RECE failed to represent all Cuban exiles, and its influence waned. Meanwhile, Mas Canosa became the main partner of Church & Tower Corporation, and in the following years he created his own corporation for communications, MasTec, which accounts for hundreds of millions of dollars in profit every year.

Once Mas Canosa understood that Washington would never support or permit Cuban exiles to fight for democracy in Cuba, he and thirteen other Cubans created, on July 24, 1981, an organization to defeat Castroist propaganda and influence in Washington and at the same time to lobby in favor of Cuban exile interests. Since its creation, the CANF has among its achievements the creation of programs like "Exodus" to bring to the United States refugees from third countries; "Misión Martí" to create a multiprofessional force to rebuild Cuban economy, education, and infrastructures after Castro; **Radio Martí** and TV Martí; the approval of the Torricelli Act; and the Helms-Burton Act (see **Appendix 13**). Mas Canosa met many of the world's leaders and obtained their support for CANF's policy against Castro. In the 1990s surveys often showed Mas

Canosa as the most popular leader of Cuban exiles and the most influential in U.S. policy making toward Cuba. A CBS-TV debate on September 5, 1996, between the Cuban **National Assembly**'s president **Ricardo Alarcón** and CANF's chairman showed Mas Canosa's stature as a political leader.

After Mas Canosa's death in 1997, the CANF lost a great deal of its influence over U.S. policy toward Cuba, and the vacuum he left was apparent during the **Elián González case** in 2000. Mas Canosa's son, Jorge Mas Santos, born in Miami and not experienced in political activism, took over the leadership of the organization that his father built. His approach has generated some internal opposition.

Further Readings

Pérez Castellón, Ninoska. *Un hombre y su tiempo: el pensamiento político de Jorge Mas Canosa.* Washington, DC: The Endowment for Cuban American Studies of the Cuban American National Foundation and the Jorge Mas Canosa Freedom Fund, 1998.

Vargas Llosa, Álvaro. *El exilio indomable: historia de la disidencia cubana en el destierro.* Madrid: Espasa, 1998.

Moisés Asís

Menéndez, Robert "Bob" (1954–)

One of the most vocal and influential voices in the Cuban exile community, Robert "Bob" Menéndez has fought in Congress to maintain and tighten the **U.S. trade embargo** on Cuba with the hope that it will pave the way for a democratic transition.

Born in New York City, Menéndez was raised in Union City, New Jersey, in an area with the largest Cuban American community outside of Miami (see **New Jersey, Cubans in**). He received his bachelor's degree from St. Peter's College in Jersey City and his law degree from Rutgers University in Newark. At the age of

Congressman Robert "Bob" Menéndez, New Jersey's 13th district since 1992. Courtesy of the Office of Congressman Robert Menéndez.

twenty, he was elected to the Union City Board of Education. He would eventually become the mayor of Union City and serve in that capacity from 1986 until 1992. From 1987 through 1992, he served in the New Jersey State Legislature, becoming the first Hispanic to serve in the State Senate.

Menéndez, a Democrat, was elected to Congress in 1992 and has led efforts to pressure the **Fidel Castro** government to make democratic reforms. He was a supporter of the Helms-Burton legislation that tightened the economic embargo against Cuba (see **Appendix 13**). He authored the section of the bill that provides funds to house and support members of the Cuban armed forces in the event that Castro leaves or is forced from power (see **Revolutionary Armed Forces**). In 1996, he was appointed by President Bill Clinton to argue for the condemnation of Cuba at a meeting of the UN Commission on **Human Rights**. A resolution condemning Cuba was passed at that meeting. Menéndez has been described as "infamous" in the Cuban media and beholden to the Cuban-American "mafia" represented by the **Cuban American National Foundation**. Critics within the United States argue current foreign policy harms the Cuban people rather than the Cuban government and does not reflect the new post–Cold War reality.

He lives in Union City with his wife and two children.

Further Reading

Torres, María de los Ángeles. *In the Land of Mirrors: Cuban Exile Politics in the United States.* Ann Arbor: University of Michigan Press, 1999.

Frank Argote-Freyre

Migration Accords

The United States and Cuba signed migration agreements in 1994 and 1995 in an effort to discourage Cubans from rafting across the Florida Straits and to encourage a pattern of safe and legal migration. In August 1994, tens of thousands of Cuban **balseros** set sail for the United States on rickety homemade rafts. Although approximately 30,000 of these rafters ultimately arrived in the United States, many died at sea. In an effort to prevent further loss of life and to open a safe channel for leaving the island, the two nations signed an accord on September 9, 1994. In the accord, the United States agreed to accept 20,000 permanent migrants from Cuba each year, and Cuba agreed to stem the flow of rafting departures from the island. Rafters rescued at sea after September were taken to camps at the **Guantánamo U.S. Naval Base**. By spring 1995, tensions were rising at the camps, and the coming summer rafting season promised to bring even more Cubans to the naval base. On May 2, 1995, a second accord was signed to alleviate the

developing problems. The two countries agreed that all rafters rescued at sea would be returned to Cuba unless they faced a credible fear of persecution. U.S. diplomats would visit those rafters who were returned to monitor their status and verify that they were not facing harassment. These agreements largely closed what had been considered by many Cubans to be the escape route from Cuba. *See also* United States, Cuban Migrations to the; Cuban Adjustment Act; United States, Cuba's Relations with the

Further Readings

Moses, Catherine. *Real Life in Castro's Cuba.* Wilmington, DE: Scholarly Resources, 2000.

Nackerud, Larry. Alyson Springer, Christopher Larrison, and Alicia Isaac. "The End of the Cuban Contradiction in U.S. Refugee Policy." *International Migration Review* 33 (Spring 1999): 176–192.

Catherine Moses

Montaner, Carlos Alberto (1943–)

Carlos Alberto Montaner is a Cuban-born exile writer, professor, and anti–**Fidel Castro** political leader whose articles, books, and active contacts with government leaders mainly in Europe and Latin America have made him the most effective intellectual foe to the Cuban communist ideologists. Founder and president since 1989 of the Unión Liberal Cubana, and a vice president of the Liberal International, he seeks a democratic transformation of Cuba by following the Cuban liberal tradition of **Francisco de Arango y Parreño, Ignacio Agramonte**, and **José Martí**, under the principle that liberty is a key component of prosperity and in concordance with the ideas of Friedrich Von Hayek and others. In 1996, Montaner received the Jovellanos Prize granted by the Fundación Foro Jovellanos for social innovation and for his contribution to liberal thought. Since leaving Cuba in 1961, he has lived

590 New Jersey, Cubans in

in Puerto Rico and Miami. He now resides in Madrid. Some of his best-known books on Cuba are *Secret Report on the Cuban Revolution* (1981), *América Latina y los Estados Unidos: propuesta para un acercamiento diferente* (1983), *Cuba, Castro, and the Caribbean: The Cuban Revolution and the Crisis in Western Conscience* (1985), *Fidel Castro and the Cuban Revolution* (1989), *Castro en la era de Gorbachov* (1990), *Cómo y por qué desapareció el comunismo* (1994), *Cuba hoy: la lenta muerte del Castrismo* (1996), *No perdamos también el siglo XXI* (1997), *Viaje al corazón de Cuba* (1999), *Guide to the Perfect Latin American Idiot* (1999), *Fabricantes de miseria* (1999), and *Manual del perfecto sinvergüenza* (1999). *See also* Puerto Rico, Cubans in; Spain, Cuba's Relations with

Further Readings

Fernández de la Torriente, Gastón. *La narrativa de Carlos Alberto Montaner*. Madrid: Cupsa, 1978.

Vargas Llosa, Álvaro. *El exilio indomable: historia de la disidencia cubana en el destierro*. Madrid: Espasa, 1998.

Moisés Asís

New Jersey, Cubans in

New Jersey is the home of the second largest concentration of Cubans in the United States after Miami, Florida. According to the U.S. Census of 2000, there are approximately 77,337 Cubans in the state, 6.2 percent of the Cuban population in the United States. Another 62,590 live in the neighboring state of New York. There was a small Cuban community in Union City, North Hudson County, before 1959, but the group's majority came after the **Revolution** as political exiles. When the initial flow of refugees in the early 1960s became unmanageable for the state of Florida, the federal government created the Cuban Refugee Program that helped relocate Cubans to other states. As a result, almost 60,000 Cubans arrived in New Jersey between 1961 and 1970, making the state's figure for the Cuban population 71,233 in 1970. Cubans came to many New Jersey counties, but Union and Hudson were top choices. The adjacent cities of Union City and West New York became so Cuban that the area was often referred to as "Havana on the Hudson" or "the second Cuban capital in exile."

The abundance of manufacturing jobs in New Jersey made the state a logical destination for the refugees. Most Cubans who resettled in New Jersey were part of the second wave of migration that left the island after a 1965 Memorandum of Understanding was signed by the United States and Cuba, which allowed 3,000 persons to leave monthly through the port of Varadero in **Matanzas** (see **Freedom Flights**). Many of these migrants were less affluent and less educated than the refugees of the early 1960s, who tended to stay in Miami. But New Jersey Cubans were entrepreneurial, and in a short period of time, they helped revive the economic and social life of many New Jersey urban areas. In Elizabeth, Union County, and especially on Bergenline Avenue, the main commercial street extending through Union City and West New York, Cuban-owned businesses flourished. A large number of New Jersey's Cubans are from the municipality of Fomento in **Las Villas** Province.

Since the 1980s, Cubans have started to move away from the state's urban areas. In 1980, 32 percent percent of Union City's population was Cuban. In 1990 that proportion decreased to 26 percent. According to the 2000 Census, 10,296 Cubans resided in Union City and 8,991 in West New York. This movement has coincided with the immigration of other groups, mainly from other Latin American countries, into the cities. The fourth wave of Cuban immigrants, those coming through the **Mariel boatlift**, arrived precisely in 1980. The *Marielitos* received assistance from North Hudson County's Refugee Settlement Program but did not have many of the benefits of the first and second wave. Many industries had left New Jersey, and jobs were not as easily available. Also, these refugees faced a great deal of prejudice because there were many non-white immigrants among them. Some 20,000 Marielitos settled in the New York–New Jersey area. In the 1990s, legal and illegal immigration continued to bring more Cubans to New Jersey cities. As the older exiles move to the suburbs or to Florida, the recent immigrants settle in old Cuban areas. Cities like Union City continue to be symbolically "Cuban," even when the majority of Latin immigrants coming there are from other countries. The new Cubans are bringing current influences of the island's culture with them. This is evident in new clubs featuring Afro-Cuban dance and music and art galleries that exhibit work of young refugee artists (see **Afro-Cubans**). *See also* United States, Cuban Migrations to the; United States, Cuban Population in the

Further Readings
Bischoff, Henry. "Caribbean Peoples in New Jersey: An Overview." *New Jersey History* 113, nos. 1–2 (Spring–Summer 1995): 1–32.
Rogg, Eleanor M, and Rosemary S. Cooney. *Adaptation and Adjustment of Cubans: West New York, New Jersey*. Bronx, NY: Hispanic Research Center, Fordham University, 1980.

Yolanda Prieto

Nuevo Herald, El

One of the fastest-growing Spanish-language newspapers in the country, Miami's *El Nuevo Herald* was established by the parent company of the *Miami Herald* to tap into the growing economic power of Hispanics, and particularly Cuban Americans, in South Florida. As of 2000, the newspaper's circulation was over 100,000 on Sundays and 93,000 during the week.

The newspaper was originally conceived in 1976 as a supplement to the *Miami Herald* and consisted of articles translated into Spanish from the English-language edition. The Cuban American community has frequently been at odds with the *Miami Herald* because of its coverage of Cuba and positions on a variety of social issues, including bilingual education. *El Nuevo Herald*, originally called *El Herald*, was part of an effort to reach out to the community and to reverse stagnant circulation figures. Initial response was lukewarm because there was little effort to diversify the content to satisfy the target audience. In 1998, a decision was made to separate the two newspapers, and *El Nuevo Herald* became editorially independent. The newspaper maintains a staff of more than eighty employees, most in the newsroom. It emphasizes coverage of the local and national Hispanic communities as well as Latin America.

Further Reading
Soruco, Gonzalo R. *Cubans and the Mass Media in South Florida*. Gainesville, University Press of Florida, 1996.

Frank Argote-Freyre

Omega 7

A right-wing extremist terrorist cell responsible for several bombings and murders in the 1970s and early 1980s, Omega 7 principally operated in the areas of New York City, Newark and Union City, New Jersey, and Miami, Florida. Headed by Eduardo Arocena, the clandestine group allegedly received funding through participation in drug trafficking, from anti-**Castro** organizations in the United States, networks of Radical Right formations, and some Latin American secret police groups. Omega 7 ostensibly united seven different counterrevolutionary factions, although because of its secretive terrorist nature, the organization never had a mass membership. Omega 7 was closely tied to, and shared members with, the Cuban Nationalist Movement

(MNC), which was involved in the assassination of the former Chilean ambassador to the United States, Orlando Letelier, and his coworker, Ronni Moffit, in a 1976 Washington, D.C., car bombing. The MNC apparently worked with Chilean dictator Augusto Pinochet's secret police in plotting the murder. Omega 7 targeted Cuban diplomats, missions, and offices as well as moderates favoring dialogue with Cuba and persons sympathetic to Cuban revolutionary goals. Omega 7 underwent internal power struggles in 1981 and was later made the subject of a Federal Grand Jury investigation in the mid-1980s.

The organization has been silenced since the arrest of Arocena in 1984. *See also* Alpha 66

Further Readings

Arguelles, Lourdes. "The US National Security State: The CIA and Cuban Émigré Terrorism," *Race & Class* 23, no. 4 (1982): 287–304.

Dinges, John, and Saul Landau. *Assassination on Embassy Row*. New York: Viking Press, 1982.

Hinckle, Warren, and William Turner. *Deadly Secrets*. New York: Thunder's Mouth Press, 1993.

David C. Carlson

Pedro Pan (Peter Pan), Operation

Operation Pedro Pan was the largest political exodus of unaccompanied children in the history of the Western Hemisphere. In Cuba it is referred to by its English name: from Peter Pan. It started on December 26, 1960, and lasted until October 23, 1962, when all flights between Cuba and the United States stopped because of the **missile crisis**. During this twenty-two-month period, 14,048 Cuban children between the ages of six and eighteen, and a few even younger, were sent out of Cuba alone by their parents. Although this exodus was not formally named at the time, the U.S. press gave it this evocative name in 1962, after the James Barrie novel of the boy who could fly, but with a Spanish

Boys in class at Matecumbe Camp, Florida, 1962. Courtesy of the Cuban Heritage Collection of the Otto G. Richter Library of the University of Miami.

twist. The reasons given by parents for taking this drastic step are always unswerving: apprehension of communist indoctrination and the fear that the government was going to usurp parental custody.

The children flew from Havana to Miami, where half of them went to live with family friends or relatives, and the others were placed under the care of the Unaccompanied Cuban Children's Program paid for by the U.S. government and mostly run by the Catholic Welfare Bureau. The Children's Service for Protestant Children and the Jewish Family and Children's Service were also involved (see **Judaism**). Under this program the Cuban children were placed in a foster home or institutions throughout the United States that received a per diem for their care until their parents left Cuba and the family was reunited, a separation that lasted anywhere from weeks to several years. Monsignor Bryan Walsh, who welcomed the children to the United States, passed away on December 22, 2001.

Further Readings

Conde, Yvonne. *Operation Pedro Pan—The Untold Exodus of 14,048 Cuban Children*. New York: Routledge, 1999.

Triay, Víctor A. *Fleeing Castro: Operation Pedro*

Pan and the Cuban Children's Program. Gainesville: University Press of Florida, 1998.

Yvonne Conde

Puerto Rico, Cubans in

Compared to the major Cuban communities in the United States, Cubans in Puerto Rico constitute a small population. In 2000, the census found 19,973 persons of Cuban origin in Puerto Rico—less than 2 percent of all Cuban émigrés in the United States. Cubans in Puerto Rico are more likely to come from the propertied classes than those on the U.S. mainland. On average, Cubans in Puerto Rico have higher occupational, educational, and income levels than either Puerto Ricans or Cubans in the United States. Moreover, Cuban immigrants tend to live in upper-middle-class neighborhoods within the San Juan metropolitan area. Cubans in Puerto Rico function primarily as a middleman minority, a culturally distinctive group specializing in the selling of goods and services within the host society. Most émigrés entered the middle and upper rungs of commerce and, in some cases, virtually monopolized entire sectors of trade and services, such as small shops, bakeries, food retailing, the mass media, real estate, and advertising. They gained a special access to certain occupations, either above the reach of the majority of the Puerto Rican population or beneath the dignity of the local elite, filling a status gap between dominant and subaltern classes. Cubans in Puerto Rico are almost exclusively urban dwellers, yet they do not concentrate in a single residential district. Nor do they focus on an ethnically enclosed market, like Cubans in Miami, but cater to the larger economy. Finally, in contrast to the situation in South Florida, Cuban enterprises in San Juan tend to employ a majority of non-Cubans.

Further Readings

Cobas, José A., and Jorge Duany. *Cubans in Puerto Rico: Ethnic Economy and Cultural Identity.* Gainesville: University Press of Florida, 1997.

Esteve, Himilce. *El exilio cubano en Puerto Rico: su impacto político-social (1959–1983).* San Juan: Raíces, 1984.

Jorge Duany

Radio in South Florida, Cuban

The influence of Cubans and Cuban Americans on radio programming in South Florida can be found on both the AM and FM dials and in the political and musical content of the programming. Cuban radio in the Miami area is a vibrant mix of talk show formats, spiced with virulent anti–**Fidel Castro** political commentary, and lively music stations that have contributed to the development of Cuban American artists. Recent ratings data (winter 2001) indicate that about 25 percent of south Florida's radio audience listens to Spanish-language stations. As of 2001, there were at least thirteen Spanish-language stations in the south Florida market, a dramatic increase from 1960 when there were only three.

In the talk show arena, the most popular station is Radio Mambí (WAQI 710 AM), which frequently draws just over 5 percent of the total audience, although that figure jumped dramatically during the **Elián González case** in 1999 and 2000. Radio Mambí, named for the soldiers who fought for Cuban independence from Spain (see **Mambises**), provides a twenty-four-hour talk format. Other popular Cuban stations include La Cubanísima (WQBA 1140 AM), a station geared to news and talk, and WCMQ 92.3 FM, which has the same call letters as a popular prerevolutionary radio network based in Havana and now dedicates itself to Latin oldies music. The most popular Spanish-language music stations are Radio Amor (107.5 FM) and Radio Romance (106.7 FM).

The growth of Spanish-language radio in south Florida can be linked directly to the mass exodus of Cubans fleeing the island's communist government in the 1960s. At first, Cubans often purchased airtime on local radio stations to get their message to compatriots. In addition to condemning the Cuban government, these broadcasts helped the new immigrants reunite with their families, find housing, and land jobs.

The radio waves soon became another front in the war against Castro. The signal of some Miami radio stations reaches well into Cuba, and that made stations such as WMIE (the precursor of La Cubanísima), which could be heard in western and central Cuba, very popular with the exile community. The Cuban exiles broadcast a steady diet of anti-Castro programming onto the island, a move the Cuban government countered by intermitently jamming radio signals from the United States.

Debates on talk radio, whether over the future of Cuba or the state of Miami politics, remain passionate and controversial. Talk show hosts and guests still reserve their greatest disdain for Fidel Castro, but U.S. political figures, particularly those perceived as soft on communism, are frequent targets as well. Radio personalities have occasionally been attacked for their views. In 1976, radio announcer Emilio Milián, a staunch critic of Cuban Americans involved in covert violent acts against the Castro government, lost both his legs when a bomb detonated in his car.

The careers of some of the most prominent Cuban American performers, including **Willy Chirino**, Hansel y Raúl, and **Gloria Estefan**, were nurtured by playtime on south Florida stations. The stations promoted and contributed to the creation of a sound unique to Miami, still influenced by Cuban rhythms but no longer dependent on them.

Further Readings

Pérez Firmat, Gustavo. *Life on the Hyphen: The Cuban-American Way.* Austin: University of Texas Press, 1994.

Soruco, Gonzalo R. *Cubans and the Mass Media in South Florida.* Gainesville: University Press of Florida, 1996.

Frank Argote-Freyre

Radio Martí

Radio Martí is the short-wave radio station sponsored by the U.S. government that broadcasts to Cuba. The station began broadcasting in May 1985 under the charter of the Voice of America. It was created to provide objective information about Cuba and the world to the island, effectively offering an alternative to the state-controlled media of the **Fidel Castro** government. Because the station is intended to promote the cause of freedom on the island, its broadcasts are jammed on various frequencies by the Cuban government. Despite that interference, many in Cuba listen to the station clandestinely. Cubans often combine information from state-controlled sources with news from Radio Martí in an effort to understand what is happening in the world. Until the late 1990s, Radio Martí programming included novelas (soap operas), news, and pop music. In late 1996, the headquarters of Radio Martí moved from Washington, D.C., to Miami. Subsequently, the programming format was changed, which spawned criticism and raised questions as to whether the station was losing its audience and whether it was fulfilling its mandate to be objective. In 2002 Salvador Lew became the director of both Radio Martí and TV Martí. *See also* Communications; Cuban American National Foundation (Fundación Nacional Cubano Americana)

Further Readings

Frederick, Howard H. *Cuban-American Radio Wars: Ideology in International Communications.* Norwood, NJ: Ablex, 1986. 24–50.

"Radio Martí: Salsa in the Wound." *The Economist,* May 25, 1985, 28.

Robinson, Linda. "Questionable Content." *U.S. News and World Report,* June 3, 1996, 36.

Catherine Moses

Ros-Lehtinen, Ileana
(1952–   )

A fierce opponent of the **Fidel Castro** government, Ileana Ros-Lehtinen has worked in the U.S. Congress to maintain and tighten the economic embargo against Cuba (see **U.S. Trade Embargo and Related Legislation**).

Born in Havana on July 15, 1952, she and her family fled the island when she was seven and settled in Miami. After receiving bachelor's and master's degrees from Florida International University, she became an elementary school teacher. Ros-Lehtinen embarked on a political career in 1982 when she was elected, at the age of thirty, to Florida's House of Representatives. In 1986, she was elected to the State Senate, where she served for two years.

Congresswoman Ileana Ros-Lehtinen, Florida's 18th district since 1989. Courtesy of the Office of Congresswoman Ros-Lehtinen.

In 1989, she won a special congressional election to a House seat in Florida's Eighteenth District, which encompasses downtown Miami, **Little Havana**, and other sections of Dade County. With the election, Ros-Lehtinen, a Republican, became the first Hispanic woman elected to the U.S. Congress. As a member of the House International Relations Committee, she has repeatedly attacked the Castro government for **human rights** abuses and its failure to enact political reforms. In turn, the revolutionary government has singled her out for criticism, describing her as a "ferocious wolf in woman's clothing" and "violently ultra-rightist." One of three Cuban American representatives in Congress, Ros-Lehtinen has formed a strong alliance with fellow Republican **Lincoln Díaz-Balart** (twenty-first District—FL) and Democrat **Robert "Bob" Menéndez** (thirteenth District—NJ). Popular with the Cuban exile community, she has received financial backing from the **Cuban American National Foundation** and other anti-Castro political groups. She is married to attorney Dexter Lehtinen, a former Florida state senator. They have two daughters.

Further Reading

Torres, María de los Ángeles. *In the Land of Mirrors: Cuban Exile Politics in the United States.* Ann Arbor: University of Michigan Press, 1999.

Frank Argote-Freyre

Salvat, Juan Manuel
(1940–   )

Juan Manuel Salvat is a Miami-based publisher who might be called the "Father of Anti-Castro Literature." The appellation is the result of the hundreds of books Salvat has published by Cuban authors writing against **Fidel Castro** and the Cuban **Revolution**.

Salvat was born in Las Villas and attended the **University of Havana**, where he studied law. In 1960, he participated in anti-Castro demonstrations and activities. The same year, he sought asylum in the Brazilian embassy. He moved to Miami in 1961. Five years later, he founded a book distributing company, Distribuidora Universal, actively promoting works written by Cubans. In 1966, he opened a bookstore, Librería Universal. Two years later he began to publish under the imprint of Editorial Universal.

Though many of the books Salvat published were subsidized by their authors, a common practice in Latin America, he has nevertheless published important volumes by such major writers as **Reinaldo Arenas** and **Lydia Cabrera** and has actively promoted the maintenance of Cuban culture and tradition in the United States.

Salvat has received numerous awards from the Cuban American and Floridian business communities. His bookstore (Librería Universal) is a popular gathering place for intellectuals from Latin America.

Further Reading
Figueredo, D.H. "Love's Labour Not Lost: Latino Publishing in the United States." *Multicultural Review* 7, no. 8 (September 1998): 24–33.

D.H. Figueredo

United States, Cuban Migrations to the

Over forty years of political migration have brought more than a million Cuban immigrants to North American soil in distinct waves of immigrants. Including those who were born in the United States, the total number of Cubans in the United States in 2000, according to the census, was approximately 1,241,685, 73 percent of which were immigrants. The Cuban exodus to the United States is characterized by four distinct waves of migration, each of which has been characterized by its own distinct social composition. The various waves of Cuban immigration brought very

different sets of social resources with them—such as their social class, race, education, family, institutional knowledge, and values. Over the course of more than four decades of exodus, they also arrived in the United States at times when the social context that greeted them presented them with vastly different levels of opportunity—such as economic growth or recession, existing government policy programs, a warm welcome or a cold reception. In 1972 researchers Nelson Amaro and Alejandro Portes portrayed the different phases of the Cuban political immigration as changing over time with the exiles' principal motivation for their decision to leave. With the unfolding of the Cuban **Revolution**, over the years "those who wait" gave way to "those who escape," and they to "those who search." Bringing their periodization up to date, one may add "those who hope" and "those who despair."

Typical of the first phase of the immigration were "those who wait." The Cuban exodus began with the triumph of the Cuban Revolution in 1959 over the dictatorship of **Fulgencio Batista** with the exit of the *Batistianos*. But at this time the majority of Cubans shared in the euphoria of the Revolution's hard-fought success. It was only when the Revolution entered a more radical phase in 1960 that the exodus of political immigrants really took force. In this first wave, those who left were mostly Cuba's elite: executives and owners of firms, big merchants, sugar mill owners, manufacturers, cattlemen, representatives of foreign companies, and established professionals. Hence, amid the economic and diplomatic war that ensued between Cuba and the United States in the first couple of years, they decided to leave. The refugees of this first wave came to the United States driven by Cuba's overturning of the old order through revolutionary measures such as the nationalization of North American industries, **agrarian reform acts**, and the silencing of the Catholic Church, as well

Miami's Freedom Tower housed the Cuban Refu- gee Program, established in 1961. Courtesy of the Cuban Heritage Collection of the Otto G. Richter Library of the University of Miami.

as by the United States' severance of dip- lomatic and economic ties with Cuba, all of which entailed serious personal losses (see **Religion under Castro**; **U.S. Trade Embargo and Related Legislation**). "Those who wait" characterized those first refugees who came imagining that exile would be temporary, waiting for the inev- itable U.S. reaction and help to overthrow Cuba's new government. In this first stage the exiles' political activity was intensely militant, supporting military counterrevo- lution against Cuba. Of these, the **Bay of Pigs Invasion** in April 1961 was the larg- est and most tragic.

"Those who escape" constituted the second phase that was set on by the grow- ing political turmoil when the Catholic Church was silenced after denouncing the communist direction the Revolution was taking; the electoral system collapsed

when the jubilant crowds chanted around **Fidel Castro**, "¿Elecciones para qué?" (What do we need elections for?) (see **Elections [1959–]**); and Castro an- nounced that he had always been a Marx- ist-Leninist and would be so until the day he died. The exodus doubled. Still largely a middle-class emigration, now it was more middle-class than upper-class: mid- dle merchants and middle management, landlords, middle-level professionals, and a considerable number of skilled union- ized workers, who wanted to escape an in- tolerable new order.

The immigrants of the first two phases were not so much "pulled" by the attrac- tiveness of the new host society as "pushed" by the internal political process of the old. When the private schools and universities began to close in 1961, fear that the children would be educated by the state and sent to the Soviet Union became prevalent. Over 14,000 children came alone through **Operation Pedro Pan**, sent by their frightened parents. Data from the 1990 census showed that of the 757,187 Cubans in the United States who immi- grated after the Revolution, 25 percent ar- rived during the first wave, 1960–1965. At this time the Cuban Refugee Program was initiated, providing assistance to most of the refugees in Miami. The higher-class origin of these early Cuban refugees has been well documented. This initial exodus overrepresented the professional, mana- gerial, and middle classes, 31 percent, as well as the clerical and sales workers, 33 percent. Likewise, the educational level of these refugees was remarkably high.

During this post–**Missile Crisis** period (October 1962), flights from Cuba ceased, forcing the migration rate to slow down. Cubans came to the United States after having previously stayed in other coun- tries, or escaping the island in boats and rafts (see **balseros**) to the shores of Key West. Close to half of these arrivals were blue-collar workers, skilled and unskilled, and a large proportion were agricultural workers and fishermen. Cuba introduced food rationing and compulsory military service at this time, further spurring the exodus (see **Nutrition and Food Rationing**). In the fall of 1965 a chaotic period ensued when hundreds of boats left from Miami for the Cuban port of Camarioca, where they picked up thousands of Cubans to come to the United States. "Those who search" characterized this next major wave of the Cuban migration. In response to President Lyndon B. Johnson's "open door" policy that welcomed refugees from communism, the Cuban exodus was organized and concerted (see **Cuban Adjustment Act**). For eight years, the United States and Cuban governments administered an orderly air bridge as the *Vuelos de la Libertad*, or **Freedom Flights**, daily brought Cubans from Varadero to Miami who the Cuban Refugee Program swiftly processed and resettled, dispersing them throughout the United States. When the refugee airlift closed, thousands of flights had brought more than a quarter of a million persons; 41 percent of all Cubans who had immigrated to the United States until 1996 came over during the years of the air bridge: 1965–1974.

Throughout this period, the Memorandum of Understanding regulated the immigrants' departure, giving the immediate family of exiles already living in the United States priority. Jointly, both governments decided who would emigrate, and the migration proceeded through family networks. Cuba barred from exit young men of military service age, as well as professional, technical, and skilled workers, such as doctors, whose exit would cause a serious disturbance in production or delivery of social services.

This wave of immigration was largely working-class and "petite bourgeoisie": employees, independent craftsmen, small merchants, and skilled and semiskilled workers. Increasingly, the Cuban commu-

nity in the United States became heterogeneous, varying widely in the social class origin of its members. The former social distinctions were perpetuated and reenacted in exile, often with little bearing to their life in North America. By 1970, only 12 percent of the new immigrants were professionals or managers. More than half, 57 percent, were blue-collar, service, or agricultural workers.

Cuban immigrants that arrived after the air bridge ended consisted of refugees who had first lived in Spain. Alejandro Portes, Juan M. Clark, and Robert L. Bach found that these migrants represented Cuba's "middling service sectors": cooks, gardeners, domestics, street vendors, shoe shiners, barbers, hairdressers, taxi drivers, small retail merchants. They had left Cuba during the period when Castro launched a new "revolutionary offensive" (1968) in Cuba, confiscating over 55,000 small businesses that were still privately owned, "pushing" out the little entrepreneurs and their employees. By and large, the refugees of this new wave believed in the promises of the Revolution until the Cuban government labeled them "parasites" and confiscated their small businesses.

In 1978, a dialogue took place between the Cuban government and representatives of the Cuban community in exile as a result of which the Cuban government agreed to release political prisoners; to promote the reunification of families separated by the exodus; and to allow Cubans in the United States to visit their families and their homeland. All at once, the counterrevolutionaries, *gusanos* (worms) of yesterday, became more respectfully known as "members of the Cuban community abroad," the release of over 3,600 **political prisoners** began, and the return visits of Cuban exiles commenced. The Cuban community split into the opposing camps of those who supported and those who opposed the dialogue, those who returned and those who refused to visit Cuba. Still, since that moment, hundreds of thousands of Cubans have returned for short visits to Cuba every year—seeking the family they love and the vestiges of the life they once led.

Since the flow of Cuban refugees had halted for many years, few expected the chaotic flotilla exodus in 1980 (see **Mariel Boatlift**). Initiated in April by those who asked for political asylum at the Peruvian embassy, within days it grew massive. When this acute refugee exodus ceased the following fall, it had brought over 125,000 more Cubans to North America. This wave lacked order and process. From Miami, thousands of boats piloted or hired by relatives sped across the ninety miles of sea to Cuba's Mariel Harbor. At times they succeeded in bringing their families; other times they brought whomever angry Cuban officials put on the boats. Toward the end, this included many of Cuba's social undesirables: those who had been in prisons (whether they had committed real crimes or had only succeeded in challenging the state), mental patients, and homosexuals (see **Gays and Lesbians**).

In Cuba, these "antisocial elements," this *escoria*, or "scum," as the Cuban government called them, represented a large public slap in the face: no longer the immigrants of the transition from capitalism to communism but the children of communism itself. In the United States they arrived in the throes of President Jimmy Carter's ambivalent government policy that both welcomed them "with open hearts and open arms" and sought to limit the flow. Among the *Marielitos'* most salient characteristics were their youth (most were young men, single or without their families) and a visibly higher proportion of blacks than ever before. Their former occupations showed that most were from the mainstream of the Cuban economy, hardly scum. Also salient was their overwhelmingly working-class origins—most were blue-collar workers. Mechanics, heavy equipment and factory machine op-

erators, carpenters, masons, and bus, taxi, and truck drivers led the list of occupations. "Those who hope" might well characterize this wave.

In the United States, the press focused heavily on the criminal element among the Marielitos. Indeed, there were many who had been in prison. According to the Immigration and Naturalization Service, of the 124,789 Mariel refugees, around 19 percent, or 23,970, admitted they had been in jail in Cuba. Of those who had been in prison, 5,486 were **political prisoners**, while 70 percent of those who had been in prison had been jailed for minor crimes or for acts such as vagrancy or participation in the extensive **black market** that were crimes in Cuba but not in the United States. Of those who had been in jail, the immigration service considered only 7 percent to be serious criminals—less than two percent of all the Marielitos.

The Mariel exodus proved so traumatic, both for the United States and Cuba, that immediately thereafter the doors to further migration closed. However, in the mid-1980s both governments signed a new migration agreement that provided for the immigration to the United States of up to 20,000 Cubans and up to 3,000 political prisoners a year, as well as for the deportation of excludable Marielitos back to Cuba (see **Migration Accords**). However, in actual practice, only around 2,000 visas were being given a year through the 1990s.

Cuba's economic crisis reached new depths when communism collapsed in Eastern Europe, particularly in the Soviet Union, on whom Cuba had been enormously dependent for trade and economic subsidies. The impact of these losses was devastating: a decline in the national product of one half and a drop in investment by two-thirds from 1989 to 1993. As a result, Cuban industry was paralyzed, public transport hardly operated, the sugar harvest was poor, and electricity service became sporadic, with Havana suffering prolonged blackouts. The economic crisis was so severe that in the fall of 1990 Castro himself declared it "a **special period** in times of peace."

In the 1990s, Cubans became so desperate that many left on *balsas*—rafts, tires, or other makeshift vessels—risking death due to starvation, dehydration, drowning, or sharks. The **balseros**, as they are called, risked the arduous crossing so regularly that from 1991 on **Hermanos al Rescate (Brothers to the Rescue)** constantly patrolled the sea in helicopters searching for them. According to the U.S. Coast Guard, 5,791 balseros managed to reach safety in the United States from 1985 to 1992. As economic conditions worsened in Cuba, the numbers rose dramatically. While in the year 1989 less than 500 balseros reached the United States, by 1991 the numbers had risen to over 2,000 and by 1993 to 3,656. In 1994, due to the crisis in August and September, over 37,000 Cubans were rescued at sea. "Those who despair" constituted this last wave of migration.

August 1994 comprised yet another historic turn in Cuba. On August 5, massive riots took place in the streets of Havana, in which thousands participated. Shortly thereafter, Castro gave orders to the Cuban Coast Guard not to discourage the illegal emigration from Cuba's shores. Immediately, thousands of balseros put out to sea, in the hopes of reaching Miami. But an abrupt U.S. policy change made the Cubans unwelcome. Under orders from President Bill Clinton and Attorney General Janet Reno, the U.S. Coast Guard blocked their progress and directed them to **Guantánamo U.S. Naval Base**, where over 30,000 people lived in tents for many months until many were gradually allowed entry to the United States.

As a result of the crisis, new Migration Accords were signed in 1994 and 1995 that promised that the United States would now actually grant at least 20,000 visas a year for Cubans to immigrate to the United

States and 5,000 additional visas were to be given through the luck of the draw (*bombo*) for those who did not meet the new, stringent family reunification criteria. Henceforth, all balseros found at sea were to be returned to Cuba. One of the most controversial balsero cases was that of six-year-old Elián González, whose mother died on a raft in 1999.

For over forty years, Cuba has been a society where the only choice possible is to "love it or leave it"—too few choices. A truly democratic society is defined not only by its party structure, constitution, delegation of authority, and electoral representation but by its capacity to tolerate and incorporate dissent. The Cuban mass exodus, now over forty years old, has been driven by the trauma of revolutionary change in Cuba, by the economic hardships caused by the inefficiencies of a new economic system and the isolation of the **U.S. trade embargo**, and by Cuba's incapacity to tolerate dissent. The Cuban Revolution's only solution to dissent has been to export it. Cuba has yet to provide political channels to express and incorporate dissenting voices. For as long as it fails to do so, the Cuban exodus will continue. *See also* Dissent and Defections (1959–   ); González Case (Elián)

Further Readings

Aguirre, Benigno E. "The Differential Migration of Cuban Social Races." *Latin American Research Review* 11(1976): 103–124.

Amaro, Nelson, and Alejandro Portes. "Una sociología del exilio: situación de los grupos cubanos en los Estados Unidos." *Aportes* 23(1972): 6–24.

Fagen, Richard R., Richard A. Brody, and Thomas J. O'Leary. *Cubans in Exile: Disaffection and the Revolution*. Palo Alto, CA: Stanford University Press, 1968.

Pedraza-Bailey, Silvia. *Political and Economic Migrants in America: Cubans and Mexicans*. Austin: University of Texas Press, 1985.

Pérez, Lisandro. "Cuban Women in the U.S. Labor Force: A Comment." *Cuban Studies* 18(1988): 159–64.

Portes, Alejandro, and Robert L. Bach. *Latin Journey: Cuban and Mexican Immigrants in the*

United States. Berkeley: University of California Press, 1985.

Portes, Alejandro, Juan M. Clark, and Robert L. Bach. "The New Wave: A Statistical Profile of Recent Cuban Exiles to the United States." *Cuban Studies* 7(1977): 1–32.

Portes, Alejandro, and Alex Stepick. *City on the Edge: The Transformation of Miami*. Berkeley: University of California Press, 1993.

Prieto, Yolanda. "Cuban Women in the U.S. Labor Force: Perspectives on the Nature of the Change." *Cuban Studies* 17(1987): 73–94.

Silvia Pedraza

States with Largest Cuban Populations, 2000		
State	Cuban Population	Percentage of U.S. Cuban Population
Florida	833,120	(67.0%)
New Jersey	77,337	(6.2%)
California	72,286	(5.8%)
New York	62,590	(5.0%)
Texas	25,705	(2.0%)
Puerto Rico	19,973	(1.6%)
Illinois	18,438	(1.5%)
Total	1,241,685	
Source: U.S. Population Census, 2000		

United States, Cuban Population in the

According to the U.S. population census of 2000, 1,241,685 Cubans and Cuban Americans live in the United States. They account for 0.4 percent of the nation's inhabitants. While in absolute terms their numbers have gone up since the previous census (1,043,922 in 1990), their share within the Hispanic and general population fell over the past decade. While in 1990 Cubans were 4.7 percent of the U.S. Hispanic population, their proportion fell to 3.5 percent in 2000.

The Cuban population of the United States is heavily concentrated in Florida, particularly Miami–Dade County, where Cubans make up about 30 percent of the population. Nearly two thirds of Cubans in the United States (837,120) reside in Florida. Over 52 percent of the Cuban population resides specifically in Miami-Dade. Other states with large Cuban populations are New Jersey (77,337), California (72,286), and New York (62,590). There is a Cuban presence in all fifty states: 550 were recorded in Alaska and 160 in Wyoming in 2000.

In terms of **racial composition**, Cubans in the United States are overwhelmingly white, particularly those who arrived during 1959 and the early 1960s. According to census data 83.5 percent of the Cuban population is white, 13.3 percent are other (most mulatto), and 2.9 black. The black and mulatto proportion among those leaving Cuba through the **Mariel boatlift** of 1980 and subsequent waves is higher, however (see **Afro-Cubans**).

One of the most salient demographic characteristics of the U.S. Cuban population is that it is considerably older than the Hispanic and general population of the United States. With a median age of 40.7, the population is nearly 15 years older than the Hispanic population and more than 5 years older than the general U.S. population. Consequently, the fertility and reproduction rates of the Cuban population are significantly lower than those of other groups. Single parenthood is also lower.

Social indicators point to the fact that Cubans in the United States have reached high levels of education and income and have assimilated successfully to U.S. society. These statistics can hide, however, that a proportion of the adult Cuban population does not have a high school diploma and lives below the poverty line. More than a quarter of all young adult Cubans and Cuban Americans hold bachelor's or higher degrees, a proportion that far surpasses that of all Hispanics. They also exhibit the highest levels of family income among Hispanics, with $37,000 in 1997, and the lowest unemployment rate with 7.3

(1993). According to the latest available census figures, 83.5 percent of Cubans live above the poverty line; among those arriving in the United States since 1980, however, the rate is about 10 percent lower. Indicators for the subgroup of U.S.-born Cubans in Miami-Dade point to even higher rates of success, surpassing the education and income level of the county's Anglo population. *See also* United States, Cuban migrations to the

Further Reading
Portes, Alejandro, and Alex Stepick. *City on the Edge: The Transformation of Miami*. Berkeley: University of California Press, 1993.

Luis Martínez-Fernández

Valladares, Armando (1937–)

A former political prisoner, Armando Valladares is a **human rights** activist and poet whose memoir was a bestselling chronicle of his twenty-two years in revolutionary Cuba's prisons. Born in **Pinar del Río**, Valladares graduated from the Instituto de La Habana and briefly studied law at the **University of Havana**. In 1961, he was an employee of the revolutionary government working within the Ministry of Communications when he was charged with counterrevolutionary activities. He denied the charges but was nevertheless convicted and sentenced to thirty years in prison. While in prison, Valladares completed a book titled *Desde mi silla de ruedas*; the book was published in 1976 and drew international attention. Amnesty International designated Valladares a prisoner of conscience, and French President François Mitterand actively lobbied **Fidel Castro** to release him from prison. In 1981, Valladares was released, and in 1984 he published *Against All Hope* (1986), a biographical account of his life in prison. The Cuban government refuted Valladares's portrayal by arguing that there were no human rights violations in Cuba's prisons and that Valladares had been a police officer under the **Fulgencio Batista** regime whose accusations were motivated by antipathy for the **Revolution**.

From 1986 to 1990, Valladares served as a U.S. representative to the United Nations Human Rights Commission, where he brought further international attention to human rights violations in Cuba. In 1989, Valladares established the Virginia-based Valladares Foundation to increase awareness of human rights violations in Cuba. Among Valladares's other books is *El corazón con que vivo* (1980). *See also* Dissent and Defections (1959–); Political Prisoners

Further Reading
Valladares, Armando. *Against All Hope: The Prison Memoirs of Armando Valladares*. New York: Knopf, 1986.

John A. Gutiérrez

World, Cubans Around the

The Cuban **Revolution** unleashed a massive exile and emigration process that resulted in a diaspora of over 1.5 million Cubans; since 1959 some estimates place the number of Cubans living outside the island at around 2 million. One out of nine Cubans lives abroad. While there is some debate regarding the appropriate terminology for Cubans living abroad, the term "exiles" is widely applied to those who left Cuba during the early years of the Revolution; increasingly, those who fled Cuba in later phases are referred to as "emigrants," whose main motivations for fleeing the island are belived to be more economic than political. Labels used by Cuban officials for those leaving the island have also changed over time. Originally dubbed *gusanos* (worms), Cubans in exile since the late 1970s have been referred to as members of "the Cuban community abroad."

Besides those who have left Cuba permanently, there is a large population of

Cubans serving in foreign countries in medical, educational, and military capacities. Furthermore, it is estimated that several thousand Cuban citizens are based temporarily in many countries around the world working as entertainers, sports coaches, and technicians. A large proportion of the salaries they earn while living abroad are funneled to the Cuban government, with the Cubans abroad allowed to keep a small percentage. In recent years many other Cubans—mostly young women—have sought marriages with foreigners as a way to resettle outside of Cuba.

Due to various historical, geographical, cultural, and political factors, most Cubans living abroad reside in the United States (see **United States, Cuban Population in the**). The 2000 U.S. Census recorded 1,241,685 Cubans and Cuban Americans. One in ten Cubans resides in the United States. Cubans, however, have found their way into many other countries. Puerto Rico, which is a U.S. territory, is home to one of the largest populations of Cubans living outside of Cuba and outside the continental United States. The 2000 census recorded nearly 20,000 **Cubans in Puerto Rico**. Several other American nations have also attracted Cuban exiles and emigrants numbering around 150,000. Mexico has the largest number of Cubans in the region, numbering over 40,000. Other Latin American countries with significant nuclei of Cubans are Venezuela (with over 30,000), Peru, Costa Rica, Argentina, Panama, and the Dominican Republic. Some 1,600 Cuban exiles have settled in Peru, the remnant of those who were granted refuge in Peru during the **Mariel boatlift**, which began with several thousand Cubans seeking political asylum in the Peruvian embassy in Havana. While their numbers may not be massive, Cubans settling permanently in Latin America have had an enormous impact on the region's media and small business communities. Many see their stay in Latin American countries as a temporary situation while awaiting passage to the United States. Around 1,000 Cubans live in Canada.

Another traditional magnet for Cuban exiles is Spain, where estimates place numbers at around 30,000 (see **Spain, Cuba's Relations with**). During most of the 1970s, when the direct flow of exiles to the United States came to a virtual halt, many Cuban families left their homeland via Spain. For reasons of birth, ancestry, and cultural affinity, Cuban emigrants have found Spain to be a welcoming setting, where Cuban cultural and political organizations have emerged. Cubans have settled in virtually every European country, with enclaves flourishing in France, Germany, the United Kingdom, and the Scandinavian nations, as well as in the former Soviet Union and the nations of the now-defunct Soviet bloc. Italy is one of the main sources of tourists visiting Cuba, and hundreds of Cuban women have married Italians and subsequently left Cuba permanently. It is likely that there are Cubans in most of the world's nations—there is knowledge of one Cuban in Cairo, Egypt, who earns a living giving tours on camels.

Further Readings

Martínez, M., and J. Hernández. *Algunas facetas de la emigración cubana*. Havana: Universidad de La Habana, 1996.

Santiago, Fabiola. "Separated Yet Together, Exiles Span Many Lands." *Miami Herald*, December 29, 1998: 1A, 10A.

Luis Martínez-Fernández

Appendix 1

Political Chronology

by Louis A. Pérez, Jr.

1000 B.C. Ciboney Indians (Guayabo Blanco) migrate to central-western regions of Cuba.

1000 A.D. Ciboney Indians (Cayo Redondo) settle eastern third of Cuba.

1100–1450 Successive migration waves of Arawak Indians (Sub-Taíno and Taíno) disperse across Cuba and displace Ciboney from all areas of the island except the western extremities.

1492 Christopher Columbus reconnoiters the northeastern coast of Cuba, establishing Spain's claim of possession.

1508 Sebastián de Ocampo completes the first circumnavigation of Cuba, thereby establishing definitively its insularity. The information gathered by Ocampo about Cuban coastlines and harbors is used in preparation for Spanish occupation of the island.

1511–1515 An expeditionary force under the leadership of Diego Velázquez departs from Hispaniola and enters eastern Cuba at Maisí. The Span-ish conquest of Cuba is completed within four years. The seven original towns (*villas*) are established: Baracoa (1512), Bayamo (1513), Havana (1514), Trinidad (1514), Sancti Spíritus (1514), Puerto Príncipe (1514), and Santiago de Cuba (1515).

1519 Havana is relocated from its original site on the Gulf of Batabanó to its present location on the north coast.

1519–1540 Migration from Cuba to Mexico, Central America, South America, and Florida threatens the island with depopulation. The last significant Indian uprisings against Spanish rule occur.

1538 Santiago de Cuba is formally selected as the capital of Cuba.

1538–1560 Cuba is subjected to attacks by French and English corsairs. Smaller coastal settlements are sacked and plundered. In 1555, Jacques de Sores destroys Havana, raising concern among Spanish authorities for the future security of the island. Plans are completed to construct fortifications for the protection of Havana. The Atlantic fleet convoy system (*flota*) is inaugurated.

Source: From Louis A. Pérez, Jr., *Cuba: Between Reform and Revolution*. 2nd ed. New York: Oxford, 1995. Adapted and updated by Frank Argote-Freyre. Used by permission.

1594   The status of Havana is elevated from town (*villa*) to city (*ciudad*).

1602–1607 Government efforts to curtail contraband in Bayamo lead to the first successful colonial rebellion against Spanish authority.

1607   In an effort to reduce contraband and improve coastal surveillance, insular administration of Cuba is organized into two governing units. Havana is formally established as the capital of the island under the authority of a captain-general and exercising juridical authority over all the colony and administrative responsibility for Mariel, Cabaña, Bahía Honda, Matanzas, and 50 leagues into the eastern interior, coast to coast. The administrative authority of Santiago de Cuba is restricted to Bayamo, Baracoa, and Puerto Príncipe.

1700   Bourbons claim the Spanish crown and place Philip V on the throne, precipitating the War of Spanish Succession (1700–1714).

1715–1730 Political administration is centralized across the island. Local town councils (*cabildos*) are deprived of the authority to distribute land to settlers. The position of *teniente de rey* is established to substitute for the captain-general upon the death of an incumbent. The measure reduces insular initiative in selecting a replacement from local government officials.

1717–1723 Spain establishes a tobacco monopoly (*factoría*), provoking a series of popular armed rebellions among tobacco farmers.

1728   The University of Havana is founded.

1733   The authority of Havana is expanded. Henceforth all administrative units on the island are placed under the jurisdiction of the capital. The division of authority between Havana and Santiago de Cuba ends in favor of Havana.

1740   The Real Compañía de Comercio is chartered for the purpose of consolidating Cuban trade and commerce into one monopoly enterprise.

1762–1763 The English seize and occupy Havana for ten months, opening the port to world trade.

1764   The intendancy system is introduced into Cuba as a means of improving efficiency in administration and increasing centralization of authority.

1776   North American colonies rebel against England, thereby encouraging increased commerce between the newly independent nation and Cuba.

1778   A free trade decree provides a score of Cuban cities with direct commercial access to Spain and its colonies in the New World.

1789   The island is divided into two ecclesiastical jurisdictions: The eastern half of Cuba is placed under the authority of the bishop of Santiago de Cuba; the western half of the island, together with Louisiana and Florida, is placed under the jurisdiction of the newly established bishopric of Havana.

A royal decree authorizes free trade in slaves.

1791   Slave rebellion in the French colony of St. Domingue precipitates the migration of French coffee and sugar planters to Cuba. The destruction of St. Domingue's vast agricultural wealth provides Cuba with the opportunity to expand sugar and coffee production.

1792   The Sociedad Económica de Amigos del País is chartered.

1800   As a result of the Haitian invasion of Santo Domingo, the *audiencia* is transferred to Cuba, conferring on the island supreme judicial authority over Puerto Rico, Louisiana, and Florida.

1800–1804 German scientist Alexander von Humboldt visits Cuba as part of a larger voyage of scientific exploration. He highlights Cuba's potential for demographic and economic growth.

1808   Napoleon invades Spain and establishes his brother Joseph Bonaparte on the throne. Colonists in Cuba proclaim their loyalty to the deposed Ferdinand VII.

1809–1810   A conspiracy is organized by attorneys Román de la Luz and Joaquín Infante. The plan joins Creoles and free people of color in an effort to establish an independent republic.

1810–1826   The wars of independence spread among Spain's mainland colonists. With the end of Spanish rule, thousands of loyalists, clerics, and soldiers migrate to Cuba, thereby reinforcing the presence of pro-Spanish elements on the island and contributing to the Cuban loyalty to Spain. Henceforth, Cuba is recognized officially as the "Ever-Faithful Isle."

1811–1812   José Antonio Aponte, a free black carpenter, leads an uprising that involves whites, free people of color, and slaves. Designed to put an end to slavery, the rebellion secures supporters across the island.

1817   Spain and England sign a treaty proclaiming the end of the legal slave trade in Spanish colonies, effective May 1820.

1818   A royal decree opens Cuban ports to free international trade.

1821–1823   A conspiratorial movement is organized by poet José María Heredia and Creole army officer José Francisco de Lemus. Known as the Soles y Rayos de Bolívar, the movement aspired to the abolition of slavery and the establishment of the independent "Republic of Cubanacán."

1824   Creole ensign Gaspar A. Rodríguez launches an ill-fated rebellion for independence.

1826   Manuel Andrés Sánchez and Francisco de Agüero Velasco organize a short-lived separatist rebellion in Puerto Príncipe.

1837–1838   The first railroad in Cuba, and the first railroad in Latin America, commences operation, linking Havana with Bejucal and Güines. The subsequent expansion of the rail system in Cuba reduces substantially the transportation cost associated with sugar production.

1844   La Escalera conspiracy is uncovered and crushed.

1847   Club de La Habana is founded. The Club emerges as the center of Creole conspiracy seeking annexation to the United States. Membership includes many of the most prestigious Creole sugar planters, including the Count of Pozos Dulces, Miguel Aldama, Cristóbal Madán, and José María Sánchez.

A government decree formally authorizes the importation of Asian indentured laborers into Cuba.

1848–1851   Three abortive filibustering expeditions are organized by Narciso López.

1851   Annexationist uprising led by Joaquín de Agüero in Camagüey Province is suppressed in May. Another rebellion led by Isidoro Armenteros in Trinidad is put down in July.

1853   José Martí is born.

1865   The Reformist Party is founded. Representing the interests of Creole property owners, the new party adopts a program urging modification of tax and tariff regulations, separation of military and civil functions in the office of governor general, and Cuban representation in the Spanish parliament.

1866   The first trade union of Cuba, the Asociación de Tabaqueros de La Habana, is founded.

1866–1867   Elections are held in Cuba for the positions of sixteen delegates in the Junta de Información, in which fourteen Creoles from the Reformist Party are elected. The Junta was expected to negotiate with the Spanish government a series of insular reforms. Shortly after its arrival in Spain, the Junta is dissolved. The Reformist program subsequently flounders.

1868–1878 On October 10, 1868, the "Grito de Yara" announces the outbreak of the Ten Years' War in Oriente Province. In 1869, insurgent representatives convoke an assembly at Guáimaro in Camagüey Province to establish a unified provisional government under a new constitution. The Republic-in-Arms is headed by President Carlos Manuel de Céspedes. The insurrection expands across Oriente and Camagüey and briefly into the province of Las Villas. The inability of the insurgents to carry the war to the western provinces dooms the rebellion.

1870 The Spanish government enacts the Moret law, whereby Madrid commits itself to the emancipation of slaves on a gradual basis.

1878 The Pact of Zanjón in February brings the Ten Years' War to an end. According to the terms of the peace settlement negotiated by Spanish General Arsenio Martínez Campos and the insurgent command, Spain pledges to institute a program of political and administrative reform and extends amnesty to insurgents. Asian contract workers and African slaves who participated in the rebellion receive guaranteed unconditional freedom. A month after the negotiations, Cuban General Antonio Maceo denounces the pact (the "Protest of Baraguá") and renews Cuban commitment to armed struggle. In May, all insurgents lay down their arms.

A new political party, the Liberal Party (Autonomist) is founded. Reviving the old Creole reformist program of the 1860s, the Autonomist Party urges gradual emancipation of slavery with indemnification to owners, juridical equality with Spanish provinces, and tax and tariff reforms. In the same year, pro-Spanish elements also form a new party, the Partido Unión Constitucional. The *peninsular* party demands the retention of traditional colonial relationships in favor of Spanish interests.

The island is reorganized into six civil provinces, each taking the name of its respective capital: Pinar del Río, Havana, Matanzas, Santa Clara, Puerto Príncipe, and Santiago de Cuba.

1879–1880 A new separatist war breaks out in Oriente in August 1879. "La Guerra Chiquita" is led by General Calixto García and involves many of the ranking veterans of the Ten Years' War. After nine months of desultory armed conflict, the rebellion is crushed.

1880–1886 Spain enacts a new law abolishing slavery, whereby emancipation is planned on a gradual basis over the course of an eight-year transition period of tutelage (*patronato*). Two years before the scheduled expiration of the *patronato*, a Spanish decree totally abolishes slavery.

1885 The first labor federation of Cuba, the Círculo de Trabajadores de La Habana, is founded, joining into one union cigar workers, shoemakers, bakers, lithographers, and carpenters.

1891 Spain and the United States sign the Foster-Cánovas Treaty, whereby Cuban agricultural products receive tariff concessions in the U.S. market in return for reciprocal duty reductions for North American imports.

1892 Under the leadership of José Martí, a new party is founded in Tampa, Florida. The Cuban Revolutionary Party (PRC) proclaims its commitment to the independence of Cuba and renews the Cuban determination to win independence by armed struggle. José Martí is elected chief delegate of the PRC.

Cuba produces the first one-million-ton sugar harvest.

The first National Labor Congress convenes in Havana.

1894   The Foster-Cánovas Treaty lapses, and old tariff rates are reinstituted.

1895   The Cuban war for independence begins on February 24. José Martí is killed in battle in May. The following September, insurgent Cubans meet at Jimaguayú (Puerto Príncipe) to establish a provisional government under a new constitution. Salvador Cisneros Betancourt is elected president of the Republic-in-Arms. In October Antonio Maceo and Máximo Gómez launch the invasion of the western provinces.

1896   In January, Maceo completes the westward march into Mantua (Pinar del Río), while Gómez commences military operations in Havana province. Spanish General Valeriano Weyler arrives in Cuba and launches the "war with war" strategy. In October, the reconcentration policy is inaugurated. Antonio Maceo is killed in battle in December.

1897   In October, Weyler is recalled. The following month autonomy is granted to the island.

1898   In July the United States intervenes in the Cuban war. One month later, Spain capitulates to the United States. In December, Spain and the United States sign the Treaty of Paris, whereby sovereignty of Cuba is transferred to the United States.

1899–1902 The formal military occupation of Cuba by the United States commences on January 1, 1899. In 1900 a constituent assembly convenes to prepare a new constitution. In February 1901 the United States enacts the Platt Amendment and requires the Cuban constituent assembly to incorporate the statute into the new constitution. In June, the constituent assembly adopts the Platt Amendment by a vote of 16 to 11, with four abstentions. In national elections in December 1901, Tomás Estrada Palma is elected president. On May 20, 1902, the United States ends the military occupation of Cuba, formally inaugurating the Cuban Republic.

1903   The United States and Cuba sign three treaties. The Permanent Treaty enacts the Platt Amendment into a formal treaty relationship. A second accord, the Reciprocity Treaty, concedes a 20 percent concession to Cuban agricultural products entering the U.S. market in exchange for reductions between 20 and 40 percent on U.S. imports. In the third agreement, Cuba leases the sites of Bahía Honda and Guantánamo to the United States. A naval base is constructed in Guantánamo.

1905   President Estrada Palma obtains a second presidential term by defeating Liberal candidate José Miguel Gómez in a disputed election.

1906   In the "August Revolution" disgruntled Liberals rebel against Estrada Palma. The Cuban government is unable to defeat the insurgents and requests U.S. military intervention.

1906–1909 The United States military occupies Cuba and governs the island through a provisional government.

1907   The Agrupación de Color is founded by Afro-Cubans protesting racism in the republic.

1908   In national elections held under U.S. supervision, Liberal candidate José Miguel Gómez wins election to a four-year presidential term (1908–1912).

1912   The United States cedes its rights over Bahía Honda in exchange for larger facilities at Guantánamo Bay.

Armed rebellion staged by Afro-Cubans protesting political, social, and economic conditions. The revolt is brutally repressed. The United States military intervenes at the site of the conflict in Oriente Province to protect North American property.

1912–1920 Conservative Mario García Menocal is elected president in 1912 for a four-year term. After a disputed presidential election in November 1916, in which Menocal wins a second term, disaffected Liberals organize a rebellion in 1917, the "February Revolution." The United States undertakes an armed intervention in the regions of the disorders and maintains a military presence in the eastern third of Cuba until 1922.

1917   Cuba declares war on Germany.

1920–1924 Popular Party President Alfredo Zayas governs Cuba. Due to political and economic problems, the first three years of the Zayas administration are under the direct control of U.S. special envoy General Enoch H. Crowder.

1920   Second National Labor Congress convenes in Havana.

"Dance of the Millions." Between February and May, the price of sugar reaches the extraordinary price of 22.5 cents per pound, only to collapse to 3.7 cents in December. The Cuban economy plunges into disarray and depression.

1923   The Veterans' and Patriots' Movement organizes to protest social, economic, and political conditions in the republic.

The first National Congress of Women meets in Havana.

Under the leadership of Julio Antonio Mella, the first National Congress of Students convenes in Havana.

1924   Gerardo Machado is elected to his first term as president (1924–1928).

1925   At the third National Labor Congress, union delegates establish the first national labor federation, the Confederación National Obrera de Cuba (CNOC). This same year, the Cuban Communist Party is founded.

1927   The Customs-Tariff law is enacted, providing Cuban manufacturers and industrialists substantive protectionist relief.

Opposition to Machado increases. Carlos Mendieta leads disaffected Liberals out of the party to organize the new Asociación Unión Nacionalista. University of Havana students establish the Directorio Estudiantil Universitario (DEU).

1928   Through unconstitutional means, Machado is elected unopposed to a new and extended six-year term of office.

1930   The U.S. Hawley-Smoot Tariff reduces the Cuban share of the U.S. sugar market, exacerbating economic conditions on the island.

The CNOC, led by Rubén Martínez Villena, organizes a general strike in March against the Machado government. In September, student demonstrations result in the death of Rafael Trejo.

1931   Old-line political chieftains led by former Conservative President Mario García Menocal and ex-Liberal Carlos Mendieta launch an abortive armed uprising against Machado at Gíbara in Eastern Cuba.

1932   The first national union of sugar workers, the Sindicato Nacional de

Obreros de la Industria Azucarera (SNOIA), is founded.

1933   The worsening political crisis in Cuba prompts the United States to dispatch Ambassador Sumner Welles to organize mediations between the Machado government and the opposition. The mediations commence in July. A general strike in August brings the brewing political crisis to a climax with a military coup ousting Machado and installing Carlos Manuel de Céspedes as president. In September, the "Sergeants' Revolt" led by Fulgencio Batista overthrows the Céspedes administration and aids the establishment of a new provisional government headed by Ramón Grau San Martín. Known as the "government of 100 days," the Grau regime inaugurates a wide range of social, economic, and political reforms.

1934   In January, Batista overthrows the Grau government and installs Carlos Mendieta as president. In May the United States abrogates the Platt Amendment.

Ramón Grau San Martín and others organize the first new post-Machado political party, the Partido Revolucionario Cubano (Auténtico) (PRC).

1935   In February and March, crippling strikes nearly topple the government. Mendieta and Batista brutally suppress the strikes.

In May, radical leader Antonio Guiteras Holmes dies in a gun battle with the Cuban Army.

Mendieta resigns in December as a result of intense pressure from the political opposition. Secretary of State José A. Barnet replaces him.

1936   In January, elections orchestrated from Washington lead to the election of Miguel Mariano Gómez.

The Cuban Congress impeaches him in December because of his opposition to the Army's bid to take over rural education. Batista works with his allies in Congress to secure his ouster. Federico Laredo Brú, who serves the balance of the four-year term, replaces Gómez.

1938   The Communist Party obtains recognition as a legal political organization. In return for recognition, the party agrees to support the presidential aspirations of Fulgencio Batista.

1939   The CNOC is reorganized as the Confederación de Trabajadores de Cuba (CTC).

1940   The constitution of Cuba is promulgated.

Fulgencio Batista is elected president for a four-year term.

1941   Cuba declares war on Germany, Italy, and Japan within days of the attack on United States forces at Pearl Harbor.

1944   Ramón Grau San Martín is elected president for a four-year term and carries the Auténtico Party into power.

The Communist Party is reorganized and changes its name to the Partido Socialista Popular (PSP).

1947   Eduardo Chibás breaks with the Auténtico Party to organize a new opposition party, Partido del Pueblo Cubano (Ortodoxo).

1948   Carlos Prío Socarrás is elected president for a four-year term.

1951   Senator Eduardo Chibás commits suicide after a national radio address. In his final speech, he warns of the decay of democratic institutions and predicts the return of military rule.

1952   Fulgencio Batista seizes power through a military coup and ousts the Prío administration, thereby ending constitutional government in Cuba.

1953   Fidel Castro attacks the Moncada barracks in Santiago de Cuba. The attack fails, and survivors are sentenced to fifteen-year prison terms.

1954   Running unopposed, Batista is elected to another four-year term as president.

1955   Batista proclaims a general amnesty in which Fidel Castro and other participants in the Moncada attack are released from prison. Castro, the leader of the newly organized 26th of July Movement, departs for Mexico to organize armed resistance against the Batista government.

1956   Fidel Castro returns to Cuba aboard the *Granma* yacht and establishes guerrilla operations in the Sierra Maestra Mountains of southeastern Cuba.

Colonel Ramón Barquín is arrested for organizing an antigovernment plot within the armed forces. More than 200 officers are implicated in the conspiracy.

1957   In January, Fidel Castro leads the first successful guerrilla operation against the Rural Guard post at La Plata in the Sierra Maestra foothills. In March, the Directorio Revolucionario led by José Antonio Echeverría attacks the Presidential Palace in an effort to assassinate Batista. The assault fails and Echeverría is killed. In September a naval uprising in Cienfuegos leads to the temporary seizure of the local naval station.

1958   In March, Raúl Castro establishes guerrilla operations on a second front in the Sierra Cristal Mountains in northern Oriente Province. In the same month, the United States imposes an arms embargo against the Batista government. The attempt by the 26th of July Movement in April to topple the Batista government through a general strike fails. In May, the government launches a major offensive against guerrilla forces in the Sierra Maestra. Government military operations fail, and the guerrilla columns mount a counteroffensive. In late December, Batista, fearing a military coup led by General Eulogio Cantillo, decides to flee Cuba.

1959   Batista flees Cuba on the morning of January 1. A general strike in early January forces the military government to relinquish power to the 26th of July Movement. On January 8, Fidel Castro arrives in Havana. The following month, Castro becomes prime minister. In May, the government enacts the agrarian reform bill.

1960   In May, Cuba and the Soviet Union reestablish diplomatic relations. The following month, the Cuban government nationalizes U.S. petroleum properties. In July, the United States cuts the Cuban quota. Between August and October, additional North American properties are seized, including utilities, sugar mills, banks, railroads, hotels, and factories. In mid-October, the United States imposes a trade embargo on Cuba. In the course of the year, a number of mass organizations are founded, including the militia, the Committees for the Defense of the Revolution (CDRs), the Federation of Cuban Women (FMC), the Association of Young Rebels (AJR), and the National Organization of Small Peasants (ANAP).

1961   In January the United States and Cuba sever diplomatic relations. In April the Bay of Pigs (Playa Girón) invasion fails, with some 1,200 expeditionaries taken prisoner.

The Cuban government proclaims the "Year of Education," inaugurating a national campaign to eliminate illiteracy.

1962	October 22–28: the Missile Crisis occurs.
1965	The PSP is reorganized as the Communist Party of Cuba (PCC).
1967	Ernesto Che Guevara is killed in Bolivia, thereby dealing Cuban advocacy of armed struggle (*foquismo*) a serious and irrevocable blow.
1968	Fidel Castro tacitly endorses the Soviet invasion of Czechoslovakia, announcing the beginning of Cuban reconciliation with the Soviet Union.
	The Cuban government launches the "revolutionary offensive," leading immediately to the nationalization of the remaining 57,000 small businesses and preparing for the Ten Million Ton Harvest of 1970.
1970	The sugar harvest totals 8.5 million tons, short of the much heralded and symbolic target of ten million tons. The economy falls into serious disarray.
1971	Poet Herberto Padilla is arrested and charged with writing counterrevolutionary literature.
1974	*Poder Popular* (People's Power) is inaugurated in Matanzas province, establishing local elections for municipal assemblies.
1975	The Family Code is promulgated, establishing a comprehensive body of law regulating family, marriage, and divorce.
	The First Party Congress convenes.
	Cuban combat troops participate in the Angolan war for national liberation against Portugal.
1976	The new socialist constitution is promulgated. The government is reorganized around a Council of Ministers headed by the president. The administrative units of the island are reorganized into fourteen new provinces: Pinar del Río, Havana, the City of Havana, Matanzas, Cienfuegos, Villa Clara, Sancti Spíritus, Ciego de Ávila, Cama-

	güey, Las Tunas, Holguín, Granma, Santiago, and Guantánamo.
1977	The United States and Cuba establish limited diplomatic relations by opening interest sections in Washington and Havana.
1978	Cuba inaugurates the family reunification program, whereby Cuban exiles are permitted to return to the island for brief family visits.
1979	At the sixth Non-Aligned Movement summit in Havana, Fidel Castro is elected president of the organization. The Soviet invasion of Afghanistan later in the year effectively neutralizes Cuban leadership of the Non-Aligned Movement.
1980	In April, some 11,000 Cubans seeking asylum storm the grounds of the Peruvian Embassy, initiating a process that will culminate in the Mariel exodus. By September 125,000 Cubans emigrate to the United States.
	The Second Party Congress is convened.
1983	The U.S. armed intervention in Grenada results in the capture and arrest of Cuban construction workers and soldiers.
1985	The United States inaugurates Radio Martí broadcasts to Cuba. Havana responds by suspending family visits to Cuba.
1986	Limited family travel to Cuba is reestablished. The Third Party Congress is held.
1987	Cuba and the United States sign a Migration Accord whereby Cuba agrees to accept the return of 2,000 "undesirables" who arrived during the 1980 Mariel boatlift. In return, the United States agrees to accept 20,000 new Cuban immigrants annually. News of accord sparks riots among Cuban inmates in U.S. detention centers.
1989	Cuban combat troops begin evacuation of Angola.

In July, General Arnaldo Ochoa, a popular leader of Cuban troops in Africa, is executed along with three others for alleged drug-running. The executions and the preceding trials produce the biggest political scandal on the island in decades and give rise to reports of serious internal disputes.

1990   The Soviet Union proposes new trade arrangements with Cuba on hard-currency basis at real market value.

The Soviet Union replaces the ruble with the dollar as the accounting unit.

The Cuban government announces a new series of austerity measures associated with the "Special Period."

1991   The Fourth Party Congress is convened.

1992   The U.S. Congress enacts the Torricelli bill, increasing trade sanctions against Cuba by prohibiting U.S. subsidiaries in third countries from trading with the island.

In the wake of the collapse of the Soviet Union and the socialist bloc, the Cuban government amends the constitution. It gives President Fidel Castro broad emergency powers. It emphasizes the establishment of new relationships with countries throughout Latin America. It allows greater freedom of religious expression and practice.

1993   The Cuban government legalizes dollar transactions and authorizes limited self-employment.

1994   A delegation of Cuban émigrés, including representatives of the opposition, hold a series of meetings in Havana with government leaders.

Havana and Washington sign an agreement whereby the United States authorizes the legal immigration of 20,000 individuals annually and in return Cuba pledges to control illegal immigration.

In March, the U.N. Human Rights Commission cites Cuba for its repressive practices.

On July 13, a Cuban coast guard vessel rams and sinks a tugboat loaded with would-be refugees trying to escape to the United States, leaving more than 30 dead. Several weeks later, on August 5, the worst riot in Havana since the overthrow of Batista erupts along the Malecón.

1995   In May, the United States reverses a decades-long policy of granting all Cubans intercepted at sea political asylum. Protests by the Cuban exile community fail to deter the Clinton Administration.

A report by the United Nations confirms that Cuba's gross domestic product has declined by 34.9 percent.

The Cuban National Assembly approves a new law that gives foreign investors more incentives to start new businesses in Cuba. It offers guarantees of investment protection and streamlined bureaucratic procedures.

1996   In February, Cuban MiGs shoot down two unarmed civilian planes belonging to the Cuban exile organization Brothers to the Rescue for allegedly violating Cuban airspace.

The incident paves the way for another confrontation with the United States. Just weeks later, President Clinton signs the Helms-Burton Act, tightening the U.S. embargo on Cuba by sanctioning foreign firms that make use of confiscated U.S. properties. The legislation codifies the economic embargo into law, bringing U.S.-Cuba relations to their lowest point in years.

1998   After years of negotiations, Pope John Paul II visits Cuba and holds a series of open-air masses. During the visit, the pope calls for an end to the United States embargo against Cuba and for greater religious freedom on the island.

1999–2000 In November 1999, six-year-old Elián González is saved by Florida fishermen after his mother and ten others die fleeing Cuba in a small boat. Florida relatives want the boy to receive political asylum, while his father in Cuba wants him returned. The custody battle ignites a fierce struggle between the Cuban government and Cuban exiles. U.S. federal courts and the Immigration and Naturalization Service ultimately rule in favor of the father, and the boy returns to Cuba in June 2000.

2001–2002 In the aftermath of the terrorist attacks on the World Trade Center and the Pentagon, President Castro voices his opposition to terrorism, although Cuba remains on the United States' list of terrorist nations. The Cuban government voices no objection to the imprisonment at the U.S. Naval Base in Guantánamo of Taliban and Al-Qaeda fighters captured in Afghanistan.

In May 2002 former U.S. president Jimmy Carter visits Cuba. During the visit he publicly calls for an end to the U.S. trade embargo and for democratic reforms on the island. The Proyecto Varela dissident group collects 11,000 signatures in a petition for democratic reforms.

Appendix 2

Columbus's Log

Sunday, the twenty-eighth day of October, 1492

He went from there in search of the nearest point in the island of Cuba to the south-south-west, and he entered a very lovely river, very free from danger of shoals or of other obstacles, and the water all along the coast, where he went, was very deep and clear up to the shore. The mouth of the river was twelve fathoms deep, and it is fully wide enough to beat about. He anchored, as he says, a lombard shot within it. The admiral says that he had never seem anything so beautiful. All the neighbourhood of the river was full of trees, lovely and green, and different from ours., each one with flowers and fruit after its kind; there were many birds and small birds, which sang very sweetly. There were a great number of palms, different from those of Guinea and from ours, of moderate height, and at their feet had no bark, and the leaves were very large; with them they cover their houses. The land is very flat. The admiral jumped into the boat and went to shore, and he came to two houses, which he believed to be those of fishermen, who fled in terror. In one of them he found a dog that never barked, and in both houses he found nets of palm fibre and cords and horn fish-hooks, and bone harpoons, and other fishing-tackle, and many fires in the houses. He believed that in

The Voyage of Christopher Columbus. Trans. Cecil Jane. London: The Argonaut Press, 1930.

each one of the houses many persons lived together. He commanded that none of these things should be touched, and so it was done. The vegetation was as abundant as in Andalusia in April and May. He found much purslane and wild amaranth. He returned to the boat sand went to see a good distance up the river, and it was, as he says, so great a joy to see that verdure and the trees and to hear the singing of the birds that he could not leave it all to return. He says that the island is the most lovely that eyes have ever seen; it is full of good harbours and deep rivers, and it seems that the sea can never be stormy, for the vegetation on the shore runs down almost to the water, which it does not generally do where the sea is rough. Up to that time, he had not experiences a high sea among all those islands. He says that the island is full of very beautiful mountains, although there are no very long ranges, but they are lofty, and the rest of the land is high like Sicily. It is full of many waters, as he was able to gather form the Indians whom he carried with him and whom he had taken in the island of Guanahani; they told him by signs that there are ten large rivers, and that they cannot do round it in their canoes in twenty days. When he went near the shore with the ships, tow boats or canoes came out, and as they saw that the sailors entered the boat and rowed about in order to see the depth of the river, to know where they should anchor, the canoes fled. The Indians said that in the island there are mines of gold, and that there are pearls; the admiral saw that the place was suited for them, and that there were mussels, which are an indication of them. And the admiral understood that there come the ships of the Grand Khan, and that they are large; and that from there to the mainland it is ten days' journey. The admiral called that river and harbour *San Salvador*.

Monday, 29 October

He weighed anchor from that harbour and navigated to the west, in order, as he says, to go to the city where he thought that the Indians told him the king resided. One point of the island ran out six leagues to the north-west; from there another point ran out to the east ten leagues. He went another league, and saw a river with a smaller mouth, to which he gave the name *Rio de la Luna*. He went on until the hour of vespers. He saw another river, larger than the former, and so the Indians told him by signs, and near it he saw fair villages of houses. He called the river the *Rio de Mares*. He sent two boats to a village to have speech, and in one of them an Indian of those he carried with him, because by now they understood something and showed themselves to be well pleased with the Christians. All, men, women and children, fled from these houses, abandoning them with all that they had, and the admiral commanded that nothing should be touched. The houses, so he says, were quite the most lovely that they had seen, and he believed that the nearer they came to the mainland, the better they would be. They were made in the manner of tents, very large, and they looked like the tents in a camp, with no regular streets, but one here and another there. Inside, they were well swept and clean, and their furnishing very well arranged; all were made of very beautiful palm branches. They found many images made like women and many heads like masks, very well worked. He did not know if they had them for their beauty or whether they worship them. There were dogs that never bark; they were wild birds, tamed, in their houses; there were wonderful outfits of nets and hooks and fishing-tackle. They did not touch one of these things. He believed that all those on the coast must be fishermen who carry the fish inland, for that island is very large and so lovely, that he is never weary of speaking well of it. He says that there he found trees and fruit with a very wonderful taste, and he says that there

should be in it cows and other herds, since he saw skulls which seemed to be those of cows. There are birds, large and small, and the chirping of the crickets went on all night, at which all were delighted; the air all night was scented and sweet, and neither cold nor hot. And further, on the voyage from the other islands to that island, he says that there was great heat, and that in this island there was not, but it was as temperate as May. He attributes the heat of the other islands to the fact that they are very flat and that the wind there blows from the south and is thus warm. The water of those rivers was salt at the mouth; they did not know where the Indians found drinking water, although they had fresh water in their houses. In this river the ships could turn to go in and go out, and they have very good signs or landmarks. The water was seven or eight fathoms deep at the mouth and five within. All that sea, as he says, seems to him to be always as calm as the river of Seville, and the water suited for the cultivation of pearls. He found large periwinkles, tasteless and not like those of Spain. He described the character of the river and the harbour, which he mentioned above and which he named *San Salvador,* as having lovely mountains near and lofty as la Peña de los Enamorados. One of them has on its summit another peak, like a beautiful mosque. There is another river and harbour, in which he then was, having on the south-east side two quite round mountains and on the west-north-west side a lovely flat cape which projects outwards.

Tuesday, 30 October

He went from the Rio de Mares to the north-west and saw a cape full of palms, and he named it *Cape de Palmas*. After having gone fifteen leagues, the Indians who were in the caravel *Pinta* said that behind that cape there was a river, and that from the river to Cuba it was four days' journey. The captain of the *Pinta* said that he understood that this Cuba was a city, and that land was a very extensive mainland which stretched far to the north, and that the king of that land was at war with the Grand Khan, whom they called "cami," and his land or city they called "Saba" and by many other names. The admiral resolved to go to that river and to send a present to the king of the land, and to send to him the letter of the sovereigns. For this purpose he had a sailor who had gone to Guinea in the same way, and certain Indians from Guanahani who were ready to go with him, on condition that afterwards they might return to their own land. In the opinion of the admiral, he was distant from the equinoctial line forty-two degrees to the north, if the text from which I have copied this is not corrupt; and he says that he must attempt to go to the Grand Khan, for he thought that he was in that neighbourhood, or to the city of Catayo, which belongs to the Grand Khan, which, as he says, is very large, as he was told before he set out from Spain. He says that all this land is low-lying and lovely, and the sea deep.

Wednesday, 31 October

All night Tuesday, he was beating about, and he saw a river where he could not enter because the mouth was shallow, and the Indians thought that the ships could enter as their canoes entered it. And navigating farther on, he found a cape which jutted very far out and was surrounded by shallows, and he saw an inlet or bay, where small vessels might enter, and he could not make it, because the wind had shifted due north and all the coast ran north-north-west and south-east. Another cape, which he saw, jutted still farther out. For this reason and because the sky showed that it would blow hard, he had to return to the Rio de Mares.

Thursday, 1 November

At sunrise, the admiral sent the boats to land, to the houses which were there, and they found that all the people had fled, and after some time a man appeared, and the admiral ordered that he should be allowed to become reassured, and they went back to the boats. After eating, he proceeded to send ashore one of the Indians whom he carried with him and who, from a distance, called out to them, saying that they should not be afraid, because these were a good people and did harm to no one, and were not from the Grand Khan, but in many islands to which they had been, had given of that which they possessed. And the Indian threw himself into the water and swam ashore, and two of those who were there took him by the arms and brought him to a house, where they questioned him. And when they were certain that no harm would be done to them, they were reassured, and presently there came to the ships more than sixteen boats or canoes, with spun cotton and their other trifles, of which the admiral commanded that nothing should be taken, in order that they might know that the admiral sought nothing except gold, which they call "nucay." So all day they were going and coming from the land to the ships, and they went to and fro from the Christians to the shore with great confidence. The admiral did not see any gold among them. But the admiral says that he saw on one of them a piece of worked silver, hanging from the nose, which he took to be an indication that there was silver in the land. They said by signs that within three days many merchants would come from the interior to buy the things which the Christians brought there, and that they would give news of the king of that land, who, as far as he could understand from the signs which they made, was four days' journey from there, because they had sent many men through the whole land to tell of the admiral. "These people," says the admiral, "are of the same character and have the same customs as the others who have been found, having no creed that I know, since up to this moment I have not seen those whom I carry with me offer any prayer, but they say the *Salve* and the *Ave Maria* with their hands raised to heaven as they are shown, and they make the sign of the cross. There is, moreover, one language for them all, and they are all friends, and I believe that all these islands are so and that they are at war with the Grand Khan, whom they call 'cavila,' and his province 'Basan'; and they all go naked also like the others." This the admiral says. He says that the river is very deep and at its mouth they could bring the ships alongside the land. The fresh water does not come within a league of the mouth and it is very sweet, and "It is certain," says the admiral, "that this is the mainland, and that I am," he says, "before Zayto and Quisay, a hundred leagues, a little more or less, distant from one and the other, and this appears clearly from the sea, which is of a different character from that which it has hitherto been here, and yesterday, going to the north-west, I found that it was becoming cold."

Appendix 3

The Conquest of Cuba

The following excerpt relates the cruel treatment of the Amerindians on the island of Cuba by the conquering Spaniards. The story of the death of the Cacique Hatuey is included in the account. His defiance of the Spaniards would convert him into a national symbol long after his death.

In the year one thousand five hundred and eleven, the Spaniards passed over to the island of Cuba, which as I have said is at the same distance from Hispaniola as the distance between Valladolid and Rome, and which was a well-populated province. They began and ended in Cuba as they had done elsewhere, but with much greater acts of cruelty.

Among the noteworthy outrages they committed was the one they perpetrated against a cacique, a very important noble, by name Hatuey, who had come to Cuba from Hispaniola with many of his people, to flee the calamities and inhuman acts of the Christians. When he was told by certain Indians that the Christians were now coming to Cuba, he assembled as many of his followers as he could and said this to them: "Now you must know that they are saying the Christians are coming here, and you know by experience how they have put So and So and So and So, and other nobles to an end.

And now they are coming from Haiti (which is Hispaniola) to do the same here. Do you know why they do this?" The Indians replied: "We do not know. But it may be that they are by nature wicked and cruel." And he told them: "No, they do not act only because of that, but because they have a God they greatly worship and they want us to worship that God, and that is why they struggle with us and subject us and kill us."

He had a basket full of gold and jewels and he said: "You see their God here, the God of the Christians. If you agree to it, let us dance for this God, who knows, it may please the God of the Christians and then they will do us no harm." And his followers said, all together, "Yes, that is good, that is good!" And they danced round the basket of gold until they fell down exhausted. Then their chief, the cacique Hatuey, said to them: "See here, if we keep this basket of gold they will take it from us and will end up by killing us. So let us cast away the basket into the river." They all agreed to do this, and they flung the basket of gold into the river that was nearby.

This cacique, Hatuey, was constantly fleeing before the Christians from the time they arrived on the island of Cuba, since he knew them and of what they were capable. Now and then they encountered him and he defended himself, but they finally killed him. And they did this for the sole reason that he had fled from those cruel and wicked Christians and had defended himself against them. And when they

Source: Taken from Bartolomé de las Casas. Translated from the Spanish by Herma Briffault. *The Devastation of the Indies: A Brief Account*. New York: Seabury Press, 1974.

had captured him and as many of his followers as they could, they burned them all at the stake.

When tied to the stake, the cacique Hatuey was told by a Franciscan friar who was present, an artless rascal, something about the God of the Christians and of the articles of the Faith. And he was told what he could do in the brief time that remained to him, in order to be saved and go to Heaven. The cacique, who had never heard any of this before, and was told he would go to Inferno where, if he did not adopt the Christian Faith, he would suffer eternal torment, asked the Franciscan friar if Christians all went to Heaven. When told that they did he said he would prefer to go to Hell. Such is the fame and honor that God and our Faith have earned through the Christians who have gone out to the Indies.

On one occasion when we went to claim ten leagues of a big settlement, along with food and maintenance, we were welcomed with a bounteous quantity of fish and bread and cooked victuals. The Indians generously gave us all they could. Then suddenly, without cause and without warning, and in my presence, the devil inhabited the Christians and spurred them to attack the Indians, men, women, and children, who were sitting there before us. In the massacre that followed, the Spaniards put to the sword more than three thousand souls. I saw such terrible cruelties done there as I had never seen before nor thought to see.

A few days later, knowing that news of this massacre had spread through the land, I sent messengers ahead to the chiefs of the province of Havana, knowing they had heard good things about me, telling them we were about to visit the town and telling them they should not hide but should come out to meet us, assuring them that no harm would be done to them. I did this with the full knowledge of the captain. And when we arrived in the province, there came out to welcome us twenty-one chiefs and caciques, and our captain, breaking his pledge to me and the pledge I had made to them, took all these chieftains captive, intending to burn them at the stake, telling me this would be a good thing because those chiefs had in the past done him some harm. I had great difficulty in saving those Indians from the fire, but finally succeeded.

Afterward, when all the Indians of this island were subjected to servitude and the same ruin had befallen there as on the island Hispaniola, the survivors began to flee to the mountains or in despair to hang themselves, and there were husbands and wives who hanged themselves together with their children, because the cruelties perpetrated by one very great Spaniard (whom I knew) were so horrifying. More than two hundred Indians hanged themselves. And thus perished a countless number of people on the island of Cuba.

That tyrant Spaniard, representative of the King of Spain, demanded, in the *repartimiento*, that he be given three hundred Indians. At the end of three months all but thirty of them had died of the hard labor in the mines, which is to say only a tenth of them had survived. He demanded another allocation of Indians, and they also perished in the same way. He demanded still another large allocation, and those Indians also perished. Then he died, and the devil bore him away.

In three or four months, when I was there, more than seventy thousand children, whose fathers and mothers had been sent to the mines, died of hunger.

And I saw other frightful things. The Spaniards finally decided to track down the Indians who had taken refuge in the mountains. There they created amazing havoc and thus finished ravaging the island. Where had been a flourishing population, it is now a shame and pity to see the island laid waste and turned into a desert.

Appendix 4

Colonial Governors (1511–1898)

1511–1524	Diego Velázquez de Cuéllar
1524–1526	Juan Altamirano
1526–1531	Gonzalo de Guzmán
1531–1532	Juan de Vadillo
1532–1535	Manuel de Rojas
1535–1538	Gonzalo de Guzmán
1538–1544	Hemán de Soto
1544–1546	Juan de Ávila
1546–1548	Antonio de Cháves
1549–1555	Gonzalo Pérez de Angulo
1556–1565	Diego de Mazariegos
1565–1567	Francisco García Osorio
1567–1574	Pedro Menéndez de Avilés
1575–1577	Gabriel Montalvo
1577–1579	Francisco Carreño
1579–1584	Gaspar de Torres
1584–1589	Gabriel de Luján
1589–1593	Juan de Tejeda
1593–1602	Juan Maldonaldo Barnuevo
1602–1608	Pedro Valdés
1608–1616	Gaspar Ruíz de Pereda
1616–1619	Sancho de Alquiza
1620–1624	Francisco de Venegas

1624–1626	Damián Velázquez de Contreras
1626–1630	Lorenzo de Cabrera y Corbera
1630–1634	Juan Bitrián de Viamonte y Navarra
1634–1639	Francisco Riaño y Gamboa
1639–1647	Álvaro de Luna y Sarmiento
1647–1653	Diego de Villalba y Toledo, Marqués de Campo
1653–1654	Francisco Jedler (or Xelder)
1654–1656	Juan de Montanos Blázquez
1656–1658	Diego Rangel
1658–1663	Juan de Salamanca
1663–1664	Rodrigo de Flores y Aldama
1664–1670	Francisco Oregón y Gascón
1670–1680	Francisco Rodríguez de Ledesma
1680–1685	José Fernández Córdoba Ponce de León
1685–1687	Manuel de Murguia y Mena
1687–1689	Diego Antonio de Viana e Hinojosa
1689–1697	Severino de Manzaneda Salinas y Rozas
1697–1702	Diego de Córdoba Laso de la Vega
1702–1705	Pedro Nicolás Benítez de Lugo
1705–1706	Luis Chirino Vandevall

Source: Adapted from David P. Henige, *Colonial Governors from the Fifteenth Century to the Present*. Madison: University of Wisconsin Press, 1970.

1706–1708	Pedro Álvarez de Villamartín	1819–1821	Juan Manuel de Cagigal y Martínez Niño
1708–1716	Laureano José de Torres y Ayala, Marqués de Casa Torres	1821–1822	Nicolás Mahy y Romo
1716–1717	Vicente Raja	1822–1823	Sebastián Kindelán y Oregón
1717–1724	Gregorio Guazo y Fernández de la Vega	1823–1832	Francisco Dionisio Vives
1724–1734	Dionisio Martínez de la Vega	1832–1834	Mariano Ricafort Palacín y Abarca
1734–1746	Juan Francisco de Güermes y Horcasitas, Conde de Revillagigedo	1834–1838	Miguel Tacón y Rosique, Marqués de la Unión de Cuba
1746	Juan Antonio Tinéo y Fuertes	1838–1840	Joaquín de Ezpeleta y Enrille
1746–1747	Diego Peñalosa	1840–1841	Pedro Téllez y Girón
1747–1760	Francisco Antonio Cagigal de la Vega	1841–1843	Gerónimo Valdés y Sierra
1760–1761	Pedro Alonso	1843–1848	Leopoldo O'Donnell y Jorris
1761–1762	Juan de Prado Mayeza Portocarrero y Luna	1848–1850	Federico Roncali Ceruti, Conde de Alcoy
1763–1765	Ambrosio Funes Villalpando, Conde de Ricla	1850–1852	José Gutiérrez de la Concha e Irigoyen
1765–1766	Diego Manrique	1852–1853	Valentín Cañedo Miranda
1766–1771	Antonio María de Bucareli y Ursúa	1853–1854	Juan Manuel la Pezuela y Cabello Sánchez
1771–1777	Felipe de Fondesviela, Marqués de la Torre	1854–1859	José Gutiérrez de la Concha e Irigoyen, Marqués de La Habana
1777–1780	Diego José Navarro y García de Valladares	1859–1862	Francisco Serrano y Domínguez, Duque de la Torre
1781–1782	Juan Manuel de Cagigal y Montserrat de la Vega y Adames	1862–1866	Domingo Dulce Guerrero, Marqués de Castell Florit
1782–1785	Luis Unzaga y Amezaga	1866–1867	Francisco Lersundi y Ormaechea
1785	Bemardo Vicente Pólinarde de Gálvez y Galardo	1867	Joaquín del Manzano y Manzano
1785–1789	José Manuel Ignacio Timoteo de Ezpeleta	1867	Blas Villate y de La Hara, Conde de Valmaseda
1789–1790	Domingo Cabello y Robles	1867–1869	Francisco Lersundi y Ormaechea
1790–1796	Luis de las Casas y Aragorri	1869	Domingo Dulce Guerrero, Marqués de Castell Florit
1796–1799	Juan Procopio Bassecourt y Bryas, Conde de Santa Clara	1869	Felipe Ginovés del Espinar
1799–1812	Salvador de Muro y Salazar, Marqués de Someruelos	1869–1870	Antonio Caballero Fernández de Rodas
1812–1816	Juan Ruíz de Apodaca y Eliza López de Letona y Lasquetty	1870–1872	Blas Villate y de la Hara, Conde de Valmaseda
1816–1819	José Cienfuegos y Jovellanos	1872–1873	Francisco Ceballos y Vargas
1819	Juan María Echéverri	1873	Cándido Pieltaín y Jove-Huelgo

1873–1874	Joaquín Jovellar y Soler
1874–1875	José Gutiérrez de la Concha e Irigoyen, Marqués de La Habana
1875–1876	Blas Villate y de la Hara, Conde de Valmaseda
1876–1878	Joaquín Jovellar y Soler
1878–1879	Arnseio Martínez Campos
1879	Cayetano Figueroa y Garaondo
1879–1881	Ramón Blanco y Erenas, Marqués de Peña Plata
1881–1883	Luis Prendergast y Gordón, Marqués de Victoria de Las Tunas
1883–1884	Ignacio María del Castillo y Gil de la Torre, Conde de Bilbao
1884–1886	Ramón Fajardo e Izquierdo
1886–1887	Emilio Calleja e Isasi
1887–1889	Sabas Marín y González
1889–1890	Manuel Salamanca y Negrete
1890	José Sánchez Gómez
1890–1892	Camilo Polavieja y del Castillo
1892–1893	Alejandro Rodríguez Arias
1893	José Arderius y García
1893–1895	Emilio Calleja e Isasi
1895–1896	Arsenio Martínez Campos
1896	Sabas Marín y González
1896–1897	Valeriano Weyler y Nicolau, Marqués de Tenerife
1897–1898	Ramón Blanco y Erenas, Marqués de Peña Plata
1898	Adolfo Jiménez Castellanos

Appendix 5

Royal Decree Granting Absolute Powers to the Captain-General of Cuba (1825)*

This royal decree of May 28, 1825, was granted to the Captain-General of Cuba to provide him and his successors with extraordinary powers to rule over the island's inhabitants. It was produced in the immediate aftermath of the loss of Spain's continental colonies of the New World. As a result, Cuba's highest colonial authorities began to rule the island despotically and capriciously.

Your Highness, having been well persuaded that at no time and under no circumstances Your Excellency's right principles and love toward your monarch will be weakened, and at the same time Your Highness wanting to avoid any inconveniences that may result in extraordinary cases, in the division of jurisdictions and confusions of prerogatives of various positions, for the important end of keeping his legitimate sovereign authority over that precious Island and preserving public peace, has decided, following the decision of his Council of Ministers, to authorize Your Excellency granting him the full faculties that royal ordinances grant to governors of sieged posts. Consequently Your Highness grants Your Excellency ample and unlimited au-

thorization, not only to remove from that Island and send to the Peninsula any employees, no matter what class, rank or condition, whose permanence in said Island be deemed prejudicial or whose public or private conduct cause you discomfort, replacing them momentarily with servants faithful to Your Highness and who deserve Your Excellency's full confidence, but also to suspend the execution of any orders or general legislation in any of the branches of administration that Your Excellency considers convenient to royal service, all of these measures being provisional and Your Excellency always notifying Your Highness for his sovereign approval. Your Highness when granting to Your Excellency this clear token of his appreciation and sign of the high trust that he has on your strong loyalty, expects that in correspondence, you will use it with utmost prudence and circumscription, as you increase your vigilance so that laws be observed, justice be administered, faithful vassals of Your Highness be protected and rewarded, and without contemplation or disguise punish those who neglecting their obligations oppose their sovereigns through sinister machinations against the laws and regulations that stem from them. This Royal Order is communicated to Your Excellency for your knowledge. May God. . . .

Madrid. . . . To the Captain-General of the Island of Cuba.

* Translated by Luis Martínez-Fernández.

Appendix 6

The Slave Code of 1842

In response to a series of slave uprisings, tighter restrictions were placed on the slave population. The Slave Code of 1842 did little to deter new revolts, which increased in the following years and led to ever greater acts of repression.

1. Every slaveholder shall instruct his slaves in the principles of the Holy Roman Catholic Apostolic Religion so that those who have not been baptized may be baptized, and in case of the danger of death, he shall baptize them, since it is known that in such cases anyone is authorized to do so.

2. The aforesaid instruction shall be given at night at the end of work, and immediately afterwards the slave shall recite the rosary or some other devout prayers.

3. On Sundays and feast days of obligation after fulfilling their religious obligations, slaveholders or those in charge of the estates shall employ the slaves for two hours to clean the houses and workshops, but no longer, nor occupy them in the labors of the landed property, except in harvest time when delay is impossible. In such cases they shall work the same as on week days.

Source: Taken from Robert L. Paquette, *Sugar Is Made with Blood*. Middletown, CT: Wesleyan University Press, 1988. Translated from the *Bando de gobernación policía de la isla de Cuba . . .* (Havana, 1844), 59–68.

4. [Slaveholders] shall heed their responsibility to those slaves already baptized who have arrived at the proper age to administer the sacraments to them, whenever the Holy Mother Church requires it or whenever *it* may be necessary.

5. [Slaveholders] shall put forth the greatest attention and diligence possible in making them [the slaves] understand the obedience that they owe to the constituted authorities, the obligation to show reverence to the clergy, to respect white persons, to behave well with the people of color, and to live harmoniously with their companions.

6. Masters shall necessarily give their slaves in the country two or three meals a day as they may think best, provided that they may be sufficient to maintain them and restore them from their fatigues, keeping in mind that six or eight plantains or its equivalent in sweet potatoes, yams, yuccas, and other edible roots, eight ounces of meat or salt fish, four ounces of rice or other pottage or meal is standardized as daily food and of absolute necessity for each individual.

7. [Masters] shall give them two suits of clothes a year in the months of December and May, each consisting of a shirt and pants of nankin or linen, a cap or hat, and handkerchief; in December shall be added alternatively a flannel shirt one year and a blanket for protection during the winter the next.

8. Newly-born or small slave children, whose mothers are sent to work in the field,

shall be fed very light food such as soups, *atoles* [a pap made from corn flour], milk, and similar substances until they are weaned entirely and have finished teething.

9. While the mothers are at work, all children shall remain in a house or room that all sugar estates and coffee estates should have, which shall be under the care of one or more female slaves, as the master or administrator may deem necessary, according to the number of children.

10. If [slave children] shall become sick during the lactation period, they shall be nursed by the breasts of their own mothers, who shall be exempted from fieldwork and applied to domestic duties.

11. Until they reach the age of three years, [slave children] shall have shirts of striped gingham; from age three to six they may be of nankin. The girls of six to ten shall be given skirts or long dresses, and the boys of six to fourteen shall be provided with trousers. After these ages the dress shall be like the adults.

12. In ordinary times slaves shall work nine or ten hours daily, the master arranging these hours as best he can. On sugar plantations during harvest time, the hours shall be sixteen, arranged in such a way that the slave shall have two hours in the day to rest and six at night to sleep.

13. On Sundays and on feast days of obligation and in the hours of rest during the week days, slaves shall be permitted to employ themselves within the estate in mechanical labors or occupations, the product of which shall be for their own benefit in order to be able to acquire the means to purchase their freedom.

14. Male and female slaves older than sixty years or less than seventeen shall not be obliged to do strenuous work, nor shall any of these classes be employed in work not appropriate to their age, sex, strength, and constitution.

15. Those slaves who because of their age or because of sickness are not fit for work shall be maintained by their owners, who shall not be permitted to give them their freedom in order to get rid of them, unless they provide them with sufficient means, according to the dictates of justice and the determination of the *procu-*

rador síndico, so that they may be able to support themselves without need of other assistance.

16. Every estate shall have a depository reserved for the placement of the instruments of labor, the key of which shall never be entrusted to a slave.

17. On leaving for work each slave shall be given the instrument he needs for the labor of the day, and later, as he returns, it will be taken from him and locked up in the depository.

18. No slave shall leave the property with any instrument of labor, much less arms of any kind, unless accompanied by his master or overseer or the family of either, in which case he may carry his machete and nothing more.

19. Slaves of one estate shall not be able to visit those of another without the express consent of the masters or overseers of both. When they have to go to another estate or leave their own, they shall take a written pass from the owner or overseer with the description of the slave, the date of the day, month, and year, the declaration of his destination, and the time he must return.

20. Any individual of whatever class, color, and condition he may be is authorized to arrest any slave if he is met outside of the house or lands of his master; if he does not present the written license he is obliged to carry; or if, on the presentation, it shows that the bearer has manifestly changed the route or direction described or the leave of absence has expired. The individual shall conduct said slave to the nearest estate, whose owner shall receive him and secure him and notify the slave's master, should he be from the same district, or the *pedaneo* [district magistrate], so that he may give notice to the interested party in order that the fugitive slave may be recovered by the person to whom he belongs.

21. Owners and overseers of the plantations shall not receive any remuneration for the fugitive slaves that they shall apprehend or deliver according to the aforesaid article, since it is a service that the proprietors are reciprocally obliged to loan and redounds to their private advantage.

22. The master shall have to pay, besides the cost of food, the cost of medical treatment,

should it be necessary, and all other costs, as expressed in the same fugitive slave law.

23. Masters shall permit their slaves modest amusement and recreation on festival days after they [the slaves] have complied with their religious obligations, but without leaving the plantation or joining with slaves of any others. They shall make do in open places and in full view of their owners, overseers or foremen, until sunset or until the bell rings for evening prayer and no longer.

24. Owners and overseers shall be charged particularly to watch vigilantly in order to restrain excessive drinking [among the slaves] and the introduction of slaves from another estate and free men of color into the amusements.

25. Masters shall take great care to construct for unmarried slaves spacious dwellings in a dry and ventilated area, with separation of the two sexes, well closed and secured with key, in which a light shall be kept burning all night. Where means permit, they shall have a separate dwelling for each married couple.

26. At the sleeping hour (which in a long night shall be at eight and in a short one at nine) the slaves' roll shall be called so that only the watchmen shall remain outside, one of which shall be appointed to see to it that everyone keeps silent and to inform the master or overseer of any disturbance on the part of his companions, of any intruders, or of any other important occurrence.

27. On each plantation there shall be a room well-closed and secured for each sex and two others besides for contagious diseases where slaves who may fall sick shall be attended in severe cases by physicians and in slight cases, where household remedies are sufficient, by male or female nurses, but always with good medicine, proper food, and with the greatest cleanliness.

28. The sick shall be placed, where it is possible, in separate beds that consist of a straw mattress, mat, or *petate* [a mat made of palm leaves], pillow, blanket, and sheet, or on boards sufficiently convenient for the healing of individuals that lie on them, but in all cases raised from the floor.

29. Masters of slaves shall avoid the illicit contact of both sexes and encourage marriages.

They shall not prevent marriages made with slaves of other owners, and they shall give to married couples the means of living under the same roof.

30. To accomplish this end and so that the consorts may fulfill the ends of matrimony, the wife shall follow the husband whose master shall buy her at a price that may be suitable to both sides or else by arbiters appointed by both sides or by a third party in case of disagreement. If the master of the husband does not want to buy the wife, then her owner shall have the power to buy the husband. In the event that neither of the owners want to make the purchase, then the married slaves shall be sold together to a third party.

31. When the master of the married male slave buys the wife, he shall also buy all her children under three years old, since according to law the mothers are obliged to suckle and nurse them until they attain that age.

32. Masters shall be obliged by the magistrates to sell their slaves when they have injured them, badly treated them, or committed other excesses contrary to humanity and the rational way with which they should be treated. The sale shall be made in these cases at the price fixed by the arbiters of both sides, or by a magistrate in case one of these should refuse to name a price, or by a third person in case of disagreement, when it may be necessary. But if there is a buyer who wants to purchase them without arbitration at the price fixed by the master, then the sale shall be made in his favor.

33. When masters sell their slaves for their own convenience or at their own determination, they shall be at liberty to fix any price that pleases them, according to the greater or lesser estimation of them.

34. No master shall oppose the *coartación* of his slaves if they present at least fifty pesos of their price on account.

35. Slaves *coartados* shall not be sold for a higher price than that fixed in the last *coartación*, and this condition shall pass from buyer to buyer. However, if the slave desires to be sold against the will of his master without just cause or by his bad conduct gives cause to be sold, the master may add to the price the amount of the sales tax and the cost of the deed of sale.

36. As the benefit of *coartación* is very personal, the children of the mothers *coartadas* cannot be participants in it, and they can be sold like any other slave.

37. Masters shall free their slaves as soon as they put together the amount of their evaluation as legitimately fixed. The price, in case the interested parties do not agree, shall be named by an arbiter appointed by the owner of the slave or in his absence by a magistrate, another by the *procurador síndico* representing the slave, and a third chosen by said magistrate in case of disagreement.

38. The slave who may discover any conspiracy plotted by another of his class or by any persons of free condition to disturb the public order shall receive his freedom and besides a reward of five hundred pesos.

If the informers should be many and present themselves in such a way as to show that the last ones did not know that the disclosure had already been made, then all such informers shall receive their freedom, and the reward of five hundred pesos shall be divided equally among them.

When the denunciation makes reference to a conspiracy of slaves or to the project of some cunning slave or free man against the owner, his wife, children, relations, the administrator, or overseer on the estate, owners are recommended to be generous with the servant or servants who have so well fulfilled the duties of a good and faithful servant, as it is much to their advantage to offer an encouragement to loyalty.

39. The price of freedom and the reward referred to in the first paragraph of the previous article shall be taken from the fund that results from fines imposed by infractions of this law or any others ordered by the government.

40. Slaves shall also acquire their freedom when it is granted them in a will or by any other legally justified means that proceeds from an honest and praiseworthy motive.

41. Slaves shall be obliged to obey and respect their owners, administrators, overseers, and all other superiors as heads of the family and to fulfill the tasks and works given them. He that shall fail in any of these obligations shall be and ought to be punished by whomever is in charge of the plantation according to the type of failing or transgression, with impris-onment, shackles, cudgel, or stocks, which shall confine by the feet and never the head, or with flogging, which must never exceed twenty-five lashes.

42. When a slave shall commit grave excesses or some crime for which the penalties referred to in the previous article may not be sufficient, he shall be bound and presented before the magistrate so that in the presence of his master, should he not give him up to justice, or before the *procurador síndico*, should he give him up and choose not to continue the proceedings, [the slave] may be proceeded against according to law. In case the owner did not relinquish or submit the slave to justice, and he is condemned to the payment of damages and costs toward a third party, the owner shall be responsible for the same, which will not exempt the slave from bodily punishment or another type as the crime may merit.

43. Only owners, administrators, or overseers shall be able to punish slaves, with the moderation and under the penalties aforesaid. Any other person who may do so without the express mandate of the owner or against his will and cause any wound or injury shall become liable under the penalties established by the laws. The case may be opened at the instance of the owner or in his absence at the instance of the *procurador síndico*, as the protector of slaves, unless the transgression should be such as to affect the public good, or, officially, if it should pertain to this last category.

44. The owner in charge or his subordinate on the estate who may disobey or infringe any of these rules shall be fined twenty to fifty pesos the first time, from forty to one hundred pesos the second time, and from eighty to two hundred pesos the third time, according to the greater or lesser importance of the infringed article.

45. Fines shall be paid by the owner of the estate or person who has been guilty of the negligence or infraction. In case he is not able to pay because of lack of funds, he shall suffer a day in jail for each peso that he has been fined.

46. If the offense of the owners or those encharged to manage slavery on the estates should consist of the excessive use of punishment causing slaves grave contusions, wounds,

or mutilation of limbs, or other serious injury, besides the monetary fines already cited, the person who may have caused the injury shall be prosecuted criminally at the instance of the *procurador síndico*, or officially, so as to impose on him the penalty commensurate with the crimes committed. The owner shall be obliged to sell the slave, if he is still able to work, or to give him his freedom, if he is disabled, and to pay him during his lifetime a daily stipend which the magistrate shall determine sufficient for his food and clothing, payable monthly in advance.

47. Fines shall be applied in this manner: a third part of their amount to the magistrate or judge who imposes them and the remaining two-thirds to the fund that is to be formed in the political administration of each district for the cases named in article thirty-eight, to be delivered under receipt, to the secretary's office at that administration.

48. The lieutenant-governors, magistrates, and *pedaneos* shall see to the punctual observance of these regulations and shall be inevitably responsible for any omissions or excesses.

Appendix 7

The Constitution
of Guáimaro (1869)*

This is Cuba's first constitution. It was drafted and ratified by representatives to the Assembly of Guáimaro in 1869 and remained in effect in insurgent-controlled territories during the rest of the Ten Years' War.

Art. 1. Legislative power shall reside in a Chamber of Representatives.

Art. 2. Each of the four states in which the island is now divided shall have equal representation in the Chamber of Representatives.

Art. 3. These states are: Oriente, Camagüey, Las Villas, and Ocidente.

Art. 4. Only those citizens of the Republic who are twenty years of age or older can serve as Representatives.

Art. 5. The position of Representative is incompatible with any other appointment within the Republic.

Art. 6. In the case of vacancies in the representation of any state, that state's executive shall dictate the necessary measures for a new election.

Art. 7. The Chamber of Representatives will name the President in charge of the Executive Power, the Commanding General, the sessions' presiding officer, and the rest of its employees.

The Commanding General is subordinated to the Executive and shall give accounts of his operations.

Art. 8. The Chamber of Representatives shall hear any accusations raised against the President of the Republic, the Commanding General, and members of the Chamber. Any citizen may file accusations; If the Chamber finds probable cause, it will be sent to the Judicial Power.

Art. 9. The Chamber of Representatives may remove any functionary under its jurisdiction.

Art. 10. The legislative decisions of the Chamber require the President's approval to be valid.

Art. 11. If these do not receive this approval, they will return immediately to the Chamber for further deliberations, in which the President's objections shall be taken into account.

Art. 12. The President must, within ten days, approve or reject all bills.

Art. 13. If the Chamber of Representatives votes in favor of a bill a second time, the President must approve that legislation.

Art. 14. The following matters must be legislated upon: taxation, public loans, ratification of treaties, the declaration and cessation of war, the President's authority to grant corsair licenses, the arming of troops, the arming of a Navy, and the declaration of penalties against the enemy.

---

* Translated by Luis Martínez-Fernández.

Art. 15. The Chamber of Representatives shall stand in permanent session upon the ratification of this constitution and until the cessation of the war.

Art. 16. The Executive Power shall rest upon the President of the Republic.

Art. 17. The President shall be at least thirty years old and a native of the Island of Cuba.

Art. 18. The President has the power to negotiate treaties with the ratification of the Chamber.

Art. 19. The President will name the ambassadors, ministers, and consuls of the Republic serving in foreign countries.

Art. 20. The President will receive ambassadors, will see that the laws are enforced, and will appoint all the employees of the Republic.

Art. 21. The secretaries of the ministries will be appointed by the Chamber upon the recommendation of the President.

Art. 22. The Judicial Power is independent and its organization will result from special legislation.

Art. 23. The requirements for voting are the same as those for being elected.

Art. 24. All the inhabitants of the Republic are fully free.

Art. 25. All of the citizens of the Republic are deemed soldiers of the Liberating Army.

Art. 26. The Republic does not recognize titles, special honors, nor privileges.

Art. 27. The citizens of the Republic may not accept honors or distinctions from a foreign country.

Art. 28. The Chamber may not restrict the freedoms of worship, press, peaceful gathering, teaching and petition, nor any other inalienable right of the People.

Art. 29. This Constitution may be amended only with a unanimous determination of the Chamber.

This Constitution was voted on in the free town of Guáimaro, on April 10, 1869, by Citizen Carlos Manuel de Céspedes, President of the Constitutional Assembly, and Citizen Deputies Salvador Cisneros Betancourt, Francisco Sánchez, Miguel Betancourt Guerra, Ignacio Agramonte Loynaz, Antonio Zambrana, Jesús Rodríguez, Antonio Alcalá, José Izaguirre, Honorato Castillo, Miguel Gerónimo Gutiérrez, Arcadio García, Tranquilino Valdés, Antonio Lorda, and Eduardo Machado.

Appendix 8

"La rosa blanca" (1891)

Published in October of 1891 in the book *Versos sencillos*, José Martí's "La rosa blanca" became one of Cuba's most popular and revered poems. Killed during the war of independence in 1895, Martí became an important symbol of Cuban patriotism. The poem's simple construction makes it easy for children to memorize it. Most Cubans in the United States and in Cuba can recite the poem, line by line.

La rosa blanca

    Cultivo una rosa blanca,
    En julio como en enero,
    Para el amigo sincero
    Que me da su mano franca.

    Y para el cruel que me arranca
    El corazón con que vivo,
    Cardo ni oruga cultivo;
    Cultivo una rosa blanca.

The White Rose

    I plant a white rose,
    In July as well as January,
    For the beloved friend
    Whose hand I hold.

    And for the enemy who tears apart
    The heart that beats in me,
    Neither thistles nor thorns I plant;
    For him, I plant a white rose.

Source: José Martí.

Appendix 9

Letter from General Calixto García to General William Shafter, July 17, 1898

General Calixto García commanded the Cuban forces that were instrumental in the fall of Santiago de Cuba in 1898 after three years of fierce fighting. U.S. General William R. Shafter, whose troops had been in action for only a few months, kept the Cubans from entering Santiago and denied their leaders any participation in the surrender negotiations and Santiago's occupation. An embittered García responded with the following letter, protesting the denial of a role to Cuban forces in the surrender of Santiago de Cuba.

To Major-General Shafter, Commander of
The 5th Army Corps of the United States Army

Sir:

On May 12, the Government of the Republic of Cuba ordered me, in my capacity as commander in chief of the Cuban Army in the Eastern Provinces, to lend my cooperation to the American Army.

Following the plans and obeying the orders of my superiors, I have done all that is

Source: From Hortensia Pichardo, ed., *Documentos para la historia de Cuba (Época Colonial)*. Havana: Consejo Nacional de Universidades, 1965: 456–459. Translated by Luis Martínez-Fernández.

possible to satisfy the desires of my government, having been, until now, one of your most faithful subordinates, and having had the honor to execute your commands and instructions to the extent of my faculties.

The City of Santiago de Cuba surrendered, at last, to the American Army, but the news of such an important victory reached me through persons not affiliated with your staff of officers, and I failed to receive a single word from you concerning the peace negotiations and the terms of surrender proposed by the Spaniards.

The important actions of surrender of the Spanish Army and this city to you, occurred later, and only reached me as a public rumor. I was also denied the honor of a single word from you, inviting me and the officers of my staff to represent the Cuban Army in such solemn occasion. Lastly, I know that you have left in place, in Santiago, the same Spanish authorities, enemies of Cuban independence, against which I have fought for three years. I must inform you that those authorities were never elected by the residents of Santiago, but rather appointed by decrees of the Queen of Spain.

I agree, sir, with the action of the troops under your command of taking possession of the city and its fortification; I would have given my most ardent cooperation to any measure you would have deemed appropriate, maintaining public order, until the moment to fulfill the solemn vote of the people of the United States, to establish in Cuba a free and independent government; but when the occasion comes for the appointment of authorities in Santiago, with the special background circumstances of thirty years of war against Spanish rule, I can not help but see, with the deepest feelings, that those authorities are not elected by the Cuban people, but are the same that the Queen and her ministers had named to defend Spanish sovereignty against the Cubans.

A rumor circulates, which is so absurd that it lacks any credibility, General, that the order to keep my army from entering Santiago de Cuba obeyed to fears of vengeance and reprisal against the Spaniards. Allow me to protest against the slightest shadow of such thinking, for we are not a savage people that are unfamiliar with civilized warfare; we are a poor and raggedy army, as poor and raggedy as that of your forefathers in the noble war for the independence of the United States of America; and like the heroes of Saratoga and Yorktown, we respect our cause and are unwilling to tarnish it with barbarism and cowardice.

In light of the reasons outlined above I deeply regret not being able to further comply with the orders of my Government, having today presented my formal resignation as commanding general of this section of our army before Major-General Máximo Gómez, Chief General of the Cuban Army.

In expectation of its resolution, I have retired, with all of my troops, to Jiguaní.

I remain respectfully yours, Major-General,
Calixto García
Countryside of Free Cuba, July 17, 1898.

Appendix 10

The Platt Amendment (1901)

This piece of legislation, which the United States forced the Cubans to accept as part of the Constitution of 1901 and later as part of a comprehensive treaty, would become a powerful symbol of U.S. imperialism on the island. It would inspire Cuban nationalists for generations to come, even after it was abrogated in May 1934.

Art. I. The Government of Cuba shall never enter into any treaty or other compact with any foreign power or powers which will impair or tend to impair the independence of Cuba, nor in any manner authorize or permit any foreign power or powers to obtain by colonization or for military or naval purposes, or otherwise, lodgement in or control over any portion of said island.

Art. II. The Government of Cuba shall not assume or contract any public debt to pay the interest upon which, and to make reasonable sinking-fund provision for the ultimate discharge of which, the ordinary revenues of the Island of Cuba, after defraying the current expenses of the Government, shall be inadequate.

Art III. The Government of Cuba consents that the United States may exercise the right to intervene for the preservation of Cuban independence, the maintenance of a government adequate for the protection of life, property, and individual liberty, and for discharging the obligations with respect to Cuba imposed by the treaty of Paris on the United States, now to be assumed and undertaken by the government of Cuba.

Art. IV. All Acts of the United States in Cuba during its military occupancy thereof are ratified and validated, and all lawful rights acquired thereunder shall be maintained and protected.

Art. V. The Government of Cuba will execute, and as far as necessary extend, the plans already devised or other plans to be mutually agreed upon, for the sanitation of the cities of the island, to the end that a recurrence of epidemics and infectious diseases may be prevented thereby assuring protection to the people and commerce of Cuba, as well as to the commerce of the southern ports of the United States and the people residing therein.

Art. VI. The Isle of Pines shall be omitted from the boundaries of Cuba, specified in the Constitution, the title thereto being left to future adjustment by treaty.

Art. VII. To enable the United States to maintain the independence of Cuba, and to protect the people thereof, as well as for its own defense, the government of Cuba will sell or lease to the United States lands necessary for coaling or naval stations at certain specified points to be agreed upon with the President of the United States. . . .

Appendix 11

"History Will Absolve Me" (Excerpts) (1953)

This famous speech given by Fidel Castro on October 16, 1953, at his trial for plotting to overthrow the dictatorship of Fulgencio Batista thrust the revolutionary into the national and international spotlight. Although the court proceedings were closed to the public, Castro's defense was smuggled from the prison and disseminated in pamphlet form by his supporters.

Opening Remarks

Honorable Magistrates:

Never has a lawyer had to practice his profession under more difficult conditions; never against an accused have more overwhelming irregularities been committed. Here, counsel and accused are one and the same. As attorney for the defense I have been denied even a look at the indictment. As the accused, I have been, for the past seventy-six days, shut away, in solitary confinement—held incommunicado in violation of every legal and human consideration.

He who is speaking abhors—with all his being—anything that might be vain or childish. Neither by his temperament nor by his present

Source: From Fidel Castro, *History Will Absolve Me*. Havana: Book Institute, 1967.

frame of mind is he inclined toward oratorical poses—or toward any kind of sensationalism. I am compelled to plead my own defense before this court. There are two reasons: first, because I have been deprived almost entirely of legal aid; second, because only he who has been outraged as deeply as I, and who has seen his country so forsaken, its justice so reviled, can speak on an occasion like this with words that are made of the blood of his own heart and the very marrow of truth. . . .

Attack on the Moncada Army Barracks

The final mobilization of men who came to this province from the most remote towns of the entire island was accomplished with admirable precision and in absolute secrecy. It is equally true that the attack was carried out with magnificent coordination. It began simultaneously at 5:15 A.M., in both Bayamo and Santiago de Cuba; and one by one, with an exactitude of minutes and seconds foreseen in advance, the buildings surrounding the barracks fell to our forces. Nevertheless, in the interests of accuracy, and even though it may detract from our reputation, I am also going to reveal a fact that was fatal: due to a most unfortunate error, half of our forces—and the better armed half, at that—went astray at the entrance to the city and were not on hand to help us at the decisive moment. Abel Santamaría, with 21 men, had occupied the City Hospital; with him went a doctor and two of our female comrades, to attend the wounded. Raúl Castro, with ten men, occupied the Palace of Justice and it was my responsibility to attack the barracks with the rest, 95 men. Preceded by an advance guard of eight who had forced Gate Three, I arrived with the first group of 45 men. It was precisely here that the battle began, when my automobile ran into a perimeter patrol armed with machine-guns. The reserve group, who had almost all the heavy weapons [the light arms were in the advance guard] turned up the wrong street and lost their way in this city, with which they were not familiar. I must clarify that I do not for a moment doubt the valour of those men; they experienced great anguish and desperation when they realized they were lost. Because of the type of action under way and because of the identical color of the uniforms of the two contending forces, it was not easy for these men to reestablish contact with us. Many of them, captured later on, met death with true heroism.

We all had strict instructions to be, above all, humane in the struggle. Never was a group of armed men more generous to the adversary. From the very first, we took numerous prisoners—eventually nearly twenty—and there was one moment when three of our men—Ramiro Valdés, José Suárez and Jesús Montane—managed to enter a barracks and hold nearly fifty soldiers prisoners for a short time. Those soldiers have testified before the court, and all without exception have acknowledged that we treated them with absolute respect, without even offending them by the use of an unpleasant word. Apropos of this, I want to give the prosecutor my heartfelt thanks for one thing in the trial of my comrades: When he made his report, he was fair enough to acknowledge as an incontestable fact that we maintained a high spirit of chivalry throughout the struggle.

Discipline among the soldiers was very poor. They finally defeated us, because of their superiority in numbers—fifteen to one—and because of the protection afforded them by the defenses of the fortress. Our men were much the better marksmen, as our enemies conceded. Courage was high on both sides. . . .

Revolutionary Program

In the brief of this cause there must be recorded the five revolutionary laws that would have been proclaimed immediately after the capture of the Moncada barracks and would have been broadcast to the nation by radio. It is possible that Colonel Chaviano may deliberately have destroyed these documents, but even if he has done so, I conserve them in my memory.

The First Revolutionary Law would have returned power to the people and proclaimed the Constitution of 1940 the supreme Law of the land, until such time as the people should decide to modify or change it. And, in order to effect its implementation and punish those who had violated it—there being no organization for holding elections to accomplish this—the revolutionary movement, as the momentous incarnation of this sovereignty, the only source of legitimate power, would have assumed all the faculties inherent to it, except that of modifying the Constitution itself: In other words it would have assumed the legislative, executive and judicial powers. . . .

The Second Revolutionary Law would have granted property, not mortgageable and not transferable, to all planters, sub-planters, lessees, partners and squatters who hold parcels of five or less "caballerías" [tract of land, about 33⅓ acres] of land, and the state would indemnify the former owners on the basis of the rental which they would have received for these parcels over a period of ten years.

The Third Revolutionary Law would have granted workers and employees the right to share 30% of the profits of all the large industrial, mercantile and mining enterprises, including the sugar mills. The strictly agricultural enterprises would be exempt in consideration of other agrarian laws which would have been implemented.

The Fourth Revolutionary Law would have granted all planters the right to share 55% of the sugar production and a minimum quota of forty thousand "arrobas" [25 pounds] for all small planters who have been established for three or more years.

The Fifth Revolutionary Law would have ordered the confiscation of all holdings and ill-gotten gains of those who had committed frauds during previous regimes, as well as the holdings and ill-gotten gains of all their legatees and heirs. To implement this, special courts with full powers would gain access to all records of all corporations registered or operating in this country [in order] to investigate concealed funds of illegal origin, and to request that foreign governments extradite persons and attach holdings [rightfully belonging to the Cuban people]. Half of the property recovered would be used to subsidize retirement funds for workers and the other half would be used for hospitals, asylums and charitable organizations. . . .

The problems concerning land, the problem of industrialization, the problem of housing, the problem of unemployment, the problem of education and the problem of the health of the people; these are the six problems we would take immediate steps to resolve, along with the restoration of public liberties and political democracy.

Perhaps this exposition appears cold and theoretical if one does not know the shocking and tragic conditions of the country with regard to these six problems, to say nothing of the most humiliating political oppression.

85% of the small farmers in Cuba pay rent and live under the constant threat of being dispossessed from the land that they cultivate. More than half the best cultivated land belongs to foreigners. In Oriente, the largest province, the lands of the United Fruit Company and West Indian Company join the north coast to the southern one. There are two hundred thousand peasant families who do not have a single acre of land to cultivate to provide food for their starving children. On the other hand, nearly three hundred thousand "caballerías" of productive land owned by powerful interests remains uncultivated.

Cuba is above all an agricultural state. Its population is largely rural. The city depends on these rural areas. The rural people won the Independence. The greatness and prosperity of our country depends on a healthy and vigorous rural population that loves the land and knows how to cultivate it, within the framework of a state that protects and guides them. Considering all this, how can the present state of affairs be tolerated any longer? . . .

The Coup

Let me tell you a story.

Once upon a time there was a Republic. It had its constitution, its laws, its civil rights, a president, a Congress, and law courts. Everyone could assemble, associate, speak and write with complete freedom.

The people were not satisfied with the government officials at that time, but [the people] had the power to elect new officials and only a few days remained before they were going to do so!

There existed a public opinion both respected and heeded and all problems of common interest were freely discussed. There were political parties, radio and television debates and forums, and public meetings. The whole nation throbbed with enthusiasm. This country had suffered greatly and although it was unhappy, it longed to be happy and had a right to be happy. It had been deceived many times and it looked upon the past with real horror. This country believed—blindly—that such a past could not return; the people were proud of their love of liberty and they carried their heads high in the conviction that liberty would be respected as a sacred right; they felt confident that no one would dare commit the crime of violating their democratic institutions. They desired a change for the better, aspired toward progress; and they saw all this at hand. All their hope was in the future.

My poor country! One morning the citizens awakened dismayed; under the cover of night, while the people slept, the ghosts of the past had conspired and now had seized the citizen body by the limbs . . . by its very throat. That grip, those claws were familiar: those jaws, those death dealing scythes, those boots. No; it was no nightware; it was a sad and terrible reality: A man named Fulgencio Batista had just committed the appalling crime that no one had expected. . . .

Closing Argument

I come to the close of my defense plea but I will not end it as lawyers usually do—asking that the accused be freed. I cannot ask freedom for myself while my comrades are suffering in the ignominous prison of Isla de Pinos. Send me there to join them and to share their fate. It is understandable that honest men should be dead or in prison in [this] Republic where the president is a criminal and a thief.

To the Honorable Magistrates, my sincere gratitude for having allowed me to express myself freely without petty interruptions, I hold no bitterness toward you. I recognize; that in certain aspects you have been humane and I know that the Presiding Officer of this court, a man of unimpeachable private life, cannot disguise his repugnance at the current state of affairs that oblige him to dictate unjust decisions.

Still, there remains for this hearing a more serious problem, the issues arising from the murder of seventy men—that is to say, the greatest massacre we have ever known. The guilty continue at liberty with a weapon in hand—a weapon which continually threatens the citizens. If all the weight of the law does not fall upon [the guilty] because of cowardice, or because of domination of the courts—and if then, all the magistrates and judges do not resign, I pity you. And I regret the unprecedented shame that will fall over the judicial system.

I know that imprisonment will be as hard for me as it has ever been for anyone—filled with cowardly threats and wicked torture. But I do not fear prison, just as I do not fear the fury of the miserable tyrant who snuffed life out of 70 brothers of mine.

Sentence me. I don't mind. *History will absolve me.*

Appendix 12

Agrarian Reform Law of the Republic of Cuba (Excerpts) (1959)

The first major reform of the Revolutionary government, this 1959 law reduced landholdings, with a few exceptions, to a maximum of 1,000 acres. This legislation initiated the cycle of confrontation between the United States and Cuba. Millions of acres belonging to U.S. corporations were expropriated and redistributed. In the months following the law's enactment, the Eisenhower Administration expressed concern about the proposed method of compensation and began to hint at economic retaliation against Cuba.

Land in General

Article 1.—Large landholding is hereby prohibited. The maximum area of land that a natural or juridical person may own shall be thirty *caballerías*. Land owned by a natural or juridical person in excess of that limit will be expropriated for distribution among the peasants and agricultural workers who have no land.

Article 2.—The following land shall be exempt from the provisions of the foregoing article:

(a) Areas planted in sugar cane, the yield of which is not less than the national average plus fifty percent.

(b) Cattle-raising areas that meet the minimum standards for support of cattle per *caballería*

fixed by the National Agrarian Reform Institute, taking into account the breed, the time of growth, the birth rate percentage, the system of feeding, the percentage of yield of meat, after slaughter, in the case of beef cattle, or of milk in the case of milch cows. The potential production of the producing area in question will be determined through physical and chemical analysis of the soils, their moisture content and the pattern of rainfall distribution.

(c) Areas planted in rice that, in the opinion of the National Agrarian Reform Institute, normally yield no less than fifty percent more than the average national production of the variety in question.

(d) Areas devoted to one or more crops or to a combination of agriculture and stockraising, with or without industrial activity, for the efficient exploitation of which, with a rational economic yield, it is necessary to have an area of land greater than that established as the maximum limit in Article 1 of this Law.

Notwithstanding the foregoing provisions, in no event may a natural or juridical person own land greater in area than one hundred *caballerías*. In cases in which a natural or juridical person owns land greater in area than one hundred *caballerías*, and there are two or more crops of the types listed under (a), (b), and (c) of this article on the said land, the benefit of the exemption that is established up to the maximum limit of one hundred *caballerías* shall be granted in such manner as the National Agrarian Reform Institute may determine, the remaining area being subject to the provisions of this Law.

With respect to the crops mentioned in sections (a) and (c), the yields referred to shall be computed by taking into consideration the last harvest. The benefits of these exemptions shall continue as long as those levels of productivity are maintained.

In the case of the exemption indicated in section (d), the National Agrarian Reform Institute shall determine which shall be the areas in excess of the maximum limit of one hundred *caballerías* subject to the provisions of this Law, and shall see to it that economic unity of production is maintained and, in cases of several crops, that the correlation between them, and between the crops and the combination of agriculture and stockraising, where it exists, is also maintained.

Article 3.—The land of the State, the provinces, and the municipalities shall also be subject to distribution. . . .

Article 6.—Privately owned lands up to a limit of thirty *caballerías* per person or entity shall not be subject to expropriation unless affected by contracts with tenant farmers who grow sugar cane, subtenant farmers who grow sugar cane, tenant farmers, subtenant farmers, and sharecroppers, or occupied by squatters, who hold parcels not larger than five *caballerías* in which case they also shall be subject to expropriation pursuant to the provisions of this Law.

Article 7.—The owners of lands subject to this Law, once the expropriations, grants, and sales to tenant farmers, subtenant farmers, tenant farmers who grow sugar cane, subtenant farmers who grow sugar cane, and squatters established on the farm have been made, may retain the remainder of the property in so far as it does not exceed the maximum area authorized by the Law.

Article 8.—Land that has not been recorded in the Property Registries up to October 10, 1958, shall be considered property of the State.

Article 9.—State lands are all those that are recorded in the inventories of national property or acquired through a preferential right to purchase or any other right, even though the titles may not have been recorded at the Property Registries.

The Ministry of Treasury shall proceed to survey and record all lands which, under the foregoing provisions, belong to the State. . . .

Article 15.—Rural property may in the future be acquired by Cuban citizens or companies formed by Cuban citizens.

Farms not larger than thirty *caballerías* which, in the judgment of the National Agrarian Reform Institute, are suitable for conveyance to foreign companies or entities for industrial or agricultural development considered beneficial to the development of the national economy are exempt from the foregoing provision.

In cases of hereditary conveyances of rural properties to heirs who are not Cuban citizens, such properties shall be considered to be subject to expropriation for purposes of the Agrarian Reform, regardless of their size.

Redistribution of Lands and Indemnification of the Owners

Article 16.—An area of two *caballerías* for fertile land, without irrigation, distant from urban centers and devoted to crops of medium economic yield shall be established as a "vital minimum" for a peasant family of five persons.

The National Agrarian Reform Institute shall be the agency charged with establishing and deciding in each case what the necessary "vital minimum" is, starting from the aforesaid base and taking into consideration the average level of annual income it is hoped to attain for each family.

The lands that make up the "vital minimum" shall enjoy the benefits of not being subject to attachment or transfer as referred to in Article 91 of the Organic Law of the Republic.

Article 17.—Private lands subject to expropriation under the provisions of this Law and lands of the State shall be transferred undivided to the cooperatives recognized by this Law or distributed among the beneficiaries in parcels no larger than two *caballerías*, without prejudice to the adjustments that the national Agrarian Reform Institute may make in order to determine the "vital minimum" in each case.

All the lands, no matter to whom they may

be transferred, shall be subject to payment of the taxes specified by law as a contribution to the public expenses of the nation and of the municipalities.

Article 18.—Privately owned lands cultivated by tenant farmers who grow sugar cane, subtenant farmers who grow sugar cane, tenant farmers and subtenant farmers, sharecroppers, or squatters shall be awarded free of charge to the persons that cultivate them when their area does not exceed the "vital minimum." When the said farmers cultivate lands having an area less than the "vital minimum," the land necessary to complete it shall be awarded to them, provided it is available and the economic and social conditions of the region so permit.

If the lands cultivated in the cases mentioned in the foregoing paragraph exceed the "vital minimum," provided they do not exceed five [*caballerías*], the tenant farmer, subtenant farmer, tenant farmer who cultivates sugar cane, subtenant farmer who cultivates sugar cane, sharecropper, or squatter shall receive two *caballerías* free of charge after their expropriation by the National Agrarian Reform Institute, and they may purchase from the owner, through a forced sale, the portion owned by him exceeding the area awarded free of charge, up to a limit of five *caballerías*.

Article 19.—Owners of parcels of land smaller in area than the "vital minimum," who cultivate them personally, shall also be awarded free of charge the land necessary to complete it, provided it is available and the economic and social conditions of the region so permit. . . .

Article 29.—The constitutional right of owners affected by this Law to receive indemnization for the property expropriated shall be recognized. This indemnization shall be determined by taking into consideration the sale value of farms as shown by the municipal assessment statements dated prior to October 10, 1958. The improvements and structures on the farms that may be affected shall be the subject of an independent appraisal made by the authorities charged with the enforcement of this Law. Likewise, an independent appraisal shall be made of the value of the stalks of the [sugar cane] crops in order to recompense their legitimate owners.

Article 31.—The indemnity shall be paid in redeemable bonds. To that end an issue of Republic of Cuba bonds shall be floated in such amount, and under such terms and conditions, as may be fixed in due time. The bonds shall be called "Agrarian Reform Bonds" and shall be considered public securities. The issue or issues shall be floated for a period of twenty years, with annual interest not exceeding four and one-half [$4\frac{1}{2}$] percent. The proper amount for the payment of interest, amortization, and expenses in connection with the issue shall be included each year in the Budget of the Republic.

Article 32.—The holders of Agrarian Reform Bonds, or the amount thereof, shall be granted ten year exemption from the Personal Income Tax on income derived from investing these bonds in new industries. It shall be the duty of the minister of the Treasury to submit to the Council of Ministers a bill regulating such exemption.

The same right shall be granted the heirs of the person indemnified in case they should be the ones who make such investment. . . .

Agrarian Cooperation

Article 43.—Whenever possible the National Agrarian Reform Institute will promote agrarian cooperatives. The agrarian cooperatives organized by the National Agrarian Reform Institute on lands available to it under the provisions of this Law shall be under its direction, and it shall reserve the right to appoint the managers thereof for the purpose of ensuring their better development during the initial stage of this type of economic and social organization and until greater autonomy is granted it by law.

Article 44.—The National Agrarian Reform Institute will give its support only to agrarian cooperatives formed by peasants or agricultural workers for the purpose of utilizing the soil and harvesting its products through the personal efforts of their members, pursuant to the internal regulations laid down by the said Institute. In the case of these cooperatives, the National Agrarian Reform Institute shall see to it that they are located on land suitable for the purposes pursued and that they are willing to accept the aid and follow the guidance of the said Institute in technical matters. . . .

The National Agrarian Reform Institute

Article 48.—The National Agrarian Reform Institute [Instituto Nacional de Reforma Agraria, abbreviated INRA] is hereby created as an autonomous entity with its own juridical personality, for the purpose of applying and enforcing this Law.

The National Agrarian Reform Institute shall be governed by a President and an Executive Director, who shall be appointed by the Council of Ministers.

The powers and functions of the National Agrarian Reform Institute shall be as follows:

1. To make studies, to order investigations, to order and put into practice whatever measures are necessary in order to attain the objectives of the Law, issuing to that end pertinent regulations and general and special instructions;

2. To propose to the Ministry of the Treasury such tax measures for stimulating saving or consumption as may be deemed adequate for promoting the development of the production of articles derived from agriculture and stockraising;

3. To propose the margin of tariff protection required in each case for better development of products derived from agriculture and stockraising;

4. To coordinate the campaigns for improving the housing, health, and education of the rural population;

5. To determine the areas and boundaries of the Agrarian Development Zones which it decides to establish and organize;

6. To direct the preliminary studies for the distribution and awarding of lands subject to this Law, installations for State aid, the administrative set-up of each zone, and conveyance of the lands and the deeds thereto to the beneficiaries;

7. To see to the implementation of the plans for agrarian development, awarding or distribution of lands, both with respect to the internal administration of each zone and with respect to the purposes of the Law, issuing such instructions and adopting such resolutions and measures as it may deem necessary;

8. To draft the regulations of the agricul-tural cooperative associations that it organizes and to appoint managers thereof, pursuant to the provisions of Article 43, to keep records and to decide questions that may arise between their members, and to take cognizance of and to decide appeals that, pursuant to the regulations, are brought as a result of opposition to resolutions or measures adopted;

9. To organize and direct the Cooperative-Training School;

10. To handle and decide, under the terms of this Law, all applications or suggestions that may be addressed to it in connection with resettlement [of agricultural workers], awards, distribution, management, and other aspects of the Reform; classifying the applications submitted for obtaining the benefits thereof;

11. To draw up its budgets and to administer its funds, as well as those intended for implementing the Agrarian Reform;

12. To organize its own statistical services and the five-year agricultural census, compiling and publishing the results thereof for purposes of general information;

13. To organize its own offices and to issue the necessary internal regulations and to establish relations with the departments of the State, the province, the municipalities, autonomous bodies and quasi-state organizations; agrarian commissions, agrarian and industrial delegations and associations in general;.

14. To establish and direct its permanent relations with such international associations as may be advisable.

Additional Final Provisions

In exercise of the constituent power vested in the Council of Ministers the present Law is declared to be an integral part of the Organic Law of the Republic, which is thereby supplemented.

Accordingly, this Law is hereby given constitutional force and effect.

Therefore: I order that all parts of the present Law be implemented and enforced.

Enacted in La Plata, Sierra Maestra, on May 17, 1959, "Year of the Liberation."

MANUEL URRUTIA LLEÓ,
President of the Republic.
FIDEL CASTRO RUZ, *Prime Minister. . . .*

Appendix 13

Helms-Burton Law (Excerpts) (1996)

Cuban Liberty and Democratic Solidarity (Libertad) Act of 1996

The Helms-Burton Law created a great deal of controversy between the United States and its allies because it was seen as an affront to the sovereignty of nations wishing to trade with Cuba. President Bill Clinton signed it into law in March 1996. It formalizes U.S. sanctions against Cuba.

Besides the controversial provisions of the bill, the legislation is intended as a blueprint for U.S. foreign policy in the aftermath of Fidel Castro's departure from power.

SEC. 3. Purposes.

The purposes of this Act are—

(1) to assist the Cuban people in regaining their freedom and prosperity, as well as in joining the community of democratic countries that are flourishing in the Western Hemisphere;

(2) to strengthen international sanctions against the Castro government;

(3) to provide for the continued national security of the United States in the face of continuing threats from the Castro government of terrorism, theft of property from United States nationals by the Castro government, and the political manipulation by the Castro government of the desire of Cubans to escape that results in mass migration to the United States;

(4) to encourage the holding of free and fair democratic elections in Cuba, conducted under the supervision of internationally recognized observers;

(5) to provide a policy framework for United States support to the Cuban people in response to the formation of a transition government or a democratically elected government in Cuba; and

(6) to protect United States nationals against confiscatory takings and the wrongful trafficking in property confiscated by the Castro regime. . . .

TITLE I—Strengthening International Sanctions Against the Castro Government

SEC. 101. Statement of Policy.
It is the sense of the Congress that—

(1) the acts of the Castro government, including its massive, systematic, and extraordinary violations of human rights, are a threat to international peace;

(2) the President should advocate, and should instruct the United States Permanent Representative to the United Nations to pro-

pose and seek within the Security Council, a mandatory international embargo against the totalitarian Cuban Government pursuant to chapter VII of the Chapter of the United Nations, employing efforts similar to consultations conducted by United States representatives with respect to Haiti;

(3) any resumption of efforts by any independent state of the former Soviet Union to make operational any nuclear facilities in Cuba, and any continuation of intelligence activities by such a state from Cuba that are targeted at the United States and its citizens will have a detrimental impact on United States assistance to such state; and

(4) in view of the threat to the national security posed by the operation of any nuclear facility, and the Castro government's continuing blackmail to unleash another wave of Cuban refugees fleeing from Castro's oppression, most of whom find their way to United States shores, further depleting limited humanitarian and other resources of the United States, the President should do all in his power to make it clear to the Cuban Government that—

(A) the completion and operation of any nuclear power facility, or

(B) any further political manipulation of the desire of Cubans to escape that results in mass migration to the United States, will be considered an act of aggression which will be met with an appropriate response in order to maintain the security of the national borders of the United States and the health and safety of the American people.

TITLE II—Assistance to a Free and Independent Cuba

SEC. 201. Policy Toward a Transition Government and a Democratically Elected Government in Cuba.
The policy of the United States is as follows:

(1) To support the self-determination of the Cuban people.

(2) To recognize that the self-determination of the Cuban people is a sovereign and national right of the citizens of Cuba which must be exercised free of interference by the government of any other country.

(3) To encourage the Cuban people to empower themselves with a government which reflects the self-determination of the Cuban people.

(4) To recognize the potential for a difficult transition from the current regime in Cuba that may result from the initiatives taken by the Cuban people for self-determination in response to the intransigence of the Castro regime in not allowing any substantive political or economic reforms, and to be prepared to provide the Cuban people with humanitarian, developmental, and other economic assistance.

(5) In solidarity with the Cuban people, to provide appropriate forms of assistance—

(A) to a transition government in Cuba;

(B) to facilitate the rapid movement from such a transition government to a democratically elected government in Cuba that results from an expression of the self-determination of the Cuban people; and

(C) to support such a democratically elected government.

(6) Through such assistance, to facilitate a peaceful transition to representative democracy and a market economy in Cuba and to consolidate democracy in Cuba.

(7) To deliver such assistance to the Cuban people only through a transition government in Cuba, through a democratically elected government in Cuba, through United States Government organizations, or through United States, international, or indigenous nongovernmental organizations.

(8) To encourage other countries and multilateral organizations to provide similar assistance, and to work cooperatively with such countries and organizations to coordinate such assistance.

(9) To ensure that appropriate assistance is rapidly provided and distributed to the people of Cuba upon the institution of a transition government in Cuba.

(10) Not to provide favorable treatment or influence on behalf of any individual or en-

tity in the selection by the Cuban people of their future government.

(11) To assist a transition government in Cuba and a democratically elected government in Cuba to prepare the Cuban military forces for an appropriate role in a democracy.

(12) To be prepared to enter into negotiations with a democratically elected government in Cuba either to return the United States Naval Base at Guantánamo to Cuba or to renegotiate the present agreement under mutually agreeable terms.

(13) To consider the restoration of diplomatic recognition and support the reintegration of the Cuban Government into Inter-American organizations when the President determines that there exists a democratically elected government in Cuba.

(14) To take steps to remove the economic embargo of Cuba when the President determines that a transition to a democratically elected government in Cuba has begun.

(15) To assist a democratically elected government in Cuba to strengthen and stabilize its national currency.

(16) To pursue trade relations with a free, democratic, and independent Cuba.

SEC. 202. Assistance for the Cuban People.

(a) AUTHORIZATION—

(1) IN GENERAL—The President shall develop a plan for providing economic assistance to Cuba at such time as the President determines that a transition government or a democratically elected government in Cuba is in power.

(2) EFFECT ON OTHER LAWS—Assistance may be provided under this section subject to an authorization of appropriations and subject to the availability of appropriations.

(b) PLAN FOR ASSISTANCE—

(1) DEVELOPMENT OF PLAN—The President shall develop a plan for providing assistance under this section—

(A) to Cuba when a transition government in Cuba is in power; and

(B) to Cuba when a democratically elected government in Cuba is in power.

(2) TYPES OF ASSISTANCE—Assistance under the plan developed under paragraph (1) may, subject to an authorization of appropriations and subject to the availability of appropriations, include the following:

(A) TRANSITION GOVERNMENT— (i) Except as provided in clause (ii), assistance to Cuba under a transition government shall, subject to an authorization of appropriations and subject to the availability of appropriations, be limited to—(I) such food, medicine, medical supplies and equipment, and assistance to meet emergency energy needs, as is necessary to meet the basic human needs of the Cuban people; and (II) assistance described in subparagraph (C). (ii) Assistance in addition to assistance under clause (i) may be provided, but only after the President certifies to the appropriate congressional committees, in accordance with procedures applicable to reprogramming notifications under section 634A of the Foreign Assistance Act of 1961, that such assistance is essential to the successful completion of the transition to democracy. (iii) Only after a transition government in Cuba is in power, freedom of individuals to travel to visit their relatives without any restrictions shall be permitted.

(B) DEMOCRATICALLY ELECTED GOVERNMENT—Assistance to a democratically elected government in Cuba may, subject to an authorization of appropriations and subject to the availability of appropriations, consist of economic assistance in addition to assistance available under subparagraph (A), together with assistance described in subparagraph (C). Such economic assistance may include—(i) assistance under chapter 1 of part I (relating to development assistance), and chapter 4 of part II (relating to the economic support fund), of the Foreign Assistance Act of 1961; (ii) assistance under the Agricultural Trade Development and Assistance Act of 1954; (iii) financing, guarantees, and other forms of assistance provided by the Export-Import Bank of the United States; (iv) financial support provided by the Overseas Private Investment Corporation for investment projects in Cuba; (v) assistance provided by the Trade and Development Agency; (vi) Peace Corps programs; and (vii) other appropriate assistance to carry out the policy of section 201.

    (C) MILITARY ADJUSTMENT ASSISTANCE—Assistance to a transition government in Cuba and to a democratically elected government in Cuba shall also include assistance in preparing the Cuban military forces to adjust to an appropriate role in a democracy.

(c) STRATEGY FOR DISTRIBUTION—The plan developed under subsection (b) shall include a strategy for distributing assistance under the plan.

(d) DISTRIBUTION—Assistance under the plan developed under subsection (b) shall be provided through United States Government organizations and nongovernmental organizations and private and voluntary organizations, whether within or outside the United States, including humanitarian, educational, labor, and private sector organizations.

(e) INTERNATIONAL EFFORTS—The President shall take the necessary steps—

    (1) to seek to obtain the agreement of other countries and of international financial institutions and multilateral organizations to provide to a transition government in Cuba, and to a democratically elected government in Cuba, assistance comparable to that provided by the United States under this Act; and

    (2) to work with such countries, institutions, and organizations to coordinate all such assistance programs.

(f) COMMUNICATION WITH THE CUBAN PEOPLE—The President shall take the necessary steps to communicate to the Cuban people the plan for assistance developed under this section.

(g) REPORT TO CONGRESS—Not later than 180 days after the date of the enactment of this Act, the President shall transmit to the appropriate congressional committees a report describing in detail the plan developed under this section. . . .

SEC. 205. Requirements and Factors for Determining a Transition Government.

(a) REQUIREMENTS—For the purposes of this Act, a transition government in Cuba is a government that—

    (1) has legalized all political activity;

    (2) has released all political prisoners and allowed for investigations of Cuban prisons by appropriate international human rights organizations;

    (3) has dissolved the present Department of State Security in the Cuban Ministry of the Interior, including the Committees for the Defense of the Revolution and the Rapid Response Brigades; and

    (4) has made public commitments to organizing free and fair elections for a new government—

        (A) to be held in a timely manner within a period not to exceed 18 months after the transition government assumes power;

        (B) with the participation of multiple independent political parties that have full access to the media on an equal basis, including (in the case of radio, television, or other telecommunications media) in terms of allotments of time for such access and the times of day such allotments are given; and

        (C) to be conducted under the supervision of internationally recognized observers, such as the Organization of American States, the United Nations, and other election monitors;

(5) has ceased any interference with Radio Marti or Television Marti broadcasts;

(6) makes public commitments to and is making demonstrable progress in—

(A) establishing an independent judiciary;

(B) respecting internationally recognized human rights and basic freedoms as set forth in the Universal Declaration of Human Rights, to which Cuba is a signatory nation;

(C) allowing the establishment of independent trade unions as set forth in conventions 87 and 98 of the International Labor Organization, and allowing the establishment of independent social, economic, and political associations;

(7) does not include Fidel Castro or Raúl Castro; and

(8) has given adequate assurances that it will allow the speedy and efficient distribution of assistance to the Cuban people.

(b) ADDITIONAL FACTORS—In addition to the requirements in subsection (a), in determining whether a transition government in Cuba is in power, the President shall take into account the extent to which that government—

(1) is demonstrably in transition from a communist totalitarian dictatorship to representative democracy;

(2) has made public commitments to, and is making demonstrable progress in—

(A) effectively guaranteeing the rights of free speech and freedom of the press, including granting permits to privately owned media and telecommunications companies to operate in Cuba;

(B) permitting the reinstatement of citizenship to Cuban-born persons returning to Cuba;

(C) assuring the right to private property; and

(D) taking appropriate steps to return to United States citizens (and entities which are 50 percent or more beneficially owned by United States citizens) property taken by the Cuban Government from such citizens and entities on or after January 1, 1959, or to provide equitable compensation to such citizens and entities for such property;

(3) has extradited or otherwise rendered to the United States all persons sought by the United States Department of Justice for crimes committed in the United States; and

(4) has permitted the deployment throughout Cuba of independent and unfettered international human rights monitors.

SEC. 207. Settlement of Outstanding United States Claims to Confiscated Property in Cuba.

(a) REPORT TO CONGRESS—Not later than 180 days after the date of the enactment of this Act, the Secretary of State shall provide a report to the appropriate congressional committees containing an assessment of the property dispute question in Cuba, including—

(1) an estimate of the number and amount of claims to property confiscated by the Cuban Government that are held by United States nationals in addition to those claims certified under section 507 of the International Claims Settlement Act of 1949;

(2) an assessment of the significance of promptly resolving confiscated property claims to the revitalization of the Cuban economy;

(3) a review and evaluation of technical and other assistance that the United States could provide to help either a transition government in Cuba or a democratically elected government in Cuba establish mechanisms to resolve property questions;

(4) an assessment of the role and types of support the United States could provide to help resolve claims to property confiscated by the Cuban Government that are held by United States nationals who did not receive or qualify for certification under section 507 of the International Claims Settlement Act of 1949; and

(5) an assessment of any areas requiring legislative review or action regarding the resolution of property claims in Cuba prior to a change of government in Cuba.

(d) SENSE OF CONGRESS—It is the sense of the Congress that the satisfactory resolution of property claims by a Cuban Government recognized by the United States remains an essential condition for the full resumption of economic and diplomatic relations between the United States and Cuba.

TITLE III—Protection of Property Rights of United States Nationals

SEC. 301. Findings.

The Congress makes the following findings:

(1) Individuals enjoy a fundamental right to own and enjoy property which is enshrined in the United States Constitution.

(2) The wrongful confiscation or taking of property belonging to United States nationals by the Cuban Government, and the subsequent exploitation of this property at the expense of the rightful owner, undermines the comity of nations, the free flow of commerce, and economic development.

(3) Since Fidel Castro seized power in Cuba in 1959—

(A) he has trampled on the fundamental rights of the Cuban people; and

(B) through his personal despotism, he has confiscated the property of— (i) millions of his own citizens; (ii) thousands of United States nationals; and (iii) thousands more Cubans who claimed asylum in the United States as refugees because of persecution and later became naturalized citizens of the United States.

(4) It is in the interest of the Cuban people that the Cuban Government respect equally the property rights of Cuban nationals and nationals of other countries.

(5) The Cuban Government is offering foreign investors the opportunity to purchase an equity interest in, manage, or enter into joint ventures using property and assets, some of which were confiscated from United States nationals.

(6) This "trafficking" in confiscated property provides badly needed financial benefit, including hard currency, oil, and productive investment and expertise, to the current Cuban Government and thus undermines the foreign policy of the United States—

(A) to bring democratic institutions to Cuba through the pressure of a general economic embargo at a time when the Castro regime has proven to be vulnerable to international economic pressure; and

(B) to protect the claims of United States nationals who had property wrongfully confiscated by the Cuban Government.

(7) The United States Department of State has notified other governments that the transfer to third parties of properties confiscated by the Cuban Government would complicate any attempt to return them to their original owners.

(8) The international judicial system, as currently structured, lacks fully effective remedies for the wrongful confiscation of property and for unjust enrichment from the use of wrongfully confiscated property by governments and private entities at the expense of the rightful owners of the property.

(9) International law recognizes that a nation has the ability to provide for rules of law with respect to conduct outside its territory that has or is intended to have substantial effect within its territory.

(10) The United States Government has an obligation to its citizens to provide protection against wrongful confiscations by foreign nations and their citizens, including the provision of private remedies.

(11) To deter trafficking in wrongfully confiscated property, United States nationals who were the victims of these confiscations should be endowed with a judicial remedy in the courts of the United States that would deny traffickers any profits from economically exploiting Castro's wrongful seizures.

SEC. 302. Liability for Trafficking in Confiscated Property Claimed by United States Nationals.

(a) CIVIL REMEDY—

(1) LIABILITY FOR TRAFFICKING—

(A) Except as otherwise provided in this section, any person that, after the end of the 3-month period beginning on the effective date of this title, traffics in property which was confiscated by the Cuban Government on or after January 1, 1959, shall be liable to any United States national who owns the claim to such property for money damages in an amount equal to the sum of—(i) the amount which is the greater of—(I) the amount, if any, certified to the claimant by the Foreign Claims Settlement Commission under the International Claims Settlement Act of 1949, plus interest; (II) the amount determined under section 303(a)(2), plus interest; or (III) the fair market value of that property, calculated as being either the current value of the property, or the value of the property when confiscated plus interest, whichever is greater; and (ii) court costs and reasonable attorneys' fees.

(B) Interest under subparagraph (A)(i) shall be at the rate set forth in section 1961 of title 28, United States Code, computed by the court from the date of confiscation of the property involved to the date on which the action is brought under this subsection.

(2) PRESUMPTION IN FAVOR OF THE CERTIFIED CLAIMS—There shall be a presumption that the amount for which a person is liable under clause (i) of paragraph (1)(A) is the amount that is certified as described in subclause (I) of that clause. The presumption shall be rebuttable by clear and convincing evidence that the amount described in subclause (II) or (III) of that clause is the appropriate amount of liability under that clause. . . .

SEC. 306. Effective Date.

(a) IN GENERAL—Subject to subsections (b) and (c), this title and the amendments made by this title shall take effect on August 1, 1996.

(b) SUSPENSION AUTHORITY—

(1) SUSPENSION AUTHORITY—The President may suspend the effective date under subsection (a) for a period of not more than 6 months if the President determines and reports in writing to the appropriate congressional committees at least 15 days before such effective date that the suspension is necessary to the national interests of the United States and will expedite a transition to democracy in Cuba.

(2) ADDITIONAL SUSPENSIONS—The President may suspend the effective date under subsection (a) for additional periods of not more than 6 months each, each of which shall begin on the day after the last day of the period during which a suspension is in effect under this subsection, if the President determines and reports in writing to the appropriate congressional committees at least 15 days before the date on which the additional suspension is to begin that the suspension is necessary to the national interests of the United States and will expedite a transition to democracy in Cuba.

(c) OTHER AUTHORITIES—

  (1) SUSPENSION—After this title and the amendments of this title have taken effect—

    (A) no person shall acquire a property interest in any potential or pending action under this title; and

    (B) the President may suspend the right to bring an action under this title with respect to confiscated property for a period of not more than 6 months if the President determines and reports in writing to the appropriate congressional committees at least 15 days before the suspension takes effect that such suspension is necessary to the national interests of the United States and will expedite a transition to democracy in Cuba.

  (2) ADDITIONAL SUSPENSIONS—The President may suspend the right to bring an action under this title for additional periods of not more than 6 months each, each of which shall begin on the day after the last day of the period during which a suspension is in effect under this subsection, if the President determines and reports in writing to the appropriate congressional committees at least 15 days before the date on which the additional suspension is to begin that the suspension is necessary to the national interests of the United States and will expedite a transition to democracy in Cuba.

TITLE IV—Exclusion of Certain Aliens

SEC. 401. Exclusion from the United States of Aliens Who Have Confiscated Property of United States Nationals or Who Traffic in Such Property.

(a) GROUNDS FOR EXCLUSION—The Secretary of State shall deny a visa to, and the Attorney General shall exclude from the United States, any alien whom the Secretary of State determines is a person who, after the date of the enactment of this Act—

  (1) has confiscated, or has directed or overseen the confiscation of, property a claim to which is owned by a United States national, or converts or has converted for personal gain confiscated property, a claim to which is owned by a United States national;

  (2) traffics in confiscated property, a claim to which is owned by a United States national;

  (3) is a corporate officer, principal, or shareholder with a controlling interest of an entity which has been involved in the confiscation of property or trafficking in confiscated property, a claim to which is owned by a United States national; or

  (4) is a spouse, minor child, or agent of a person excludable under paragraph (1), (2), or (3). . . .

Appendix 14

The Homeland Belongs to Us All
(*La Patria es de todos*)
(Excerpts) (1997)

On July 16, 1997, this manifesto was sent to the Central Committee of the Cuban Communist Party by its authors, among whom was Vladimiro Roca, son of legendary communist leader Blas Roca. The four signers of the document were immediately arrested and imprisoned. In March 1999, they were convicted of sedition and given prison sentences varying in length from three and a half to five years. This document and its authors' stance have become symbols of Cuban dissidence.

When you finish reading this document, you will be able to support us if we agree on this initial statement: Men cannot survive on history, which is the same as surviving on tales; material goods are necessary, spiritual needs require satisfaction, and there is a need to being able to look to the future with hope, and also enjoying a space that we call freedom.

The Cuban government ignores the word "opposition": those who do not agree with its policies or simply do not support them are considered enemies and [have] received a host of other demeaning appellatives. They have also

produced a new meaning for the word *Patria* (Homeland), which has been linked in a distorting manner with Revolution, Socialism, and Nation. They pretend to ignore that, by definition, *Patria* is the country of one's birth.

Not accepting this, our Working Group has analyzed the Project Document produced in anticipation of and for the consideration of the Fifth Congress of the Cuban Communist Party. Since we are unable to emit public reactions about it (because all media are controlled by the State), we have decided to put them in writing so that they be known to Cubans in and out of the island, and in so doing, defend our right to have an opinion, because we are convinced that: *the Homeland Belongs to Us All.* . . .

To sustain the arguments [of the Project Document], they recur to the figure of [José] Martí; which they use to insist on the old and absurd idea that the existence of a single party is an idea of Martí's, because he founded only one party. There has never been a political leader who has simultaneously founded several parties; . . . .

Although they want to present the democratic republic as a series of uninterrupted failures and acts of treason, we find in it the socioeconomic results gained between 1902 and 1958 that placed our country among the three

Source: Translated by Luis Martínez-Fernández.

most advanced of Latin America, even above, according to some indicators, great Old World nations like Spain and Italy. . . .

The distortion of facts plagues the document. If we consult statistics prior to 1959, we can see that the illiterate population of Cuba at the time reached 16%, not 40% as was stated. . . .

Each year, with a growing number of votes, the General Assembly of the UN demands the ending of the so-called blockade; this is true, but they do not say that, with the same insistence, the current Cuban government is condemned for its systematic violations of Human Rights. . . .

The Party insists on unity, but forgets that in order for unity to be valid and real (not a parody) it must emerge from a freely formed consensus reached by its citizenry; the contrary is a crass imposition, unity only in name. We stand here as an opposition to demonstrate that there is no consensus in our country. . . .

If, as its leaders affirm, the citizenry supports the Communist Party, there is no reason not to call for free elections under international supervision, a move that would silence all of the system's opponents. . . .

Also, when it was deemed useful, that unity was appealed to welcome as members of the "Cuban community abroad" our exiled brethren after having kept families separated and having obstructed mail communications to avoid the establishment of any effective links. Because of the effects of that policy on the weakened finances of the country, party members were later allowed to welcome to their homes those who had previously been insulted as "traitors" and "worms" (*vende patrias* and *gusanos*) and who had endured the tossing of eggs and physical aggressions under the infamous "manifestations of the people's dignity" which led to the Rapid Response Brigades and the detestable "acts of repudiation."

In the name of unity "captive towns" were created, believers were persecuted, churches were left without priests. The document states that: "the Congress approved the membership to the Party of revolutionaries with religious beliefs." This implies that they are proud of a decision that reminds of the shame of thirty years of persecuting those who professed religious ideas. If we look back, all of this was motivated by opportunism, because some party militants embraced religion in order to be expelled from the Party. . . .

The government's philosophy is not to serve the people, but rather its dictator. Its main objective is not to guarantee its citizens a quality of life with a minimum of dignity. Power, through totalitarian control, is the ultimate end of politics. Nobody believes in the notion of social justice that has been so widely heralded. Salary levels and the crisis of other financial factors, make the population's situation more difficult with each passing day. As they deteriorate further, economic activities are increasingly militarized and politicized. . . .

Nobody wants to return to the negative aspects of the 1950s, contrary to what the government sustains. Reality has changed dramatically throughout the world, as it has in our country. The transition to democracy that we want to accomplish, is based on the principles of the Constitution of 1940, which establishes social rights that have nothing to do with the impact of neoliberalism. In reality, the present situation, whereby foreign companies hire their workers through state agents so they can be exploited and not offered stable employment, could in fact be deemed as neo-totalitarian. The document does not provide for the rule of law, nor an independent and impartial judiciary that can protect individual rights and liberties as well as political pluralism. . . .

The document mentions rule of law. Yet we cannot find any of its defining characteristics. Laws are not respected as is demonstrated by the recently issued Decree 217, which violates the Constitution and the General Housing Law, and by flagrant violations of the laws governing associations. Non-governmental associations are required to submit multiple applications in order to be legalized.

The State does not serve its citizens. Neither is there equality of rights nor a system of mutual obligations; on the contrary, citizens are at the service of the State.

Laws do not respect the rights inherent to human beings, as attested by numerous denunciations of human rights violations and recurrent condemnations by the United Nations. . . .

Havana, June 27, 1997
Félix Antonio Bonne Carcassés
René Gómez Manzano
Vladimiro Roca Antúnez
Martha Beatriz Roque Cabello

Appendix 15

Presidents from 1868 to the Present

At times throughout Cuba's tumultuous history, maximum power has not always rested in the hands of the president. Fulgencio Batista, as chief of the army, exerted enormous power in the period between 1934 and 1940 and was arguably the most powerful man in Cuba in those years. The same can be said of Fidel Castro in the period from 1959 through 1976 when he lacked the title of president but effectively retained the power of the office.

The Republic-in-Arms (1868–1878)

Carlos Manuel de Céspedes y del Castillo	April 12, 1869 to October 27, 1873
Salvador Cisneros Betancourt	October 27, 1873 to June 28, 1875
Juan Bautista Spotorno	June 28, 1875 to March 29, 1876
Tomás Estrada Palma	March 29, 1876 to October 19, 1877
Francisco Javier de Céspedes	October 19, 1877 to December 13 1877
Vicente García González	December 13, 1877 to February 10 1878
Manuel de Jesús Calvar (Titá)	March 16, 1878 to May 21, 1878

The Republic-in-Arms (1895–1898)

Salvador Cisneros Betancourt	September 13, 1895 to September 13, 1897
Bartolomé Masó y Márquez	September 13, 1897 to January 1, 1899

First United States Intervention (1899–1902): Military Governors

General John R. Brooks	January 1, 1899 to December 31, 1899
General Leonard Wood	December 31, 1899 to May 20, 1902

The Cuban Republic (1902–1959)

Tomás Estrada Palma	May 20, 1902 to September 28, 1906
William Howard Taft	September 29, 1906 to October 2, 1906 (Provisional Governor Second United States Intervention)

Charles E. Magoon	October 2, 1906 to January 28, 1909 (Provisional Governor Second United States Intervention)	José A. Barnet y Vinajeras	December 11, 1935 to May 20, 1936
José Miguel Gómez y Gómez	January 28, 1909 to May 20, 1913	Miguel Mariano Gómez y Arias	May 20, 1936 to December 24, 1936
Mario García Menocal	May 20, 1913 to May 20, 1921	Federico Laredo Brú	December 24, 1936 to October 10, 1940
Alfredo Zayas y Alfonso	May 20, 1921 to May 20, 1925	Fulgencio Batista y Zaldívar	October 10, 1940 to October 10, 1944
Gerardo Machado y Morales	May 20, 1925 to August 12, 1933	Ramón Grau San Martín	October 10, 1944 to October 10, 1948
Alberto Herrera	August 12, 1933	Carlos Prío Socarrás	October 10, 1948 to March 10, 1952
Carlos Manuel de Céspedes y Quesada	August 12, 1933 to September 4, 1933	Fulgencio Batista y Zaldívar	March 10, 1952 to April 6, 1954
The Pentarchy (Ramón Grau San Martín, Sergio Carbó Morera, Porfirio Franca, José Miguel Irisarri, Guillermo Portela)	September 4, 1933 to September 10, 1933	Andrés Domingo y Morales del Castillo	April 6, 1954 to February 24, 1955
		Fulgencio Batista y Zaldívar	February 24, 1955 to January 1, 1959
Ramón Grau San Martín	September 10, 1933 to January 15 1934		
Carlos Hevia y Reyes Gavilán	January 15, 1934 to January 18, 1934		
Manuel Márquez Sterling	January 18, 1934		
Carlos Mendieta Montefur	January 18, 1934 to December 11, 1935		

The Revolutionary Era (1959 to the Present)

Manuel Urrutia Lleó	January 1, 1959 to July 16, 1959
Osvaldo Dorticós Torrado	July 16, 1959 to February 14, 1976
Fidel Castro Ruz	February 14, 1976 to the Present

Bibliography (A Selective Listing of Works in English)

General Reference

Kufeld, Adam. *Cuba*. New York: W. W. Norton, 1994.

Pérez, Louis A., Jr. *Cuba: An Annotated Bibliography*. Westport, CT: Greenwood Press, 1988.

Pérez, Louis A., Jr. *A Guide to Cuban Collections in the United States*. Westport, CT: Greenwood Press, 1991.

Schroeder, Susan. *Cuba: A Handbook of Historical Statistics*. Boston: G. K. Hall, 1982.

Suchlicki, Jaime. *Historical Dictionary of Cuba*. 2nd. ed. Lanham, MD: Scarecrow Press, 2001.

Williams, Stephen. *Cuba: the Land, the History, the People, the Culture*. Philadelphia: Running Press Books, 1994.

Geography, the Environment, and Urbanization

Silva Lee, Alfonso. *Natural Cuba*. St. Paul, MN: Pangaea, 1997.

Stout, Nancy, and Jorge Rigau. *Havana/La Habana*. New York: Rizzoli, 1994.

History—Colonial

Casanovas, Joan. *Bread, or Bullets!: Urban Labor and Spanish Colonialism in Cuba, 1850–1898*. Pittsburgh: University of Pittsburgh Press, 1998.

Chaffin, Tom. *Fatal Glory: Narciso López and the First Clandestine U.S. War against Cuba*. Charlottesville: University of Virginia Press, 1996.

Díaz, María Elena. *The Virgin, the King, and the Royal Slaves of El Cobre: Negotiating Freedom in Colonial Cuba*. Stanford, CA: Stanford University Press, 2001.

Ferrer, Ada. *Insurgent Cuba: Race, Nation, and Revolution, 1868–1898*. Chapel Hill: University of North Carolina Press, 1999.

Helg, Aline. *Our Rightful Share: The Afro-Cuban Struggle for Equality, 1886–1912*. Chapel Hill: University of North Carolina Press, 1995.

Howard, Philip A. *Changing History: Afro-Cuban Cabildos and Societies of Color in the Nineteenth Century*. Baton Rouge: Louisiana State University Press, 1998.

Humboldt, Alexander von. *The Island of Cuba: A Political Essay by Alexander von Humboldt*. Princeton, NJ: Markus Wiener, 2001.

Johnson, Sherry. *The Social Transformation of Eighteenth-Century Cuba*. Gainesville: University Press of Florida, 2001.

Kuethe, Alan J. *Cuba, 1753–1815: Crown, Military and Society*. Knoxville: University of Tennessee Press, 1986.

Martínez-Fernández, Luis. *Fighting Slavery in the Caribbean: The Life and Times of a British Family in Nineteenth-Century Havana*. Armonk, NY: M. E. Sharpe, 1998.

Martínez-Fernández, Luis. *Torn between Empires: Economy, Society, and Patterns of Political Thought in the Hispanic Caribbean, 1840–1878*. Athens: University of Georgia Press, 1994.

Montejo, Esteban. *Autobiography of a Runaway Slave, Esteban Montejo*. New York: Vintage Books, 1973.

Pané, Ramón. *An Account of the Antiquities of the Indians*. Durham, NC: Duke University Press, 1999.

Pérez, Louis A., Jr. *Cuba between Empires, 1878–1902*. Pittsburgh: University of Pittsburgh Press, 1983.

Pérez, Louis A., Jr. *Lords of the Mountain: Social Banditry and Peasant Protest in Cuba, 1878–1918*. Pittsburgh: University of Pittsburgh Press, 1989.

Pérez, Louis A., Jr. *The War of 1898: The United States and Cuba in History and Historiography*. Chapel Hill: University of North Carolina Press, 1998.

Rouse, Irving. *The Taínos: Rise and Decline of the People Who Greeted Columbus*. New Haven, CT: Yale University Press, 1992.

Schmidt-Nowara, Christopher. *Empire and Antislavery: Spain, Cuba and Puerto Rico, 1833–1874*. Pittsburgh: University of Pittsburgh Press, 1999.

Scott, Rebecca J. *Slave Emancipation in Cuba: The Transition to Free Labor, 1860–1899*. Princeton, NJ: Princeton University Press, 1985.

Zanetti Lecuona, Oscar, and Alejandro García Álvarez. *Sugar and Railroads: A Cuban History, 1837–1959*. Chapel Hill: University of North Carolina Press, 1998.

History—Republican Era

Ameringer, Charles D. *The Cuban Democratic Experience: The Auténtico Years, 1944–1952*. Gainesville: University Press of Florida, 2000.

Argote-Freyre, Frank. "The Political Afterlife of Eduardo Chibás: Evolution of a Symbol, 1951–1991." *Cuban Studies* 32 (2002): 74–97.

Ayala, César J. *American Sugar Kingdom: The Plantation Economy of the Spanish Caribbean, 1898–1934*. Chapel Hill: University of North Carolina Press, 1999.

Batista, Fulgencio. *The Growth and Decline of the Cuban Republic*. New York: Devin-Adair, 1964.

de la Fuente, Alejandro. *A Nation for All: Race, Inequality, and Politics in Twentieth-Century Cuba*. Chapel Hill: University of North Carolina Press, 2001.

Pérez, Louis A., Jr. *Cuba under the Platt Amendment, 1902–1934*. Pittsburgh: University of Pittsburgh Press, 1986.

Pérez, Louis A., Jr. *On Becoming Cuban: Identity, Nationality and Culture*. Chapel Hill: University of North Carolina Press, 1999.

Stoner, Lynn K. *From the House to the Streets: The Cuban Woman's Movement for Legal Reform, 1898–1940*. Durham, NC: Duke University Press, 1991.

Whitney, Robert. *State and Revolution in Cuba: Mass Mobilization and Political Change, 1920–1940*. Chapel Hill: University of North Carolina Press, 2001.

History—Revolution

Anderson, Jon Lee. *Che Guevara: A Revolutionary Life*. New York: Grove Press, 1997.

Chang, Laurence and Peter Kornbluh, eds. *The Cuban Missile Crisis, 1962: A National Security Archive Documents Reader*. New York: The New Press, 1998.

Domínguez, Jorge I. *To Make a World Safe for Revolution: Cuba's Foreign Policy*. Cambridge, MA: Harvard University Press, 1989.

Fursenko, Aleksandr, and Timothy Naftali. *One Hell of a Gamble: Khrushchev, Castro, and Kennedy, 1958–1964*. New York: W. W. Norton, 1997.

Geyer, Georgie Anne. *Guerrilla Prince: The Untold Story of Fidel Castro*. Boston: Little, Brown, 1991.

Gleijesse, Piero. *Conflicting Missions: Havana, Washington, and Africa, 1959–1976*. Chapel Hill: University of North Carolina Press, 2002.

Kennedy, Robert F. *Thirteen Days: A Memoir of the Cuban Missile Crisis*. New York: W. W. Norton, 1971.

Kornbluh, Peter, ed. *Bay of Pigs Declassified: The Secret CIA Report on the Invasion of Cuba*. New York: The New Press, 1998.

Leonard, Thomas M. *Castro and the Cuban Revolution*. Westport, CT: Greenwood Press, 1999.

Mead, Walter Russell. "Castro's Successor?" *The New Yorker*, January 26, 1998, 42–49.

Mesa Lago, Carmelo, and June Belkin, eds. *Cuba in Africa*. Pittsburgh: University of Pittsburgh Press, 1982.

Moses, Catherine. *Real Life in Castro's Cuba*. Wilmington, DE: Scholarly Resources, 2000.

Nathan, James A. *Anatomy of the Cuban Missile Crisis*. Westport, CT: Greenwood Press, 2000.

Oppenheimer, Andrés. *Castro's Final Hour*. New York: Simon & Schuster, 1992.

Patterson, Thomas G. *Contesting Castro: The United States and the Triumph of the Cuban Revolution*. New York: Oxford University Press, 1994.

Pérez-Stable, Marifeli. *The Cuban Revolution: Origins, Course, and Legacy*, 2nd ed. New York: Oxford University Press, 1999.

Quirk, Robert E. *Fidel Castro*. New York: W. W. Norton, 1993.

Suchlicki, Jaime. *Cuba, Castro, and Revolution*. Coral Gables, FL: University of Miami Press, 1972.

Szulc, Tad. *Fidel: A Critical Portrait*. New York: Morrow, 1986.

Triay, Víctor Andrés. *Bay of Pigs: An Oral History of Brigade 2506*. Gainesville: University Press of Florida, 2001.

Valladares, Armando. *Against All Hope: A Memoir of Life in Castro's Gulag*. San Francisco: Encounter Books, 2001.

White, Mark J., ed. *The Kennedys and Cuba: The Declassified Documentary History*. Chicago: Ivan R Dee, 1999.

Wyden, Peter. *Bay of Pigs: The Untold Story*. New York: Simon and Schuster, 1979.

Economy and Society

Arenas, Reinaldo. *Before Night Falls*. New York: Viking Press, 1993.

Carr, Kimberly. "Cuban Biotechnology Treads a Lonely Path." *Nature: The Weekly Journal of Science* 398 (1999): A22–23.

Feer, Jason L., Teo A. Babun, Jr., et al. *CubaNews Business Guide to Cuba*. Washington, DC: CubaNews, 2000.

Leiner, Marvin. *Sexual Politics in Cuba: Machismo, Homosexuality, and AIDS*. Boulder, CO: Westview Press, 1994.

Lumsden, Ian. *Machismo, Maricones and Gays: Cuba and Homosexuality*. Philadelphia, PA: Temple University Press, 1996.

Medea, Benjamin. *No Free Lunch: Food and Revolution in Cuba Today*. San Francisco: Institute for Food and Development Policy, 1984.

Pérez Sarduy, Pedro, and Jean Stubbs. *Afro-Cuban Voices: On Race and Identity in Contemporary Cuba*. Gainesville: University Press of Florida, 2000.

Schwartz, Rosalie. *Pleasure Island: Tourism and Temptation in Cuba*. Lincoln: University of Nebraska Press, 1997.

Smith, Lois M., and Alfred Padula. *Sex and Revolution: Women in Socialist Cuba*. New York: Oxford University Press, 1996.

Literature and Social Sciences

Álvarez Borland, Isabel. *Cuban-American Literature of Exile*. Charlottesville: University of Virginia Press, 1998.

Arenas, Reinaldo. *Before Night Falls*. New York: Viking Press, 1993.

Behar, Ruth, ed. *Bridges to Cuba: Puentes a Cuba*. Ann Arbor: University of Michigan Press, 1995.

Cortina, Rodolfo J., ed. *Cuban American Theater*. Houston: Arte Público Press, 1991

Luis, William. *Literary Bondage: Slavery in Cuban Narrative*. Austin: University of Texas Press, 1990.

Luis, William. *Dance Between Two Cultures: Latino Caribbean Literature Written in the United States*. Nashville, TN: Vanderbilt University Press, 1997.

Martínez, Julio A., ed. *Dictionary of Twentieth-Century Cuban Literature*. Westport, CT: Greenwood Press, 1990.

Mullen, Edward J., ed. *Critical Junctures*. Westport, CT: Greenwood Press, 1998.

Pérez Firmat, Gustavo. *Next Year in Cuba*. New York: Anchor Books, 1995.

Rodríguez-Luis, Julio, ed. *Re-reading José Martí (1853–1895): One Hundred Years Later*. Albany: State University of New York Press, 1999.

Smorkaloff, Pamela María. *Cuban Writers on and off the Island*. New York: Twayne Publishers, 1999.

Williams, Lorna Valerie. *The Representation of Slavery in Cuban Fiction*. Columbia: University of Missouri Press, 1994.

Performing Arts

Acosta, Leonardo. "The Rumba, the Guaguancó, and the Tío Tom," in *Essays on Cuban Music: North American and Cuban Perspectives,* ed. Peter Manuel. Lanham, MD: University Press of America, 1991. 51–73.

Chanan, Michael. *The Cuban Image: Cinema and Cultural Politics in Cuba*. London: British Film Institute, 1985.

Díaz Ayala, Cristóbal. *The Roots of Salsa: A History of Cuban Music*. Westport, CT: Greenwood Press, 1996.

Gerard, Charley. *Mongo Santamaría, Chocolate Armenteros, and Other Stateside Cuban Musicians*. Westport, CT: Praeger Publishers, 2001.

Moore, Robin D. *Nationalizing Blackness: Afrocubanismo and Artistic Revolution in Havana, 1920–1940*. Pittsburgh: University of Pittsburgh Press, 1997.

Storm Roberts, John. *The Latin Tinge*, 2nd ed. New York: Oxford University Press, 1999.

Terry, Walter. *Alicia and Her Ballet Nacional de Cuba*. Garden City, NY: Anchor, 1981.

Plastic Arts

Camnitzer, Luis. *New Art of Cuba*. Austin: University of Texas Press, 1994.

Fuentes-Pérez, Ileana, Graciella Cruz-Taura, and Ricardo Pau-Llosa, eds. *Outside Cuba: Contemporary Cuban Visual Artists*. New Brunswick, NJ: Rutgers University Press, 1989.

Gómez Sicre, José. *Art of Cuba in Exile*. Miami: Editorial Munder, 1987.

Martínez, Juan A. *Cuban Art and National Identity: The Vanguardia Painters, 1927–1950*. Gainesville: University Press of Florida, 1994.

Murphy, Jay. "The Young and the Restless in Habana." *Third Text* 20 (Autumn 1992): 115–132.

Sims, Lowery Stokes. *Wifredo Lam and the International Avant-Garde, 1923–1982*. Austin: University of Texas Press, 2001.

Popular Culture and Religion

Asís, Moisés. *Judaism in Cuba, 1959–1999*. Miami: University of Miami Institute for Cuban and Cuban-American Studies, 2000.

Brandon, George. *Santería from Africa to the New World: The Dead Sell Memories*. Bloomington: Indiana University Press, 1993.

Kirk, John M. *Between God and the Party: Religion and Politics in Revolutionary Cuba*. Tampa: University of South Florida Press, 1989.

Levine, Robert M. *Tropical Diaspora: The Jewish Experience in Cuba*. Gainesville: University Press of Florida, 1993.

Luis, William. *Culture and Customs of Cuba*. Westport, CT: Greenwood Press, 2001.

Martínez-Fernández, Luis. *Protestantism and Political Conflict in the Nineteenth-Century Hispanic Caribbean*. New Brunswick, NJ: Rutgers University Press, 2002.

Matibag, Eugenio. *Afro-Cuban Religious Experience: Cultural Reflections in Narrative*. Gainesville: University Press of Florida, 1996.

Peritore, Patrick N. *Catholicism and Socialism in Cuba*. Indianapolis, IN: Universities Field Staff International, 1989.

Yaremko, Jason M. *U.S. Protestant Missions in Cuba: From Independence to Castro*. Gainesville: University Press of Florida, 2000.

Sports

González Echevarría, Roberto. *The Pride of Havana: A History of Cuban Baseball*. New York: Oxford University Press, 1999.

Pettavino, Paula J., and Geralyn Pye. *Sport in Cuba: The Diamond in the Rough*. Pittsburgh: University of Pittsburgh Press, 1994.

Price, S.L. *Pitching around Fidel: A Journey into the Heart of Cuban Sports*. New York: Ecco Press/HarperCollins, 2000.

Diaspora

Ackerman, Holly. *The Cuban Balseros: Voyage of Uncertainty*. Miami: Cuban American National Council, 1995.

Cobas, José A., and Jorge Duany. *Cubans in Puerto Rico: Ethnic Economy and Cultural Identity*. Gainesville: University Press of Florida, 1997.

Conde, Yvonne. *Operation Pedro Pan: The Untold Exodus of 14,048 Cuban Children*. New York: Routledge, 1999.

García, María Cristina. *Havana USA: Cuban Exiles and Cuban Americans in South Florida, 1959–1994*. Berkeley: University of California Press, 1996.

González-Pando, Miguel. *The Cuban Americans*. Westport, CT: Greenwood Press, 1998.

Levine, Robert M., and Moisés Asís. *Cuban Miami*. New Brunswick, NJ: Rutgers University Press, 2000.

Masud-Piloto, Félix. *From Welcomed Exiles to Illegal Immigrants*. Lanham, MD: Rowman & Littlefield, 1995.

Masud-Piloto, Félix. *With Open Arms: The Evolution of Cuban Migration to the U.S., 1959–1995*. New York: Rowman & Littlefield, 1998.

O'Reilly Herrera, Andrea, ed. *Remembering Cuba: Legacy of a Diaspora*. Austin: University of Texas Press, 2001.

Pedraza-Bailey, Silvia. *Political and Economic Migrants in America: Cubans and Mexicans*. Austin: University of Texas Press, 1985.

Pérez Firmat, Gustavo. *Life on the Hyphen: The Cuban-American Way*. Austin: University of Texas Press, 1994.

Portes, Alejandro, and Alex Stepick. *City on the Edge: The Transformation of Miami*. Berkeley: University of California Press, 1993.

Portes, Alejandro, and Robert L. Bach. *Latin Journey: Cuban and Mexican Immigrants in the United States*. Berkeley: University of California Press, 1985.

Santiago, Fabiola. "Separated Yet Together, Exiles Span Many Lands." *The Miami Herald*, December 29, 1998: 1A, 10A.

Soruco, Gonzalo R. *Cubans and the Mass Media in South Florida*. Gainesville: University Press of Florida, 1996.

Torres, María de los Ángeles. *In the Land of the Mirrors: Cuban Exile Politics in the United States*. Ann Arbor: University of Michigan Press, 1999.

Tray, Víctor Andrés. *Fleeing Castro: Operation Pedro Pan and the Cuban Children's Program*. Gainesville: University of Florida Press, 1998.

Index

Note: Page numbers in **bold** indicate the major discussion of the topic; page numbers in *italic* indicate illustrations.

Contributors

ROBERT J. ALEXANDER is professor emeritus of economics at Rutgers University. Over his career he has written and edited over forty books on Latin American politics and economics; the vast bibliography of his work is included in *Robert J. Alexander: The Complete Bibliography of a Pioneering Latin Americanist* (1995).

EMMA ÁLVAREZ-TABÍO ALBO is an architect and essayist. She has studied and taught at the schools of architecture of the University of Havana and the University of Barcelona. She has worked on architectural projects in Cuba and has authored numerous works of criticism and history of architecture. In 1990 she published *Vida, mansión y muerte de la burguesía cubana* and in 2000 *La invención de La Habana*. Her essays have appeared in several edited volumes and journals.

ALEJANDRO ANREUS is associate professor of art history at William Paterson University, where he teaches modern and Latin American art. He is the author of *Orozco in Gringoland* (2001) and coeditor of the forthcoming *The Social and the Real: Art and Politics in the Americas* (2003). He is currently working on a manuscript titled "The Cuban Complex: Exile and Ethos in the Visual Work of Cuban-Americans."

FRANK ARGOTE-FREYRE is a Ph.D. candidate in history at Rutgers University. His dissertation "Fulgencio Batista: The Making of a Dictator" is based on research in Cuba and the United States. He served as assistant editor of this encyclopedia.

LOHANIA J. ARUCA ALONSO is currently an independent researcher and writer with specialty in the history of Cuba's architecture. She taught history of architecture between 1976 and 1989 at ISPJAE and co-authored several architecture textbooks, among them *Historia de la arquitectura y urbanismo III. América Latina y Cuba* (1982) and *Arquitectura y urbanismo: de los orígenes al siglo XIX* (1987).

MOISÉS ASÍS is a scientist and attorney who has written sixteen books, among them *Cuban Miami* (2000), coathored with Robert M. Levine. He works for the Florida Department of Children and Families.

MARÍA DEL CARMEN BARCIA ZEQUEIRA is a historian specializing in Cuba's nineteenth century and professor at the University of Havana. Her books include *Burguesía esclavista y abolición* (1987) and *Élites y grupos de presión: Cuba, 1868–1898* (1998).

NILO JORGE BARREDO received a bachelor's degree in Latin American Studies from Rutgers University, where he presided over the Cuban-American Students' Association. He currently attends the Law School of the University of Pennsylvania.

RAY BLANCO is president and executive producer of Cutting Edge Entertainment. A television producer, his productions include *Black and White in Exile, Artists in Exile, Culture Shock*, and the A&E Biography of Gloria and Emilio Estefan.

YAVET BOYADJIEV COLLADO is a violinist. She is currently a doctoral candidate in music at the Graduate Center of the City University of New York.

ADRIAN BURGOS, JR., is an assistant professor who teaches U.S. Latino history at the University of Illinois. He is currently working on a book manuscript titled "Playing America's Game: Baseball, Race, and Latinos, 1868–1959." He has contributed chapters in anthologies, and his articles have appeared in *Centro: Journal of Puerto Rican Studies* and the *Journal of Negro History*.

WILFREDO CANCIO ISLA is a literary critic and journalist. He taught at the University of Havana between 1983 and 1994. In Cuba he collaborated with various publications, among them *Revolución* and *Cultura y Cine Cubano*.

In 1994 he left Cuba and joined the faculty of Barry University until 1997. The following year he received his Ph.D. in communications from the Universidad de La Laguna (Spain). He is currently a member of the editorial staff of *El Nuevo Herald*, and he served on the advisory board of this encyclopedia.

DAVID C. CARLSON is a history Ph.D. candidate at the University of North Carolina. His current research focuses on the Cuban War of Independence (1895–1898) and the Oriente Province.

BARRY CARR directs the Institute of Latin American Studies at La Trobe University in Melbourne, Australia. He is researching the history of Cuban sugar workers and Cuban communism. Together with Avi Chomsky and Pamela Smorkaloff, he is the editor of *The Cuba Reader* (2003).

ILIA CASANOVA-MARENGO received her Ph.D. from Rutgers University at New Brunswick and is assistant professor in the Department of Modern Languages and Literature at St. Lawrence University.

JOAN CASANOVAS is associate professor of Latin American history at Florida State University. He is the author of numerous articles on Cuban history and the book *Bread, or Bullets!: Urban Labor and Spanish Colonialism in Cuba, 1850–1898* (1998).

ALMA CONCEPCIÓN is an independent scholar and artist and an adjunct instructor at Rutgers University. She is currently researching the musical and dance traditions of Cuba and Puerto Rico.

YVONNE CONDE is a freelance journalist and a columnist for *Hoy* newspaper in New York City. She is the author of *Operation Pedro Pan: The Untold Exodus of 14,048 Cuban Children* (1999).

PABLO JULIÁN DAVIS has a Ph.D. in Latin American history from Johns Hopkins University. He is assistant dean of students at the University of Virginia, where he also teaches courses on Latin American history and culture.

NANETTE DE JONG is an assistant professor of music at Rutgers University, where she specializes in Latin American music. She also directs the Rutgers University Salsa Band.

CRISTÓBAL DÍAZ AYALA is a researcher and author whose books include *Música cubana del areyto a la nueva trova* (1981); *Si te quieres por el pico divertir* (1988); *Cuba canta y baila* (1994); *Cuando salí de La Habana: 1898–1997* (1998); *La marcha de los jíbaros, 1898–1997* (1998); and *Cien canciones cubanas del milenio* (1999). He served on the advisory board of this encyclopedia.

EDGARDO DÍAZ DÍAZ is an ethnomusicologist who has served as music critic for the newspapers *El Mundo, Claridad*, and *El Nuevo Día*. His research on dance, popular music, and ritual in Latin America and the Caribbean has appeared in specialized journals. A French horn player, he has been soloist and assistant soloist in the State Band of Puerto Rico, Puerto Rico's Symphonic Orchestra, and the Casals's Festival Orchestra. He now teaches at Rutgers University and the City College of New York.

JULIO DOMÍNGUEZ GARCÍA is a journalist and historian. He specializes in the Cuban Republican Era and is currently at work on a chronological history of Cuba, 1900–1958.

JORGE DUANY is professor of anthropology at the University of Puerto Rico in Río Piedras, where he previously directed the *Revista de Ciencias Sociales*. He is the coauthor of *Cubans in Puerto Rico: Ethnic Economy and Cultural Identity* (1997) and the author of *Nation on the Move: Representations of Puerto Rican Identity on the Island and in the United States* (2002).

ALFREDO DURÁN is a founding member of the Committee for Cuban Democracy (CDC) and is currently serving as president of the CDC (2001–2002). He is an attorney at law and served as state chairman of the Florida Democratic Party from 1976 to 1980. Durán is a veteran of the Bay of Pigs Invasion and has been active in Cuban American politics for over two decades.

MARIOLA ESPINOSA is a Ph.D. candidate in the Department of History of the University of North Carolina at Chapel Hill. She is currently completing her dissertation on the health and sanitation reforms implemented in Cuba by the U.S. occupation government of 1899 to 1902.

JASON FEER was editor of the monthly publication *CubaNews*, which includes articles and valuable information on all aspects of Cuba's economy and society. He coedited with Teo A. Babun the *CubaNews Business Guide to Cuba* (2000) and served on the advisory board of this encyclopedia.

DAMIÁN J. FERNÁNDEZ is professor and chair of the Department of International Relations at Florida International University. He is the author of *Cuba and the Politics of Passion* (2000) and the coeditor of *Cuba, the Elusive Nation* (2000), among other books.

ADA FERRER is associate professor of history at New York University. She is the author of *Insurgent Cuba: Race, Nation, and Revolution, 1868–1898* (1999).

D.H. FIGUEREDO is the director of the Library and Media Center at Bloomfield College, New

Jersey. He has published over sixty articles on Latin American studies in anthologies, books, and journals. He has also published four children's books and several short stories. He is a frequent contributor to the *Multicultural Review* and *Booklist* and is one of the editors of this encyclopedia.

ARACELI GARCÍA CARRANZA has worked at the Biblioteca Nacional José Martí in different capacities since 1962, currently heading its Department of Bibliographical Research. She is chief editor of the Biblioteca Nacional's journal and an adjunct professor at the University of Havana. Her bibliographical studies appear in dozens of books and journals published in Cuba and other countries.

ARMANDO GARCÍA GONZÁLEZ teaches biology at the Instituto Pedagógico Enrique José Varona in Havana. He is a historian of science in Cuba, specializing in the eighteenth and nineteenth centuries. His published work includes several books and articles on Darwinism, racism, immigration, and eugenics in Cuba as well as biographies of Cuba's naturalists.

LUIS MIGUEL GARCÍA MORA is adjunct director of the Reference Center of La Fundación Histórica Tavera in Spain. A specialist in nineteenth-century Cuban history, with Alejandro García Álvarez he coedited *Textos clásicos de la historia de Cuba* (2001).

JORGE L. GIOVANNETTI studied sociology at the University of Puerto Rico and history and Caribbean studies at the University of North London. His research interests are popular culture and music, and migration and race relations in the Caribbean. He is the author of *Sonidos de condena: sociabilidad, historia, y política en la música reggae de Jamaica* (2001).

LUIS GONZÁLEZ is president of González & Associates, a publishing consultancy. He has contributed to numerous reference works during more than fifteen years in publishing. He was project manager of the critically acclaimed work Scientific American; *Triumph of Discovery* (1995). González originally conceived the idea of this encyclopedia and served as one of its editors.

GERARDO GONZÁLEZ NÚÑEZ is an economist who teaches at Inter American University in San Juan. The author of numerous articles and the books *El Caribe en la política exterior de Cuba* (1999) and *¿Intelectuals vs. Revolución? (2001)*, he previously worked in Havana's Centro de Estudios sobre América.

JULIO CÉSAR GONZÁLEZ PAGÉS is a professor in the Department of History of the University of Havana. He is the author of *Buscando un espacio: historia de las mujeres en Cuba* (2001).

MARÍA DOLORES GONZÁLEZ-RIPOLL NAVARRO is a researcher at the Consejo Superior de Investigaciones Científicas in Madrid. A historian, she authored *Cuba, la isla de los ensayos. Economía y sociedad (1790–1815)* (1999).

JOHN A. GUTIÉRREZ is a doctoral student in history at the Graduate Center/City University of New York, where he is also administrative director of the Center for Latin American, Caribbean, and Latino Studies. His research interests center on social policy and public health in late-nineteenth- and early-twentieth-century Cuba.

ROGER E. HERNÁNDEZ is a syndicated columnist and coauthor of *Cubans in America* (2002). He is writer-in-residence at the New Jersey Institute of Technology and also teaches journalism at Rutgers University.

MANUEL HERNÁNDEZ GONZÁLEZ is professor of history at the Universidad de La Laguna, Tenerife, Canary Islands. He is the author of several books, among them *La emigración canaria a América (1765–1824)* (1996) and *Los canarios en la Venezuela colonial (1670–1810)* (1998). He has also coauthored *Cultura y vida cotidiana en América Latina (1763–1898)* (2000) and *La esclavitud blanca* (1993).

ELENA HERNÁNDEZ SANDOICA is professor of contemporary history at the Universidad Complutense de Madrid. She is the author of *Pensamiento burgués y problemas coloniales en la España de la Restauración, 1875–1887* (1982).

DENNIS R. HIDALGO is assistant professor of history at Adelphi University. The author of several articles, his doctoral dissertation focused on early Protestant communities in the Hispanic Caribbean.

PETER T. JOHNSON is Princeton University's bibliographer for Latin America, Spain, and Portugal, and he periodically visits Cuba to conduct research on intellectual life. His broader Latin American interests include civil society and social movements. He served on the advisory board of this encyclopedia.

SHERRY JOHNSON is an associate professor of history at Florida International University. She serves as one of the editors of *Cuban Studies* and is the author of *The Social Transformation of 18th-Century Cuba* (2001).

ELOISE LINGER teaches in the Department of Politics, Economy, and Society at the State University of New York—College at Old Westbury. She authored the introduction for and co-edited *Cuban Transitions at the Millennium* (2000) and is working to complete a book on political contention, revolution, and state formation in Cuba, 1953–1963.

WILLIAM LUIS is professor of Spanish at Vanderbilt University. He is the author of *Literary Bondage: Slavery in Cuban Narrative* (1990), *Dance between Two Cultures: Latino Caribbean Literature Written in the United States* (1987), and *Culture and Customs of Cuba* (2000).

JUAN A. MARTÍNEZ is associate professor of art history at Florida International University. The author of *Cuban Art and National Identity: The Vanguardia Painters, 1927–1950* (1994), he advised the editors of this encyclopedia in the visual arts.

LUIS MARTÍNEZ-FERNÁNDEZ is professor and chair of the Department of Puerto Rican and Hispanic Caribbean Studies at Rutgers University. The senior editor of this encyclopedia, his books include *Torn between Empires: Economy, Society, and Patterns of Political Thought in the Hispanic Caribbean, 1840–1878* (1994), *Fighting Slavery in the Caribbean: The Life and Times of a British Family in Nineteenth-Century Havana* (1998), and *Protestantism and Political Conflict in the Nineteenth-Century Hispanic Caribbean* (2002).

MARIKAY McCABE is a Ph.D. candidate in anthropology at Columbia University. She is currently completing her dissertation titled "Urban Topographies, Social Commerce, and the Limits of Law in Havana, Cuba."

MARISA MÉNDEZ holds a degree in literature and philosophy from the University of Havana. Since 1987 she has served as curator for the discographic collection of Fundación Musicalia in San Juan, Puerto Rico.

ROBIN MOORE is an assistant professor of music history at Temple University. He is the author of *Nationalizing Blackness: Afrocubanismo and Artistic Revolution in Havana, 1920–1940* (1997).

CATHERINE MOSES teaches political science at Georgia College and State University and is the author of *Real Life in Castro's Cuba* (2000). She served as a U.S. diplomat in the U.S. Interests Section in Havana, 1995–1996.

CONSUELO NARANJO OROVIO is a researcher at the Instituto de Historia of the Consejo Superior de Investigaciones Científicas in Madrid. She directs the team that conducts research on the Hispanic Caribbean (nineteenth and twentieth centuries). Her books and articles have focused on the social and cultural history of the Caribbean, including migration, exile, race relations, and culture. She also served on the advisory board of this encyclopedia.

ISABEL NAZARIO is the executive director of the Office of Intercultural Initiatives at Rutgers University, where she also directs the Center for Latino Arts and Culture. She has extensive experience curating and lecturing on Latin American and Latino art history.

MANUEL DE PAZ SÁNCHEZ is professor of history of the Americas at the Universidad de La Laguna, Tenerife, Canary Islands. The author of numerous books on Cuba, he specializes in the subjects of banditry, Freemasonry, and Cuba's relations with Spain.

SILVIA PEDRAZA is professor of sociology at the University of Michigan. Her research interests are the sociology of immigration, race, and ethnicity in the United States and the Cuban Revolution and its exodus. Pedraza is the author of two books: *Origins and Destinies: Immigration, Race, and Ethnicity in America* (1996) which she coedited with Ruben G. Rumbaut; and *Political and Economic Migrants in America: Cubans and Mexicans* (1985). She served on the advisory board of this encyclopedia and is currently working on a book entitled *Political Disaffection: Cuba's Revolution and Exodus*.

GUSTAVO PELLÓN is associate professor of Spanish and comparative literature at the University of Virginia. He is the author of *José Lezama Lima's Joyful Vision* (1989).

LOUIS A. PÉREZ, JR., is J. Carlyle Sitterson Professor of History at the University of North Carolina at Chapel Hill. He is the author of several books on Cuban history, among them *Cuba: Between Reform and Revolution* (1995) and *On Becoming Cuban: Identity, Nationality, and Culture* (1999). He served as editor of this encyclopedia and chaired its advisory board.

PAULA J. PETTAVINO is an adjunct professor of government at American University in Washington, D.C., where she leads the study abroad trip to Cuba each year. She served on the advisory board of this encyclopedia and coauthored with Geralyn Pye *Sport in Cuba: The Diamond in the Rough* (1994).

JULIO CÉSAR PINO is associate professor of history at Kent State University in Ohio. He is the author of *Family and Favela: The Reproduction of Poverty in Rio De Janeiro* (1997). Currently, he is researching the origins and practice of Islam among African slaves in Bahia, Brazil, in the nineteenth century.

JOSÉ ANTONIO PIQUERAS ARENAS is professor of history at Jaume I University in Castellón, Spain. He is the editor of *Diez nuevas miradas de la historia de Cuba* (1998).

ARMANDO H. PORTELA holds a Ph.D. in geography from the Russian Academy of Sciences. Coauthor of the *New National Atlas of Cuba* (1989), he has also published numerous geographical papers and original maps in Cuban, Russian, and American scientific institutions. He has also authored over a hundred articles on Cuban geography and economy in the United States and served on the advisory board of this encyclopedia and produced several of its maps.

YOLANDA PRIETO is professor of sociology at Ramapo College of New Jersey, Mahwah, New Jersey. Her work has focused on the Cuban migration to the United States, particularly women and the role of religion. She is writing a book on the Cuban community in Union City, New Jersey.

MIGUEL ÁNGEL PUIG-SAMPER MULERO is a researcher at the Consejo Superior de Investigaciones Científicas, Madrid. He specializes in the history of science and has written extensively about the history of science in Latin America and the history of biology and anthropology.

KEVIN RENTE holds a master's degree in sociology from the New School University Graduate Faculty. His current areas of interest are urban studies, popular culture, and cyberspace.

JOHN RIPTON is adjunct professor at Rutgers University and Centenary College. He is currently history chairperson at Gill St. Bernards's School in Gladstone, New Jersey.

INÉS ROLDÁN DE MONTAUD teaches history at the Universidad de Alcalá, Spain. She is the author of several works on Cuban colonial history, among them *La hacienda en Cuba durante la Guerra de los Diez Años* (1990), *La Restauración en Cuba. El fracaso de un proceso reformista* (2001), and *Historia del Banco Español en La Habana* (2002).

ERNESTO SAGÁS teaches in the Department of Puerto Rican and Hispanic Caribbean Studies of Rutgers University. He is a political scientist and author of *Race and Politics in the Dominican Republic* (2000).

ANTONIO SANTAMARÍA GARCÍA is a researcher at the Consejo Superior de Investigaciones Científicas in Madrid. The author of over forty articles and essays, he has published *Sin azúcar no hay país. La industria azucarera y la economía cubana, 1919–1939* (2001). Currently he researches Spain's relations with its former colonies after 1898.

ZENÉN SANTANA DELGADO is reading for a Ph.D. in the Department of Politics, University of Durham, United Kingdom, where he researches Cuban foreign policy and its interaction with the international community. He has published reviews of recent books about Cuba in the journals *International Affairs* and *Millennium*.

DAVID A. SARTORIUS is a Ph.D. candidate in history at the University of North Carolina at Chapel Hill. He is completing a dissertation titled "Limits of Loyalty: Race and the Public Sphere in Cienfuegos, Cuba, 1850–1898."

LOIS MAMIE SMITH is a National Science Foundation graduate research fellow in sociology at the University of Texas at Austin. She wrote, with Alfred Padula, *Sex and Revolution: Women in Socialist Cuba* (1996) and is currently researching the role of legal marriage in national development in Latin America and the Caribbean.

PAMELA MARÍA SMORKALOFF is assistant professor of Spanish and Latin American/Latino Studies at Montclair State University. She has authored and edited numerous volumes on Cuban and Caribbean literature and is coeditor of *The Cuba Reader*, forthcoming from Duke University Press in 2003.

MIGUEL SOCARRÁS is a poet and legal translator. He has authored *Visiones* (1983) and *Los desaparecidos* (1986). His collection of short stories, *Alucinaciones de la vagancia*, awaits publication.

CAMILLA STEVENS is assistant professor of Spanish at Rutgers University, where she teaches Spanish American theater and literature of the Hispanic Caribbean. She is currently researching family and national identity in Cuban and Puerto Rican drama.

JO-ANN VAN EYCK is a Ph.D. research student at the School of Oriental and African Studies (SOAS), University of London. She is currently writing her dissertation based on the contemporary visual art practices of a selection of Cuban female artists: Marta María Pérez, Magdalena Campos-Pons, Belkis Ayón, Tania Bruguera, and Sandra Ramos.

WILLIAM VAN NORMAN, JR., is a doctoral candidate in history at the University of North Carolina at Chapel Hill. He is currently researching slave life and experience on Cuban coffee plantations during the first half of the nineteenth century.

JESÚS VEGA is a Miami-based author and film critic. His books include *Wunderbat, maravilloso* (1994), *Zavattini en La Habana* (1995), and *El cartel de cine cubano* (1996).

ALAN WEST-DURÁN is a professor at Northeastern University. A poet, writer, and translator, he won the Latino Prize for Poetry with *Dar nombres a la lluvia* (1996) and authored *Tropics of History: Cuba Imagined* (1997). Recently he translated Alejo Carpentier's *Music in Cuba* (2001). He also served on the advisory board of this encyclopedia.

ROBERT W. WHITNEY is an assistant professor of Latin American history at the University of New Brunswick at Saint John in Canada. He is the author of several scholarly articles on Cuba and of the book *State and Revolution in Cuba: Mass Mobilization and Political Change, 1920–1940* (2001). His current research focuses on the study of the British West Indian population in Cuba's Oriente.